Indian Political Thinkers
Modern Indian Political Thought

N. Jayapalan

ATLANTIC
PUBLISHERS & DISTRIBUTORS (P) LTD

ATLANTIC
PUBLISHERS & DISTRIBUTORS (P) LTD
7/22, Ansari Road, Darya Ganj, New Delhi
Tel.: +91-11-4077 5252, 2327 3880
E-mail: orders@atlanticbooks.com
Web: www.atlanticbooks.com

Reprint 2010, 2012, 2018, 2021, 2022, 2024, 2026

Published by Atlantic Publishers & Distributors (P) Ltd.

Printed & bound in India by Atlantic Print Services

PREFACE

I take pleasure in placing the book "Indian Political Thinkers—(Modern Indian Political Thought)" in the hands of the readers. It is quite comprehensive and covers all aspects and the entire syllabus prescribed by various Universities. I have narrated all the events chronologically from the beginning to the end. I have also made a serious attempt to present the matter in a simple and lucid style.

There is a plethora of books on "Indian Political Thinkers." Most of them are bulky. Hence, I have written this book in a sizable volume *i.e.* neither too small nor too big. In addition, special attention has been given to Gandhian thought.

My experience of teaching the subject at the college level for several years has prompted me to write this book to meet the requirements of students of our universities and that of the examinees of Civil Services Examination in History and Political Science. I hope that 'the present book will prove to be more useful to the students than any other book on the subject available in the market.

I am thankful to the M/s Atlantic Publishers and Distributors, New Delhi for readily agreeing to publish this book and bringing it out expeditiously and efficiently.

Suggestions, if any, for improving the book in the subsequent edition will be highly appreciated.

N. JAYAPALAN

CONTENTS

	Preface	iii
1.	Introduction	1
2.	Raja Ram Mohan Roy (1772-1833)	5
3.	Dadabhai Naoroji (1825-1917)	19
4.	Mahadeo Govind Ranade (1842-1901)	32
5.	Pherozeshah Mehta (1845-1915)	45
6.	Surendranath Banerjee (1848-1925)	52
7.	Gopal Krishan Gokhale (1866-1915)	61
8.	Bal Gangadhar Tilak (1856-1920)	78
9.	Bipin Chandra Pal (1858-1932)	104
10.	Lala Lajpat Rai (1865-1928)	115
11.	Shri Aurobindo Ghosh (1872-1950)	131
12.	Mahatma Gandhi (1869-1948)	150
13.	Vinoba Bhave (1895-1988)	213
14.	Jaya Prakash Narayan (1902-1979)	229
15.	Manavendra Nath Roy (1886-1954)	242
16.	Jawaharlal Nehru (1889-1964)	258
17.	Acharya Narendra Dev (1889-1956)	292
18.	Dr. Ram Manohar Lohia (1910-67)	300
19.	Ashok Mehta	304
20.	Dutt, Dange and Ranadive	306
21.	Sayyid Ahmad Khan (1817-1898)	310
22.	Mohammad Iqbal (1873-1938)	321
23.	Rabindranath Tagore (1861-1941)	325
24.	Sarvapalli Radhakrishnan (1888-1975)	344
	Index	353

1
INTRODUCTION

The advent of Indian Independence and the framing of the new Constitution are glorious events in the recent History of India and the World. The intellectuals as well as the masses plunged into the freedom struggle in their own way. Right from the times of Vasudev Balwant Phadke and Gopal Krishna Gokhale to the recent times of Mahatma Gandhi and Subhas Chandra Bose, it is an inspiring and thrilling scene of struggles and sacrifices. The Western influence had its impact on them, they accepted and adopted their political ideas and practices. Those amongst them who were westernised to a degree, also drew upon the national heritage, with pride, used it to stimulate change in social outlook and to eliminate superstition from religion, which in turn strengthened the national movement. They contributed in diverse manner to the national main stream. To them, patriotism was their religion. Then their do or die spirit secured to the nation, their best.

The most distinguished amongst the distinguished leaders were Dadabhai Naoroji, Mahadev Govind Ranade, Pheroze Shah Mehta, S.N. Banerjee, Gokhale, Tilak, Bipin Chandra Pal, Lala Lajpat Rai, Aurobindo Gosh, Gandhi, Nehru and a host of others. Gokhale and Gandhi, *i.e.*, the Guru and the disciple played a significant role. Both came from diverse background. Their contribution has been distinct in several fields. The circumstances that brought both Gokhale and Gandhi to the national politics were not similar. In their thinking too they were similar. They can be clubbed together in very many fields. Their detestation of the political subordination and their sacrifices for freedom were their characteristics.

As one of the pillars of the Congress organisation during the period of moderates, he believed that the British rule was a necessity for the good of India. Gandhi, the Saint, came from South Africa with experience and ideology, name and image. He generated the national political tide as God's own man; involved the people in the national cause and that too at his will, binding and choosing.

Gokhale wanted a better and benevolent Government under the British yoke, but not a self-government for which Indians were not yet fit. He was a staunch advocate of the constitutional method of agitating for reforms within the system of Government. As a legislator, he made history and drew the attention of the British rulers on important issues.

As the potter on the wheel shapes the revolving clay after his ideas, so did Gandhi with human material available to him. He picked up his very close team and made them into his servant followers and the effective instruments to fulfil the high objectives. He was, man the maker. This "practical idealist", hold Sarvodaya, as the ideal social order. Technology in such society, would serve man, make life easy, eliminate competition and ensure contentment to individual in his requirements; yet one has to be active and progressive; earnest in effort to realise ones best and seek thus, the salvation. Being essentially a religious man, Gandhi wanted *Dharma* to guide the exercise of the political power.

The diversity in the background of both has its importance. But, the unity of their purpose, between Gokhale and Gandhi was very strong.

The leaders worked on a well prepared ground. By the time, they appeared, political consciousness has come to the people, patriotism had seized them; the importance of Swadeshi had come to be well realised and the idea of Independence had gained prominence; A birds eye-view of the circumstances in which he British, have got at the helm of political authority; the growth of new political ideas in Europe, and their creeping into our country; the response of our leaders and the manner they communicated them to the people, is both interesting and enlightening.

The presence of the British here, coupled with the expanding means of transport and communication, printing press and the newspaper, and due to the expanding influence of English Language, facilitated the import of this crop of western political ideas into our country. This is the real and perhaps the only acquisition, one have from the West. Not that we had no political ideas.

Here the political theory was based on supremacy of the society, and not of state; on duty alone and not on right. The balance between individual society and state had been well established in terms of *Varnashramadharma.* This, despite all its merits, had now been forgotten; and was dead over the thousand years and more. But Gokhale and Gandhi appeared on the Indian scene and pointed out their concepts on the basis of the ancient heritage.

Between Ram Mohan Roy and the establishment of the Republic is a long period of renaissance, reformation and resurgence, well accomplished. The leadership that guided these currents contributed in a varigated manner to the national reconstruction.

The emergence of the Indian National Congress provided a common platform for the exchange of views; it also provided a very good opportunity for planning of action; further it paved the way to appeal and approach the people for cooperation and for the common good.

It is early beginning the Congress funtioned in the leadership of Dadabai Naoroji, S.N. Banerjee Mehta and Gokhale. They educated the people in Nationalism and National unity. They introduced them the concepts like Modern State', 'Civil Liberty' and 'Progressive Society. They 'believed in liberalism and moderation', "compromise and fairness."

During this period, their highest aim was as Gokhale said, "Self-government within the empire." At the same time, the British Government's measures like the officialisation of Calcutta Corporation and of the University Senate broadened the scope of the Official Secret Act and brought about the partition of Bengal to kill nationalism. These measures made the people realise the true nature of imperialism.

Extremists like Bal Gangadhar Tilak and Lala Lajpat Rai believed in self-reliance and not in mediocre politics. They laid emphasis on passive resistance and non-cooperation; Swadeshi and on recognition of education to serve the national ends better. Their ultimate aim was national freedom.

They used the medium intelligible to the people to bring them under one umbrella for national struggle. They interpreted their ideas and actions through the common and popular religious symbols, mythical personages and historical heroes. They used religious concepts to educate the people. On public festivals, when people assembled in large numbers, they contacted them, and gave wider base to their political ideas. They aroused, by their selfless work, enthusiasm of the masses. The concept of 'Indian Nation', in the guise of 'Mother India', made deep and wide appeal; words like 'Swadeshi' and 'Swaraj' gained wide currency. They made self-confidence and self-reliance props of their strength. They stood for constitutionalism and progress.

The administration and the unpopular acts of Curzon created a tense atmosphere in India. The public resented it; demonstrated against it and carried out a long agitation like of which had never been launched before. The repressive measures of the Government provided the appropriate nourishment to the extremists. The difference between the leadership in consequence became deep and then followed in 1907, the Surat split.

A new factor, *i.e.*, the Muslim communalism emerged at this time. Adding fuel to the fire, Curzon by partitioning, Bengal gave a communal tilt; the officials, encouraged some amongst the Muslims in East Bengal to resort to the communal killings, mass rape and arson. The communalism that was in the brooding now burst out in the open. So this finally led to the birth of Muslim League in 1906.

The Indian Councils Act of 1909, that followed, this long drawn repression, and suppression, was frustrating to the extremists, and disgusting to the moderates. The displeasures of all, due to it, was unbound. Still worse was the Muslim separatist movement became very serious and severe.

Meanwhile, the moderates had lost their appeal, the extremists were in defusion, the Home Rule League that had come that had come-up recently had limited appeal and that the political stage was vacant. All eyes were eagerly waiting for someone to come up.

At this juncture Gandhiji, the disciple of Gokhale took-up the leadership of our Freedom Movement. He made the Congress an organisation of masses. He stood for the principles of truth, non-violence, Harijan upliftment and Hindu-Muslim Unity. He invented the weapon of Satyagraha to liberate the country from the foreign yoke. In subsequent pages, we are going to see how Gandhi thought like a saint, spoke like a saint and lived likes a saint.

The Political thinkers gave their political ideas according to needs of the time. As already mentioned they were both Moderates and Extremists. But all these thinkers had one aim of seeing India an independent nation. In the following pages we shall discuss the political philosophies of some of the prominent political thinkers of Modern India.

2

Raja Ram Mohan Roy (1772-1833)

Life Sketch

Raja Ram Mohan Roy is considered as the "Father of Indian Renaissance." He was the creator of the mental climate which contributed to the birth of the Indian Renaissance. He was the pioneer of religious and social reforms. He was the first advocate of the introduction of Western education in modern India. Moreover, Roy was the father of Constitutional Agitation in India. He was the first Indian to condemn religious and social malpractices like idol-worship, enforced widowhood, *sati* and girl infanticide, etc. No wonder he was also the first to speek to the government about the rights and the privileges of the people.

According to Max Muller, "Ram Mohan Roy was the first to complete a connected life current between the East and the West."

According to B. Majumdar, "He is the father of the modern political movement."

As the history of Western political thought practically begins with the name of Aristotle, so the history of modern Indian political thought begins with the name of Raja Ram Mohan Roy. He is regarded as the father of modern Indian political thought.

Raja Ram Mohan Roy was born in a well-to-do orthodox Brahmin family in Hugli District of West Bengal on 22nd May 1772.

His great grandfather, Krishan Chander Banerjee was given the title of Roy for good services rendered to the local government. His grandfather. Braja Binod Roy attained high position of responsibility under the Mohammedan Governor of Murshidabad. Ram Kanta, Ram Mohan's father, was a man of property — the revenue of which was lakhs of rupees. He was described as the most respectable man in the district. Ram Mohan's father and mother were devout Hindus and so was he. Ram Mohan received the first elements of native education at home in accordance with the prevalent system and then in the village school or pathshala Since the knowledge of Persian and Arabic was essential for becoming a respectable and successful citizen in those days, Ram Kanta, his father, to ensure for his son a bright career, engaged a Maulvi to teach him Persian. After he had learn Persian at home, Ram Mohan was sent to Patna at the age of nine, then a famed centre of Persian and Arabic learning. His receptive mind very quickly acquired deep and extensive knowledge of the two languages and he got himself the title of Zabardust Maulvi, He 'studied the works of Sufi Poets like Saadi and Hafiz. At the age of 14 he was sent to Banaras to learn Sanskrit. He became a profound scholar of Sanskrit and of the theological works written in it. It was the study of Koran which opened his eyes to the error of idol-worship, and he became highly critical of idolatry and polytheism. He made up his mind to purify Hinduism of all the social and religious evils. After finishing his studies at Patna and Banaras, Roy composed a manuscript condemning idolatry. This led Roy's expulsion from his father's house. After leaving his ancestral home he travelled far and wide. In his own words, he passed through different countries, chiefly within, "but some beyond the bounds of Hindustan". Roy also visited Tibet where he acquired the knowledge of Buddhism. In Tibet, he spent two or three years where he criticised strongly the worshippers of the living Lama. This irriated the Lamas so much that they thought of even killing him. However, he was saved by a kind-hearted woman. After his travel, Roy settled down in Varanasi where he devoted himself to the study of Sanskrit.

After his reconciliation with his father in 1794, Roy returned home. As he says, in his autobiography, "My father recalled and restored me to his favour."

This is the period when Roy first made his acquaintance with Europeans and made himself familiar with their laws and forms of government. In the beginning he had strong feelings about the British people, but the contact with them made him revise and abandon this idea. He writes in his autobiography, "I gave up my prejudices against them (British people) and became inclined to their favour, feeling persuaded that their rule, though a foreign yoke, would lead more speedily and surely to the amelioration of the native inhabitants."

In the words of Dr. Verma "Ram Mohan Roy was a many sides genius. He was a prophet of monotheism, keen ardent champion of liberty in all its phrase, and a political agitator for the freedom of press and the right of tenents. He was a great scholar of comparative religions and the freedom of Bengali prose literature and Bengali Journalism."

He entered into the civil service under the East India Company as a Sheristadar. During his 10 years service he saved sufficient money and became a landlord (zamindar). His income from land was to the tune of Rupees ten thousand per year.

In 1814 Raja Ram Mohan Roy settled down in Calcutta. He was a scholar of Vedas. He published his first translation of Vedanta Sutra into Bengali in 1815 and also published translation into English and Hindustani. He translated Kena, Isha, Katha, Mudka Upnishads into English and distributed free of charge to the countrymen.

Apostle of Social Reform

In 1815 he formed a society by his name Atmiya Sabha for the purpose of spiritual purification and enlargement. He made a very powerful campaign against the custom of Sati (Sacrifice of life by wife on the death of husband). He used to go to such of the ladies himself and persuaded them not to sacrifice their lives. He used to call it the greatest sin of the life. He was an apostle of social reforms. He addressed an appeal for freedom and regeneration of woman final in the words, Women are in general inferior to men in bodily strength and energy. Consequently the male part of the community taking advantage of their corporal weakness have denied to them those excellent merits that they are entitled to by nature and afterwards they are apt to say that women are naturally incapable of acquiring those merits. But if we give the subject consideration, we may easily ascertain whether or not your accusation against them is consistent with justice. As to their inferiority in point of understanding when did you even afford them opportunity of extending their natural capacity? How then can you access them of want of understanding. On the contrary Pilawati, Bhanumati are celebrated for their thorough knowledge of *shastras,* Moreover, in the Brihadaranyka Upanishad of the Yujurveda, it is clearly stated that Yajnvalkya imparted divine knowledge of the most difficult nature to his wife Maitrayi who was able to follow and completely attain.

Secondly, you charge them with want of resolution, at which I feel exceedingly surprised, for we constantly perceive that in a country where the name of death makes the male shudder, that the female from the firmness of mind, offers to burn with the corpse of her deceased husband and yet you accuse those women of deficiency in point of resolution.

Thirdly, with regard to their trustworthiness, let us look into the conduct of both the saxes and ascertain which of them is the most frequently and quietly of betraying from friends, If we enumerate such women in each village or town as have been betrayed by women I presume that the number of deceived women would to found ten time greater than that of the betrayed men. Men are in general able to read and write and manage public affairs by which means they easily promulgate such faults as women occasionally commit but never consider as crime that mis-conduct of men towards women. One fault they have it must be acknowledged, which is by considering others equally void of duplicity as themselves, to give their confidence too readily, from which they suffer much misery even so for that some of them are misled to suffer themselves to be burnt to death.

In the fourth place with respect to their subjection to passions, this may be judged of by the custom of marriage as to the respective sexes, for one man may marry two or three sometimes even ten wives and upwards, while a woman who marries but one husband, desires at his death to follow him forsaking all worldly enjoyments or to remain leading the auster life of an asectic.

Raja Ram Mohan Roy wrote pamphlets, petitions against the system of *sati,* which had really great effect on people. He also became the founder of the Brahma Samaj and the social reform school of Sati Ranade. The Government was obliged to prohibit Sati.

In the words of Tagore "Raja Ram Mohan Roy inaugurated the modern age in India. He was born at the time when our country, having lost its link with the inmost truths of its being struggled under a crushing usage, in politics, in the realm, of religion and art, we have entered the zone, uncreative habit of decadent tradition and ceased to exercise our humanity. Through the dynamic power of his personality, his in compromising spirit of freedom he vitalised our material being with the urgency of creative endeavour and launched into arduous adventure of self-realisation. He is the great path maker of this urgency of creative endeavour who has removed ponderous obstacles that impeded our progress at every step and initiated into the present era of worldwide co-operation of humanity."

According to Shri S.N. Banerjee, "Raja Ram Mohan Roy was not only the founder of Brahma Samaj and pioneer of all social reforms in Bengal, but he was also the father of the constitutional agitation in India. He fought tooth and nail for the separation of judiciary from executive so that Judiciary may function independently and the work load in court may also be reduced. The importance of the separation of judiciary was well realised after his death and what he could not achieve during his life was done after his death."

Raja Ram Mohan Roy was the founder of Brahma Samaj which he formed in 1828, He went to England in 1830. He was the father of the Indian liberalism and was contemporary of the great English thinker Bentham.

Raja Ram Mohan realised the need of education in English. He opened Anglo-Indian School for imparting free education of English to boys and girls. He laid the foundation of the social transformation of Hindu on the footing of equality and individual judgement. In addition to the various religious reforms that he advocated very successfully he also championed the right of liberty for women and the establishment of classless society — no big, no small, all are equal. Appropriately he may be called father of Hindu reformation. The Brahma Samaj which he founded represented synthesis of the doctrines of European enlightenment with the philosophical view of Upanishads. The main idea was to purge Hinduism of the bad custom crept in which were writing adverse criticism and resulting the weakening of Hinduism. Truly speaking, Raja Ram Mohan Roy embodies the new spirit, freedom of all the oppressed ones including women, thirst for science, large human sympathy for all, uplift of the masses, preacher of education in English, an apostle of religious revival, removal of all the social impurities that had crept into Hinduism revival of Vedantism, love for motherland, a true patriot, and a noted writer. In fact, Raja Ram Mohan Roy stands as the tribune and prophet of new India.

In the words of Jawaharlal Nehru "Raja Ram Mohan Roy was a new type combining in himself, the old learning and the new. Deeply served in Indian thought and philosophy, a scholar in Sanskrit, Persian and Arabic, he was the product of mixed Hindu and Muslim culture that was there dominant among the cultural classes of India. He was more than a scholar and investigator. He was a reformer above all. Influenced in his early days by Islam and later to some extent by Christianity he struck nevertheless to see foundations of his own faith. But he tried to reform that faith and rid it of the abuses and evil practices that had become associated with it. It was largely because of his agitation of the abolition of Sati practice that the British Government prohibited it".

Freedom of Press

Raja Ram Mohan Roy advocated the cause of the freedom of Press. We can rightly attribute and honour him by saying that he was one of the founders of modern press. He emphasised that freedom of thought and expression thereof without any fear is most vital for the governors and the governed and for democratic rule in the country. His views could best be known and understood by a minute study of his writings such as (a) Petitions against the Press Regulations to the Supreme Court and to the King-in Council, (b) Letter to Lord Amherst on English education.

Lover of Freedom

He raised the voice of freedom of the country. In accordance with the versions of Mr. Arnot that Raja Ram Mohan Roy laid the limit of 40 years for working out England's cultural and humanitarian mission in India because he,believed that during this period British rule would bring up to the level of other civilized and free countries of the world. He advocated religious toleration and firmly believed in compassion.

Other Reforms

Raja Ram Mohan Roy advocated and stood for Constitutional Government. He wanted right of private property and freedom of conduct. He stood for the right of tenants.

His Writings

Raja Ram Mohan Roy was a noted writer and journalist. He started :

(1) *Jufit Muwahhidin* in 1803. A text in Persian with Arabic introduction.

(2) *Vedanta Grantha* (1815). It is a commentary on Brahma Sutra in Bengali.

(3) *Vedantasara* (1815) in Bengali.

(4) *Kenopanishads* (1816) in Bengali

(5) *Isopanishads* (1816) in Bengali.

(6) *Kathopanishads* (1817).

(7) *Mandukyopanishad* (1817) in Bengali.

(8) *The Precepts of Jesus* — the guide to peace and happiness.

(9) Political Writings :

  (i) Petitions against the Press Regulation to Supreme Court and to King-in Council.

  (ii) Letter to Lord Amherst on English education.

  (iii) A tract on the Religious Toleration.

  (iv) Rights of Hindus over ancestral property according to the Law of Bengal.

  (v) Remarks on Settlement in India by Europeans (1831).

Political Ideas

Like Aristotle and Machiavelli, Roy followed the indicative and historical methods and like them was interested in practical political problems rather than in general theories. Raja Ram Mohan Roy was a prolific writer. His political ideas are to be found mainly in his following writings:

(a) Petitions against the Press Regulation to the Supreme Court and to the King-in-Council (1823).
(b) A tract on Religions Toleration (1823).
(c) A Letter to Lord Amherst on English Education (1823).
(d) Rights of Hindus over ancestral property according to law of Bengal (1830).
(e) Remarks on Settlement in India by Europeans (1831).
(f) An Exposition of the Revenue and Judicial System of India.

Admirer of British Rule

Raja Ram Mohan Roy was a realistic thinker and had liberal attitude towards every problem of life. In the beginning Roy had a feeling of great aversion to the establishment of the British rule in India but contact with Europeans made him revice this idea. He gave up his prejudices against Europeans and became inclined to their favour, feeling persuaded that their rule, "though a foreign yoke, would lead more speedily and surely to the amelioration of the Indian People." He also enjoyed the confidence of them even in their public capacity. In this way, he was an admirer of British rule in India. He wanted the continuance of the British rule in India for the advancement of India. He appreciated and admired the British rule for introducing progressive measures on political and social reforms. According to Roy, the British rule was a blessing in disguise. No doubt Roy was an admirer of the British rule in India and wanted it to continue for centuries to come, but he never hesitated to criticise the wrong policies of the government, Raja Ram Mohan Roy demanded that Indians should be given more share in the administration of the country.

Faith in Peaceful and Constitutional Methods Raja Ram Mohan Roy was an ardent advocate of peaceful and constitutional methods for achieving political goals. According to S.N. Banerjee, "Raja Ram Mohan Roy was the father of constitutional agitation in India". Majumdar says, "Raja Ram Mohan Roy was the first apostle of a political creed based on constitutional agitation in this country."

Lover of Liberty like Voltaire, Montesquieu and Rousseau Raja Ram Mohan Roy was a passionate lover of liberty in all the spheres of life. As B.C. Pal points out, one of Ram Mohan's most favourite text was that which declared the essential divinity of man as man. Man was by his nature and constitution, 'eternally free'. To deny this freedom was an out rage upon his nature and a sin against his maker. This was the fundamental philosophy of Ram Mohan.

B.B. Majumdar says that Roy's interest in politics sprang from his love of liberty.

According to Bipin Chandra Pal, "Ram Mohan Roy was the first to deliver the message of political freedom to India. His outstanding contribution towards the political advancement of his people was the new 'self-consciousness and self-confidence' that he tried to create in his countrymen by his multifarious works theological, social, educational and juridical". Roy was the most unhesitant advocate of religious toleration and spiritual individuality. Thus, in his 'Tract on Religious Toleration' he says, "We should feel no reluctance to cooperate with them (the Christians) in religious matters, merely because they consider Jesus Christ as the Messenger of God and their spiritual teacher, for oneness in the object of the religious practice should produce attachment between, the worshippers". Raja Ram Mohan Roy was always a staunch lover of liberty. In a letter to J.S. Buckingham, the editor of the Calcutta Journal, written on August 11, 1821, Ram Mohan expressed his belief in the eventual restoration of the liberty of the European nations and Asiatic colonies. He sympathised with the demands of the Greeks and Neapolitans for liberty. When in 1821, autocracy was restored in Naples, Roy felt perturbed. He wrote, cancelling an engagement with Buckingham on 11th August 1821, "I consider the cause of the Neapolitans as my own and their enemies as ours. Enemies of liberty and friends of despotism have never been and never will be ultimately successful". In 1821 when Ram Mohan heard the news of the establishment of a constitutional Government in Spain, he gave a dinner at the Town Hall in Calcutta to celebrate the occasion. Miss Collet, the editor of the Life and Letters of Raja Ram Mohan Roy also tells us how "at Cape colony on his way to England, the right of the tricolour flag on two French ships lying at anchor in Table Bay fired his enthusiasm", As in the spiritual world he stood up as the prophet of universal religions, so in the sphere of politics, he wanted to see the triumph of the principles of liberalism everywhere in the world.

His views on the Freedom of the Press According to S.N. Banerjee. "Raja Ram Mohan was the first political agitator. He worked tirelessly, not only for increasing democratisation of the administration of India, but also helped forge that indispensable instrument for the working of democracy, a powerful press". The Raja was one of the earliest champions of the press, Like Milton, he championed the concept of Freedom of

Expression and the Freedom of the Press. Roy mentioned his views on the freedom of the press in his Memorial to the Supreme Court and to the King-in Council, He expressed the view that freedom of the press was equally necessary for the sake of the governors and the governed. It is good for the government as it becomes acquainted with the views and wishes of the people concerning the various measures adopted by it. Freedom of the press is good for the governed because it promotes mental improvement. According to Roy, a free press is a safety valve. Thus, he says, "a I free press has never yet caused a revolution in any part of the world, because, while men can easily represent the grievances arising from the conduct of the local authorities to the Supreme government and thus, get them redressed, the grounds of discontent that excite revolution are removed. Moreover a free press is also necessary to improve their minds and ameliorate their condition." Thus, according to Majumdar, the Raja's views on the freedom of the press are regarded 'as the Areopagitica of Indian History.'

B.B. Majumdar remarks that Roy did not claim absolute liberty for the Indian press. In fact, he was not against restraints but was against arbitrary restrictions. Roy also demanded that various restrictions imposed on the press should be removed. In the beginning government's policy towards the press was a combination of severe discouragement on the one side and strict control on the other. However, during the administration of Lord William Bentinck, the law against the press was endorsed.

His views on the Judicial System of India In a Pamphlet' An Exposition of the Revenue and Judicial Systems in India', Raja Ram Mohan Roy discussed some of the most important questions relating to the administration of India, such as, the reform of courts, the jurisdiction of the courts of the country over Europeans, the jury system, the separation of the executive and judicial offices, the consulting of the people in legislation, the codification of laws, the larger, employment of natives, the establishment of a native militia, the age and education of civil servants, the amelioration of the conditions of the ryots, and the making of laws for their protection and the permanent settlement, etc. Roy urged the separation of the legislative and judicial power. He also protested against the union of the offices of the Revenue Commissionership and the Judgeship of the Circuit Court. Thus, in his eassy on the Rights of Hindus over Ancestral Property according to the Law of Bengal, Ram Mohan wrote. "In every civilised country, rules and codes are found proceeding from one authority, and their execution left to another. Experience shows that the unchecked power often leads the best men wrong, and produces general mischief."

Raja Ram Mohan Roy was opposed to the appointment of immature persons to the civil services. He suggested 22 years as the minimum age qualification for the appointment of covenanted service.

Raja Ram Mohan Roy also advocated Jury System. He suggested that the jurors should be appointed from the retired judicial officers and retired lawyers. He also favoured the formation of the Indian code of criminal law, which would be based on principles, common to and acknowledged by all the different sections of the people of the country. The language of this should be simple, precise and clear.

His Views on Civil Rights Raja Ram Mohan Roy was a great champion of rights, Like Locke, Grotius and Paine, he accepted the theory of natural rights. Roy not only advocated the natural rights of life, property and liberty but also believed in the moral rights of the individual. The Jury Act of 1827 introduced religious discrimination into the structure of the judiciary. Under the provision of the Act, Hindus and Muslims could not sit on the jury when a Christian was being tried. Ram Mohan Roy protested against this because it introduced the pernicious element of "religious distinction into the judicial system of the land". Roy initiated a petition on August 17, 1829 against the Act, which was signed by distinguished Hindus and Muslims and the same was submitted to the British Parliament. Though the petition failed the matter was taken up by Mr. Grant, the then President of the Board of Control. Grant's Bill was passed in 1832, making Hindus and Muslims eligible not only to sit both on petty and grand juries but also for appointment as justices of the peace. Roy always fought for the cause of right of the people.

His Remarks on Settlement in India by Europeans In 1882, Roy was asked by the Select Committee of the house of Commons to give his opinion on the question of the settlement in India by the Europeans, Under the provision of the Charter Act of 1813, the Europeans were excluded from settling in India. It was a very complicated problem. Being a liberal, Ram Mohan recommended that educated Europeans "of character and capital" should be permitted and encouraged to settle in India. By the Charter Act of 1833 all the existing restriction were abolished.

His Views on the Scope of State Activity Raja Ram Mohan Roy was not an advocate of the theory of *laissez faire.* He pleaded for state-intervention in suppressing evil practices like Sati and others. In the economic sphere, Roy held that it was the duty of the state to protect the tenants against the rapacity and greed of the landlords, Thus, he advocated state-regulation for improving the moral, social cultural economic and political conditions of India.

His Views on Law, Custom and Morality Though not a jurist, Roy had a clear understanding of the principles of law and its relation to custom on the one side and to morality on the other. He considered both custom as well as command as constituting the sources of law but he did not identify either with law itself, Roy, but his independent thinking arrived at a conclusion, essentially modern, in 1830, *i.e.*, two years before the Publication of Austin's famous work 'Lectures on Jurisprudence'. In his Essay on Rights of Hindus over Ancestral Property according to the Law of Bengal, Roy says, "In every country, rules determining the rights of succession to and alienation of property first originated in the conventional choice of the people, or in the discretion of the highest authority, secular or spiritual and these rules have been subsequently established by the common usage of the country, and confirmed by judicial proceedings". According to Roy, law originates in customs and usage and is confirmed by the courts.

Like his English contemporaries, Austin and Bentham, Roy also made a broad distinction between the spheres of law and that of morality. It is maintained by Austin, says Willoughby, that a custom becomes a law at the time when it is applied by a court and not before, but Roy arrived at the true nature of law by means of his forceful intellect even before Austin. Roy asked, "How shall we draw a line of distinction between those immoral acts that should not be considered invalid and those that should be regarded as null in the eye of the law" and replied "We must refer to the common law and the established usages of every country as furnishing the distinctions admitted between the one class and the other." That is, Roy admitted, the right of the Supreme authority to make whatever changes or modification it thought fit, but at the same time, he insisted that the long standing customs of India be lightly set aside, If the people had followed a particular custom for centuries, Ram Mohan was of the opinion that the people must have found that custom reasonable other-wise, they would not have followed it for such a long time. But Roy advocated adherence to those customs only which satisfied two important conditions : (a) these must be reasonable and (b) these must lead to the general welfare of the people. He had not the least hesitation in rejecting any custom which was unreasonable.

Raja Ram Mohan Roy maintained that the father had an absolute right to sell or mortgage the ancestfal property without consulting his sons even though such an act might cause distress to the family and thus become morally unjustifiable. According to Roy, all laws are legally binding, though some of them may be morally bad (sale of liquor, etc.) Some practices may be very sound morally, but cannot be given legal force; for example — obedience to parents, etc;

These illustrations clearly show how the Raj knew about the distinction between law and morality. This has been described as a capital discovery of Roy by B.B. Majumdar credit for which has been given to John Austin. The distinction between law and morality was not a capital discovery of the Raja. "In the essay itself" as Dr. Goyal remarks, "the Raja makes no secret of how he has borrowed this distinction between law and morality from Hindu legislators of repute. However, what is significant is that he has borrowed this not from Austin or Bentham but from the authors of the Hindu law."

His views on Educations Raja Ram Mohan Roy was a great scholar. He studied Arabic, Persian, Hebrew, Greek etc. He was also a profound scholar of Sanskrit. Roy studied English language only after 1794 and became the admirer of this rich language. So much so, Roy protested against the establishment of a Sanskrit College in 1823 by British government in India and demanded of instead that the college might be utilised for importing a liberal and enlightened system of instruction embracing Mathematics. Natural Philosophy, Chemistry, Anatomy and other useful sciences through the medium of English. In his letter to Lord Amherst on English education Roy wrote, "The Sanskrit system of education would be the best calculated to keep this country in darkness if such had been the policy of the British legislature". Raja Ram Mohan also pleaded that education should be practical in nature and character.

His Social Ideas Raja Ram Mohan was a great social reformer. He realised that before any political advancement of the people, it was necessary to carry out religious and social reforms, He said, "I regret to say that the present system of religion adhered to by the Hindus is not well calculated to promote their political interest. The distinction of castes, introducing innumerable divisions among them, has entirely deprived them of political feeling. It is, I think, necessary that some changes should take place in their religion at least for the sake of their political advantage and social comfort." Raja Ram Mohan Roy began with the denouncement of idolatry as the root cause of all the evils in Hinduism. At the age of sixteen, Roy composed a manuscript condemning idol-worship. According to Roy, idolatry was not only posed to reason and commonsense, but also had no support in the Vedas and the Upanishads, He held the view that idolatry was of recent origin.

The second great reform of Raja Ram Mohan Roy was the task eradicating the revolting custom of burning Hindu widows on the funeral pyre of their husbands. He was shocked to see his sister in-law being immolated. Roy lunched a systematic campaign against this inhuman custom. He cited the *shastras* to disprove the contention of orthodox Hindus, Roy sought government's help in the religious reforms of India.

In 1829, lord Bentinck's enactment made burning of widows illegal. Roy also advocated to cause of widow re-marriage.

Raja Ram Mohan Roy raised a voice against polygamy and caste system. Roy pointed out in an article "We have been subjected to such insults for about nine centuries and the cause has been our excess in civilisation as well as our division into castes which has been the source of want of unity among us". Ram Mohan made efforts to encourage inter-caste marriage. He also voiced against girl-infanticide and child marriage.

Raja Ram Mohan Roy's basic approach to social reforms, rested on a synthesis between the East and West. Dr. Seal pointed out that Ram Mohan had aimed at reconciling the good of the individual with the good of the greatest number-in other words harmonising individualism and socialism.

His Economic Ideas Raja Ram Mohan Roy also took keen interest in the economic problems of India. According to Bepin Chandra Pal "Ram Mohan sought to work out the problems of economics by economic methods along their own lines to solve financial and political questions by the highest principles of the sciences of politics and government, ant thus he struck out a happy balance between these different departments of national life". Roy recognised the co-relationship between cultural regeneration and economic growth. It was clear from his suggestions for administrative reforms to improve the condition of the people, his opposition to the East India Company's monopolistic trading rights, the monopoly enjoyed by the servants of the company in the matter of Salt trade, his support to the principle of free trade and colonisation of Europeans, Roy wanted that the drain of wealth from India to England should be stopped. There should be industrialisation of the country. He also demanded that the poor tenants should be protected from the big zamindars.

Roy was also a champion of the right of Hindu females to inheritance. He criticised the existing law of inheritance which deprived women of property. In his Essay 'Modern Encroachments on the Ancient Rights of Females according to the Hindu law of inheritance'. Roy quoted learned jurists to support his view. According to Roy, the mother was entitled to a share equal to that of her son, in the property left by her husband, and the daughter to one fourth.

Estimate Raja Ram Mohan Roy had been assessed very highly by different great personalities.

According to Bepin Chandra Pal, "He (Rammohan) was the first to affiliate political and social freedom to religious and spiritual emancipation and to initiate the present freedom movement in all its aspect in Modern

India". Roy's unshakable faith in the ability, intelligence and capability of his countrymen to attain the same heights as was reached by any other civilised nation was clear in all his writings in regard to political reforms.

S.N. Banerjee described Ram Mohan as the first political agitator.

Writing on Ram Mohan Roy, Jawaharlal Nehru said, "He was more than a scholar and investigator; he was a reformer above all. There was no aspect of national life which was left untouched by Ram Mohan Roy."

According to V.P. Naik, "In the field of social and religious reform no less than in journalism and in politics his one endeavour was to awaken his countrymen not only to their rights as free men, but also to their obligation to society."

Dr. Brajendra Nath Seal sums up his assessment of Roy as under :

> "He (Raja Ram Mohan Roy) gave a modern meaning and purpose to these ancient and medieval elements of Indian polity. He went on to link them up with representative government, trial by jury, and freedom of the press, and he corrected and completed the Hindu personal law of marriage, inheritance, religious worship, women's status, *stri-dhan* and *varnashramadharma,* by introducing the most liberal principles of justice and equity, for which, he found sanction also in the old codes, thus, working out a synthesis between Eastern and Western social values and postulates against the common background of universal humanity."

Raja Ram Mohan Roy was a great humanist and internationalist. Bentham, the great British liberal thinker greeted him as 'his intensely admired and dearly beloved collaborator in the service of mankind.' According to Miss Collet, "Whatever future the destinies may have in store for India, that future will be largely shaped by the life and work of Ram Mohan Roy, and not the future of Indian alone, we stand on the even of an unprecedented intermingling of the East and the West."

3

Dadabhai Naoroji (1825-1917)

Dadabhai Naoroji, popularly known as the Grand Old Man of India, was a member of the British Parliament in the 19th century. He was engaged for long years in multifarious beneficial activities in Britain and served the cause of India from there. He brought together Indians and Englishmen interested in India through the forum 'London Indian Society' founded by him. He was an expert in Indian economy and exposed the Un-British rule in India which impoverished India. He was a haven of refuge to overseas Indians for many years. He commanded the respect of giants like Tilak and Surendranath Banerjee. His was a simple but heroic life dedicated to the service of his motherland. He was a great social reformer as well. He pioneered women's education vigorously.

His Life Sketch

At the advent of the nineteenth century India was governed by the East India Company whose officers enriched themselves in the name of administering the country. They did nothing to educate the Indians; the lamp of knowledge was burning dimly in a few parts of our country. But even in this period some British administrators appreciated the just aspirations of a few enlightened Indians, and set up some English schools for the first time. The Governor of Bombay Mount Stuart Elphinstone was the foremost among them. He interested himself in the education of Indians. He assisted a lot in the establishment of education institutions in Bombay. During his Governorship of the Bombay Presidency, a child was born in a Parsi Priestly family in Bombay on the 4th September, 1825. The child was destined to wield enormous influence in the political sphere.

The child was Dadabhai Naoroji, the first and only son of Naoroji Palanji Dordi, a simple Parsi Priest and his wife Manekbai. He lost his father when he was only an infant. His mother had great difficulty in bringing him up. She was quite young and there were none to help her except a brother who was very affectionate to her. Mrs. Naoroji lived for her child and aspired to make him a virtuous and celebrated person. She trained him to think and act rightly. He was proficient in studies and possessed sterling character. No doubt his mother was illiterate and doted on her son. Yet she did not fail to have a firm hold upon him and save him from the evil influences of the surroundings. He owed his greatness to her upbringing.

In those days free education was in vogue in Bombay. This was a tremendous facility and blessing for Naoroji; otherwise chill penury would have denied him education. In later years this made him a doughty champion of free education and of the principle that every child should be enabled to receive all the education which he can assimilate. At first he was put in a school where only Indian languages were taught. Even in his childhood he beamed with intelligence and learnt everything more quickly than the other boys. If some dignitary visited the school, the boys were kept in a row. Questions would be put to them by the teacher. As soon as a question was put, Dadabhai would quickly advance and answer the question correctly. With an overhanging forehead and small sparkling eyes, the little Parsi boy Dadabhai, impressed Mrs. Poston, an English visitor to the school immensely. He finished his problems in a trice and gave out the solution in a flash.

Dadabhai was extremely fond of books. He read a lot of stories. He loved games and sports as well. He took delight in playing gilli-danda which was later described by him as cricket. At the age of fifteen there was a strange incident. As he was walking along the road one day, he suddenly realised his foible of carelessly using bad words. He paused there immediately and swore not to use bad words again. He watched himself vigilantly and kept the promise most faithfully. As time passed, he made many other promises to himself and implemented them carefully.

After completing his study at school, Dadabhai passed his matriculation examination and joined the Elphinstone College which had been started a short time before. He was a very intelligent pupil and acquitted himself with distinction. At the age of twenty he held the top most rank. He created such an impression on Sir Erskine Perry, the then Chief Justice and President of the Board of Education that he volunteered to bear half the expense of sending him to England to study Law so that he could be qualified for the Bar. Sir Jamshetjee Jeejibhoy agreed to bear the other portion of the expenses but withdrew the offer on the score that in England Dadabhai might change his religion. So his overseas studies did not materialise. He could not become a luminary in the firmatment of Law.

Dadabhai had to content himself with the position of a teacher in Elphinstone School. Soon he rose to be an Assistant Professor of Mathematics in the College and two years later he became the full-blown Professor of Mathematics. This was a very rare distinction conferred on an Indian for the first time in any college in India. Dadabhai was an exemplary professor and he was affectionately called "Dadabhai Professor". Besides teaching, Dadabhai participated in multifarious movements promoting social reform in Bombay and specially among the Parsi community. He actively associated himself with the demand for political freedom. In furtherance of this great cause, he edited a Gujarati, magazine, called Rast Goftar (Truth Teller). Dadabhai Naoraji's dynamic activities had much impact on the social and educational life of Bombay. He took up the question of religious reforms with great zeal and induced the Parsis to shed many frills and accretions to the Zorastrain faith. In this he succeeded, notwithstanding diehard opposition. In 1852 he was instrumental in establishing the Bombay Association with a view to ventilating political grievances. He pioneered women's education. He went round with his companions asking the permission of parents to teach their girls in the varandahs of their houses. Women's education gradually picked up and institutions sprang up. He felt that he owed his education and all the benefits accruing from it to the people and that he should return to them the best he had in him and so he devoted himself heart and soul to the service of the people.

In his thirtieth year, Naoroji's life underwent a change. This changed his destiny and also the destiny of India. A Parsi business firm called Cama & Co wanted to establish a branch in England, and they requested Dadabhai to serve as their representative in England. He took up the offer. It looked as though worldly advantages weighed with him and he abandoned the noble profession of teaching. But the real inducement was that he could forge an intimate new connection established between England and India. Particularly he could afford a home for young Indians. They could freely go to England and compete for the Indian Civil Service and other services.

In England Dadabhai carried on the business of his firm and simultaneously engaged himself in efforts to educate the British people on Indian affairs. He founded a society and christened it The East India Association. Indians and Englishmen interested in India met together under the auspices of this forum. He kept contact with numerous English institutions and wrote and talked a great deal. He was made a Professor of Gujarati in the University. College, London, and was elected a member of its Senate. As ill luck would have it, all was not well with Dadabhai's firm. It closed down the English branch and sent Dadabhai back to

India in 1869. His native city of Bombay arranged a grand welcome in appreciation of the excellent work done by him in England to promote the interests of India, the citizens presented an address along with a purse of Rs. 30,000. Dadabhai did not use the money for his benefit but utilised all the amount for the service of his countrymen. A young Parsi artist painted and Justice Ranade unveiled this in the hall of the Framjee Cowasjee Institute, Bombay. He went about mobilising public interest in the East Indian Association and educating the people on the need for reform. Within a short period he again sailed for England where he plunged into activities to advance Indian interests. Now he gave evidence before the Parliamentary Committee on Indian finance. Nobody had any clear knowledge of the actual income of India and the average income of Indians. Dadabhai made independent calculations and declared that the average income of Indians was not more than Rs. 20 per annum per head. Other expert did not approve of his figures but after some years the Government of India almost accepted his conclusions.

In 1874 Dadabhai returned to India and Mulhar Rao the Maharaja of Baroda, appointed him Dewan of the State. The affairs of the State were not in good shape. Corruption and mismanagement were rampant. Dadabhai undertook to redress everything. Many a difficulty confronted him. The corrupt officials resented his reforms. The Maharaja was eccentric and the British Resident in the State was a very tough man to tackle. Notwithstanding all these hurdles, Dadabhai carried on his work, set up a sound administration in the State and his sincere efforts were crowned with success.

Dadabhai's sixtieth year was memorable in several respects. Lord Reay, Governor of Bombay, invited him to serve on the Legislative Council. This was an unusual and rare distinction for an Indian and this appointment was widely welcomed by the whole country. Another very important event took place in the same year. The first session of the Indian National Congress was held in Bombay with Umesh Chander Banerjee in the Chair. It became the instrument for India's severance from the British yoke in later times. A small group of people had founded it. Allan Octavian Hume, a retired member of the Indian Civil Service and a staunch supporter of India's struggle for increased self-government, was the most prominent of those people. Dadabhai associated himself closely with the inauguration of the Congress and took a leading part its session in Bombay. As time went on, his connection with this body grew closer and closer.

Now Dadabhai realised that the best way to way India's battle was to capture a seat in the British Parliament. So, he went to England again in 1886. He allied himself with the Liberal Party and the Holborn Liberal

Association declared him as its candidate. That was no insignificant event. Though he lost the election, he polled 1950 votes which was no mean achievement. At the end of 1886, he got back to India and got elected as the President of the second session of the Indian National Congress held in Calcutta. The Congress was still a 'faithful' body. Dadabhai as president declared that the members of the Congress were not rebels against the British Government but very loyal to the backbone. He appealed to the Government of India to introduce immediate reforms and to admit Indians to the legislatures as elected members. He helped in the drafting of a proper scheme for council reform.

At the age of sixty-six, Dadabhai returned to England once again and attempted an entry into the House of Commons. He toiled hard for five years and at length, on July 6, 1891 he became a full-fledged Liberal Member of Parliament for Central Finsbury Constituency defeating his conservative opponent. This election to Parliament was an astounding triumph for Dadabhai and for India. He was the first Indian ever to be elected a member of Parliament. This event is a great landmark in the annals of India's march towards independence. In his maiden speech in the House of Commons he expressed his grateful thanks to the British people for enabling him to enter the Parliament and solicited their support for the just causes he would expose. He involved himself in many important happenings which affected the improvement of India. In 1893 he visited India to take the chair in the ninth session of the Congress to be held at Lahore. His journey from Bombay to Lahore was a triumphant march befitting a king and he was welcomed with great jubilation. At Lahore his carriage was not drawn by horses but by the enthusiastic crowd of young men. At every station where the train halted large numbers of people assembled and applauded him lustily. In his presidential address he stated that he aimed at the promotion of good fellow — feeling among all his countrymen and he appealed to the people to remember that all were the children of the same soil. His clarion call to them was given as follows. "I am an Indian. I am above all an Indian. Our Country is India. Our nationality is Indian."

Dadabhai returned to England and remained an M.P. till 1895. In that year the Liberals were defeated in the General Election and Dadabhai's seat was lost. Nevertheless, he was no less active. In 1901 a selection of his writings and speeches was published by him under the caption 'Poverty and Un-British Rule in India.' He again tried to enter the House of Commons but an unfortunate split in the Liberal Party spoiled his chances. He was eighty years of age. His countrymen and friends in England admired him for his long record of service to his motherland and held him in great regard. He was now popularly known by the affectionate appellation of "The Grand Old Man of India". At a meeting of the Congress Reception Committee held in Calcutta in 1906 his name was proposed for the presidentship of the Congress as a mark of honour and appreciation. He left England after a ceremonial send off and arrived in Bombay. Large crowds gathered on the water-front and in the streets and cheered him heartily. The people took him a motor car to Malabar Hill in a slowly moving procession. They had decorated the streets gaily. The procession had to halt a number of times to permit the people to garland him. There were strings of precious pearls among the garlands. Later, in Calcutta, the people greeted him with similar marks of honour and enthusiasm. In his eloquent presidential speech Dadabhai remarked as follows : "Freedom is the very breath of our lives. We stand for liberty. The whole of the administration must be in the hands of the people. Had this been in Indian hands there should have been no present misery, poverty and discontent of the Indian people. Hindus and Muslims are the twin eyes of Mother India. We are all in one boat. We should sink or swim hand in hand. United we stand, divided we fall."

The session of Congress over, Dadabhai sailed to England notwithstanding his advanced age, he did not cease to be active and alert. Soon heavy work and lack of rest told on his health. He was taken ill and his friends advised him to get back to his motherland. So he left England for the last time and landed in Bombay. Large crowd of people surged forward to meet him. He was ailing miserably. He was taken quietly to his home in Versova, a suburb of Bombay. He did not fail to interest himself in the affairs of his country. He still wrote many letters. The people celebrated his birthday throughout the length and breadth of India. He became the President of the Home Rule League started by Mrs. Annie Besant on his ninetieth birthday. The Bombay University conferred on him the honorary degree of Doctor of Laws in 1916. The non-agenarian veteran attended the convocation in person. On his return home after the convocation the streets were lined with people who had gathered to have *darshan* of the Grand Old Man of India. His sole desire was that he should be spared to witness the beginning of the reforms culminating in self-government. But this was not fulfilled. On 1st June his condition became critical. The best doctors attended on him but they could do little. The great apostle who had lived for right and truth passed away peacefully on June 30th, 1917. The great chapter of the great son of India who was born of the people, trusted by the people and who toiled and moiled ceaselessly for his motherland, came to a close.

In his funeral oration Sir Narain Chandravarkar echoed the thoughts of millions of his admirers in the following words. "The Sun that rose just ninety-three years ago over India is set; but it is set to rise again in the form of a regenerated India, for Dadabhai lived and worked for us with a rare devotion which must endure as an inspiring example for all of us."

Admirer of the British Rule Dadabhai Naoroji was a great admirer of the British rule in India like his contemporaries. He had faith in the British fair-paly and justice. He considered the British rule in India as a blessing. Thus, he said, "I, for one, have not the shadow of a doubt that in dealing with such justice-loving, fair-minded people as the British, we may rest fully assured — that the time will come when the sentiments of the British nation and our gracious Queen's proclamation of 1858 will be realised." Dadabhai was of the opinion that India could progress only if the British rule continued. He never thought of a complete severance of the political connection with England. The self-government of his conception was self-government under the British paramountcy. Dadabhai Naoroji had firm faith in British sense of justice and fair play.

In spite of Dadabhai's admiration of the British Rule in India, he pointed out that the relations between England and India had to be established on the basis of justice, righteousness and liberality He wanted that England should rule India for India's good rather than the good of England. Dadabhai never hesitated to criticise the evils of the British administration in India. However, he was of the firm conviction that the British people possessed deep traditions of equality, justice and fair play, that they loved freedom and would help India to obtain Swaraj.

His Political Goal According to Dadabhai Naoroji, self-government was the only remedy for the ills of India. He said at the gathering of the London Indian Society. "Thdre is only one remedy to the present dishonourable, hypocritical and destructive system. That remedy is self-government under British paramountcy."

On November 10 at a dinner party in U.K. Dadabhai said, "The colonies were prospering with self-government whereas India was perishing without it. After all great events have been happening abroad, Japan and Russia and I do not think our present statesmen will shut their eyes to the obvious results of these great events....If the whole population of India said once for all that they were determined to have self-government their claim would not be and could not be made in vain."

Dadabhai demanded self-government under the British empire. He said, "The moment a people came under the British flag, they are free and fellow British citizens. We Indians have been free citizens as if it were out birth-right... from the first moment we came under the British flag."

Dadabhai Naoroji also demanded Indianisation of Services, introduction of representative institutions and just and equal financial relations between India and England.

His Political Method Dadabhai Naoroji believed in the method of prayers and petitions. He advocated peaceful and constitutional methods for achieving the political goal, Dadabhai said, "The whole parliament, press and platform is simply all agitation; small agitation is the civilized peaceful weapon of moral forces and infinitely preferably to brute physical force when possible." Dadabhai had complete confidence in the justice and fairplay of the British people and he was sure that our demands would be conceded gracefully. However, Dadabhai never believed in the politics of mendicancy nor he considered prayers and petitions as a method of political mendicancy. He explained "these petitions are not any begging for any favour any more than that the conventional 'Your Obedient Servant' in letters makes a man an obedient servant. It is the conventional way of approaching higher authorities. The petitions are claims for rights or for justice or for reforms — to influence and put pressure on Parliament by showing how the public regard any particular matter."

Dadabhai also emphasised educating the British people about the Un-British character of the British rule in India. He was of the opinion that the British public did not know the pitiable conditions of Indians. So, he suggested that Indian delegations should be sent to England to educate the British people about the terrible mental, moral and economic drain to which India was being subjected. To achieve the political goal, the Indians must agitate, otherwise the Britishers would naturally conclude that they were satisfied. According to Dadabhai, thus, agitation was the life and soul of political life, but it should be peaceful.

Lover of Liberty Dadabhai Naoroji was a passionate lover of liberty in all the sphere of life. He demanded that the Indian people must enjoy some basic liberties as the British themselves enjoyed. Dadabhai said, "British is the parent of free and representative government and, that we as her subjects and children are entitled to inherit the great blessings of freedom and representation." To deny these basic liberties, according to Dadabhai, was an unhealthy character of British administration in India. Like Raja Ram Mohan Roy, Dadabhai Naoroji was always a staunch lover of liberty.

His views about Rights Dadabhai Naoroji was a great champion of rights. He demanded certain basic rights for the Indian people. Dadabhai proceeded to enumerate them in the form of demands.

First, he wanted Indianisation of services, *i.e.*, the Indians should be given more share in Indian administration particularly in higher jobs. Dadabhai explained, "They (Indians) could not rise, they could not develop their capacity for higher government, because they had no opportunity : the result was, of course, that their faculties were stunted". He strongly advocated that there should be simultaneous examination in India and England for recruitment to the civil services.

Secondly, Dadabhai demanded the introduction of representative institutions in India. The Indians should be given more representation to the legislative bodies. He was opposed to the idea of limited franchise. Thus, he said, "just as the administration of the U.K. in all services, departments and details is in the hands of the people themselves of that country, so should we in India claim that the administration in all services, departments and details should be in the hands of people themselves of India."

Thirdly, Dadabhai demanded just and equal financial relations between Indian and Britain.

His Faith in the Moral Basis of Authority Dadabhai Naoroji had deep-rooted faith in the moral foundations of political authority. Like Prof. T.H. Green, he believed that the political authority should be based on moral foundations rather than on brute force. In his Presidential Address at the Lahore session of the Congress in 1893, Dadabhai said, "You can build up an empire by arms or ephemeral brute physical force; but you can preserve it by the eternal moral forces only. Brute force will, sometime or another, break down; righteousness is everlasting." Justice, generosity and humanity alone constitute the real basis of political power. According to Dadabhai, if England would embark upon a policy of irritation, it was bound to lead to the disintegration of the empire.

Change in His Political Out-look In the beginning Dadabhai Naoroji was an admirer of the British rule in India. He had deep faith in British fairplay and justice. Dadabhai considered the British rule in India as a blessing. But in his later days, a transition took place in his political outlook. Due to the reactionary activities of the British government in India, Dadabhai showed considerable interest in the activities of the extremist leaders Lal, Bal and Pal. The whole matter, Dadabhai said, "could be compressed in one word, "Self-government" — Swaraj. The time had, however, arrived for the transfer of power to begin. "In his presidential address at the Calcutta session of the Congress (1906) he said "If I can leave a word of affection and devotion for my country and countrymen. I say, be united, persevere, and achieve self-government, so that the millions now perishing by poverty, famine and plague... may be saved, and India may once more occupy her proud position of yore among the greatest and civilised nations of the world."

Dadabhai's Drain Theory According to Dadabhai Naoroji the Indian economy was subjected to a heavy drain. The inevitable consequence of foreign domination was the drain of wealth from India to Britain. Dadabhai pointed out that India had the lordliest and costliest administration in the world. The extravagant cost of Indian administration intensified the disastrous effect of the drain. The British people had no idea about the pitiable and miserable conditions of the Indian people. So, Dadabhai set himself to the difficult task of exposing the astounding expenditure of the rulers. It was a very difficult task as official data were inadequate and misleading. In spite of this, Dadabhai dedicated all his energy to the task.

According to Dadabhai Naoroji, the existing financial relations between India and England were unjust and unfair. He said, the existing system of government was despotic for Indians and Un-British and suicidal to Britain. In the first paper of his book 'Poverty and Un-British Rule in India'. Dadabhai calculated that the yearly average, income per head in India was 40 shillings, roughly equivalent to Rs. 20 and commented, "even for such food and clothing as a criminal obtains there is hardly enough of production even in a good season, leaving alone all luxuries, all social and religions wants, all expenses of occasions of joy and sorrow and any provision for bad season." Dadabhai did not accept the view that India's poverty was due to over-population or the interplay of economic laws. In this connection he said, "There is the strong argument of over-population. They taste and so far truly of the increase by British peace, but they quite forget the destruction by the British drain. They talk of the pitiless operations of economic laws, but some-how they forget that there is no such thing in India as the natural operation of economic law... It is not the pitiless operation of economic laws, but it is the thoughtless and pitiless action of the British policy, it is the pitiless eating of India's substance in India, and the further pitiless drain to England, in short, it is pitiless perversion of economic laws by the sad bleeding to which India is subjected that is destroying India."

Examining the figures of imports and exports from India between the years 1835 and 1872. Dadabhai pointed out that the value of exports exceeded that of imports by £ 500,000,000. Thus, according to Dadabhai, this did not represent the total tribute which India annually paid to Britain. Had interest been calculated the drain would have amounted to a higher figure. In a letter sent to the Daily News on April 3, 1905, he pointed out that during 10 years from 1892 to 1899 and 1902 to 1903, England imported from India goods worth £ 4,988,913,359 and exported worth £ 3,421,438,153 thereby making a net gain of £ 1,467,441,206, the average drain in India was £ 34 million. The drain was in the form of vast amount of wealth taken away by the Britishers to England. This was as under :

(a) Expenditure of European officials in England for their various wants both there and in India, *i.e.*, expenses of the Government of India in England,

(b) Payment of pensions to the British officers,

(c) Payments to the war office for the maintenance of British troops in India,

(d) Money sent by the British professionals to England from India.

Thus, Dadabhai wrote in his book, "this drain consists of two elements — first, that arising from the remittances by European officials of their savings, and for their expenditure in England for their various wants both there and in India, from pensions and salaries paid in England, and from government expenditure in England and India. And the second, that arising from similar remittances by non-official Europeans. Calculated in terms of statistics, Dadabhai pointed out that this drain came to 30 to 40 million pounds annually.

According to Dadabhai, this drain of wealth from India to England was the basic evil that prevented just and fair relations between India and England. Another evil which Dadabhai referred to was as to how this drain from India was being brought back in the shape of British Capital in India. Thus, Dadabhai said, "As the drain prevents India from making any capital, the British by brining back the capital which they have drained from India itself secure almost a monopoly of all trade and important industries, and thereby further exploit and drain India, the source of the evil being the official drain."

In his evidence before the Indian expenditure commission, Dadabhai said, "At present we suffer it as an evil because we are helpless and on the ground, and foreign capital comes in and develops the resources for their benefit, and carries away the whole profit that is obtained out of these resources. We are simply used as common labourers, mere hewers of wood and drawers of water. That is the only position to which we are reduced." He demanded that the British capital in India should complete on fair and equal terms and that it should not enjoy a monopoly position. Dadabhai again pointed out, 'In India in the construction of the rail road, a large amount of the loan that goes towards the payment of Europeans goes out of the country. Then, again in the working of the railway there is the same drawback, leaving therefore, hardly any benefit at all to India itself and the whole interest of the loan must also go out of the country.'

Dadabhai Naoroji believed in the policy of free trade, but the conditions in which India was placed, he felt that could only be disastrous. Free trade between England and India was, said Dadabhai, "something like a race between a starving, exhausting invalid, and a strong man with a horse to ride on. Before powerful English interests, India must and does go to the wall." However, he felt that free trade was possible only between countries which had equal control over their own resources. But in India, the infant industries were rained in the name of free trade. They needed protection. Dadabhai accepted that India could be prepared for free trade in case the drain of wealth from India was brought within reasonable limits.

In addition to the economic drain Dadabhai also referred to 'The Moral Drain' of the country. Thus, he said, 'all experience and knowledge of statesmanship, of administration or legislation, of high scientific or learned professions, are drained away to England when the persons possessing them give up their service and retire to England. This migration of experience amounted to moral drain'. This was not the position under Mughal rule. The Muslims made India their home and contributed to her culture and progress.

On the role of the state in creating the condition of economic progress, Dadabhai closely followed Mill's enunciation of economic development in the underdeveloped countries. He enquired how far these pre-conditions of economic development were present or could be created in India. According to Dadabhai, India's problem was one of production rather than of distribution. He said, "Any poverty in the countries of Western Europe is not from want of wealth or income, but from unequal distribution. In India with such a low level of production or income, the question of its right distribution is very far off indeed." He recognised the importance of the over-heads of economic development in a pre-dominating agricultural country. Dadabhai Naoroji was a sincere believer in state initiative in the economic sphere.

Dadabhai's Views about Colonialism Dadabhai was also a socialist in his views. He had love and sympathy for the labourers and workers. Dadabhai attended an international gathering of socialists at Amsterdam from the 14th August to the 20th August, 1904. At the Conference of Democrats, held on July 29, 1905, he moved a resolution demanding the establishment of a universal system of old-age pensions. Dadabhai also formulated and published a scheme for setting up of industrial Commissioner's Courts for the recognition and protection of labour and to ensure justice to all wage-earners.

Dadabhai was opposed to the policy of imperialism and colonialism. He said, "Colonial possession alone gives the monopoly guarantee against all contingencies in the struggle with competitors. Including the contingencies, the latter will defend themselves by means of a law establishing a state monopoly. The more the capitalism is developed, the more strongly, the shortage of raw-material is felt, the more intense the competition and the hunt for sources of raw-materials throughout the world, the more desperate is the struggle for acquisition of colonies."

4

Mahadeo Govind Ranade (1842-1901)

According to D.G. Karve, "M.G. Ranade was a great man, a fervent patriot, a religious reformer, a leader of thought, a guide of men, an able historian and an eminent economist."

Mahadeo Govind Ranade a distinguished jurist, economist, historian, social reformer, a fervent patriot and a great educationist, was one of the stupendous figures of modern India.

According to Gopal Krishan Gokhale, "Mr. Ranade was a pre-eminently great and a pre-eminently good man — a great thinker, a great scholar, a great worker, a saintly man in private life.... But he was more — a man so equipped could worthily undertake the task of moulding the thoughts and hopes and aspirations of his country men".

Justice M.G. Rande occupies and important place in the history of Indian modern political thought. He has been also described as a political Rishi. Like Raja Ram Mohan Roy and Dadabhai Naoroji, Justice Ranade was also the advocate of liberalism and contitutionalism. In his opinion, India could advance politically, socially and economically only if the British Rule continued in India. He regarded the British Rule in India as a blessing in disguise.

Mahadeo Govind Ranade was a staunch advocate of individual liberty and demanded maximum rights for the Indians. He believed in the positive conception of the role of the state. M.G. Ranade took keen interest in all the spheres of life. He expressed his views on the role of the state, religion, social reforms, Maratha History, liberty, rights, economic affairs, etc. He was the political Guru of Mr. A.O. Hume, the founder of the Indian National Congress.

His Life Sketch Mahadeo Govind Ranade was born in the Chitpavan Brahmin family, on January 18, 1842, at Niphad in the Nasik District of Maharashtra. Govindrao, his father held an important post in the service of the Kolhapur state. Ranades were in the service of the British for a long time and had administrative experience. Ramabai Ranade wrote, "the men of the Ranade family were tall, brilliant, strong and valiant, industrious, and generous of heart."

M.G. Ranade received his early education at Kolhaphur. He was married at the age of thirteen in 1854. In 1856 Ranade was sent to Elphinstone Institution at Bombay. In those days, he was a very studious student. Bhandarkar wrote, "I came to know Mahadeo Ranade near about 1856 when he came from Kolhapur to Bombay and joined the Elphinstone College... He never wasted time in gossips. He did not know any one intimately nor did he cultivate intimacy with anyone. Day and night he was absorbed in reading."

At the age of 17 years, Ranade wrote two essays expressing his views about the decline of Maratha power and the establishment of the British Rule in India. He wrote, "To wrote the history of one's own country is always a pleasing task. The felicity and pleasure are yet still greater when one sits to write about the rise and progress of his own nation."

Mahadeo Govind Ranade had a very brilliant career at the college and passed all examinations with distinction. He passed his senior scholarship examination in 1861, B.A. in 1862, B.A. Honours in 1863, M.A. in 1864, LL.B. in 1865 and LL.B. Honours in 1866 with first class first. As a student, Ranade was so brilliant that his papers were sent to England as model papers for the University students there. In 1866, he was appointed Marathi translator in the education department. From 1868 to 1871, Ranade acted as Professor of English Literature in the Elphinstone College. In 1871, he was appointed as a judge of the Bombay High Court. From 1885 to 1893, Ranade was the additional law member of the Bombay legislative council.

Justice Ranade took a very keen interest in social and political activities of his times. In 1862, he began to work as the editor of the English section of the daily Induprakash. He took active part in the establishment of the Deccan Education Society. In 1870 Ranade founded the Poona *Sarvjanik Sabha*. He also actively participated in Paramhans Mandli, which later on became the basis of the *Prarthana Samaj*, the Widow-re-marriage Association and the Indian Social Conference. Ranade was one of the 72 delegates who attended the first session of the Indian National Congress. The Indian National Social Conference, a social organisation played very important role covering all aspects of human progress. It viewed that there could be no real economic, social or political progress until the individual was renovated and uplifted. Indians would not advance politically unless they advanced socially. Commenting on the aims and objects of the Indian National Social Conference, James Kellock wrote; The object of the National Social Conference was to stimulate and to strengthen the forces of reform by bringing together every year in mutual consultation representation of the various associations and movements which, scattered all over India, were struggling with the social evils. A great deal of good and hopeful work in the way of social reform was being done here and there throughout the country. The conference brought such work to a focus and made the inspiration and example of it available for others. It strengthened the hands of local societies, formulated methods and guided the reforming aspirations. This unifying of the social movement in India was achievement of great importance. It brought the ideas of social reform home to a much larger public, and it gave powerful reinforcement to the scattered reformers in their struggle with inertia and reaction. Ranade threw himself into the work with immense zeal and with untiring perseverance..., Raghunath Rao was its secretary, but Ranade was the guiding hand and the inspiring mind."

His works :

Ranade was a prolific writer. He wrote (a) *Essays on Indian Economics* and (b) *Rise of the Maratha Power.* It is through these two works that we know the main political ideas of justice Ranade.

Political Ideas

Like Dadabhai Naoroji and Ram Mohan Roy, Mahadeo Govind Ranade was also a liberal. Like his contemporaries, he regarded British rule in India as a boon and a blessing. He had deep faith in the British fair-play and justice. It was through British Rule that India could progress in all the spheres of life. Ranade appreciated many points of the British rule and opined that the British had a mission in India for good of her people. As T.V. Parvate remarked, "Like the Muslim domination, he (Ranade) regarded the British domination also as a necessary discipline for the evolution of a better India, the British association with India was to him a superior educative process which he expected to last long enough for India to realise her real soul". In an article to the journal of the Sarvjanik Sabha, Ranade expressed his views about the British rule as. follows; 'the rationale of British rule is its capacity and its providential purpose of fostering the political education of the country, on the largest scale, civil and public activities.' No doubt Ranade was a great admirer of British rule in India but he never hesitated to criticise the wrong policies of the government, *e.g.*, the system of land tenure and land revenue, the exclusion of Indians from higher positions and the industrial policy. He also opposed the highly centralised system of British administration which left little scope for local initiative.

Like his contemporaries Raja Ram Mohan Roy and Dadabhai Naoroji, Mahadeo Govind Ranade also believed in the peaceful and constitutional method of making representation to the government. In 1874, he sent a petition to the British Parliament demanding that the Indians should be given representation in the British Parliament in London. It also demanded the introduction of self-governing institutions in India. Justice Ranade adopted the method of prayers and petition as the best way of educating the Indian people politically. He was also in favour of sending deputations of Indians to England to educate the British electors in regard to Indian affairs. Ranade used to arrange public meetings, inviting people for discussions and delivering lectures on the current questions of his times.

Ranade's Views about State Mahandeo Govind Ranade was the first modern Indian political thinker who gave his ideas about the nature and functions of the state. He believed in the positive conception of the role of the state. Justice Ranade regarded state as "representing the highest and most disinterested wisdom of the times working to give effect to the other tendencies, capacity represents the power, the wisdom, the mercy and charity of its best citizens". Like German idealist thinkers. Ranade believed in the organic nature of the state. Thus, he said, "The state after all exists only to make individual members composing it nobler, happier, richer and more perfect, in every attribute with which we are endowed". But the realisation of this noble object could not be brought about unless the individuals made earnest efforts. It shows that basically Ranade was an individualist. He regarded the individual as end and the state as means to promote the well-being of the individual. But his individualism was individual-in-society. Ranade never wanted maximum liberty for the individuals. Thus, he said, "State help is after all a subordinate factor is the problem. Our own exertion and resolutions must conquer the difficulties which are chiefly of our own creation."

Ranade believed in the positive conception of that state and advocated state initiative in matters of industrialization, colonization, planned organisation of economic life, Social reform legislation and its protection.

In modern India, Justice Ranade was the first thinker who gave the idea of the welfare state. Thus, he said, "The state is now more and more recognized at the national organ for taking care of national needs in all matter in which individual and co-operative efforts are not likely to be so effective and economical as nation's effort. This is the correct view to take all the pure functions of a state. To relegate them to the simple duty of maintaining peace and order is in reality to deprive the community of many of the advantages of the social unions". The state should not function for the welfare of the people. In the economic sphere also, Ranade opposed the policy of Laissez-faire. He considered the policy of state indifference as the root cause of India's poverty.

Mahadeo Govind Ranade was staunch lover of liberty. He believed in the positive conception liberty. According to him, liberty was not mere absence of restraint but was a positive concept of doing work under the framework of law. He said in 1893, "Freedom means making laws, levying taxes, imposing punishment and appointing officials The true difference between a free country and an unfree one is that in the former before punishment is given, a law must has been made : before taxes are levied, consent must have been secured : before making a law, opinions must have been taken". According to Ranade, liberty can be realised only through the system of Rule of Law and the parliamentary form of government. He demanded the introduction of self-government, decentralisation of administration, educational reforms, social reforms, etc. for the betterment of India. Justice Ranade also supported the independence of judiciary and considered it as the backbone of a free country.

Mahadeo Govind Ranade believed in the democratic constitutional type of government. He supported decentralised administration and healthy growth of local institutions. Ranade openly condemned the highly centralised system of British administration in India. He wanted that Indians should be given representation in British parliament. So far as state-centre relations were concerned, Ranade said, "the central government is to give instructions and to lay down fixed principles and it should leave the local bodies to apply them in practice". Moreover, it is the magisterial and police functions which represent the distinctive features of a sovereign authority, and these must be localized if local government is not to be a misnomer and a certain failure. Ranade also suggested that existing local bodies be empowered to borrow from the government at low interest the money required and advance them as loans for the improvement of the rural and urban industries. He wanted to grant enormous function to the local bodies.

M.G. Ranade was an advocate of Hindu-Muslim Unity, the two major communities of India. He said that India could progress only if there was Hindu-Muslim Unity. He wanted that both these communities should live in harmony. At the Indian National Social Conference held at Lucknow, Ranade said, "If the lessons of the past have any value, one thing is quite clear that in this vast country no progress is possible unless both Hindus and Mohammedans join hands together and determine to follow the lead of men who flourished in Akbar's time and were his chief Advisors and councillors and sedulously avoided mistakes which were committed by his grandson, Aurangzeb. Join again from a sense of common interest and a desire to bring about the fusion of thoughts and feeling of men so as to tolerate small differences and bring about concord. These were the chief aims kept in view by Akbar and formed a principle of new divine faith formulated Din-i-Illahi". He advised the Hindus, not to regard their culture and civilisation alone best in the world. They should also realise the importance of the culture and civilisation of others, In the words of Ranade, "Besides the source of strength, there can be no doubt that in a hundred other ways the Mohammedan domination helped to refine the tastes and the manner of the Hindus. The art of government was better understood by the Mohammedans than by the old Hindu sovereigns."

Mahadeo Govind Ranade had faith in Indian culture and civilisation. He wanted to revive what was best in the past. He said, "We could not break with the past if we would, we must not break with it if we could". But he did not wish to live in the past and opposed the concept of Revivalism as preached in the name of Golden Age in the past. Thus, Justice Ranade said, "What shall we revive?.. Shall we review the twelve forms of sons, or eight forms of marriage which included capture and recognised mixed and illegitimate intercourse? Shall we revive the Niyoga System of procreating sons on our brother's wives when widowed? Shall we revive the old liberties taken by the *Rishis* and by the wives of *Rishis* with the marital tie?... In a living organisation, as society is, no revival is possible. The dead and the buried or burnt, are dead, buried and burnt once for all, and the dead past cannot, therefore, be revived except by a reformation of the old materials into new organised beings. If revival is impossible, reformation is the only alternative open to sensible people".

Mahadeo Govind Ranade was a religious man and had profound faith in the kindness of Providence. He was influenced by the theistic ideal of Maharashtra saints. Like Kant, Ranade believed that the moral laws of conscience vindicated the existence of God. He had faith in the teachings of religious scriptures. Justice Ranade said, "When favoured souls in all times and countries are born, inspired with a prophet's vision, piet's fire, or a great preacher's eloquence, a philosopher's wisdom, or a martyr's self-surrender, then the vision and the fire and the eloquence and the wisdom and the heroism are Divine, *i.e.*, special gifts of God, and what these favoured men see, feel and teach, and their whole life, are a special sort of a higher and a truer revelation in the only tenable sense of the word". He believed in the purification of the human heart in accordance with the dictates of conscience. Like Tulsidas, Ranade believed in the forceful power of prayers. He believed in the existence of God even in the working of external natural but He could not be demonstrated by reason.

In his essay on the 'Philosophy on Indian Theism' Ranade wrote; 'All the proof that we can attain to in religious matters is that practical or moral conviction is all that is needed and, therefore, attainable by the human mind in its search after the Absolute and in that case the demand for logical proof may itself be an unreasonable demand. Ranade also believed in the concept of Moksha eternal blessedness and fellowship with God, However, Moksha for Ranade did not mean absolute merging in God but salvation was only for bodily lusts. It lay in the love of mankind and fellow-beings. In the words, of G.V. Joshi, "Mr. Justice Ranade did all his work not simply from patriotic motives but as religious work, and with religious zeal.... He was one of the most religious of men and what most struck and impressed me during my association with him was his simple, exalted, and fervent piety. He always seemed to feel that he was in the presence of the Almighty, a humble servant doing his appointed task as best as he could, and with the light of faith that was vouchsafed to him."

Champion of Social Reforms Before Justice Ranade, the idea of social reform originated with Raja Ram Mohan Roy. According to Ranade, "Raja Ram Mohan Roy had turned the flow of the national current in the right direction by his long fight for the abolition of Sati and other religious atrocities, and by his endeavour to remove the false accretion of ages and to return to the pure monotheism of Vedic times."

When Ranade came to Bombay, a society named Paramhans Mandli was doing work with the object of eliminating the social evils like caste system, ban on widow-remarriage, idolatry, etc.

In 1867, Ranade became the active member of the *Prathana Samaj*, the organisation which concentrated attention on propagating interdining and intermarriage of widows and other social activities.

He also became the member of Widow-Marriage Association. In support of widow re-marriage Ranade remarked, "The advocates of re-marriage have never maintained that a woman after her husband's death should not live a life of single devotion to her deceased husband. They freely allow that such heroic self-sacrifice to sentiments is peculiarly meritorious. But a woman who cannot live this species of life, a woman who is widowed when a girl before she knew who her husband was, before she knew what her duties as a wife were surely such a woman cannot practise this devotion. It is on behalf of such women that this reform is a pore-emptory and crying want, and to require them to live a life of devotion is a simple mockery of all religion and justice."

He also raised voice against child marriage. He suggested that the boys should not marry before the age of 20 and the girls before the age of 14. In 1894, at Ranade's initiative, a circular regarding social reform was circulated, on questions like compulsory education, school playgrounds, school boarding houses, libraries and gymanasia, begger problem, etc. He opined, unless these social evils are removed, the Indian society cannot progress.

According to him, social reform was a means for the solidification and purification of the character of the nation.

Hence, Ranade laid stress on promoting social evolution. This social evolution was to take place side by side, if it was not to precede the political growth.

Like Hegel, Comte and Spencer, Justice M.G. Ranade believed that society was a complex organism. He felt that there was very close relationship between economic, social and political system. It was impossible to separate politics from social reform as to separate the beauty of a rose from its perfume, or the light of the sun from its heat. Ranade said, "You cannot have a good social system when you find yourself low in the scale of political rights, nor can be fit to exercise political rights and privileges unless your social system is based on reason and justice. You cannot have a good economical system when your social arrangements are imperfect. If your religious ideas are low and grovelling, you cannot succeed in social, economical or political spheres. This interdependence is not an accident, but is the law of nature. Like the members of our body, you cannot have strength in the hands and the feet if your internal organs are in disorder; what applies to the human body holds good of the collective humanity we call society or state. It is a mistaken view which divorces considerations political from social and economical."

Ranade on the Methods of Social Reform Justice M.G. Ranade was a great champion of social reforms, but he never advocated rebellious or violent methods to bring about the same. Like Raja Ram Mohan Roy, he was also a liberal and believed in peaceful and constitutional methods. Mahadeo Govind Ranade enumerated four methods to bring about social reform:

(a) *The Traditional Method* : It means, the basing of reform on the old texts. The reformer interpreted the old texts in a next way so as to support a social reform. This method was used by Swami Dayanand Saraswati in his disputations with the orthodox people. Justice Ranade made considerable use of this method. He wrote essays 'Vedic Authorities for Widow Marriage' and "The Shastric Texts on the subject of Infant Marriage."

(b) *The Consience Method* : The second method for social reform was that of direct appealing to the conscience of the people, to their sense of right and wrong. Ranade regarded conscience as the Voice of God. He said, "Until the conscience is stirred up, nothing great or good can be accomplished by the agencies from outside, which hardly touch the surface. It is not an easy thing to stir up the conscience of a nation such as ours, but to judge from the signs around us the obvious indications that the dead bones are heaving with a new life, and that the cold limbs are reviving with a warmth hither to despaired of."

(c) *The Legislation Method* : The third method was to enforce reform through the agency of the state by legislation or by means of penalties of cast *panchyats, i.e.,* through social boycott. Justice Ranade advocated the first two methods and supported the third only where absolutely necessary. He said, "It is a coercive method, which should not be resorted to, until other ways have been tried." It could not be treated as a permanent method. Thus, Ranade remarked, "though legislation is a simple and quicker method, its effects are usually not permanent and also not through. Legislation cannot also deal with customs and practices which have deep roots in the social organism."

(d) *The Rebellion Method* : The last method about which Ranade was reluctant was that of rebellion. Justice Ranade never applied this method in practice.

With some reluctance, Ranade believed in the method of state legislation when the people are not able to succeed in bringing about a desired social change. In some cases, it was the duty of state to remedy evils like *sati,* infanticide, slavery, etc. Thus, Ranade said, "the diseased corruptions of the body cannot and should not be dealt with in the same way as its normal and healthy developments. The sharp surgical operation and not the homeopathic infinitesimally small pill, is the proper remedy for the first class of the disorders and the analogy holds good in the diseases of the body politic, as well as the material body as also in dealing with the parasitical growth of social degeneration."

In the year 1890, a circular on social reform was drafted by Justice Ranade which contained the following reforms :

(a) That not more than a year's income should be expended on the marriage ceremonies of a son.
(b) That not more than a year's income should be expended on the marriage ceremonies of a daughter.
(c) That boys should not marry before the ages of 16, 18 or 20.
(d) That daughter should not be married before the ages of 10, 12 or 14.
(e) That polygamy should be prohibited.
(f) That no one should marry after the age of 60.
(g) That liquor should be taken medicinally only.

(h) That every possible endeavour should be made to promote female education.

Hence, Ranade wanted to seek the help of state in social matters, specially in removing some chronic social evils.

Tilak and Ranade on Social Reform Tilak opposed the intervention of the state interference for the simple reason that reform to be durable must be a growth from within. Not only this as Athalye wrote', but Tilak was fully convinced that no social reform shall be durable unless political reform precedes it. Since there was political backwardness with no intention or little intention on the part of our rulers to give us political reform, there was no sense in asking that very government to improve our social set up. Tilak also opposed the idea because he felt that each society has its own religion which is the very life of that community. It has many things though not based on reasons, yet based on sentiments. Such sentiments have value in that community and might appear useless to those who are asked to reform the society. It is very dangerous to play with the sentiments of a community and as such he felt that each community should be left to improve its own social system. Thus, it is clear that both Tilak and Ranade were opposed to each others as far as the question of state-intervention in social affairs was concerned. But it must be noted that Ranade accepted legislation for social reform as a last resort. Tilak was also not against social reform but against foreign interference. We will discuss in detail the social ideas of Tilak. Ranade also agreed with Tilak that foreign interference in social and religious matters was not a good sign, but he drew a line between interference due to foreign initiation and interference due to Indian initiation. Thus, he said, 'The initiative is to be our own and based chiefly upon the example of our venerated past and dictated by the sense of the most representative and enlightened men in the community and all that is sought at the hands of the foreigners is to give to this responsible sense as embodied in the practices and usages of the respectable classes, the force and the sanction of law.' Both Justice Ranade and Lokmanya Tilak had deep faith in Indian culture and civilisation. Both desired to reform the society but differed in their approach.

Economic Ideas Mahadeo Govind Ranade was not only a social and political thinker, but he was also expounder of an economic theory. He was deeply moved by the poor economic conditions of the Indians. Ranade said, "We need only to walk through our streets, and study the most superficial aspects of our economic situation, and the fact forces itself upon us that we are a people of little resources. Many millions among us scarcely earn a couple of annas a day, many millions more are always underfed and live on the border land of famine and slow death into which the failure of a single monsoon precipitates them". He studied thoroughly every aspect of Indian economy and gave suggestions for its improvement.

Justice Ranade had dynamic, inductive and positive approach towards the study of economic problem. He studied the economic views of Smith, Recardo, Malthus, McCullough and Bastiat. Ranade opined that the economic ideas of Adam Smith and Recardo could not be applied to the Indian conditions. They advocated the theory of *laissez-faire* or free trade and condemned the policy of governmental management and intervention. They also favoured the freedom of capitalists and labourers in the market. Ranade opposed the state policy of *laissez-faire* in the case of India. He remarked, "Political economy, as a hypothetical, a priori science is one thing, while practical political economy as applied to the particular conditions of backward countries is a different thing altogether." Ranade said that the state policy of *Laissez-faire* and that of state indifference was the root cause of India's poverty. He denied the view point that India's poverty was due to any single reason. He also did not accept the importance of the Drain theory as the true explanation of India's poverty. According to Ranade, the lack of industrialisation and predominantly agricultural pattern of Indian economy was the real cause of India's poverty. If India was to get rid of poverty, it must industriablise.

As mentioned earlier, Ranade did not agree to the Drain theory of Dadabhai Naoroji as the sole cause of India's poverty. In his inaugural address at the first Industrial Conference at Poona in 1890, he remarked, "There are some people who think that, as long as we have a heavy tribute to pay to England, which takes away nearly twenty crores of our surplus exports, we are doomed and can do nothing to help ourselves. This is, however hardly a fair or manly position to take up. A portion of the burden represents interest on money advanced to, or invested in our country, and so far from complaining, we have reasons to be thankful that we have a creditor who supplies our needs at such a low rate of interest. Another portion represents the value of stores supplied to us, the like of which we cannot produce here. The remainder is alleged to be more or less necessary for the purpose of administration, deviance and payment of pensions, and though there is good cause for complaint that it is not all necessary, we should not forget the fact that we are enabled by reason of this British connection to levy an equivalent tribute from China by our opium monopoly. It would not, therefore, desire you to divert and waste your energies in the fruitless discussion of this question of tribute which had better be left to our politicians."

M.G. Ranade mentioned the following factors responsible for India's poverty :

(1) *The dependence on Agriculture* : According to Ranade the dependence on agriculture was one of the major factors of India's poverty. The condition of peasants in India was worse. They were overburdened due to heavy land-revenue. Moreover, the peasants were not being given any credit facility. Ranade said in 1881, "We have for the last fifteen years, exposed the failure of the peasant system and advocated a permanent settlement of land as the only alternative open to the government by the side of which reform by all other agencies sinks into insignificance." According to Ranade, the state acted as a landlord owning all land in its territory. He wrote, "The state monopoly of land its right to increase the assessment at its own discretion are the two most prominent obstacles in the way of growth of our national prosperity."

(2) *Lack of Industrialisation* : Lack of industrialisation in the country was another cause of India's poverty. The Indian handicrafts and indigenous industries were completely ruined due to her large exports of raw materials and her imports of manufactured goods. It led India to extreme backwardness in industry. Thus, Ranade wrote, "The industry and commerce of the country, such as it was, is passing out of our hands and... the country is fed, clothed, warmed, washed, lighted, helped and comforted generally by a thousand arts and industries in the manipulation of which its sons have every day a decreased share."

(3) *Lack of Capital* : Lack of capital for investment in agriculture and new industries was one of the major reasons of India's poverty. Ranade said, "The industry of the country is parched up for want of capital". The Indian capitalists were not prepared to invest money in new industries. They were not in favour of taking risks. Moreover, the credit facilities in India were inadequates, there was no encouragement to the creditors for coming in the market.

Ranade's suggestions for removing India's poverty : Mahadeo Govind Ranade observed that if India was to get rid of poverty. It must promote industry, trade and agriculture. The following suggestions for the agriculture and industrial sector were given by Justice Ranade :

(a) *Agriculture* : On the agricultural side, Ranade suggested that, the state must reduce the burden of land revenue. He said, "Every effort must be made to develop in India manufacturing industries. This would indirectly help the agriculturists also. But to help him more directly in raising his standard of living, land revenue should be reduced and be permanently fixed at the reduced level. Next in importance was the setting up of an organisation of credit at low interest for the cultivator. Another remedial measure was legal protection to the cultivator against the greed and wiles of the money-lender". He further said, "Judicial reform, increased banking and loan facilities and the guarantee of a permanent settlement : these are the three-dold elements in that organic constitution of our agricultural economy which will alone rescue the country from its present sad plight". Ranade wanted that the government should create additional supply of credit to the agriculturists. It should give financial help. Ranade supported the establishment of agricultural banks to lend money at low rate of interest to small farmers. He also wanted the government to introduce reforms in the land revenue system.

(b) *Industrialisation* : Justice M.C. Ranade wanted that the government should actively encourage the establishment of industries in the country. He wrote, "When factories and mills on a small or large scale were set up all over the land, the present paralysis would give way to a play of energies which would... give a new birth to the activities of the nation". Ranade suggested that Local or Municipal Boards or Corporate Boards of Trade and commerce should undertake the development of industries in their areas. He advocated the policy of state initiative in the economic sector. He suggested that the state could also very well be asked to produce its own stores here, just as it produced certain minor articles required by its military and postal departments. It could also undertake to buy leather, wooden goods, etc., from the Indian producer, and thus, secure the benefit of sure custom at remunerative rates to new undertakings. It could finally help people to join their capital together under such guarantees and official supervision, and afford such facilities as the governments of Europe had extended to land improvement banks.

In 1890, at the industrial conference at Poona, Ranade said, "Each district might thus have a fund to develop its sources in its own way and several districts might combine together to start a strong undertaking for common advantage. If the powers of these Boards were thus enlarged, there would be no risk of loss to government, and the Boards might make considerable profit by the use of money, and thus relieve the burden of local taxation." He also advocated the flow of foreign capital. He wanted that in India, foreign capital should be encouraged in the interest of industrial development. Ranade wanted that the burden of taxation should be lessened. He also suggested that the distribution of produce among the needy many and the powerful few had to be arranged to a spirit of equity and fair-play.

5

Pherozeshah Mehta (1845-1915)

Pherozeshah Mehta was one of the great personalities of modern India. Like Raja Ram Mohan Roy, Dadabhai Naoroji and Justice M.G. Ranade he also belonged to the liberal school of thought. He had deep faith in British fair-play and justice. He believed in continuance of the opinion that India could develop only by remaining under the British Empire. He was one of the founding fathers of the Indian National Congress. He was one of the greatest leaders of the Congress. Sitarammyya writes, "Sir Pherozeshah Mehta was one of the those who had been associated with the Congress from its very inception and played a leading part in moulding its policies and programmes." He was a scholar, an educationist, and a great orator. He advocated the introduction of local-self government.

His Life Sketch Pherozeshah Mehta, the uncrowned King of Bombay, was born on August 4, 1845 in a well-to do family. He received his early education in Ayrton's school established by Mr. Dunjibhoy, who took keen interest in the education of children. He passed his Matriculation Examination in 1860 at the age of fifteen. Shortly after, he joined the Elphinstone College, Bombay where he passed his B.A. Examination in 1864. As a student, he was very shining and brilliant. Sir Alexander, an eminent educationist wrote about Pherozeshah Mehta: "I have great pleasure in tastifying that Mr. Pherozeshah Merwanji is in every way worthy of the benefaction which he seeks. He is on the whole the best student of all I have had to do with in the Elphonistone college. He has good abilities, industry, good sense, modesty, an excellent moral character, and remarkable gentlemanly and pleasing manners." Pherozeshah passed his M.A. Examination in six months of his passing the B.A. Examination. In December, 1864, he sailed for England to qualify himself for the bar. He stayed there from 1865 to 1869. He started his public career in 1867. In England he came under the benign and inspiring influence of Dadabhai Naoroji, and Grand Old Man of India. Pherozeshah Mehta regarded Dadabhai as the greatest parliamentarian and became his admirer. Under his inspiration he also became a member of the East India Association and the London Indian Society. In England, he came in contact with all that was healthy in Western life and thought. That four year stay in England laid the foundations of the political career of Pherozeshah Mehta.

As mentioned earlier, Pherozeshah Mehta began his public activities as early as 1867 under the guidance of Dadabhai Naoroji in London. In 1872, he became a member of the Bombay Corporation and was thrice elected its chairman. He actively participated in the debates of the corporation to solve the then problems of drainage, medical relief, primary education, water supply, etc. In 1886, he became a member of the Bombay Legislative Council. He was also one of the founding fathers of the Indian National Congress. He was elected the President of the I.N.C. in 1890. He was also the chairman of the Reception Committee of the Indian National Congress in 1889 and in 1904. From 1894 to 1897 he was a member of Imperial Legislative Council. In its meetings, he boldly and frankly criticised the wrong policies of the government. Dr. V.P. Verma says, 'He was noted for vigorous and brilliant education and his fearlessness. He was a superb dialectician, a master of biting and caustic sarcasm and satire and a splendid politician; Pherozeshah Mehta took an active part in the Ilbert Bill Agitation. He was also one of the foremost speakers of his times." Gladstone remarks, "when he spoke, he uplifted debate from whatever rut of mediocrity it may have fallen into. That was the power of the orator, when he sat silent, his mere presence communicated to the House a sense of dignity and a moral strength easier to feel than to describe. That was the quality of the man." Pherozeshah died on November 5, 1915. His death plunged the whole country into gloom as if a great light had gone out, leaving darkness and confusion behind.

His Political Ideas Like Dadabhai Naoroji, Justice M.G. Ranada and other Indian liberals, Pherozeshah Mehta was a great admirer of the British rule in India. For him, the British rule was a boon and blessing in disguise. He had deep faith in the British fair-play and justice : He was influenced by the English culture and statesmanship. In this connection, he wrote, 'I have undoubted faith in the living and the fertilizing principle of the English culture and English civilisation. It may be that, at times, prospect may look dark and gloomy. The Anglo-Indian opposition may look fierce and uncompromising but my faith is large.'

He accepted British rule in India as the will of the Divine Providence. In his speech delivered in connection with the Ilbert Bill. Pherozeshah Mehta said, 'If I entertain one political conviction more strongly than another, it is that this country in falling under the British rule, has fallen into the hands of a nation than which no other is better qualified to govern her wisely and well. Look among all the leading nations of the world, and you would not find one who, both by her faults and her virtues, is so well adapted to steer her safe on the path of the true progress and prosperity. It was his firm conviction that England would help India to stand on her own legs. He was of the opinion that India could progress only if the British rule continued.

Pherozeshah Mehta had loyalty to the British crown and believed in the permanence of the British Empire. He regarded the British connection with India as beneficial for its peace, prosperity and progress. In 1904, he said, 'My steadfast loyalty is founded upon this rock of hope and patience.' Seeking the will of providence, like Oliver Cromwell, in dispensation rather revelations seeing God's will like him in fulfilment of events, I accept British rule, as Ranade did as a dispensation so wonderful, a little island set at one end of the world establishing itself in a far continent as different as could be, that it would be folly not to accept it as a declaration of God's Will. He was sure that the British would do justice to Indians. In spite of his deep faith in the British rule, Mahta never hesitated to criticise the wrong policies of the government. He was always prepared to fight for reforms.

Like other Indian liberal thinkers, Pherozeshah Mehta had faith in constitutional methods to solve political questions. Because of his conservatism, he opposed the quick method of violence. He was of the view that violence would never succeed in the long run. He was convinced that all the problems could be solved through constitutional means by the method of persuasion and appeals. He did not accept the idea that the roots of power lay in the cult to military force. In fact, there was no place for force in his political thought. He believed that the foundations of the British rule in India were based on ethical considerations. He wrote, "Englishmen don't do justice themselves when they read Indian History in this way though it cannot be denied that there are many pages in this history blotted by error and crime. England has won India not simply by the sword, but in a large measure by the exercise of high moral and intellectual qualities which have not only guided its victories but have always been on the alert to neutralise its baneful influences." Mehta was in favour of making people conscious of their rights and privileges. In all his speeches and addresses delivered at various political conferences, he tried to awaken the minds of the Indian people. He wanted the government to solve file problems, instead of resorting to repression.

Pherozeshah Mehta wanted self-government under the British Empire. He had deep love for local-self-government. He was in favour of decentralisation of authority. According to him, the centralisation of authority was not suited to India. So he pleaded for local autonomy and demanded that there should be extension of power of local authorities. Though, a great believer of local-self-government institutions, he never opposed the government to exercise some control over them. According to his view-point the government control up to some degree was necessary on local bodies. Pherozeshah also advocated the introduction of elective principles in local-bodies. He demanded that the strength of the elected members in the local-bodies should be increased. In support of his demand he quoted J.S. Mill and Spencer, the great thinkers. He said, 'We know that the highest authorities on the subject — Herbert Spencer and John Stuart Mill — have pointed out that you must have external or internal check on the working of these municipal bodies, you must not have both.' Pherozeshah also wanted that Indians should get more share in the administration.

Pherozeshah Mehta was a staunch lover of liberty. In all his speeches and addresses, he made the people conscious of their rights and privileges and to fight for them. He opposed injustice, despotism and oppression with all his might and fought for their removal. He fought in the Bombay Legislative Council and the Imperial Legislative Council for the right and liberty of the people. He boldly and frankly opposed the Arms Act, the Press Act and supported the Ilbert Bill. He pleaded for the introduction of the elective principle in the Bombay Corporation and in the local-bodies. He believed in the parliamentary system of government with its characteristic of responsible executive. Pherozeshah Mehta imbibed his love of liberty from the writings of J.S. Mill and Spencer and the Liberal Indian leaders of his times.

Pherozeshah Mehta attached great importance to the moral basis of politics. It is very difficult to divorce morality form politics. They should go side by side. Like G.K. Gokhale, Pherozeshah also wanted to spiritualise politics. He was of the opinion that politics could become healthy only if it was based on the principles of morality. Politics without morality was like a body without life. Hence, Pherozeshah emphasised the need of moral foundations of political power.

Pherozeshah Mehta was also a lover of education. Like other Indian Liberals, he regarded education as the key to creative life. He pleaded for the extension of educational opportunities for all. He supported the cause of both intellectual and moral education. He believed that only educated and intelligent people could lead the nation. He wrote, 'There is no doubt that an intelligent and educated population is the best means of developing indefinitely, the resources of a country. On the continent this idea has of late gained immense ground. It was first started by those grand statesmen of the French Revolution, even as they were hurling defiance and armies at a coalition of almost all the crowned heads of Europe. And though the original plans of Condorcet and Robespierre fell through the time, yet ever since France, Germany, Italy, and Switzerland, have been sparing no efforts even in times of trouble and difficulty, to reconstruct their system of public education under the direct administration, management and support of the state. 'Mehta' demanded that the educational institutions should be free from government's control and kept above politics. He boldly opposed Lord Curzon's policy of bringing universities under the control of the government. He actively participated in the education sphere. He did a yeomen's service to the cause of education. He worked as the Dean of Arts Faculty and later as the Vice-Chancellor of Bombay University.

His Interpretation of History Like Hegel, Pherozeshah Mehta believed in the concept of the divine dialectic in the historical movement. He had faith in the divine governance of the historical process. He realised that it was due to the kindness of God that the British Rule in India introduced the concepts of freedom and individual dignity and the benefits of a scientific civilization.

As the Chairman of the Reception Committee for the Indian National Congress Sessions at Bombay in 1904, he said, ...let me lay before you the confession of faith of a devout and irreclaimable Congressman like myself. I am an inveterate, I am a robust optimist like my late friend Mahadeva Govinda Ranade. I believe in divine guidance through human agency. It may be the fatalism of the East, but it is an active, not a passive fatalism, a fatalism which recognise that the human wheels of the machinery must actively work to fulfil their appointed task. My humility saves me from the despair that seizes more impatient soul like those who have recently preached a gospel of despondency — I always seek hope and consolation in the words of the poet : "I have not made the world and He that has made it will guide." I derive patience from the same poet's teaching : 'My faith is large in time, and that which shapes it to some perfect end.' My steadfast loyalty is founded upon this rock of hope and patience. Seeking the will providence, like Oliver Cromwell, in dispensation rather than revelations, seeing God's will like him in fulfilment of events, I accept British rule, as Ranade did as a dispensation so wonderful... as a declaration of God's will.

The similar ideas on the process of history were held by Ranade, G.K. Gokhale, Hegal and Borsuet.

As Dr. V.P. Varma writes, 'Thus, although in their belief in reason, science, progress, constitutionalism and education the Indian Moderates are the inheirtors of the legacy of Diderot and Voltaire, in their belief in divine instrumentality behind the British Empire in India they resemble the exponents of a Christological interpretation of history. Like St. Augustine, Borsuet or Toynbee.'

According to Pherozeshah Mehta, there was nothing static in this world, history is a process of ever-expanding progress. He was of the opinion that there is a law of widening progress in all ages and in all countries. In his speech as President of the fifth Bombay Provincial Conference held at Poona in November 1892, he said, ... the old Hebrew fallacy, 'the thing that has been is the thing the shall be. History does not repeat itself, its lessons are invaluable for teaching us to guide the experiments' by which alone human progress makes way! they only mislead, if we use them for vain speculations as to the repetition in the future of the phenomena of the past. Mehta hoped the finest prospects of a gradual development of political progress of India.

His Role in the Indian National Congress As mentioned earlier, Sir Pherozeshah Mehta was one of the founding fathers of the Indian National Congress. He served the Congress with spirit of selflessness and dedication till the end of his life.

In 1889, he was elected Chairman of its Reception Committee and its President in 1890. He was again elected Chairman of the Reception Committee of the Congress in 1904 and its President in 1909. Pherozeshah Mehta was of the view that 'the Congress was Indeed not voice of the masses, but it was the duty of their educated compatriots to interpret their grievances and offer suggestions for their redress'. He further said.... It is, I repeat, the glory of the Congress that the educated and enlightened people of the country seek to pay the debt of gratitude which they owe for the priceless boom of education by pleading and pleading temperately for timely and provident statesmanship.

Pherozeshah Mehta was the real force behind the Congress. He was one of the great leaders of the Congress. He did commendable service through it various committees; deputations and delegations. He was a very familiar figure in the Congress, his advice was sought on important problems.

In his address over the sixth session of the I.N.C. held at Calcutta in 1890, he condemned the view-point of Lord Salibury that 'Government by representation did not fit Eastern traditions of Eastern minds'.

In 1892, he was one of the members of the committee to draw up a petition to be presented to parliament regarding the Public Service Commission. At the historic Surat session of the Congress in 1907, Pherozeshah was the key figure in the moderate camp.

After the Surat split, the so called 'Extremists' were expelled from the Congress. Some National leaders did make efforts to unite both wings of the Congress. Pherozeshah Mehta strongly opposed the readmission of extremists because he distrusted their methods and policies. He said, "I cannot help saying that there is a great deal of mawkish sentimentality in the passionate appeals for union at all cost. For my part, I think it is most desirable that each set of distinct convictions should have its separate Congress. To jumble them up in one body confuses the real understanding of the extent to which opinion really tends in one direction or another.... It is, therefore, desirable that persons holding nearly the same opinions and principles should organise themselves into bodies where they can expound them and lay them before the public in a clear and consistent form .... For God's sake let us have done with all inane and slobbery whine about unity where there is none." Thus, he advocated two separate wings of the Congress. In 1910, he was again elected the President of the Indian National Congress, but due to his ill health he resigned.

6

Surendranath Banerjee (1848-1925)

According to Bipin Chandra Pal, "Surendranath is the only person who may justly claim an all-India leadership."

Shri Surendranath Banerjee was another worthy son of India. He played a very significant role in the development of the liberal tradition in modern India. His life and activities form an integral part of the history of the Indian National Movement. He did commendable service for the enlargement of the rights and liberties of the people.

Like Raja Ram Mohan Roy, Dadabhai Naoroji, Justice M.G. Ranade and Gokhale, he belonged to the liberal school of thought. He was also an admirer of the British rule in India. He had faith in the British fair play and justice. According to Surendranath Banerjee, India could get peace, prosperity and advancement only under the British Empire. Like other liberal thinkers, he also had faith in the institutional methods. He was a good orator and writer. He was regarded by many as the life and soul of the national movement in India.

His Life Sketch Surendranath Banerjee was born on November 10, 1848 in the Jaltola region of Calcutta. The atmosphere in the Banerjee family was one of a tie between the old world forces and the new. Surendranath's grandfather was an orthodox Hindu and his father Durga Charan had deep faith in Western Culture and Civilisation. He wrote in his autobiography, 'A Nation in Making', "Thus, in our home the two conflicting forces of those times met.." However, the peace of the family was not disturbed by this conflict. Brought up in such an atmosphere, Surendranath Banerjee represented a fine synthesis between the two extremes of Hindu conservatism and Western civilisation. He inherited his father's revolutionary zeal and his grandfather's basic traditionalism.

Surendranath received his early education in a village Pathshala. Afterwards, he was admitted to the Dovetone college where he graduated in 1868. He had a distinguished educational career both in school and college. He was sent to England in 1868 where he joined the University

College. He competed successfully for the civil service examination but was rejected on the ground of being over-age. Surendranath appealed to the court of the Queen's Bench. The court asked the Civil Service Commissioner to show reasons for his rejection. The result was Surendranath was restored and sent to India.

Later on, he was appointed as Assistant Magistrate at Sylhet. But after two years, he was dismissed from service on some charges. Then, he went to London to plead his case before the authorities at the Indian Office, but he could not achieve success. Surendranath Banerjee's dismissal from service created a nation-wide resentment. In this connection, he wrote, "My case excited very strong feelings in the Indian community and the general belief among my country men was that if I were not an Indian I could not have been put to all this trouble and that the head and front of my offence was that I had entered the sacred premises of the Indian Civil Service, which so far had been jealously guarded against invasion by the children of the soil. Many years afterwards a Lieutenant Governor stated that it was a wicked proceeding." But his removal from the service proved a blessing in disguise so far as the country was concerned. As C.Y. Chintamani remarks, "the loss of the government became the gain of the country."

In 1876, Surendranath was appointed Professor of English in the Metropolitan Institution. In 1881, he joined the Free Church College as Professor of English literature. For 37 years, *i.e.*, from 1875 to 1912, Surendranath Banerjee was fully engaged in active teaching work. He loved his students. He was a great educationist with a missionary zeal.

Surendranath attached more importance to education than politics. Thus, he wrote, "political work is more or less ephemeral though nonetheless highly useful. Educational work has in it the element of permanent utility. The empire of a teacher is an ever enduring empire, which extends over the future. The teachers are the masters of the future. I cannot think of a nobler calling than theirs."

Surendranath Banerjee began his political career sometimes in 1875. He founded the Indian Association in Calcutta on July 26, 1876. The main object of this association was to agitate for the introduction of representative government in India. The Indian Association played a very significant role in the political life of the country. In 1876, Surendranath was elected a Member of Culcutta Corporation. Four times, he was elected a Member of Bengal Legislative Council in 1894, 1896, 1898 and 1900. In 1913 Surendranath was elected to the Imperial Council. For several years, he also edited the Bengalee Journal.

Surendranath was one of the founders of the Indian National Congress and was its president at Poona in 1895 and again at Ahmedabad in 1902. He served the Indian National Congress till 1918. Afterwards, he along with other moderate leaders, organised a party, the liberal federation. Surendranath also gave evidence before the Joint Select Committee. In 1921, he became the minister for Local Self-government and Public Health in Bengal.

Surendranath visited England several times; in 1890 as a member of a delegation sent by the Calcutta Corporation, in 1896, to give evidence before Welby Commission, and in 1910 to represent Indian in the Imperial Press Conference. He died on August 6, 1925 at the age of 77 years.

His Works The main elements of his political thought are to found in his autobiography, "A Nation in the Making."

His Political Ideas The views and thought of Surendranath Banerjee are available to us through his work "A Nation in the making." "He discussed in detail the political, social and economic problems of his times in this book. Surendranath was influenced by the self-sacrificing career of Joseph Mazzini. He imbibed the teachings of English liberal political thinkers, like Burke, J.S. Mill, Macaulay etc. He was also inspired by the Indian liberals. His main political ideas are mentioned below :

Admirer of the British Rule Like Raja Ram Mohan Roy, Dadabhai Naoroji, Justice Ranade, etc., Surendranath Banerjee was an admirer of the British rule in India. For him the British rule was a blessing in disguise and was in the interest of the people India. He had deep faith in the British fair-play and justice. Thus, he said, "To England we look for inspiration and guidance... We have been fed upon the strong food of English constitutional freedom. We have been taught to admire the eloquence and genius of the great masters of English Political Philosophy." He further wrote, "The noblest heritage which we can leave to our children and our children's children is the heritage of enlarged rights, safeguarded by the loyal devotion and the fervent enthusiasm of an emancipated people. Let us so work with confidence in each other, with unwavering loyalty to the British connection, that we accomplish this great object within a measurable distance of time."

Surendranath Banerjee regarded the British rule in India as providential, as one of the dispensations of the God of History.

At the anniversary meeting of the Bhawampur Students Association held on April 28, 1877, he referred that there were three main categories in England's mission to India:

(i) To help towards the eradication of those evils which afflict Indian Society.

(ii) To help in the formation of a manly, energetic, self-reliant Indian character.

(iii) To introduce the art of self-government in India.

It was the British Empire which brought the dynamic political concepts of the West into contact with the old idealism of the East.

In 1878, While addressing a meeting of the Students Association, Surendranath said, "It was England's mission in the East to save, to regenerate, to emancipate from the chains of ignorance, error and superstitution, 250 millions of human beings, to heal the wounds that have been inflicted on them by the rapacity of their former rulers, to develop in them a selfreliant, manly energetic character, to separate through the land, the great blessings of peace, contentment and happiness; but above all it is England's noble mission in the East to help towards the consummation of Indian Unity to reconcile the jarring conflicts of the diverse Indian nationalities, to bring them nearer together, to evoke in them a sentiment of brotherhood and make them feel that they have to make common cause for the redress of common grievances." Hence, Surendranath regarded the British rule in India beneficial for its peace, prosperity and progress.

His faith in Constitutional Methods Like other Indian liberals, Surendranath was also an advocate of the constitutional agitation. He believed in peaceful and constitutional methods. He was deadly against the use of violence. Thus, he, said, "Constitutional agitation will secure for us those rights and privileges, which in less favoured countries are obtained by sterner means. Blit peaceful are the means to be enforced, there is a stern duty to be performed by every Indian. And he who fails in that duty is a traitor before God and man." But he observed that this method was slow and needed great patience. In his presidential address at Ahmedabad in 1902. Surendranath said, "Yet there are those who take a desponding view of the situation — who say that our methods are faulty, that we wasted our time and breath, or that at any rate the results achieved have not been commensurate with the sacrifices incurred or the efforts put-forth... The question is asked — what is the good of persevering in methods and in sacrifices, when the out-turn of them all is so insignificant....I ask — Has the time come for the final judgment? I ask — Are the results inadequate? Even if they were, what are twenty years in the life-time of a nation? The triumphs of liberty are not won in a day. Liberty is a jealous goddess, exacting in her worship and claiming from her votaries prolonged and asiduous devotion. Read history, learn from it the inestimable lesson of patience and fortitude and the self-sacrificing devotion which a constitutional struggle for constitutional liberty involves."

His Political Goal-Self-government Surendranath Banerjee demanded self-government under the British Empire. In the legislature, he did commendable service for the enlargement of the rights and liberties of the Indian people. Thus, he observed that political rights were conductive to the material progress of the country. Throughout his life, Surendranath Banerjee had fought for the Indianisation of the services. He demanded that Indians should get more share in the administration. The Civil Service Examination should also be held simultaneously both in England and India. In support of self-government in India, he wrote, "Political inferiority involves moral degradation... A nation of slaves would never have produced a Patanjali, a Buddha, or a Valmiki. We want self-government in order that we might wipe off from us the badge of political inferiority and life our heads among the nations of the earth and fulfil the great destinies that are in store for us under the blessing of Divine Providence. We want self-government not only in our own interest but for the sake of humanity at large... It is our mission to become once again the spiritual guides of mankind, but we cannot fulfill that mission unless and until we ourselves are emancipated, we ourselves are free. That is the first indispensable equipment for the discharge of that great mission." To him, self-government was the essential condition for national reconstruction.

Lover of Liberty Babu Surendranath Banerjee was a staunch advocate of the concept of Liberty. He imbibed love for liberty from the writings of Burke, Macaulay, Mill, Fox, Pitt, Sheridan, etc. He, realised that people could learn from the British constitutional history the idea of freedom and liberty. Surendranath demanded maximum rights and privileges for the Indian people. It was in the interest of the ruled and the rulers. Thus, he said, "Every nation must be the arbiter of its own distinies — such as the omnipotent fact inscribed by nature with her own hands and in ther own eternal book." According to Banerjee. "If power were vested in us to legislate, to control the finance and to carry on the administration through and by our own men, in accordance with principles laid down by our own representatives, we should have self-government in the truest sense, and possess the simplest facilities for developing our powers and faculties and taking our legitimate place among the nations of the earth."

His Views about Politics and Morality Like Gopal Krishna Gokhale, Surendranath Banerjee wanted to spiritualise politics. According to him politics and Morality should not be separated. They should go side by side. In his speech at Calcutta on 27th September 1888, on the Ram Mohan Roy Memorial Meeting he said, "Politics based upon religion or deep moral earnestness is the one thing that is needed for this country. Politics divorced from a high moral purpose becomes the paltry squabble for power in which humanity can feel no interest. Take the case of the Home Rule agitation. Withdraw from it the personality of Mr. Gladstone and his intense moral earnestness, withdraw from it the deep favour of the Irish Patriots, and it becomes a miserable struggle for political power in which the deeper interest of humanity are lost sight, of. Take again the case of the Pilgrim Fathers, the founders of American greatness.... They preferred exile to the miseries of a life where their conscientious convictions had to be sacrificed.... They developed themselves into statesmen, and became the founders of the noblest government and the freest race that the world has ever seen." Like Cicero and Burke, he emphasised the need of moral foundations of political power. He did not accept the Machiavellian concept of state and politics. In his presidential address at the Poona Congress of 1895, Surendranath Banerjee said, "I desire to place the moral consideration in the forefront : that which is morally indefensible cannot be politically expedient. Politics divorced from morality is no politics at all. It is political jugglery of the worst description."

His Views on Human Nature He believed in the goodness and nobility of human nature. At the meeting of the Students's Association, held on July 15, 1876, at Calcutta, he said, "there is a divinity in human nature which admidst our most precipitate flights downwards ever arrests us with the warning voice — Thus, far shalt thou go and no further'. The majesty of human nature will always vindicate for itself the position which rightly belongs to it. Human nature will allow itself to be tainted, to be polluted, to be infected but its divine image can never be effaced, can never be blotted out." In this respect, he was very near to Rousseau.

His faith in India's Past Surendranath Banerjee had deep faith in India's past. According to him, India was the cradle of religions and the holy land of the east. It produced great *saints* like Valmiki, Vyasa, Buddha, Sankara, Panini, Patanjali, etc. He wrote, "In the morning of the world on the banks of the Ganges and on the banks of the Jamuna the Vedic Rishis sang those hymns which represent the first yearning of infant humanity towards the Divine ideal... we were the spiritual preceptors of mankind.... our past takes us back to the dim twilight of history. In those days, when the world was sunk into barbarism we were the guides and instructors of mankind." In his speech on 'The Study of Indian History' delivered on 24th June 1876 at Calcutta, he said, "Let us sit at the feet of our ancestors and hold communion with the master-minds of ancient

India. Such communion is pleasing in these days of gubernatorial repression, in these days of political lifelessness and political stagnation, and when the future outlook is indeed so truly gloomy....in studying the past history of your country, you will find much that is antiquated, much that is obsolete, much perhaps, that will excite ridicule and laughter. But let not nay such feeling overcome you. Approach reverentially the sacred records of your sires. Remember, that you are studying the sayings and doings of your revered ancestors, of those for whose sake alone you are now remembered, for whose sake alone the intellectual elite of Europe even now feel a deep and an ardent interest in your welfare. If you cannot attain the intellectual eminence of your ancestors, why not strive to emulate their moral grandeur. The road to moral greatness is not so steep or so slippery... upon the moral regeneration of your country depends its intellectual, its social and its political regeneration."

Advocate of National Unity Surendranath Banerjee was a great lover of National Unity. According to him, national unity was the path to the promised land of freedom, hope and faith. He said, "I have a strong conviction and an assured belief that there comes a time in the history of a nation's progress, when every man may verily be said to have a mission of his own to accomplish. Such a time has now arrived for India.... the celestial mandate has been issued that every Indian must now do his duty, or stand condemned before God and man." Surendranath wanted all-India Unity on the political plane too. He toured the whole of the country and got remarkable success. He wrote, "For the first time under the British rule, India with its varied races and religions had been brought upon the same platform for a common and unified effort. Thus was it demonstrated... that whatever might be our differences in respect of race and language or social and religious institutions, the people of India could combine and unite for the attainment of their common political ends...the ground was thus prepared for this great national and unifying movement." He also did positive efforts to promote friendly feelings between Hindus and Muslims. He believed that progress peace and prosperity could be attained only in United India.

His views on the role of Students in Politics According to Surendranath Banerjee, "The students should certainly discuss politics and may even subject to proper control and guidance, take part in political work. But the students should not indulge in party politics which were against the principles of morality and righteousness". According to Banerjee, true politics must be based on moral principles. It is said that once he refused to join the Calcutta University Institute because the students were excluded from discussing politics there. He was of the view that it was unwise to exclude students from politics. He also emphasised on the need of student discipline.

Social Ideas Surendranath Banerjee was not only a political thinker but was also interested in the social reform movement. He supported the cause of widow-remarriage, inter-caste marriage, abolition of child marriage, removal of restrictions of foreign travel, etc. He raised a voice against all these social evils. According to Banerjee, India could advance politically only if all these evils were eradicated. He wanted that the process of social change should be slow and gradual. There should not be a sudden change. He believed that the Hindu society was changing and moving forward. He said, "the question of sea-voyage, or child marriage, or even enforced widowhood is not today where it was in the later part of the nineteenth century". Fifty years ago I was on out-caste (being an England-returned Brahmin) in the village where I live. Today I am an honoured member of the community.

Economic Ideas Like Dadabhai Naoroji and Justice M.G. Ranade, Surendranath Banerjee also discussed causes on the growing poverty of India. He was moved by the deplorable and miserable conditions of the Indian people. According to him, 'the economic condition of the people has an intimate bearing upon their political advancement'. In his presidential address at the Poona Congress in 1895, Surendranath outlined a five-point scheme for the stoppage of the material retrogression of the country :

(i) the rivival of old Indian industries and the setting up of new ones;
(ii) moderation in the assessment of land tax which would be fixed for a fairly long period so that the peasants could be free from economic harassments;
(iii) the remission of those taxes, which adversely affect the poor people;
(iv) the stoppage of the economic drain and bleeding of India by the adoption of suitable governmental regulations and
(v) the increasing employment of Indians in the public services in place of a costly foreign administrative agency.

Surendranath suggested the government to improve the economic conditions of the people. He also preached the use of Swadeshi goods in place of Videshi goods. In this connection, he said, Swadeshism will save us from famine and pestilence and the nameless horrors which follow in the train of poverty. Take the Swadeshi vow and you will have laid broad and deep the foundations of your industrial and political emancipation. Be Swadeshi in all things, in your thoughts and actions, in your ideals and aspirations. Bring back the ancient days of purity and self-sacrifice.

Restore the Aryavarta of olden times when the Rishis sang the praises of God and did good to men... Swadeshi does not exclude foreign ideals or foreign learning or foreign arts and industries, but insists that they shall be assimilated into the national systems, be moulded after the national pattern and be incorporated into the life of a nation. Such is my. conception of Swadeshism." In this respect, the Swadeshi movement was many-sided. It touched the three principal aspects of life, economic educational and political.

7

Gopal Krishan Gokhale (1866-1915)

(i) Introduction

Gopal Krishna Gokhale (1866-1915) was one of the prominent personalities of modern India. He was a great disciple of Ranade, the mentor of Gandhi and the idol of Motilal Nehru. Gokhale was one of the most respected of India's statesmen. About Gokhale, Aga Khan said, "Gokhale was more than a statesman. He was essentially a creative artist of genius. His oratory was a work of art in words, but he was not only an artist in words, but an artist in works and conceptions, and like every great artist, he did not disdain in the search for his material to go wherever he could find it...He was not only broadminded but charitable. His sense of human solidarity made him full of personal sympathy not only to his opponents but to the selfish and the snobbish self-seekers. But his wrath and contempt were reserved for the poisonous and deadly vice of hypocrisy." He belonged to the liberal school of thought in modern India. He was the admirer of British rule in India, believed in the British fair-play and justice. But Gokhale never hesitated to criticise the wrong policies of the government. Mahatma Gandhi accepted him as his Political Guru. He described Gokhale as the ideal servant of India and the most perfect man in the political field. Gokhale was a scholar, a politician, a social reformer, an economist and one of the most brilliant parliamentarians. He devoted his whole life for the service of the motherland. Dr. Radhakrishnan wrote, "When the comforts of the world were in Gokhale's reach and could be his, he left them and gave his great talents to his service of the country. Renunciation is the principle of good life. Men are great not by what they acquire but what they renounce. Those engaged in public work should not look upon it as a career with glittering prizes."

(ii) Life Career

Gopal Krishan Gokhale was born on May 9, 1866, at Kotluk a village in Ratnagiri district in a Chitpavan Brahmin family. The Gokhale family had played an honourable part in the national history of the Marathas. Gopal Krishan Gokhale belonged to a middle class family. "Waste not, want not" was the motto of the caste of which he belonged. Gokhale received his education at his home village. After the death of his father, the Gokhale's family shifted to Kolhapur, Gopal Krishan Gokhale passed his matriculation examination in 1881 at the age of fifteen. In January, 1882, he joined the Raja Ram College at Kolhapur. In the beginning, Gokhale was a shy student but afterwards he gained a reputation for a exceptionally sharp memory. He graduated in 1884 at the age of 18. In 1886, Gopal Krishan Gokhale became a member of the Deccan Education Society and was appointed Professor of History and Economics at the Fergusson College, Poona. He was a selfless and dedicated worker of Deccan Education Society. He served the society for 20 years on a salary of Rs. 75 per month.

Gokhale took keen interest in all the activities of public life. For several years he acted as the editor of the journal of the *Sarvajanik Sabha.* At the age of 22, Gokhale became the member of the Bombay Legislative Council. In 1904, he received the title of C.I.E. At the age of 39, Gokhale became the President of the Indian National Congress. He also visited England seven times; in 1897, 1905, 1906, 1908, 1912, 1913 and in 1914. In 1905, Gopal Krishan Gokhale, founded 'The Servants of India Society'. The main object of this organisation was to train young men in the responsibilities of public service. Gokhale "said, "A sufficient number of our countrymen must forward to devote themselves to the cause in the spirit in which religious work is undertaken and public life must be spiritualised. Love of country must so fill the heart that all else shall; appear as of little moment by its side." The Servants of India Society played a very significant and important role in the political life of India. In 1905, he was one of the delegates of a commission sent to England by the I.N.C. to persuade the British Parliament not to enact the Partition of Bengal. In his Budget speech of 1907 in the Indian Legislative Council, Gokhale demanded the introduction of free primary education. In 1911, he introduced a bill in this connection in the Indian Legislative Council. In 1908 he also gave evidence before the Hobhouse Decentralisation Commission. In 1910 and 1912, Gokhale fought for the cause of Indian labourers in Natal. He also visited South Africa in 1912 on the request of Mahatma Gandhi to help in his Satyagrah movement there. Gokhale died at the premature age of 49, on 19th February 1915.

(iii) Political Ideas

Gopal Krishan Gokhale was one of the most respected of India's statesmen. He was a great disciple of Mahadeo Govind Ranade, the mentor of Gandhiji and the idol of Pt. Moti Lal Nehru. Mahatma Gandhi described him as the ideal servant of India and accepted him as his political Guru. He wrote in his book, *The Story of My Experiments with Truth* that "Sir Pherozeshah Mehta had seemed to me like the Himalaya and Lokmanya like the ocean, but Gokhale was like the Ganges, one could have a refreshing bath in the holy river. The Himalaya was unscalable and one could not easily launch forth on the sea, but the Ganges invited one to its bosom." Gokhale was and remained for Gandhiji, the most perfect man in the political field because the latter employed pure, truthful and straight-forward means in the pursuits of his political objectives. It was the ambition of Gokhale to spiritualize public life.

For his political faith, Gokhale got inspiration from many sources. He was much influenced by the lives and activities of Justice M.G. Ranade, Dadabhai Naoroji and Sir Pherozeshah Mehta and under their influence, he joined the Indian National Congress. Gokhale was highly influenced by the philosophy and work of Ranade, specially by his social and economic ideas and, moreover, by his pure and fervent patriotism. As Ramaswami Aiyer wrote, 'Ranade was the prime factor to growth of instructed Indian political and economic thought.' He was himself a scholar-politician and he (Ranade) trained Gokhale to follow his foot steps.

At the same time, Ranade and Gokhale alike, transformed politics of India and spiritualised it by insisting on self-surrender, complete dedication to the cause of the country and purity of motive and action. Gokhale also got inspiration from the life and thought of Dadabhai Naoroji, the Grand Old Man of India, particularly by his nationalism and by his pure, simple and self-sacrificing life. Ishwar Dutt remarks, "There were three men in particular to whom Gokhale felt spiritually drawn and yielded reverence from his very soul-partiarchal Dadabhai Naoroji, his great master, Mahadev Govind Ranade, and the incomparable Gandhiji (though his junior). In their presence he felt elevated." In matters of party organisation and technique, Gokhale was inspired by Sir Pherozeshah Mehta. He was influenced, up to some extent, by the philosophy of Tilak too. In addition to this, he was influenced by his personal circumstances. His forefathers, the Chitpavan Brahmins had certain distinctive qualities. They were practical, ambitious, personable and industrious. Gokhale inherited his uprightness and habits of unselfish application from his family.

Gopal Krishan Gokhale was also influenced by the Western culture and civilisation. He was described by many as the child of the Western traditions. He imbibed his liberalism from the study of English literature. According to him, the European history presented a well-marked evolution of the democratic principles. He was impressed by Burke's 'Reflections on French Revolution'. Gokhale studied the works of British liberals like J.S. Mill, Gladstone and others, and derived his concept of nationalism and liberalism from them. He was also influenced by the German economist, Prof. List. Gokhale was a practical-minded and realistic political thinker. He combined idealism with realism. The following are the main elements of the political faith of Gokhale :

Faith in British Rule

Like Dadabhai Naoroji, Justice M.G. Ranade, Pherozeshah Mehta and other liberals, Gokhale was also an admirer of British rule in India. He had deep faith in the British culture and civilisation. He accepted the British rule in India as divinely obtained. He was of the firm conviction that through the British rule God was preparing India for self-government. In 1912 he remarked, 'Not England's profit but India's moral and material well-being was to be the object of the rule; Englishmen were not to form a governing caste in the country; the people of India were to be helped to advance steadily to a position of equality with them so that they might in due course acquire the capacity to govern themselves in accordance with higher standards of the West.' According to Gokhale, the British rulers gave peace and order and Western education to the country. He believed itr the harmonious relations of India and England. He wanted that India should remain a member of the British Empire. In his budget speech of 1903, Gokhale said, 'The India of the future will, under providence, not be an India of diminishing plenty, of empty prospect, or of justifiable discontent, but one of expanding industry, of awakened faculties, of increasing prosperity, and of more widely distributed comfort and wealth. I have faith in the conscience and purpose of my own country, and I believe in the almost illimitable capacities of this. But under no other conditions can this future be realised than the unchallenged supremacy of the paramount power, and under no other controlling authority is this capable of being maintained than that of the British crown.' Thus, Gokhale accepted the supremacy of the Paramount Power and considered the British connection with India as a blessing. Hence, he was a typical moderate.

Gopal Krishan Gokhale had deep faith in British liberalism. Like Dadabhai Naoroji, he held the view that the British would do justice to India. In his budget speech of 1902, he said, 'what is needed is that we should be enabled to feel that we have a Government national in spirit though foreign in personnel — a government which subordinates all other consideration to the welfare of the Indian people, which resents the indignities offered to Indians abroad as though they were offered to

Englishmen, and which endeavours by all means in its power to further the moral and material interest of the people in India and outside India. The statesman who evokes such a feeling among the Indian people will render a great and glorious service to this country and will secure for himself an abiding place in the hearts of our people. Nay, he will do more — he will serve his own country in a true spirit of Imperialism — not the narrower imperialism which regards the world as through it was made for one race only and looks upon subject races as if they were intended to be mere foot stools of that race — but that nobler imperialism which would enable all who are included in the Empire to share equality in its blessings and honours'. Gokhale had deep faith in the British fair-play and justice. He was of the opinion that the British rule alone could secure peace and prosperity to the country. He advocated a policy of loyal co-operation to the British crown.

His Political Goal

Gokhale stood for Dominion Status for India as integral part of the British Empire. He also wanted to attain Swaraj like Tilak but he knew that the attainment of Swaraj was not immediately possible under the existing political circumstances. However, he used the term self-government instead of Swaraj. Gokhale recognised that our advance towards self-government could only be gradual because 'at each stage of the progress, it must be necessary for us to pass through a brief course of apprenticeship before we are enabled to go to the next one, for it is a reasonable proposition that the sense of responsibility, required for the proper exercise of the political institutions of the West can be acquired by an eastern people through practical training and experiment only. Though, Gokhale was admirer of the British rule and considered its connection with India as beneficial, he never hesitated to condemn the wrong policies of the bureaucracy. He observed that, 'the bureaucracy in India was becoming frankly selfish and openly hostile to national aspirations.' He strongly criticised the ruling bureaucracy for its gross irresponsibility and extreme callousness to public will in partitioning Bengal. He made strong protests against the oppressive rule of the bureaucracy. Pt. Moti Lal Nehru described Gokhale as a great apostle of self-government.

His Political Programme

Gopal Krishan Gokhale wanted Indianisation of services and demanded Indians to be given more representation in the legislative councils. At the Banaras session of the Congress, Gokhale categorised a set of nine demands : (i) a reform of the legislative councils by raising the proportion of elected members to one-half and by requiring that the budgets be passed by the councils; (ii) the appointment of at least three Indians to the India Council; (iii) the creation of advisory boards in all districts throughout the country; the district magistrates were to consult these boards compulsorily in important matters of administration; (iv) the recruitment of the judicial branch of the Indian Civil Service from the ranks of the legal profession; (v) the separation of judicial and executive administration; (vi) the reduction of the heavy military expenditure; (vii) the expansion of primary education; (viii) the growth and extension of industrial and technical education and (ix) the alleviation of rural indebtedness.

In 1905 and afterwards, Gopal Krishan Gokhale supported the Swadeshi Movement. But he did not subscribe to Boycott. In his presidental address to the session of the Banaras Congress in 1905, he said, "...the true Swadeshi movement is both a patriotic and an economic movement. The idea of Swadeshi or 'one's own country' is one of the noblest conceptions that have stirred the heart of humanity....The devotion to Motherland, which is enshrined in the highest Swadeshi, is an influence so profound and so passionate that its very thought thrills and its actual touch lifts one out of oneself. The Swadeshi Movement, as it is ordinarily understood, presents one part of this gospel to the mass of our people in a form which brings it within their comprehension. It turns their thoughts to their country, accustoms them to the idea of voluntarily making some sacrifice for her sake, enables them to take an intelligent interest in her economic development and teaches them the important lesson of co-operating with one another for a national end....But the movement on its material side is an economic one; and though self-denying ordinances, extensively entered into, must serve a valuable economic purpose, namely, to ensure a ready consumption of such articles as are produced in the country and to furnish a perpetual stimulus to production by keeping the demand for indigeneous things largely in excess of supply, the difficulties that surround the question economically are so great that they require the co-operation of every available agency to surmount them." However, Gokhale distinguished the Swadeshi movement from the movement of boycott of British goods. He also worked at improving relations among different communities. This was the programme that Gokhale set for himself and worked unselfishly throughout his life.

Constitutional Methods

Like Dadabhai Naoroji, Justice M.G. Ranade, Pherozeshah Mehta, Surendranath Banerjee and their followers, Gopal Krishan Gokhale also believed in the peaceful and constitutional methods for attaining his political goal of self-government. He was not a political mendicant. His method was that of constitutional agitation. In the words of Gokhale, 'constitutional agitation is agitation by methods which we are entitled to adopt to bring about the changes we desire through the action of constituted authorities. Thus, to define it, the field of constitutional agitation is a very wide one. But there are two essential conditions — one that the methods adopted are such as they are entitled to employ, and secondly that the changes desired must be obtained only through the action of constituted authorities by bringing to bear on them the pressure of public opinion.' This method included free speech, free association, free press, meetings, processions, delegations, constructive criticism of the government etc. The method of constitutional agitation also included prayers and petitions but it did not include the use of violence, preaching of hatred, etc. Gokhale believed in the method of persuasion. He said, '.... redress must be obtained through the constituted authorities.... the idea that we should leave the authorities, severely alone and seek to attain our goal independently of them is inadmissible and absurd.'

However, Gopal Krishan Gokhale was opposed to adopting the method of passive-resistance of the type preached by Tilak. He did believe in passive-resistance, but pleaded that it should be used only as a measure of defence rather than of attack. He wanted that the passive resistance movement should be moral, spiritual and to be carried on without any intention of vindictiveness. However, Gokhale wanted that this method should be used only when all other means of redress have failed.

His Views on Spiritualisation of Politics

Gopal Krishan Gokhale believed that the political authority should be based on moral foundations. On June 12, 1905, he established the Servants of India Society to spiritualise public life. He wanted that "a sufficient number of our countrymen must now come forward to devote themselves to the cause in the spirit in which religious work is undertaken. Public life must be spiritualised..." Gokhale firmly declared that unless our political movement was informed by the spirit of religion it would be barren. He said, 'The principal moral interest of this institution (Servants of India Society) is in the fact that it represents an idea and embodies an ideal. The idea is that Indians of the present day combined themselves together, and putting aside all thoughts of wordly interests, work for a secular purpose with the zeal and enthusiasm which we generally find in the sphere of religion alone.'

To Gokhale, Spiritualisation of public life' meant the adoption of a religious attitude towards politics. He wanted to raise politics to the level of religion. But Gokhale never understood religion in its dogmatic sense but in the sense of Ethics and moral principles. In the words of Mahatma Gandhi, "I have not the least doubt that Gokhale was well-acquainted with the inner spirit of religion. He never pretended to observe any religious practice, but his life was full of the true spirit of religion." To Gandhi, spiritualisation of public life meant that our means to achieve our ends should be pure and noble. He observed, 'It is not true that we shall be able to progress if our political conditions undergo a change by any means and in any manner. If the means employed are impure, the change will not lie in the direction of progress but very likely in the opposite direction. Only a change brought about in our political condition by pure means can lead us to real progress.' Thus, Gokhale believed in the purification of means for achieving his political ideals. 'He believed that political activities could lead to salvation and freedom only when they were based on religion or in other words spiritualised.' Gokhale did not believe in the Machiavellian concept that the ends justify the means. To Gokhale, political field demanded the highest qualities. It should not be regarded as domain of the irreligious. Hence, the principle of the purity of means is thus very much clear in the political thought of Gokhale.

As a State-Intervenist

Gokhale believed in the positive attitude towards the role and functions of the state. The main purpose of the state is to further the moral and material interest of the people. 'The state after all exists to make individual members composing it nobler, happier, richer and more perfect in every attribute with which we are endowed.' Gokhale wanted that the state should remove cramping and unnatural restrictions from the path of their development. The state should provide the opportunities to the people for their proper development. He said, 'What the Indians need is, a government which subordinates all other considerations to the welfare of the Indian people, which regents the indiginities offered to Indians abroad as though they were offered to Englishmen, and which endeavours by all means in its power to further the moral and material interests of the people in India and outside India....I want our people to be in their own country what other people are in their own country. I want our men and women without distinction of caste or creed to have opportunities to grow to the full height of their statures unhampered by cramping and unnatural restrictions.'

Gokhale believed in the concept of the welfare state. He wanted that the state should remove hindrances and hardships from the path of the development of the personality of the individual. Gokhale demanded free and compulsory education. In his own words, 'Elementary education for the mass of the people meant something more than a more capacity to read and write. It meant for them a keener enjoyment of life and a more refined standard of living. It meant the greater moral and economic efficiency of the individual. It meant a higher level of intelligence for the whole community generally.' He demanded that the use of liquor, opium and tobacco should be stopped and wanted the state to legislate to stop these evils. Gokhale also suggested state intervention in the industrial and agricultural sphere. It is clear that Gokhale was a moderate par excellence.

His Faith in Western Education

Gokhale attached great importance to Western system of education for the liberation of the Indian mind. He observed, 'In 1833 England was called upon to make her choice between two courses — to try to bring up the people of India in ignorance and superstitution, or to open to them the flood gates of Western knowledge thereby aiming at gradually raising them to the level of her own noble traditions. Guided by her noblest instincts, she deliberately preferred to instruct the people of the country in Western learning.' Gokhale was of the view that Western learning was essential for our progress in science and industry. He wanted that the social and political institutions of the country should be reformed in the image of the West.

As Lover of Liberty

Gopal Krishan Gokhale was a great lover of liberty. He was highly influenced by J.S. Mill, the great English liberal thinker. To Gokhale liberty did not imply absence of restraint. He was the view that liberty could be allowed only to the individuals with a certain sense of self-restraint, self-discipline and self organisation. While framing the rules of the Servants of India Society, he wrote, 'My difficulty for some time was the one to which you have so prominently referred — the danger of individual liberty. But in the end it was accessary to run the risk involved in it, as otherwise there was but small chance with disorganised and undisciplined public life and the want of self-restraint which characterizes most of our young men of any really useful work being done by the society.' Gokhale wanted the freedom of contact and free criticism of the government. He pleaded for the freedom of the press. Thus, he said, 'The press is in one sense like the government, a custodian of public interests and any attempt to hamper its freedom by repressive legislation is bound to affect these interests prejudicially and can't fail in the end to react upon the position of the government itself.' Like J.S. Mill, Gokhale pleaded for the establishment of representative institutions in India. Thus, Gokhale had abiding faith in the principle of liberty. He considered it essential for the progress of humanity. He also advocated the right to private property.

As Advocate of Hindu-Muslim Unity

Gokhale was a great advocate of the Hindu-Muslim Unity. He was of the view that unless these two communities developed a spirit of co-operation, no progress was possible. Gokhale was against those movements which tended to develop among the Hindus the spirit of class consciousness against the Muslims. That is why, he never appreciated the Ganapati and Shivaji festivals started by Tilak. Gokhale also opposed the principle of special representation of the religious minorities. He wanted the union of all communities in public matters. So he pleaded for separate representation of the Muslims in order to secure their co-operation. Thus, he said, 'There are acute class differences in the country today, and any scheme of representation by means of election by men in whom they have confidence, any scheme of description which secures this really, in my opinion, promotes the true interests of unity in the country.' He wanted to decrease communal differences between the Hindus and the Muslims.

Gopal Krishan Gokhale's works and activities mark him as a man of rare qualities. He believed in the nobility of human nature. Mahatma Gandhi described him as pure as a crystal, as gentle as a lamb, as brave as a lion and the most perfect man in the political field. In the words of Hoyland, 'He (Gokhale) was a great master of the possible, a constructive statesman of the first rank and bringer together of East and West in the common service of the needy, above all an idealist, a foreseer, a prophet of the new era of inner racial goodwill and co-operation.'

(iv) Economic Ideas

Under the inspiration of Justice M.G. Ranade, Gokhale was led to take an active interest in the economic affairs of the country. He devoted time and energy to study India's economic problems. Gokhale's contribution to the economic field was massive and significant. It was expounded in his writings and speeches — his evidence before the Welby Commission, his speeches in the Bombay legislative Council and the Imperial Legislative Council on budgets and his addresses on various conferences. Gokhale was pained to see the 'deep and deepening poverty' of the country. He realised that if India was to make any constitutional advance, the people must acquire progressive control over the national finances.

According to Gokhale, India was essentially poor because she was agriculturally backward. Not only this, the British were killing Indian industries with the result that there was increasing unemployment and lower living standard of the Indian people. While the British rule provided security of life and property, England's policy of developing the Indian market for her own advancement of industries brought about a rapid decline of the Indian urban handicrafts. The result was, increased pressure on agricultural prosperity. He wanted the government to undertake useful and constructive policy towards the agriculturists. In his budget speech in the Imperial Legislative Council in 1905, he said, 'Everywhere in India, and particularly in the temporarily settled districts, the resourcelessness of the agricultural classes is the most distressing fact of the situation. The cultivator has no capital and has but little credit and is simply unable to make proper use of nature's wealth that lies at his door, with the result that his cultivation is of the rudest and most exhausting type. The yield of the soil has been steadily diminishing, being simply 8 to 9 bushels an acre, about the lowest yield in the world.' Gokhale wanted the government to help the agriculturalists. He demanded that the government should open co-operative societies and agricultural banks. These banks should provide facilities to the peasants to borrow at the lower rate of interest for their constructive and productive expenditure. Gokhale also wanted to decrease land-revenue. He also wanted the government to give primary importance to irrigation and scientific agriculture as measures for agricultural prosperity.

Gopal Krishan Gokhale also wanted the state to protect infant industries in India, on the ground that she was an industrially backward country. Thus, quoting Prof. List of Germany, the great economist, he said, "The great German Economist, List, points out in one place what happens when a country like India comes into the vortex of universal competition. He says that when a country industrially backward with antiquated methods of manufacture depending largely upon manual labour comes into the vortex of universal competition — competition with countries which use stream and machinery and the latest researches of science in their production — the first effect is to sweep off local industries and the country is thrust back on agriculture for some time. But then, he says, comes in the duty of the state, when such a situation is reached, the state, he says, should step forward and by a judicious system of protection it should foster such industries as are capable of being fostered so that the country may once enter on its industrial path with the aid of the latest appliances and ultimately stand successfully the competition of the whole world....I certainly would strongly advocate that the Government of India should follow this advice of List." Gokhale pleaded for a more balanced adjustment of the expenditure and income of the government. He demanded the reduction of expenditure on the functions of the state. Thus, Gokhale said in his Budget speech of 1903,

"As things stand at present, Indian finance is virtually at the mercy of military considerations and no well-sustained or vigorous effort by the state on an adequate scale for the material advancement or the moral progress of the people is possible while our revenues are liable to be appropriated in an ever-increasing proportion for military purposes."

Gokhale opposed the policy of over-taxation. He wanted the government to decrease its expenditure. He suggested four remedial measures : (i) 'the spirit of economy,' would be installed in government spending, in place of the spirit of expenditure; (ii) substantial reduction should be effected in military expenditure; (iii) there should be a greater employment of the Indian agency in public service and (iv) provision should be made for an independent audit of public expenditure. In his budget speech of 1907, Gokhale demanded the total abolition of salt duty. In his budget speeches of 1903 and 1904, he sponsored the abolition of excise duty on cotton goods. Gokhale also raised his voice against the accumulation of the Gold Standard Fund for the purpose of Indian rupees into British Sovereigns on the introduction of gold currency in India. Thus, Gokhale worked for a large and comprehensive scheme for the moral and material well being of the Indian people.

(v) Educational Ideas

Gopal Krishan Gokhale took keen interest in the educational sphere of the country. He was of the view that a proper system of education can help in improving the future of a nation. He wanted the government to pay more attention to introducing a developed and enlightened system of education in the country. In his budget speech of 1902, Gokhale said, 'Then the question of mass education must be taken in right earnest and if it is so undertaken, the present expenditure of government on public education will require a vast increase. My Lord, it is a melancholy fact that while with us nine children out of every ten are growing up in ignorance and darkness, and four villages out of every five are without a school, our educational expenditure had been almost marking time for many years past, whereas in England where every child of school going age must attend a school, the Government's expenditure on education has mounted from 4.5 million to 11.25 million sterling in the course of fifteen years....It may be asked how can the two things that I advocate simultaneously be achieved together, namely, a considerable reduction of taxation and a large increase in the outlay on education and other domestic reforms? My answer is that the only way to attain both objects simultaneously is to reduce the over-grown military expenditure of the country.' In 1910, Gokhale moved a resolution demanding 'free and compulsory' elementary education in the country. He proposed, 'That this council recommends that a beginning should be made in the direction of making elementary education free and compulsory throughout the country, and that a mixed commission of officials and non-officials be appointed at an early date to frame definite proposals. Again, in 1911, he moved his famous Elementary Education Bill. Gokhale also pleaded for the expansion of technical and higher liberal education.

Gokhale had deep faith in the Western system of education. In his own words, 'No striking problems in any particular field are looked for, unless there be room for the free movements of the energies of people in all fields. To my mind, the greatest work of Western education in the present state of India is not so much the encouragement of learning as the liberation of Indian mind from thraldom of old world ideas and assimilation of all that is highest and the best in the life and thought and character of the West. For this purpose, not only the highest, but all Western education is useful.' Gokhale opposed Lord Curzon's policy of bringing universities and colleges under the government's control. In this connection, the University Bill was introduced in December 1903. Gokhale made six speeches at various stages of its discussion against the bill. Gokhale also pleaded for improving the living conditions of teachers. In the educational sphere, Gokhale's contribution was great. In the legislative councils, he spoke on the issues and causes of education.

(vii) The Servants of India Society

The most characteristic gift of Gopal Krishan Gokhale to India, was the establishment of the famous, the Servants of India Society. The foundation stone of the Servants of India Society was laid in Poona on 12th June, 1905 by Shivram Hari Sathe, an old-time colleague of Gokhale in *Sarvajanik Sabha*. The main object of Gokhale in establishing this society was to train the educated youngmen in the responsibilities of Public Service in a spirit of self-sacrifice. As Srinivasa Sastri said : Mr. Gokhale had long felt that what was most needed for the furtherance of the objects of our public work was a select, compact and trustworthy corps of young men who had fully prepared themselves by study, by patient observation, by travel through different parts of India and by work of a probationary character, young men who had in these ways trained themselves to take a real part on their own initiative in public life. For let me tell you at once, Mr. Gokhale loved India and her welfare so intensely and so deeply that he would not willingly see it injured by the labours of unprepared, immature, crude workers, whose only equipment consisted in a genuine call of patriotism. Patriotism by itself is not enough. It is a noble, powerful, exalted emotion. It has got to be directed into useful, fruitful channels and that can only be if every worker prepares himself by arduous study, patient survey of the realities of Indian life and by an appreciation on the spot of the variety of things and circumstances of each particular locality. He, therefore, laid it down that when young men came to him for training they should remain for five years with him, during all that time studying and travelling and working under trusted leaders, but never making themselves responsible for either a speech or a newspaper article or for any public action. When you remember that admission to the society was open only to graduates of distinction and high calibre, you can see what a five year's further preparation, superimposed upon this university equipment, must have meant to the young men whom Gokhale had in view as genuine, trustworthy public workers. Moreover, his even observations led him to the belief that in India deeply imbued with religion and the religious spirit as its people were, a religious or moral appeal must be made before they would trust a person who approached them on weighty and delicate matters. Therefore, his desire was that the young men whom he admitted to the Society should take upon themselves a vow of a simple and pure life; that they should as a principle openly eschew channels of profitable employment, that they should be contented with just that provision that the Society's 'funds may allow, from time to time, and that in a pure missionary spirit they should devote their whole lives to the work that he assigned to them. From the above passage, it is clear that Gokhale wanted that the public worker must have the knowledge of the needs of the situation and practical work, must serve the people for their improvement and lead the life of dedication, simplicity and purity. He also believed in the close relations of public life with morality and religion. He emphasised the purity of means. Thus, the preamble of the Society said, 'The Servants of India Society' has been established to meet in some measure these requirements of the situation. Its members frankly accept the British connection ordained, as the inscrutable dispensation of providence, for India's good self-government within the empire for their country and a higher life generally for their countrymen is their goal. This goal, they recognise, cannot be attained without years of earnest and patient effort and sacrifices worthy of the cause. Much of the work must be directed toward building up in the country a higher type of character and capacity than is generally available at present and the advance can only be slow. Moreover, the path is beset with great difficulties, there will be constant temptations to turn back; bitter disappointments will repeatedly try the faith of those who have put their hand to the work. But the weary toil can have but one end if only the workers grow not faint-hearted on the way. One essential condition of success in this work is that a sufficient number of our countrymen must now come forward to devote themselves to the cause in the spirit in which religious work is undertaken. Public life must be spiritualised. Love of country must so fill the heart that all else shall appear as of little moment of its side. A fervent patriotism which rejoices at every opportunity of sacrifice for the motherland, a dauntless heart which refuses to be turned back from its object by difficulty or danger, a deep faith in the purposes of providence which nothing can shake equipped with these, the worker must start on his mission and reverently seek the joy which comes of spending oneself in the service of one's country.

The Servants of India Society will train men prepared to devote their lives to the cause of the country in a religious spirit, and seek to promote, by all constitutional means, the national interests of the Indian people. Its members will direct their efforts principally towards :

(1) creating among the people, by example and by precept, a deep and passionate love of the motherland, seeking its highest fulfilment in service and sacrifice;

(2) organising the work of political education and agitation, basing it on a careful study of public questions, and strengthening generally the public life of the country;

(3) promoting relations of cordial goodwill and co-operation among different communities;

(4) assisting educational movements, especially those for the education of women, the education of backward classes and industrial and scientific education; .

(5) helping forward the industrial development of the country and

(6) the elevation for the depressed classes.

Every member of the society was required to take pledges at the time of admission. Those seven vows were :

(1) That the country will always be the first in his thoughts and he will give to her service the best that is in him.

(2) That in serving the country he will seek no personal advantage for himself.

(3) That he will regard all Indians as brothers and will work for the advancement of all, without distinction of caste or creed.

(4) That he will be content with such provision for himself and his family, if he has any, as the society may be able to make. He will devote no part of his energies to earning money for himself.

(5) That he will lead a pure personal life.

(6) That he will engage in no personal quarrel with any one.

(7) That he will always keep in view the aims of the society and watch over its interests with the utmost zeal, doing all he

can to advance its work. He will never do anything which is inconsistent with the objects of the society. The members were given an allowance of Rs. 50 per month and they were to receive a five years training, covering, economic and social studies and practical work. The Society had its branches at Bombay, Nagpur, Madras and Allahabad. The society played a very commendable role in uplifting the people of the country in economic social and political spheres.

(vii) Estimate

Gokhale was a great son of India. He dedicated his whole life for the service of the country. His last words to the members of the Servants of India Society were, 'Don't waste your time in writing a biography or setting up a statue but put your whole soul into the service of India. Then only shall you be counted her true and faithful servants.' In the words of Hoylanad, 'In regard to broad general principles; he (Gokhale) knew exactly what the next step ought to be, and where the deficiencies of things, as they were, called most urgently for practical redress. So much was this so that Gokhale ceased, during his later years of greatness, to be merely a leader of opposition. Technically he remained such, but in fact he became a leader and in some relations almost a dictator of the best elements in government policy. His moral stature was so commanding, his personal ascendancy became so marked, that men of enlightenment and good will who found themselves responsible for directing the destinies of the Indian people were glad to accept his guidance whenever they could.....that his recommendations in the great Budget speeches had year after year decisive effect in shaping the financial policy of the government, that his unceasing advocacy of the Indianisation of the services bore definite fruit, that after his death much of what he had striven for was achieved in the Montagu-Chelmsford reforms, and that in a great number of other particulars his practical idealism was justified by the formation of enlightened policies and definite measures of reform.' Aga Khan wrote about Gokhale, 'Gokhale was more than a statesman. He was essentially a creative artist of gendus. His oratory was a work of art in words, but he was not only an artist in words but an artist in works and conceptions.... He was not only broad-minded, but charitable. His sense of human solidarity made him fully of personal sympathy, not only to his opponents, but to the selfish and the snobbish self-seekers.' In the words of M.A. Jinnah, 'Gokhale was a fearless critic and opponent of the measures of the government and the administration of the country, but in all his actions and utterances, he was guided by reason and true moderation. Thus, he was a help to the government and a source of great strength and support to the cause of the people. One of the greatest lessons that his life and work teach is the example of what one single individual can achieve, how powerfully and materially he can help and guide the destinies of his country and his people and from whom millions can derive true lead and inspiration.' In the words of V.S. Srinivasa Sastri, 'In Mr. Gokhale's character there was a great element of reverence and gratitude to those that taught him, nothing but admiration for those who had done great things and undergone great trials for the sake of the country....there is no man who has shown grit and patience and courage so rare that several times in course of these struggles he lost his fortune and by his indomitable will put it all together again.' Mahatma Gandhi said about Gokhale, 'I was by the side of that saintly politician (Gokhale) to the end of his life and I found no ego in him. If he wanted to shine in the political field of the country, he did so not in order that he might gain. He developed every particular faculty in him, not in order to win the praise of the world for himself but in order that his country might gain. He did not seek public applause but it was showered upon him, it was thrust upon him.' According to R.R. Diwakar, 'The name of Gokhale emerges as a brilliant star which shone for a century and contributed substantially to the purity and an orderly advance of public life and political opinion in India'. In the words of Lord Curzon : 'In fact he was the leader of the opposition and in that capacity I had often to suffer from the weight of Mr. Gokhale's blows.... widely as we differed, I never failed to recognise either his ability or his high character.' In Lord Hardinge's words, 'He was the leader of the opposition in the Legislative Council, really a good orator and debater, a statesman and a man for whom I had the highest respect. I have always regarded him not merely as an important member of the council but also as a friend.' In the words of Ramsay MacDonald, 'In him India had a faithful and devoted son. He belonged to that race of Indian who retained that calm dignity of mind and spirit which comes from an unassailable belief in their own race and its dignity.' After Gokhale's death Tilak said, 'Gokhale had many virtues in him. The chief amongst them was his complete dedication at a very young age to the service of the country, with selfless devotion....he was the Diamond of India, the Jewel of Maharashtra and Prince of Workers.'

8

Bal Gangadhar Tilak (1856-1920)

Lokamanya Bal Gangadhar Tilak was one of the supreme leaders of India's struggle for freedom. He was born in Maharashtra. Even from his boyhood, he detested British rule. He established the 'Deccan Education Society' for the promotion of education and nationalism among the people. *The Maratha* an English language newspaper and *Kesari* a Marathi language daily were started by him. Patriotism and nationalism permeated Indian sub-continent through these two newspapers.

Tilak condemned the partition of Bengal in 1905 in strong terms. He convened public meetings protesting against the British policy. At the Calcutta Congress held in 1906 he proposed the boycott of foreign goods and raised the demand for Swaraj. He exhorted the people not to co-operate with the government. The extremists in the Indian National Congress regarded him as their unquestioned leader. Under his guidance and leadership many a protest rally was held all over India criticising and condemning the British administration. The rulers were bent on splitting the Congress by arresting the extremists and sentencing them to long spells of imprisonment and dealing with the moderates leniently. Tilak was arrested in 1907, sentenced to six years imprisonment and kept at Mandalay jail in Burma. It was Tilak who gave the Taraka Mantra : "Swaraj is my birth right and I will have It."

Bal Gangadhar Tilak was born at Ratnagiri on the West coast of India on 23rd July, 1856. The Tilaks belong to a Chitpavan Brahmin community of Ratnagiri district. Bal's original name was Keshav. Even as a child he was called Bal, the short form of Balwant. Keshav was the name of his great grandfather who had distinguished himself as a good swimmer, good shot, and a great rider. Bal seemed to have inherited his fighting temperament and boundless energy and he had to conduct his fighting in speech and writing. His father, Gangadhar Pant, was a teacher who was widely respected for his superior talents in teaching Sanskrit and Mathematics. Bal Gangadhar derived his father's scholarly gifts and intellectual faculties. He lost his father in his sixteenth year. He was already married; his studies had not yet been completed. Luckily, for him one of his uncles came forward to look after him and enabled him to pursue his studies without interruption.

In 1872, Tilak came out successfully in the Matriculation Examination in flying colours and joined the Deccan College at Poona in 1873. In the first year at college, he resolved to improve his physique. He spent his mornings in the gymnasium and the evenings in long walks in the fresh open air.

He was extremely fond of swimming and like his great grandfather he developed into an excellent swimmer. He delighted in remaining in water for hours on end. At college Tilak was an independent student doing things as he liked. He loved Sanskrit very much and composed Sanskrit verses. He liked Mathematics also greatly. He ignored the other subjects but was none the worse for it. He managed to pass his B.A. degree examination in the first division. He then went to Bombay so that he might prosecute his studies by joining the M.A. course. But he abandoned the idea in a short while and turned to the study of Law. In 1879 his efforts were crowned with success and he secured the L.L.B. degree.

During this period Tilak and a young man Agarkar by name, became friends and they made up their minds not to seek employment under the government but to devote their entire time to the service of their motherland. They felt that the wisest thing to do was to establish a school and provide cheap education to all. This plan was not very successful. They did not lose heart. They approached Vishnu Krishna Chiplunker who was a renowned prose writer of the time. Chiplunker and some other good friends assisted the two young men in starting a new English School at Poona at the beginning of 1890.

Agarkar could not join the staff at the inception but Tilak became a teacher in the school. There were many difficulties; nevertheless the school flourished and in about five years it could boast of a thousand students. In addition to the hardwork in the school Tilak and his friends had plans for starting a printing press and bringing out a newspaper. Soon they could execute their plan. They started a press and called it 'The Arya Bhushan Press'. They published two newspapers. One was called Kesari and it was in Marathi. The other was called the Maratha and it was in English. Agarkar and Tilak contributed excellent articles regularly to the newspapers. They wrote boldly about the burning topics of public interest.

The new English School was making great studies in the field of education. They were now seized with a great desire to establish a college. In order to translate their desire into action they founded a society called the Deccan Education Society. It consisted of seven life-members who vowed to serve the society for twenty-five years.

They commenced their work in the school itself and soon shifted to new buildings. Sir James Fergusson, the then Governor of Bombay laid the foundation stone of the new college building and so the college was named Fergusson College in his honour. Soon it grew to be one of the outstanding colleges of India. But an unfortunate difference of opinion cropped up between Tilak and Agarkar and caused a split. Agarkar aimed at swift changes in the customs and manners of his countrymen while Tilak favoured slow and steady change. Thus, they were diametrically opposed in their stands and this ended in a parting of ways of these two friends.

Tilak spared no points in working for the good his country with his forceful writings in *Kesari.* He left no stone unturned in bringing to light all the misdeeds of the government and this resulted in his courting trouble very often. His writing was powerful and impassioned but fetched no substantial amount. He required more funds. So, in the midst of all these activities he started a cotton factory and opened a Law class in Poona. The factory was a failure but the Law class was a thriving concern and afforded him ample funds. He also stole time to conduct research into the ancient Hindu Scriptures and he contributed some valuable papers on the Vedas; and his papers are highly appreciated.

During this period a Bill known as The Age of Consent Bill' was introduced in the Legislature. The Bill provided for raising the marriageable age of Hindu girls from ten to twelve. Tilak was of the firm opinion that such reform could not be brought about by law. So, though he was not averse to the principle of raising the age of marriage, he opposed this Bill. He wanted Hindu society to make changes stage by stage and that they themselves must feel the urgent need for the changes.

During this period Tilak involved himself intimately with the affairs of the Indian National Congress. He was in the forefront of its activities. The Secretaryship of the Deccan Standing Committee of the Congress went to him unsought. His displayed his superior talents by organising the first-five sessions of the Bombay Provincial Conference. The last session was conducted as Poona and It was a very grand affair. It was a tremendous success as well. He was twice elected to the Bombay Legislative Council and was also elected a Fellow of the Bombay University. He became a Municipal Councilor in Poona. In 1895 he was requested to serve as the Secretary of the Eleventh Session of the Indian National Congress which was to be held in Poona. But unfortunately there arose sharp differences amongst Congressmen before the Session was held. Tilak left the field and made way for others to occupy the office. He, however, continued his co-operation unofficially.

In 1896, a severe famine stalked through the Bombay Presidency and other parts of India. The people suffered untold misery. Tilak's heart bled for the people. He girded up his loins and braved the famine as it were. He did a lot to relieve the distress of the people. He set up cheap grain shops in Poona and in other places. He did not mind functioning in co-operation with the government. He established relief centres in a number of places These great effort showed his abundant love for the people. To make matters worse, plague broke out in Poona about the same time. Generally there was panic everywhere on account of this. Tilak remained undaunted. His determination inspired others also. So Tilak and his comrades stuck to Poona. They organised a hospital. Tilak published in his paper various useful methods to be adopted both by the government and. the people whereby they could eradicate that epidemic completely. He rose very high in the estimation of the common people on account of his great love for them and his enormous concern for their well-being. They naturally adored him.

Tilak understood that the craving for hero worship was inherent in people. He inaugurated a movement for celebrating Shivaji Day year after year as an instrument of promoting the patriotism of the people. Shivaji is the most outstanding 'hero' of the Maharashtrians and, therefore, this movement soon captured the imagination of the people and became very popular. The initial celebration of Shivaji Day was held on 13th June 1897 and a great deal of ceremony, pomp and splendour accompanied it to the great delight of the people. A few days later Tilak published a full report of the proceedings and a hymn sung on the occasion in *Kesari.* On the 22nd of June two Enligshmen were killed in Poona. This struck terror in the minds of Europeans. They attribute it to the consequence of what had been written in *Kesari* by Tilak. The government arrested him in Bombay on the 27th of June and instituted legal proceedings against him for sedition. He was refused bail not only by the Chief Presidency Magistrate but also by the High Court. Nevertheless a second application was made in the Court of Justice Tyabji who released him on bail. The case went on. The jury who were asked to give their verdict on Tilak consisted of six Europeans and three Indians. The six European majority found him guilty. The Judge accepted the verdict of the jury and awarded him eighteen months' rigorous imprisonment. All the efforts made to have this sentence modified were of no avail. Then some acquaintances of Tilak in England, Professor Max Muller and William Hunter, appealed the Queen Victoria to show mercy to Tilak. They represented that Tilak was a renowned scholar and his release would gladden the hearts of the people of India and make her regime popular. After sometime, on September 6, 1898, Tilak was set free. During his stay in prison Tilak continued his study of the Vedas. Some years later the results of his study were published. His stay in prison affected his health. So he stayed for some time in a sanatorium in order to recuperate his health.

Tilak never failed to attened all the meetings of the Indian National Congress when he was not in prison. He became the leader of the party in the Congress which demanded total home rule. This party was known as the Home Rule Party. The moderates charged Tilak with extremism. One of Tilak's sayings has become very famous as a Political Taraka Mantra. It was, "Swarajya (Independence) is my birthright and I will have it". Some Indians believed that they could liberate India from foreign yoke only through violent acts. So violence burst out in some parts of India. Tilak wrote articles in Kesari asking the Government of India to give Indians Home Rule and thus prevent violence from spreading in India. Tilak's articles were misinterpreted as encouraging acts of violence and so he was arrested and brought to trial. In the course of the trial, Tilak argued his own case with extraordinary skill which amazed all the lawyers. The case dragged on for about five days and ultimately the verdict went against him. He was sentenced to transportation for six years. This severe punishment awarded to this distinguished servant of the country infuriated the people greatly and brought about a total *hartal* in Bombay.

When the sentence was delivered in his case, Tilak said, "All that I wish to state is that, notwithstanding the decision of jury, I am clear that I am innocent. There are higher powers ruling over this world and it may be the will of God that the acts for which I stand may be made more successful by my suffering than by my remaining free". He maintained equanimity and patience in the teeth of all his difficulties. Thus, he became a famous hero.

Tilak was a great scholar besides being a great national leader. He based his works on deep study. While he was languishing in Mandalay jail, he continued the study of the Hindu scriptures, especially the *Bhagavad Gita*. He brought out a book called *Gita Rahasya*, or the secret of the *Gita*, in Marathi. This book has seen translations into many languages. It is read all over the world as an important modern commentary on the *Gita*.

The period of transportation came to an end in 1914. Tilak came back to India. He plunged once again in his work in connection with Kesari and the Maratha. He contributed articles attacking acts of violence which had been ravaging the country. He did not fail to show that the English had gone some good to the Indian people. His writings exhibited his liberal out-look and magnanimous spirit. His generosity was also displayed by what he did after the death of Gokhale in 1915. Gokhale was the staunch supporter and leader of the moderates and the political mentor of Gandhi who had just then returned to India from South Africa. Tilak had no use for Ghokale's ideas and ways. But when Gokhale passed away, Tilak paid him a glowing tribute. In the funeral oration Tilak said, "This is not the time for tears. This is the time for bemoaning the great loss we have suffered in the death of Mr. Gokhale. This diamond of India, the jewel of Maharashtra, the prince of workers is resting for ever on the funeral ground. Look at him and try to be like him."

There came about a split in the Indian National Congress between the extremists and the moderates. The two parties found it impossible to function together. When Tilak came back from Mandalay, he exerted his enormous influence in cementing the two parties. At last in 1916, the two parties were once again amalgamated, thanks to Tilak's initiative and drive. He persevered to get Home Rule for India. To propagate his cherished ideas on Home Rule he travelled widely in all the parts of the country. He delivered lectures in many places. Wherever he went he drew large crowds of people. The people understood every word he uttered and their hearts were deeply moved.

Tilak attended the Congress Session held in Lucknow in 1916. The people gave him a rousing reception. He spoke at this session and explained in detail what he meant by Home Rule. He employed very simple language and said, "Home Rule means that I should be in my own country what an Englishman feels himself to be in his." The people of Maharashtra celebrated his sixty first birthday grandly and bestowed a gift on him on that occasion. It was a purse of one lakh of rupees. They called him the uncrowned monarch of Maharashtra. Tilak was overwhelmed with their love and regards for him. In a fitting speech he expressed his deep sense of gratitude to the people for their generous gift and mentioned his insatiable desire to serve the country.

In 1918 Tilak felt that he would be well to present the case of Home Rule before the English people in England. Tilak achieved his object of reaching England. He wrote and spoke a lot about the urgency for Home Rule in India. He contacted numerous political leaders in England and briefed them about India.

Tilak returned to India in 1919 at the age of sixty-four and was in excellent health. He attended the session of the Congress at Amritsar that year. The joy of the people knew no bounds but next year his health failed and after a brief spell of illness he breathed his last on 31st July 1920. The tidings of his death spread like wild fire and the whole country was in profound grief. Thousands of people poured into have the last *darshan* of this great leader and to pay homage to him. A number of special trains plied to and from between Poona and Bombay. The body of

Tilak was taken through the streets of Bombay to the seashore where it was cremated. A statue was erected at that place.

The people of India held Tilak in such high esteem and revered him so much that they called him Lokamanya, *i.e.,* "Worthy of the honour of the entire world."

Tilak was one of the greatest Indians of our time. He dedicated all the gifts of his mind and all his tile and energy to the service of his motherland. Though this great leader is dead and gone, he will live for ever in he hearts of his countrymen.

Tilak's Political Philosophy

Lokmanya Bal Gangadhar Tilak was a leader of such qualities by which destiny of India was changed. His heroic deeds made Indian National Congress a mass organization. In the words of Pattabhi Sitaramayya in the book on the History of Congress who spoke of him "Lokmanya was the first nationalist who took the movement for freedom struggle to the common man."

Before the entry of Tilak to the Congress, the body as cornered by few moderate educated persons who were ignored by the Britishers. They were cautious in their actions. They only liked to have certain concessions to the educated class from the English rulers. While advocated a strong fight against the unjust foreign government. At the same time Gokhale liked constitutional ways to gain something.

The economic condition of the country was quite depressing Economic resources were utilised for their own good. The credit of being a first mags leader goes to Tilak. Pandit Jawaharlal Nehru said of him, "The early founders of Congress were great men. But they rather made the intellectual foundation in the early stages of the freedom movement. I don't think that it is unfair to them to say that they were not mass leaders in the sense that some subsequent state leaders became. I think the first great mass leader of this new state of our revolutionary movement was Lokmanya Tilak."

Tilak had to work under the unfavourable state as opposed by moderates. But he could merge as a national leader.

He was of the opinion that keeping on the constitutional methods of struggle was without foundation as India had not own constitution. Moderates gave importance to administration and its improvements. Moderates tried to win over the foreign government through love, goodwill and sympathy. While Tilak liked it through non-co-operation, obstruction and passive resistance, politicians of Pre-Tilak period depended on alien Government's benevolence, sense of equity, justice and fairplay. Tilak trusted self-sacrifice, suffering and service of the people. Most leaders appealed to intelligent class while Tilak appealed to the masses in millions. The moderates wanted to voice their resentments and feelings through the Council Chambers. Tilak used village Mandaps for voicing the feelings as platform. Leaders used English as their medium of expression, Tilak used Indian dialects. Other leaders wished to participate in the administration step by step. Tilak declared, "Swaraj is my birth-right and I will have it." He thought of freedom to be never achieved by charity but was to be demanded as a right. Freedom was quite necessary for social, political and economic uplift of the public. Freedom was a political and spiritual necessity of the people for by that they can remove their misery, starvation and degradation. Tilak liked Indian National Congress not be a body of general public for mass movement against the British Government: Congress meetings should be hold more frequently and not once in a year. Its message should reach everywhere in India through towns, cities and villages. Because of these reasons English called him the father of "Indian Unrest."

Influence on Tilak Tilak was influenced by his father. He was one of the persons born of an orthodox Brahmin family. This caused him influenced throughout his life. D.P. Karmarkar wrote, "Tilak inherited something more precious from his father a strong determination and will, a clean and healthy mind, a capacity of industry and achieving and a way of methodical work". He was also influenced by Swami Dayanand, Swami Vivekanand, and Swami Ramkrishna Paramhansa. He liked their philosophy much. At the same time the views and philosophy propagated by Mahadeo Govind Ranade were liked by Tilak. His idea of liberation provided much to Tilak. Tilak wrote about him in the following words, "Mahadeo Raoji's life was educative and important on account of his extraordinary intelligence, long and continued labour, genuine devotion to national cause, unquenchable thirst for knowledge and his rare imaginativeness. In fact that Maharashtra later had showed greater life and greater public activities, it was all due to unremitting labours of Ranade for more than a quarter century". Besides this Tilak was greatly influenced by Ancient Indian culture and civilization. Hence he was careful to revive the Indian's past glory.

His Works He gave four classical works.

(1) *The Orion*

(2) *The Arctic Home and the Vedas*

(3) *Vedanga Jyotisha*

(4) *Gita Rahasya.*

Religious Festivals and Tilak Tilak found Indians to be more religious. He thought over that religious festivals can prove mass media to appeal the people against foreign government. Hence, he arranged for the Shivaji and Ganeshotsava and gave long speeches to revive nationalism. He gave Shivaji a patriotic colour and national honour. He spoke "Our ancestors have created national opportunities in the form of these festivals for people to get together."

His Concept, Views and Philosophy of Swaraj Tilak is said to be one of the movers of the Indian Nation. He talked of Swaraj from the year 1896. While most of the moderates praised the English rule. He gave the call of Swaraj. He gave the slogan for complete freedom. That slogan was no doubt too earlier but it paved the way for it, and it became reality of the future. He awakened the mass to national politics. He gave the words, "Swaraj is my birth right and I shall have it", Tilak gave it like a mantra at the Lucknow Congress Session in 1916. He meant "Home Rule" for Indians. That means ruling power was to be handed over to Indians by the English people. He never meant the negation of the British King Emperor. He only meant the replacement of the British rulers by the Indians.

By Swaraj he meant a Dharma Rajya It was not only a transfer of political power but beyond that, as it was required to build a superstructure on Indian culture and civilisation. It was a Swaraj in which every Indian would get all the rights natural to man. He also revealed the federal structure of the country so that all races, languages, religion and culture could be accommodated. This all can be done under British Emperor and would lead to the end and independent existence.

Swaraj meant the operation and management of domestic affairs of India by Indians. According to his definition, "Swarajya as possessing these rights which the native princes had in the Indian States with this difference that instead of hereditary chiefs under Swarajya there would be an elected President". Foreign policy was to remain in English hands. British King Emperor was not to be replaced. Further he put forward "the idea of Swarajya is an old one. Of course, when Swarajya is spoken of, there is some kind of rule opposed to swa *(i.e.,* our) and this idea arises at that time. This is a plan when such a condition arises it begins to be thought that there should be Swarajya and even make efforts for that purpose", "The question of Swarajya really means in whose hands should be vested the control of our affairs. I have said that we do not wish to change the immutable government or the king but what we demand is that the management of our affairs should not be, as it now is the hands of invisible government, the bureaucracy, but should be transferred to our hands".

According to him, Swarajya was the necessity. He meant by Swarajya a federal type of political set up. Like the American Congress, the Government of India should have similar power and the same powers be used through the Imperial Council. He accepted the possibilities of linguistic provinces. As he said "India is a big country", divide it, if you want according to languages.

To attain Swarajya, many sufferings and sacrifices are required but not the prayers and petitions. We proposed some effective methods Swadeshi and Boycott movements prove for it. Karmarkar spoke of him, "Tilak attached a great importance to boycott as a means of exercising pressure on Britishers to compel them to grant Indian's legitimate rights". Tilak spoke, "We have neither the strength nor the desire to rise in arms against our rulers, but should it not be possible for us to stop the drain of crores of rupees which we are giving to the British merchants, labourers by purchasing British goods". He told of the national education children should be sent to such schools that would reach them or rationality and patriotism. For Swadeshi movement he said once, "We send our boys to schools and completely aloof from the national movement. On the other hand our object is that they should get an education that will inspire them with patriotism."

Other method was of Boycott or passive resistence. People should not obey these laws that go against justice and morality. Passive resistence was the means to an end but was not the goal in itself. "Public has to see its merits and demerits. More the demerits they should be fought but not by violence or anarchism for attaining Swarajya thought he had no faith in constitutional methods. Constitutional agitation was out of question as there was no Constitution of India. He said "There is no Constitution in India. The Government in India is irresponsible and non-constitutional constituted authorities in India are irresponsible and we have to take our rights from them. The legality of our action may be illegal according to their point of view but we should not worry whether our agitation is legal or illegal. We must see whether justice, morality and historical traditions are in our favour or not and if our actions are correct according to these standards we should not care whether they come within the law or not because the power making of law is in hands of foreigners".

Tilak gave birth to Home Rule League in 1916 with Mrs. Annie Besant's collaboration. During April 1916, he started the movement which aimed Home Rule under British Empire. British Parliamentary Act can do this by introducing a Bill in Parliament to this effect and so propaganda and agitation was required to be started in England also.

Tilak's Method of Struggle Tilak condemned the method already 'adopted by the moderates who were dominating the Indian National

Congress at that time. As their method depended completely on prayers, petitions and memoranda. Independence could not be got by these methods in charity. English people were selfish. They were bent upon unking torture and economic exploitation of the Indians. They tried to such the toils of Indians to the benefit of their home country. He had no faith for such people and justice from them. Hence, he put forward his methods for conducting struggle. He put forth Swadeshi, boycott, national education and passive resistance. Swadeshi meant the use of India-made goods this would stop the British goods' consumption and their earnings would be reduced.

Secondly, he wanted to boycott the English made goods though their superiority was established due to machine-manufacture.

Thirdly, he supported the impartation of National Education in stead of the British system of education prevalent at the time as it only produced clerks to work for the British administration in India. Hence, National Education would bring the growth of patriotism and nationalism.

Forthly, passive resistence was the effective method whereby public could resist bad laws and maladministration. He avoided constitutional methods of struggle as there was none of Indian Constitution, The Government of India was irresponsible and unconstitutional. Our legal actions were decided by an illegal government.

Lastly, the English bureaucracy in India was corrupt and misused the authority. Hence, Tilak condemned the British official engaged in India for mal-administration and spook thus, "To deport national leaders without rial, to prohibit peaceful meetings...to sentence editors of newspapers like criminals...to keep respectable people under trial for months together and such like action being taken in India are similar to autocratic policy adopted by Czars of Russia, This repressive policy is likely to result in consequences similar to those of Russia."

His Political Views

Basic Foundations He had before him the political freedom of India and it brought realism to his thoughts. He was understanding the Sanskrit Philosophy. So he brought forward the Indian thought of the heritage and coupled it with the nationalist and democratic ideas of the West.

He believed in the Indian philosophy of Vedanta regarding supremacy of the soul. Hence, the soul was supreme and all human beings were same hence all were equal in all respects. Hence, all were entitled to spiritual freedom. In *Geeta Rahasya* he gave the concept of freedom like this :

> "Divine instinct of freedom never aged... Freedom is the very life of the individual and which Vedanta declares to be not

separate from God but indentical with him. Thus, freedom was a principle that could never perish Swaraj was not only a right but a Dharma. Politically Swaraj meant home rule. Spiritually it meant realization of inner freedom. Morally Swaraj aimed are perfect self-control so very essential for performance of one's duties (Swadharma)".

In this way Swaraj in Tilk's opinion presented an essential ingredient of good life. He emphasized that without Swaraj people would suffer in life on earth as well as in future life.

Hence, Advaitism taught the supremacy of the concept of freedom. He told "Freedom was the soul of the Home Rule movement. The divine instinct of freedom never aged, freedom is the very life of the individual soul and which Vedanta declares to be not separate from God but identical with him. The freedom was a principle that could nêver perish". Hence according to him freedom as a divine attribute.

Tilak gave his base for nationalism on Western theories of national independence and self-determination. In his historical trial speech of 1905 he quoted J.M. Mill's views about nationalism. In 1919 he accepted Wilson's idea of self-determination and applied it to India. Hence, his philosophy of nationalism has base on the mixture of Western and Eastern thoughts : This was given the word 'Swarajya' which was used by Shivaji also in his Maratha Policy.

It was because of his spiritual approach and outlook that Tilak regarded it as right as well as Dharma. He gave Swaraj ya a moral as well as spiritual interpretation.

According to him, politically it meant Home Rule, morally it meant attainment of the perfection of self-control which was required for the performance of Swadharma (One's duty). Spiritually it meant the attainment of inner freedom and delight. He defined spiritually, "It is a life centred in self and dependent upon self. There is Swaraj in this world as well as in the world thereafter. The Rishis who laid down the law of duty be took themselves to forests because the people were already enjoying Swarajya or people's dominion which has administered and defend in the first instance by Kshatriya Kings. It is may conviction; it is my thesis that Swaraj in the life to come cannot be the reward of the people who have not enjoyed in this world". Hence, Tilak wished political and spiritual freedom.

Nationalism and His Views Hence, Tilak meant by Nationalism psychological and spiritual requirements it was a tribal instinct that cannot be suppressed. Modern states were big in sizes. To control the vast population in a single nation some conditions are required, unity of race, religion, language and geography come under these. Common history and culture also promoted the cause of unity of India had it the past.

Thus, he wanted to review the past and hence we can say that it was revivalism. Hence he reminded the Vedic culture and caused to know the spiritual energy and moral enthusiasm by the people. He said, "A true nationalist desires to build on old foundations. Reform based on utter disrespect for the old does not appeal to him as constructive work. We do not want to anglicize our institutions and so denationalize them in the name of social and political reforms". Hence, he revived the festivals of Ganapati and Shivaji. In terms these festivals made to look timely events and movements with historical traditions.

According to him, nationalism was a psychological and spiritual means. It is the modern version of old patriotism in tribal form. Now it covers the whole nation. Moreover, nationalism flourished with common language, descent, religion habitation and territory. All these lead to unity of nation. These factors are objective. At the same time subjective psychological factor is not present. It is required to be created by heritage of historical traditions. From immemorable past this had halped to built India. Economic grievances against the foreign power existed though demand for independent existence of the soul of nationalism through the past culture.

Spiritual side of nationalism was spread by the sages like Vivekananda, Tilak, Aurobindo Ghosh, Bipin Chandra Pal and Mahatma Gandhi. Secularism was spread by Dadabhai Naoroji. Pherozeshah and Gokhale. Tilak meant "Festivals are symbolical adjuncts of nationalism. The festivals meant for unity of participators and can be utilized by leaders for national purposes, Ganapati and Shivaji festivals thus started by Tilak led to nationalism and unity.

Ganapati festivals were celebrated from the past by the donations received from chiefs. Tilak gave it a public character and this helped to foster nationalism in the masses.

Shivaji festivals were started through the initiative of English rulers. Grave of Shivaji was reconstructed at Rajgarh. Tilak called him 'Vibhuti' of Geeta. Vibhuti was said to have all creative powers of divine nature. After his release in 1900 grand celebration was held at Rajgarh. This festival spread up to Bangal and Japan in the 20th century beginning.

In *Kesari* dated 8th April 1901, Tilak spoke of Congress movement for getting some rights, Shivaji festival worked as a tonic. Tilak said, "Nationalism is not a visible any concrete entity but is kind of symbolism, an idea and in generating this idea, the historic memorises of the great figures of the country play a significant past". Indian nationalism should come from the heart of public and not by the western writers. So he thought that the memories of Shivaji would foster the national sentiments among the public. Shivaji gave the symbol for resistance against the oppressors.

Tilak was a Revivalist Some say him to be a Hindu nationalist as he loved Hindu culture but he never opposed Muslims. Zakarias in his book "India — a Restatement" spoke of him as an anti-Muslim retaliation. Palme Dutt said to him as mixing Hindu revivalism and cut off from Muslim masses from National movement. Prominent Muslim personalities like Jinnah, Dr. M.A. Ansari and Hasan Imam had admired him. As for his advice Lucknow pact was done in 1916. Shaukat Ali and Hasrat Mohani regarded him as political Guru. Shaukat Ali said, "I would like to meiltion again for the hundred times that both Mohammed Ali and myself belonged and still belong to Lokmanya's political party". Hasrat Mphani wrote, "I even at that early as choose the Lokmanya as the ideal leader for me — during that period I had ample opportunities of appreciating the thought and abilities of almost all political leaders and basing my remarks on that close personal study. I can state without the least fear of contradiction that I found the Lokmanya the greater and superior to every other leader in every respect when I declare that all through Tilak's life I was both intellectually and practically a blind follower of his, any one can well judge thereby of that love that I cherished towards him."

Though Tilak advocated national movement through strong cultural and religious revival still he accepted the economic reasons of Dadabhai Naoroji. In an artical written by Tilak in June 1887, he said Indian art and industries were suffering and declining under the English reign. Foreign investment has created a setback to the Indians and poverty is the ultimate result. In 1907, interview with Newinson gave the economic drain of India. The same year, Allahabad speech of Tilak asked for protection of Indian trade and boycott of the English goods. He pleaded for Swadeshi, boycott and national education.

In his commentary to Gita be wrote of his love to Mother country. For him whole world was a one big family. This proves his love of internationalism.

His views on Representation under Reforms Act of 1919

Mont-Ford Reforms of 1919 gave a great controversy among the Indian political thinkers. Even the Moderates thought it unwise to act according to it and take part in legislative bodies. Though Tilak had no belief in representation to such bodies but still he thought it should act as as check to the bad laws and hence elections should be fought to take initiative under the law-making of the nation.

Tilak did not believe in representations but still he sent a memorandum to Peace Conference Paris in March 1919 as he could not attend it due to cancellation of the passport. He asked the conference to extend the principle of self-determination to India also for which English people had fought the war. He wanted right share in the family of nations. He said, "It is necessary for me to doll upon the imperative importance of solving Indian question for the purpose of ensuring the future peace of the world and the progress of the people of India. India is self-contained, harbours no design against the integrity of other states, and had no ambition outside. With the vast area, enormous resources, prodigious population, she may well aspire to be a leading powers in Asia. She could, therefore, be a powerful Steward of the League of Nations in the East for maintaining the peace of the world and the stability of the British Empire against all aggressors and disturbees of peace whether in Asia or elsewhere."

Indian problems could only be solved by Indians. Their fitness had been recognized by Notingham Conference of the Labour Party of England. He asked the Peace Conference to make two pronouncements :

(1) India would be accorded all the rights of representation in the League of Nations which have been given to British self-governing colonies.

(2) It should be declared that Indians are fit for carrying on their government and the principle of self-determination should be a plied to India so that Indians could establish a democratic form of government. He said that such a pronouncement would generate sentiments of enthusiasm in the hearts of Indians.

Seeing the opposition stand of the moderate Tilak founded Congress Democratic Party to fight the elections to demand from within and struggle from outside.

His Concept of Rights He meant that Indians should claim rights. Demand of rights was not an act of sedition. It was a sacred duty of the citizens to claim it and those who fail claim did disservice to the nation. According to him rights were essential for the healthy life of the nation. He said, "What do we ask for? Do we say, Drive away the English Government, but I ask what is it to the Emperor? Does the Emperor lose anything? Whether the administration is carried on by the Civil Servants or by our Delhi Sahibs? The rule still remains, the Emperor still remains. The Difference will be that the white servants who were with them would here be placed by black servants. From whom does this opposition come?

This opposition comes from those people who are in power. It does not come from the Emperor. From the Emperor's point of view there is neither anarchy nor want of loyalty nor sedition in this. What does sedition means, hatred of the King. Does king mean a police Society." Thus, Tilak meant for the demand or rights and it should not be dislocate the political set up.

His Views about Revolution Historians of Indian National Movement were of different opinions about Tilak. Revolutionary is one who brings revolution in the socio-economic system in the country. But it is to remember that he was neither a socialist nor a communist. His aim was to get the Home Rule. By Home Rule he meant attainment of Indianization to the existing civil and military administration under the British Emperor.

Japan's victory over Russia and partition of Bengal were printed in his papers *Kesari* and *Maratha* but the unrest in India was the outcome of the political and social conditions mixed with economical circumstances which was all brought about by the foreign rule.

Chirol in his book, *Indian Unrest* spoke, "Tilak had been the first to create, the atmosphere which breeds murders." John S. Hoyland spoke, "Tilak had been conquering with doctrine of physical force." Branson, the Advocate General in 1908, while conducting the case spoke, "Tilak's articles contained a covert threat of mutiny and he was preaching Swaraj or Bombs." Dr. P.S. Khankhoje, a prominent revolutionary of Nagpur said to Tilak being a revolutionary in the articles under Kesari during August 1903 and February 1904 he spoke him, "a teacher and preceptor of the revolutionary youth of India."

No doubt Tilak was an extremist in his views as compared to moderates of his time. He was fearless for his attack on bureaucracy. He spoke petitions and prayers as useless. Though he advocated passive resistance still he returned while the force was to be used. It was known that he had established an arms factory in Nepal in 1903. He was more advanced than the times. English control was to a great extent and only Tilak could dare to oppose the Government. He was not a believer of Ahimsa. He was in touch with the revolutionaries of the calibre of Shyamji Krishana Verma and B. D. Savakar. He spoke that todays extreme might be a moderate of tomorrow. He never tried to murder anybody nor he incited anybody to murder. He adopted the legal, methods of political organization and agitation. He said once, "from begging to open rebellion choose any one according to your ability and do it but remember the supremacy of *Swadharma*." He accepted that Gita gave the theory of righteous violence for the doing of an act. A revolution means a change fundamental in the socio-political field. He wanted only the management of ones own affairs by themselves favouring the retention of king Emperor. He only liked to replace British bureaucracy by Indian Civil Service.

Tilak said, "I may say once for all that we were trying in India as the Irish Home Rulers have been doing in Ireland for the reforms of a system of administration and not for the overthrow of government and I have no hesitation in saying that the acts of violence which have been committed in different parts of India are not only repugnant to me but have, in my opinion, actually, unfortunately retarded to a great extent, the cause of out political progress". His activity was mainly bound to Maharashtra. His only aim was emancipation of India from foreign domination. Through his paper *Kesari* he preached political liberty, natural rights and justice. He was at best a political agitator and the Britishers regarded him as the leader of Indian Unrest.

His Views About Social Reforms

The important problem before India was the social reforms during the British and pre-British period. With the decline of the Mughals, the Indian social life was neglected and with the arrival of Britishers, it was quite destroyed. They thought their own culture to be superior. They ridiculed the prevailing customs of sati, caste, untouchability, child marriage, ban on widow marriage. Leaders like Raja Ram Mohan Rai took the British help to introduce social reforms, Lord Bentinck abolished Sati system through law. So also were the views of Ranade and Gokhale. But Tilak did not accept the idea of state intervention in social field and religious life.

Social and Political Reforms Tilak did not favoured the idea of British intervention in the social and religious fields. The Brahma Samaj, Prarthna Samaj and the Arya Samaj supported the English rulers in passing the age of Consent Act, 1891, which raised the consent age from 10 to 12 years. So also Arya Samaj obtained the Sharada Act, Arya Samaj Act. But Tilak did not favour this.

On the whole Tilak was not against the social reforms. He spoke that he was not the anti-social reformer. He was of the opinion that reforms should come from the people. He spoke of political liberty first. Earlier in Congress both these activities were mixed together. In 1915 Congress Session it was said, "Authoritative record, after this has been carefully elicited, by the fullest discussion of the matured opinions of the educated classes in India on some of the more important and pressing of social questions of the day."

At the Calcutta Session of the Congress held under Dadabhai Naoroji's presidentship it was held that "A national Congress must confine itself to questions in which the entire nation has a direct participation and it must leave the adjustment of social reforms and other class questions to the class Congress."

Tilak's opinion about social reforms and political liberty were quite apart as they were different. He wanted social reforms to be gradual by education. Before the political rights, social reforms were not valuable. He quoted Ireland, Ceylone and Burma where religious reforms were carried on and later they became independent.

Though he was against the Age of Consent Act, he followed the spirit and arranged his daughters' marriages at the age of fifteen. He also allowed untouchables to participate in the festivals arranged by him. He also advocated widow marriage. He congratulated Prof. Karve when he married a widow after the death of his first wife.

He was in favour of social reforms still he did not prefer the government interference.

These prove that Tilak was not a social reactionary or a champion of Hindu orthodoxy. He was a full supporter of the social reforms but he wanted that we must have first political independence. He wanted that ancient Hindu culture should be preserved. He said, "Once the political soul of India was free, the Indian councillors could decide the problem of social changes in atmosphere of free criticism."

The people themselves would bring about the required change in social set up. After political reforms social changes will automatically follow. Government head by Indian people would automatically be concerned with the social problems of the country and will thus take necessary stemps for the improvement of social set up in the country. He, therefore, wanted that the Indians should first struggle for political freedom rather than hankering after social questions. Political freedom was primary and social reforms were secondary. Hence, he was of the opinion that political reforms must precede the social reforms.

Views about Social Reforms According to Tilak, social reforms should be evolutionary and not revolutionary. It should from within the people and should not be imposed on them by the leaders. The leaders should regard themselves as members of the society and not above the society in his own words, "The leaders are not the masters but the servants of the people. So long as the opinion of the leader is not much different from the people they are receptive. But if a leader's stand point is entirely different from the people, then on a particular issue at least there has to be a divorce between the two."

He was against social reforms on Western lines. Hence, the opposed the idea of a foreign Government interfering in the sphere. Progressive education was the first necessary in this field. Hence, he liked the change in educational system. The educated mass will discard the prevailing social evils. The same we expect of the social leaders and they should act according to that. They should be persons of saintly kinds like Nanak and Kabir. He spoke, "There has been much talk about our social reforms but we have to bear in mind that we have to reform the masses and if we dissociate ourselves from them, reforms would become impossible. The outstanding example of this is that the widow-remarriage is a desirable reform but most of the reforms do not practice it in their family. I, therefore, think that each one should begin reforms with himself and convert others through practice rather than by theory. The reforms should live up to this preaching". Hence, he asked the social reformers not to violate the public sentiment. Hence, Tilak also accepted the punishment awarded to him by the society (award of Shankaracharya) for taking tea at the missinary's house on 4th October 1890 at Poona with Gokhale and Ranade.

He believed in the social reforms but first he wanted political changes. Again he wanted these changes should come from within and not from outside, He opposed the Age of Consent Bill on this ground that it was done by Government. So he opposed untouchability. In Ganapati festivals lowest classes were permitted to attend the function. He addressed in Bombay in March 1918, the First Depressed Classes Conference. He spoke of all-Indians as children of the same parents. He said, "If a God were to tolerate untouchability, I would not recognize him as god at all." Hence, Tilak was never opposed to social reforms. Tilak did not oppose the State Intervention in social life. He was opposed to the Intervention at such a period of existence. The present state had no authority to interfere in the social traditions. As such Britishers were claiming their superiority in culture but at the same time Indian culture was no more inferior to theirs. He was proud of the past of Indian inheritance He, hence, could not tolerate the Government intervention. The government interference was to disturb the religious and social pattern of society. So he disliked the government sponsored changes. If government makes social changes then it is their duty to see them executed and the offenders should be punished. Again he spoke of the judges who would decide the cases will be foreign in morals.

He said of Hindus requesting the Britishers to formulate the rulers for social affairs and it was a shameful act for them to do this, as they were unable to do it, if the government was composed of popular elected representatives, he would have adopted different attitude. To say in the end he was against the bureaucratic social legislation which was against his patriotic sentiments. Hence he opposed State intervention.

Tilak and Gokhale Bal Gangadhar Tilak was a great personality of Modern India. He was the leader of the people's movement in Maharashtra. He was of the extremist views. His opinions and methods of working differed from that of the moderates who were quite in effective in their efforts. He was convicted several times and paid penalties for that. For his free spokesmanship the under went many trial and tribulations. Thus, he is quite different from the personalities like Gokhale and Gandhi.

Similarities between Gokhale and Tilak Gopal Krishna and Bal Gangadhar Tilak are both prominent personalities of the Modern India. Both are the sons of Maharashtra and belong to the same family of Chittapawan Brahmins. They were contemporaries. Both were pioneers of Indian struggle for emancipation. Poona was the centre of activity of both of them. After completing their education both worked for. The Deccan Education Society for some years. They started as teachers in the Fergusson College Poona. They were the life members of the Deccan Education Society. Both were leaders of the national level. They were both top-ranking patriots and worked ceaselessly for India's freedom. Though in different ways, both were great leaders in their own ways. Both were imbued with the spirit of sincere patriotism. Both made heavy sacrifices for the sake of the country in and through the Indian National Congress. They joined and worked in the National Congress but belonged to different groups in the Congress and to different schools of thoughts. Pattabi Sitaramayya, a great political historian of national struggle, brought out the contrast between the two stalwarts of freedom agitation as such:

(1) Gokhale was the leader of Moderate school of thought in the Indian National Congress whereas Tilak was the leader of Extremist section of the same organization.

(2) Gokhale along with other moderate believed in the British sense of justice, equity and fair play. He, therefore, appealed to the sense of reason of the Britisheres through petitions, prayers and memoranda. He believed in what the Moderates called as constitutional methods for achievement of their goal. Tilak, on the other hand, was a typical Maharashtrian full of valiant spirit of struggle. He along with Aurobindo Ghosh, Lala Lajpat Rai, Bipin Chandra Pal did not believe in any sense of reason of the Britishers who ruled over India with a clear and simple intention of exploiting the economic resources of India to the benefit of their mother country. He ridiculed the idea of constitutional methods on the ground that India had a constitution as such. He

believed the political freedom could never be achieved through an appeal to mercury. No nation, however, good it may be, would grant freedom just for asking. Freedom is something which had to be won from unwilling hands. Tilak wanted to mobilize the Indian masses for attainment of freedom. Instead of trying to win favours from British bureaucracy he believed in the fact of putting up a fight. He believed in self-help, self-reliance, self sacrifice and self-suffering.

(3) Gokhale and other moderates were admirers of British rule and believed that it was a blessing in disguise and that India made trendemous progress under benevolence of British rule. Tilak regarded British rule as the greatest curse and sooner the people got rid of the same, better it would be.

(4) Gokhale believed in improving the British administration but Tilak wanted to replace it.

(5) Gokhale believed in offering co-operation to the British bureaucracy but Tilak's wanted to fight it out.

(6) Gokhale was mostly concerned with administration and its reforms but Tilak's concern was his country and her uplift.

(7) Gokhale believed in love and sweet reasonableness but Tilak believed in suffering and sacrifice.

(8) Gokhale looked to the classes but Tilak looked to the masses. Gokhale and his moderate associates tried to mobilize the intelligentsia and win concession and favours for them. Tilak made a direct approach to the masses and generated political consciousness amongst them and prepared them for a great struggle for national liberation.

(9) Gokhale's field was the Council Halls whereas Tilak would use village Mandap as his platform for expression of his opinions.

(10) Gokhale delivered his speeches in English but Tilak mostly expressed himself in vernacular.

(11) Gokhale wanted to bring about reforms in British administration in India step by step but Tilak fixed Swaraj as his political goal and he would not be satisfied with anything less than that.

(12) Gokhale aimed at the mobilization of the educated classes in India and England but Tilak believed in moblization of world public opinion against the British rule in India. He had his visit to London, he presented the Indian case to the Labour and Liberal Leaders of England and tried to win over their support.

Though they both differed in political ideals still they were great friends and paid respect to each another. Tilak received hearlity Gokhale when he returned from England after giving Indian opinion in 1905. He even recommended Gandhiji to see Gokhale when he met him after return from South Africa. Tilak paid his high tributes to Gokhale at his death.

Gokhale admired British rule and relations and it can be judged from the reply to Lord Hardinge's question, "How would you like it, if I were to tell you that all-British officials and British troops would leave India within a month?" Gokhale replied, "I would be very pleased to hear the news but before you had all reached Aden, we would be telegraphing to you to come back". In this way Gokhale regarded the British as guardian of the Indian public and advocated a policy of loyal co-operation.

In his budget speech in 1902 in the Indian Legislative Council he said about the expectation of justice from Britishers "What is needed is that we shall be enabled to feel that we had a government national in spirit though foreign in personnel-government which subordinates all other consideration to be welfare of the Indian people."

While Tilak though of constitutional methods were no solution as he said, "There is as such no constitution in India. The Government of India is irresponsible and non-constitutional. Constituted authorities in India are irresponsible and we have to take our rights from them. The legality of our actions is decided by this government. Our actions may be illegal according to their point of view, but we should not worry whether our agitation is legal or illegal. We must see that the justice. Morality and historical traditions are in our favour or not and our actions are correct according to these standards. We should not care as to whether they came within the law or not, because the power of making law is in the hands of foreigners. Of course, it is true that the infringement of law will result in punishment but if law is repressive it will be resisted by suffering such punishment, there is not other way. This is bound to happen when law and morality are conflict with each other."

At the same time Tilak advocated the self-reliant way for the achievement of one's end. He asserted that "Swaraj is my birth right, I shall have it." About the method of moderates Tilak said, "Political rights have to be fought for. The moderates think that these can be won by persuation." He suffered imprisonment thrice and "won for himself the crown of martyrdom."

Mahatma Gandhi had in his book, *Stories of My Experiments with Truth* compared "Tilak to the ocean and Gokhale to the Ganges."

Tilak had great regard for Gokhale. He said about him, "It requires a great self-restraint, it requires a great will, to turn out one's back on the temptation of the life, with prospect of sure happiness especially when one is confident of more than normal achievements. And to devote oneself ceaselessly to national work and to find life's fulfilment in such work, with a perfect willingness to suffer, in the force of all adversities that may come."

Tilak has deep regard for Gokhale as he has commented at the funeral pyre "This is not the time of cheers, this is the time for shedding tears. This diamond of India, this gem of Maharashtra, this prince of workers is laid to eternal rest in the funeral ground. Look at him and try to emulate him."

Tilak and Gandhi

Similarities Bal Gangadhar Tilak and Mohandas Karmachand Gandhi were the remarkable leaders and brave sons of India. For Swarajya sake they did the great sacrifices. Both believed in the attainment of Swaraj from the British Government, they both thought it in terms of politically and spiritually attainments. They tried to bring ethics in politics Both believed in ancient Indian culture. Both loved India and Indian ways of living and thinking Both worked in Congress but differed at times in approach and programme. They both thought Swadeshi and boycott as instruments of politics. Both believed in conditions of India not favourable for revolution. Both covered masses and not classes. They preferred that only mass movement could only bring the desired object. By the sufferings of the people and selfless sacrifice, Britishers could give Independence.

Tilak could not live long to see his long cherished Independence but Gandhiji lived for a very short time after Independence. Both believed in the non-co-operation with the British rulers. Politics thrived on spirituality and morality Both condemned the western civilization I and culture as it depended on materialism.

There is a truth in the statement that mantle of Tilak fell on Gandhiji since the latter used all those methods which were advocated by the former. Gandhiji adopted the method of non-violence, non-co-operation as means for the achievement of the freedom. Passive resistance, Swadeshi, Boycott and National Education were also adopted by Gandhiji.

According to J.P. Suda, in Gandhiji's own words, "I cannot claim the honour of being a follower of the late Lokmanya. I, admire him like millions of his countymen for his indomitable will, his vast learning, his love of country and above all, the purity of his private life and great sacrifice. Of all the modern men of time he captivated the imagination of the people. He breathed into us the spirit of Swaraj. No one perhaps realized the evils of the existing system as Tilak did. And in all humanity I claim to driver his message to the country as truly as the best of his disciples. But, I am conscious that my method is not his method".

Thus, we find that Gandhiji praised Tilak but not followed accordingly. Gandhiji was more near to Gokhale than to Tilak. The differences can be brought as hereunder.

Differences between Tilak and Gandhiji

(1) Tilak believed in democratic realism while Gandhiji believed in ethical realism. Tilak derived his inspiration from *Mahabharata, Gita* and *Upnishads* for politics and action. Gandhiji was influenced by Tolstoy, Thoreau, Ruskin, Narsi Mehta and Raichand Bhai. Tilak thought of Ahimsa for political expendiency but Gandhiji has absolute faith in Ahimsa. Tilak would not use force and diplomacy for dealing with opponent till the opponent is not mischievous. As quoted by V.R. Verma, Tilak, at Shivaji Festival said in *Kesari* dated 15th June 1857 "Let us even assume that Shivaji first planned and then executed the murder of Afzal Khan. Was this act of Maharaj good or bad? This question which has to be considered should not be viewed from the stand point of Indian Penal Code or even Smirities of Manu or even the principle of morality laid down in the western or eastern ethical systems. The laws which bind society are for common man like yourself and myself... Great men are above the common principle or morality. Did Shivaji commit a sin in killing Afzal Khan? The answer to this question can be found in *Mahabharata* itself : Krishna's advice to Arjuna to kill his Guru and Kinsmen for the sake of the conquest of Dharma over the evil. No blame attaches to any person if he is doing deeds without being actuated by a desire to reap the fruits of his deeds. Shivaji did nothing with a view to fill the small void of his own belly from interested motives. With benevolent intentions he murdered Afzal Khan for the good of others. If thieves enter our house as we have no sufficient strength in our wrist to drive them out, we should, without hesitation, shut them up and burn them alive. Do not circumscribe your vision like a frog in a well, get out of the Penal Code, enter into the extremely high atmosphere of the *Bhagwat Gita* and then consider the actions of the great men."

Tilak never believed in ethical aspect of non-violence. To protect good and destroy the evil is a divine quality. A policy of forgiveness and meekness cannot be practised in this world full of sins. Tilak was a realist and not an idealist. He once wrote to Gandhiji that politics was not the game of *Sadhus* and *Sunyasis.* It was a game of wordly people. He would like Gandhiji to follow Krishna than to follow Buddha. Krishna gave priority to the practically of the situation and would destroy evil and restore Dharma. Buddha would return evil with goodness. Gandhiji followed later and regarded violence for good or evil as unethical.

(2) Both had different methods for the achievement of their goal. Tilak was a lawyer first and so he preferred legal methods though he ridiculed constitutional method and spoke of India having no constitution at all expect the Indian Penal Code. Mahatma Gandhi spoke of secred rights to resist bad laws. In South Africa he asked Indians to have the basic civil rights. And as such he started *Satyagraha* in India to revoke such laws. Thus, he gave Civil Disobedience as the weapon.

(3) Tilak was an orthodox Sanatan Hindu by faith. While Gandhi was a rationalist in religious thoughts and praised that looked good in world religions.

(4) Tilak believed in representative democracy while Gandhi believed in moral sovereignty. Gandhiji gave moral supremacy of a single man superiority over big parliament.

(5) Realism of Tilak and ethical idealism of Gandhiji were clear as to their approaches to the Reforms Act of 1919. Mahatmaji was against contesting elections while Tilak condemned the reforms but advocated contesting of elections to Assemblies and participate. He wanted more and more of the rights for which he aimed to work both inside and outside. He agreed to Mahatma's Non co-operation, but did not agree to boycott the Councils.

No doubt that they differed in their views still they were the torch bearers of the Indian struggle for Independence.

Tilak appreciated the programme of non-co-operation. He spoke to Mahatma Gandhi at Sardar Griha Hotel, Bombay in 1920 before his death, "I like the programme well enough but I have my doubts as to the country being with us in the self-denying ordinance which non-co-operation presents to the people. I will do nothing to hinder progress of the movement. I wish you every success and if you gain the popular ear, you will find in me an enthusiastic supporter."

About entering the legislative councils, Tilak said to Gandhiji, "I personally believe that it will be better to go to the councils and to obstruct when it was necessary and to co-operate also of necessary."

According to some, Gandhiji was the follower of Tilak and completed the remaining task left by him. This is wrong. Gandhiji wrote about this in *Young India* dated 23rd July 1921 "A Confession of Faith." "I cannot claim the honour of being the follower of the late Lokmanya. I admire him like millions of his country men for his indomitable will, his vast learning, his love of country and above all the purity of his private life and great sacrifice. Of all the men in modern times he captivated most of the imagination of his people. He breathed into us the spirit of Swaraj. No one perhaps realized the evil of the existing system of government as Mr. Tilak did and in all humanity I claim to deliver his message to the country as truly as the best of his disciples. But I am conscious that my method is not Mr. Tilak's method, that is why I have still difficulty with some of the Maharashtra leaders. But I sincerely think that Mr. Tilak did not disbelieve in my method. I enjoyed the privilege of his confidence. And his last word to me in presence of the several friends was, just a fortnight before his death, that mine was an excellent method, if people could be persuaded to have it. But he said he had doubts."

9

Bipin Chandra Pal (1858-1932)

Bipin Chandra Pal, who has rightly been described by Sri Aurobindo as one of the mightiest prophets of Nationalism, and perhaps the best and most original thinker in the country at that time, and by Professor Benoy Kumar Sarkar as 'the father of revolutionary thought in Bengal' was one of the learned thinkers of modern India.

According to B.C. Roy, Mr. Pal was a born orator and his eloquence in the early part of this century roused the youths of their country. Even the aged and the wise listened to him with respect and he was always prepared to convince them, as he often used to say, "not by magic, but by logic."

According to Prof. Paravate, those who push the pen powerfully are said to be shy of the platform. This is not all axiomatic because numerous examples of those who wielded their tongue and pen with equal power could be easily cited. In the case of Bipin Chandra Pal, perhaps his tongue was more effective and sharper than his pen. But this differentiation could be easily dismissed as that between Tweedledom and Tweedledee. His oratory was not mere command over words.

As Aurobindo Ghosh said, "he spoke under an inspiration which he himself was unable to resist." Srinivasa Sastri remarked with reference to Bipin Chandra Pal's Madras speeches of 1907, "oratory had never dreamt of such triumphs in India. The power of the spoken word had never been demonstrated on such a large scale."

His Life Sketch Bipin Chandra Pal was born in a village in Sylhet district, now in East Pakistan, on November 7, 1858. His father, Ramchandra Pal, was a man of strong character.

In 1875, after passing his Entrance examination, Bipin Chandra Pal joined the Presidency College, Calcutta. His college career was not distinguished by any brilliance. In fact, he was seldom seen in the classrooms. About a couple of hours every day, he says in his autobiography, and some days only an hour, I used to be in my class. The rest of the time I played truant.

The period which covered his public life (1882-1932) was also a period of great changes in the religious, social and political life of the people in India. As Lord Ronald Shay said, "His pen played a not inconsiderable part in the social and political ferments that have stirred the waters of Indian life" during the period.

Being sensitive, his mind quickly responded to the influences of the movements of his time. Sir Francis Younghusband, described him as "of fine spiritual disposition as well as of high intellectual attainments."

His journalistic career, which began at the age of 22, continued till his death in 1932. He was on the editorial staff of the Bengal Public Opinion, Calcutta, edited *The Tribune,* Lahore (1887-88) started and edited the English weekly journal *New India* (1901), started and edited the English daily *Bande Mataram* in 1906 (later suppressed by the government), published the English weekly journal *Swaraj in London* during his exile from India (1908-11), founded the English monthly journal *Hindu Review* (1912), edited the daily *Independent, Allahabad* (1919-20). He was also a regular contributor to the *Modern Review, Amrita Bazar Patrika, Statesman,* etc. till his death.

His father made his will on his death-bed and made over all his property to him. To those present he said, "For ten years I did not see Bipin's face. By a previous will I disinherited him absolutely. All those years I would not allow him to come near me. But I am convinced that while he went his own way, out of regard for what he believed to be his dharma, he did not by practising one thing and professing another destroy my *dharma.* He is not a *haramzada.* Besides I thought this also; that thought there are people who would like to have what little property I may leave behind me, there is no one except Bipin, whatever may be his religious principles, who would after my death protect with all his life, the honour of my wife and my daughter. This is why I called him back."

What Bipin wrote in *Bande Mataram* of September 8, 1906 would be very typical of what he spoke and wrote in those days. He was quite frank about it as usual. Bipin said, 'the time has come when in the interest of truth and civic advancement and the freedom of the people, our British friends should be distinctly told that while things they have done for us already, the sacrifices they have made to make our lot easy and their yoke light, we cannot any longer suffer ourselves to be guided by them in our attempt at political progress and emancipation. Their point of view is not ceasing in any sense to be essentially British; we desire to make it autonomous, absolutely free of British control.'

He was a nationalist and wanted to see India as a free nation. To achieve this, he emphasised the method of passive resistance. In a speech in Madras in 1907, he declared, "Our programme is that we shall so in the country, so combine the resources of the people, so organise the forces of the nation, so develop the instinct of freedom in the community, that by these means we will compel the submission to our will of any power that may set itself against us. If you ask me to state in general terms what are the methods and the means, what are the instruments that will further this ideal of Swaraj in this country, my reply shall be that these means and methods are in what is known in political science as the methods of Passive Resistance. It means not resistance that is not active, but non-aggressive resistance. We stand within the limits of the law that we have still in this country. We shall respect that law as long as that law shall respect our primary rights which constitute the authority of every government whether that government be a despotic government or a constitutional government, right which no government can create and which, therefore, no government can destroy. As long as the laws of this government will respect our primary rights of life, person and property and other similar primary rights, so long we purpose ourselves to be within the bonds of law; and passive resistance means resistance offered by a people from within the limits of such law."

His Political Ideas B.C. Pal was a great nationalist. According to B.C. Roy, he made great sacrifices for his love of country, truth and God. It was perhaps the great sacrifice of his life when on account of his strong convictions he lived in splendid isolation from his erstwhile colleagues and friends during the last few years of his life. His greatness lay in the fact that he never yielded to anyone in his devotion to truth and God and to his country. With him, as it was with many other politicians of this country, service of the country was a religion and a service to God.

The Historian's History of the World spoke of him as "the chief purveyor of seditious ideas who promulgated the doctrine of Swaraj or complete political independence."

His political ideas can be broken down as under :

On Nationalism Sri Aurobindo Ghosh referred to him as "one of the mightiest prophets of nationalism." Prof. Benoy Kumar Sarkar regarded him as "the father of revolutionary thought in Bengal."

The nationalist propaganda of Bipin Chandra Pal made, however, the opponents of freedom extremely uneasy. They could not deny that he was "a man of great intellectual force and high character, who had the peculiarity of expressing extreme views in modest language."

To Pal 'Nationalism implies that, collectively, we the composite Indian community are a distinct, and individual social organism : and as such, we have a distinct end unto ourselves and a specific law of our own National Being, through which we must seek to reach and realise that end'.

Bipin Chandra's patriotism was free from any hatred of the British. In an article in Bande Mataram in 1906, he said; 'The time has come when in the interest of truth and civic advancement and the freedom of the people, our British friends should be distinctly told that while we are thankful for all the kind things they have done for us already, the sacrifices they have made to make our lot easy and their yoke light, we cannot any longer suffer ourselves to be guided by them in our attempts at political progress and emancipation. Their point of view is not ours they desire to make the Government of India popular without ceasing in any sense to be essentially British; we desire to make it autonomous, absolutely free of British control.'

Bipin Chandra notes an important difference between the old and the new Nationalism. 'The new Nationalism was intensely realistic, it had a strong grip on the actualities of Indian life and thought as against the imitative character of the older and earlier social and political activities. The older generations drew their inspiration of freedom and progress from European, and specially British history and literature. The old patriotism did not feed upon the actualities of Indian thought and life but upon the idealisties of Europe and America...' There was scarcely any sense of political wrong. On the contrary there was the general impression that the British had established peace where there was turmoil, and a settled government where there was anarchy. Tire old patriotism, therefore, simply represented an awakening of the educated classes to consciousness of their inferior position in the modern world... it was just beginning of a reaction, but not the birth of a new life'.

On Swaraj B.C. Pal said : 'The idea, of Swaraj is that true freedom does not lie in isolation but fellowship and association with the rest of creation. This is the first idea involved in the conception of Swaraj in our ancient spiritual experience. That is the first implication of the Upanishadic idea on this subject. And the second idea involved in it is that this freedom can never be attained in a state of war or conflict, with other object or persons in the universe. As long as I have any enemies so long, I cannot be free to regulate my life and activities just as I like. Self-determination is really a meaningless term for any people or nation which stands perpetually in fear of rival, or enemy peoples or nations'.

Mr. Pal is of the view that Swaraj, it must, therefore, be clearly realised, is not a spiritual condition, not a state of the mind, but an objective system of government and administration. And it must be sought and attained by such methods as have been tested by political science, which means the generalisation of universal political experience and not even the vanity of doing something which nobody has ever done or attempted, should be a permitted to tempt us form the approved and verified generalisation of the experience of the race in matter pertaining to political life and organisation.

The term Swaraj is the compound of the words, SWA and RAJ. The Swa in Swaraj means the Swa or self to the nation. And a nation is a group of human beings who stand differentiated from other social units by its geographical habits, its cultural history and evolution, as well as by its political history and constitution. This Swa is not the Universal or the Absolute Self or Swa. This Swa is no doubt a revelation of the Universal Swa or Self of the Absolute, to use a philosophical term but so are all the other national was or Selfs. And these different national Swas stand differentiated from one another by their geographical borders, their state authority and by those numerous other things which constitute what has been described as their respective 'Nationalities'. This nationality has been very aptly defined by Joseph Mazzini as the individuality of a people. And the moment we understand the undeniable character or our own National Swa, we see that Swaraj is not, and cannot be in reality and truth, something that admits of no definition.

Bipin Chandra said that the Swaraj which we desire to secure for India must, in the first place, be the Raj of the people of India and not Raj of any particular individual or community belonging to India, or it must be a Democratic Swaraj. In the next place, this Swaraj must be the government of the country by agents who shall be responsible to and removable by the common authority of every class and section and community of India, exercised through such arrangements and instruments as shall secure to every individual Indian irrespective of wealth or rank or culture or creed or caste or sex, his or her right to direct and control the machinery of the administration set over them; provided those classes or communities renounce their allegiance to all outside countries and communities upon any pretence whether it be racial or cultural or religious affinity of association, so far as their political life and obligations are concerned.

In the next place B.C. Pal further said that to ensure to every individual and community the fullest share of the direction and control of the machinery of administration or the common state-life established over them, the unit of this Swaraj Administration must be the village, or groups of adjacent villages having a social solidarity and the members of which live in intimate association with one another and are bound together by old and hereditary associations and a thousand common interests —

economic and social and among whom it may, therefore, be possible to establish real self-government. And these village administrations must be joined into a federation to form the district administrations, while these district administrations must be federated to form the Provincial Federations. This is the only conceivable ideal to reasonably ensure a true Swaraj in modern India.

Non-violence in our present Swaraj said, B.C. Pal, must not, therefore, be understood as non-resistance. It must not be confused with mere absence of physical violence. This non-violence here must not be judged and determined by our inner motives. But that alone must be accepted as non-violence which preserves the continuity of the present law and order in the country while seeking to remove the alien Bureaucracy which has made itself responsible for it now. There must not be violent break in this Law and Order. The authority of the government as the government, must represent this authority now must be replaced by others who's all be responsible to and removable by the governed.

Two Roads to Swaraj B.C. Pal said that the attainment of the true Democratic Swaraj in India in the existing condition is only possible, therefore, through friendly settlement with the present foreign power, which holds political authority over us. Friendly settlement means a compromise without any appeal to the arbitrament of physical force. It does not mean anything more in the present context. This compromise must come also through mutual consultation between the Government of India and the British Cabinet and British Parliament on the one side and accredited leaders of the Indian people on the other. The first step towards this compromise is the creation of conditions which will convince the present government of the necessity of coming to terms with the Indian Swarajists for the preservation of their own reasonable interest.

How to Realise Swaraj The realisation of the ideal of this democratic Swaraj, writes B.C. Pal, requires the existence of a truly political-minded people. This condition is as yet absent in India. The creation of this political-minded people is the supreme need of the hour here.

And this education, B.C. Pal said, will have to be imparted not merely by means of books or lectures but with the help of organisations which will be real nurseries of political self-government among the people. This may be done in two ways, first, by covering the whole with a network of voluntary political associations and secondly, by using the existing legislative constituencies for this purpose. In this way, partly with the help of voluntary organisations aiming to build up what has been aptly described as a state, and partly with that of the existing legislative constituencies, and work up a real political mass-awakening in the country upon which, and upon which alone, can the true and solid foundations of democratic Swaraj be laid.

On Passive Resistance He declared in a speech in Madras in 1907, "Our programme is that we shall so work in the country so combine the resources of the people, so organise the forces of the nation, so develop the instinct of freedom in the community, that by these means we shall — shall in the imperative — compel the submission to our will of any power that my set itself against us."

He said, "If you ask me to state in general terms what are the methods and the means, what are the instruments that will further this ideal of Swaraj in this country, my reply shall be that these means and methods are included under what is known in political science as the method of Passive Resistance. It means not resistance that is not active, but resistance that is not aggressive. Passive Resistance is not non-active but non-aggressive resistance. We stand within the limits of the law that we have still in the country. We shall respect that law as long as that law shall respect our primary rights which constitute the authority of every government whether that government be a despotic government or constitutional government — rights which no government can create and which, therefore, no government can destroy. As long as the laws of this government shall respect our primary rights of life and person or property and other similar primary rights, so long we propose ourselves to be within the bounds of law; and passive resistance offered by a people from within in the limits of such law."

"The broad application of this method of passive resistance has brought out two or three special movements in India. One movement is the boycott movement. It is a movement of passive resistance. The other movement is the movement of national education; and the third movement is the movement of organisation of our public life building it up from our village life."

On Freedom To B.C. Pal freedom means the supreme right of each individual human soul. It asserts the dignity of the person as a person. But this personal self-realisation is only possible through individual self-realisation of other persons, with whom each individual stands in an organic relation, in the larger social organism of which both are constituent and organic elements. Therefore, Freedom is not all-sufficient, even for individual self-realisation, which is its logical and aim, but must be allied to Fraternity, to a sense of organic kindship with and responsibility for the well-being of brother-man and sister-woman associated with the organic life of their common society or nation.

On Races and Nationalities B.C. Pal said that there is a very wide difference between a race and a nation. In the first place, territorial unity is an essential condition of nationality but not of raciality. A race may spread over different and distant territories, and occupy various parts of the globe; but a nation must be confined to a definite habitat. A race is essentially a homogeneous thing. It has a special physical structure, a special thought-structure, and a special social structure. This threefold structural affinity is of the very essence of the race-idea. This structural affinity is observed among the different branches of the so called Aryan family.

To B.C. Pal a nation is, however, a more complex and heterogeneous thing. More than one race can go to the making of a nation. There is a good deal of racial intermixture in all the developed nationalities of the world. The growth of nationalities indicates a higher stage of social evolution and a more developed order of social life than is found in mere racial units. There may, therefore, by primitive race, but hardly and primitive nation'.

On Empire Idea B.C. Pal said that the empire idea is essentially larger and broader than the nation idea. It aims at the unification of widely separate territories, of widely divergent interests, of widely different cultures into one organic whole. As families combine into tribes, each family contributing its peculiar characteristics and possessions to the common life of other families, in and through the unity of the tribe-life; as at a subsequent social synthesis, tribes combine to form races, which though divided by space, controlled by different environment evolving under divergent historic epoches, still pursue a common ideal and, are moved mainly by a common regulative-idea, and thus make for a larger union of mankind than had been realised before; and, as at the next synthesis, different racial units combine to form a larger, more complex and yet more intimate unity, namely, that of the nation; so the unification of these national units into an imperial organisation or organism is really a higher and larger social synthesis than even what has been attained through the nation idea. It is impossible to deny, therefore, that the empire idea is positive : lager, grander, nobler than the nation idea. This is the fundamental truth of the concept of empire.

Pal said that the empire idea, offers a broader ground for the unification of humanity than the nation-idea, even as the nation idea offers a broader basis of human fellowship than the unity of tribal or racial relations. This is the fundamental claim to superiority of the empire idea. It is the claim, really, of a broader generalisation and a higher synthesis. The family, the tribe, the race, the nation, all these are what may be called, social synthesis; each succeeding synthesis being broader and higher than the preceding ones. The social synthesis offered by the empire-idea is broader and higher than all others. The first condition, therefore, of the realisation of the true empire idea is a correct and clear understanding of the nature of this synthesis.

An empire is a much larger unit than a nation; and the smaller can never hold the larger. Nay more, the family the tribe, the race, the nation, the empire, all these are distinct social categories; and one cannot, therefore, be converted into the other. A family might multiply to a hundred members, still it would be nothing more than a family; a very large family, no doubt, but never a tribe. Similarly, a tribe might contain a hundred thousand or even a million individuals, but it would still be a tribe, as much as the smallest tribe, but never a race. So with races and nations also. A nation might multiply itself to any extent, might expand its territorial possessions to any length, but it would still be a nation and not an empire. Even the possession of sovereign authority over many nations would not convert a nation into an empire. When a nation assumes the name of an empire on these grounds, it only adds what may be a terminological usurpation to its already achieved territorial usurpations. This is all.

On Socialism B.C. Pal believed in Socialism in the highest and trust sense of the term, and not merely what it is understood to mean by the followers of Marx; this socialism and not individualism.... are the rudimentary concepts of our social and political philosophy.

He suggested that we must immediately demand these three things :

(1) High wages for labour,

(2) equal hours of work and

(3) the appropriation by the state of excess profits... If it comes to the state we shall have enough money to pay for every thing that we want-enough money to improve all our sanitation, enough money to educate the people, enough money to grow to the full stature of our manhood through the help of our government. In view of this conflict, writes B.C. Pal, of interest between the government and the people of India, the policy of Indian patriotic politics ought to be the old liberal policy of *Laissez-faire*, that is to restrict the government to its primary responsibilities only because every beneficent work that a despotic government does, increases the hold of that despotism upon the affections and the allegiance, upon the acquiescence of the people...Therefore, our policy is a policy of *Laisez-faire*...by restricting the activities of the government to the primary functions of granding protection to the people of this country, we hope to develop the

spirit of self-sacrifice, the spirit of self-reliance, and the spirit of self-determination in the people, and by this means we hope to attain the ideal of Swaraj.

Estimate Bipin Chandra Pal a journalist, essayist, orator and thinker was one of the leaders who awakened India to a new sense of inner strength.

Bipin Chandra Pal was a journalist throughout his life. At the age of 22, he started *Sylhet Weekly,* Bengali Journal *Paridarshak;* and the career thus begun in his native town, he retained till the end of his days. He edited *The Tribune* in 1887-82 started *New India* in 1901 and the *Bande Mataram* in 1906, published fortnightly journal *Swaraj* in London in 1909, and founded the monthly *Hindu Review* in Calcutta in 1912. He edited the daily *Independent,* and the weekly *Democrat* in 1919-20, and the *Bengalee* in 1924-25; besides he was a regular contributor to the *Modern Review,* the *Amrita Bazar Patrika* and many other journals."

Jiten Sen writes that Bipin Chandra Pal, architect of the Bengal renaissance, strode the country like a giant in the last quarter of the nineteenth century and first-two decades of the twentieth. Through the written word and the spoken, through a long life a suffering and sacrifice, an unrelenting adherence to the principles he professed, and with a rare clarity of vision, he reawakened his countrymen to a consciousness of inner strength. With Lokmanya Tilak and Lala Lajpat Rai, he played a leading role in the early freedom movement.

Bipin Chandra's oratory was not mere command over words. He spoke, said Aurobindo Ghosh, "under an inspiration which he himself was unable to resist." commenting on his famous Madras speeches of 1907, Mr. Srinivasa dreamed of such triumphs in India, the power of the spoken words had never been demonstrated on such a scale.

In fact, Mr. Pal was a born orator and his eloquence in the early part of this century roused the youths of this country. Even the aged and the wise listened to him with respect and he was always prepared to convince them, as he often used to say "not by magic, but by logic."

> 'He made great sacrifices for his love of country, truth and God. It was perhaps the great sacrifice of his life when on account of his strong convictions, he lived in splendid isolation from his erstwhile colleagues and friends during the last few years of his life. But his greatness lay in the fact that he never yielded to any one in his devotion to truth and God and to his country. With him, as it was with many other politicians of this country, service of the country was a religion and a service to God.'

Bipin Chandra Pal was a born publicist. His contributions used to appear regularly in practically every important organ of the nationalist opinion of his day. In them he, time and again reverted to his theme that the ultimate interests of Indian Nationalism and British Imperialism were identical. "It is in the interests of Indian nationalism to seek to perpetuate the British connection, so it is equally important to the interest of British Imperialism itself to help and foster the spirit of Nationalism, and to co-ordinate these great forces with those of Great Britain and her Dominions."

10

Lala Lajpat Rai (1865-1928)

Mahatma Gandhi rightly summed up the life and achievements of Lala Lajpat Rai in *Young India.* He said, "Men like the Lala cannot die so long as the Sun shines in the Indian sky. Lalaji means an institution. From his youth, he made his country's service his religion. His patriotism was no narrow creed. He loved his country because he loved the world. His nationalism was internationalism. Hence, his hold on the European mind. He claimed a large circle of friends in Europe and America. They loved him because they knew him. His activities were multifarious. He was an ardent social and religious reformer. Like many of us he became a politician because, his zeal for social and religious reforms demanded participation in politics. He observed at an early stage of his public career that much reform of the type he wanted was not possible until the country was freed from foreign domination. It appeared to him, as to most of us, as a poison corrupting every department of life. It is impossible to think of a single public movement in which Lalaji was not to be found. His love of service was insatiable. He founded educational institutions. He befriended the suppressed classes. Poverty, wherever found, claimed his attention. No young man appealed to him in vain for help. In the political field he was indispensable. He was fearless in the expression of his views. He suffered for it when suffering had not become customary or fashionable. His life was on open book. His extreme frankness embarrassed his friends; it also confounded his critics. But he was incorrigible."

His Life Sketch Lala Lajpat Rai (1865-1928) was the greatest man produced by Punjab. He was born on 28 January, 1865 in village Dhudhike in Ludhiana district. His father Radha Krishan was a school teacher.

In his school days, he acquired a passion for reading, writing and speaking and that proved very serviceable to him in his later life. In 1895 he finished his school education by becoming a pleader and starting legal practice at the District Court of Hissar. Later he moved to Lahore and soon rose to a high position in the profession.

He gave his entire surplus to the Arya Samaj to whose social reform and social service work he was greatly devoted.

Lajpat Rai soon became a leading figure in the Arya Samaj movement. After the death of Swami Dayanand, Lajpat Rai and his associates founded the Dayanand Anglo-Vedic College Lahore, in his memory after the pattern of the Fergusson College in Poona.

The influence of the Arya Samaj on him can better be expressed in his own words when he says, "In short, I learned my lessons in public life from, and in, the Arya Samaj. It was there that I saw the models of purity in public life and there that I made my dearest friends. I am under enormously heavy debt to the Samaj I should not be able to pay back what I owe."

He came to make friends with Mahatma Hans Raj and Pt. Guru Datt, and these played a vital part not only in each other's lives but also in the life of the province. At the same time the Punjab was electrified by the gospel that Arya Samaj preached. To ardent spirits it brought a message of national regeneration and spiritual uplift.

On him was the influence of Mazzini who continued to remain his Guru for quite some time. Lalaji says, that "at about this time I happened to come across the English speeches of Babu Surendra Nath Banerjee. Amongst those was his speech on Guiseppe Mazzini which moved me to tears several times as I read it. It made a deep impression on my tender heart and I determined that all my life I would follow the teachings of Mazzini and serve my nation. I made Mazzini my Guru and so he continues to be this day." At another place he says about Mazzini's influence on his ideas, "I read Mazzini's biography from cover to cover, and I was moved by it far more intensely then I had been several years before by Babu Surendra Nath Banerjee's speech about Mazzini. The profound nationalism of the great Italian is terrible, his moral superiority, his broad humanitarian sympathies enthrilled me. I began to translate his 'Duties of Man' into Urdu."

Lala Lajpat Rai soon took keen interest in politics. He formed the trinity of militant Indian nationalism with Bal Gangadhar Tilak and Bipin Chandra Pal during the anti-partition agitation. Yet he did not neglect constructive work in his own province. The Dayanand College soon became an important educational institution in India and won the admiration of all as a privately managed efficient institution. Lajpat Rai had a great share in building it up.

"After the split in the Congress at Surat, Lajpat Rai did not choose to walk out with his Nationalist friends. He continued to take part in what came to be known as the Convention Congress in subsequent years, yet he found that he was treated as a suspect by the moderates and the

Government. He felt it was unsafe to remain in India, and therefore, left for Japan in 1913 and from there he want to England. The First World War broke out and he went to America in 1914. For six years he remained in America and did much work in favour of building up opinion in favour of Indian Nationalism."

In 1916 he established Indian Home Rule League in the U.S.A. and in 1917 he started his Magazine Young India. In 1920 he presided over an emergency session of the Congress held at Calcutta.

Lajpat Rai was arrested in 1921 because he broke the ban on addressing public meetings by presiding over a meeting of the Punjab Provincial Congress Committee. He was tried and sentenced to one year's rigorous imprisonment.

After a few months he was released, but was arrested again. Later on due to illness he was released unconditionally. He went to Solan to recoup his heath. After he was well, he joined the Swaraj Party founded by Deshbandhu Das and Moti Lal Nehru. He was elected to the Central Legislative Assembly as a Swarajist. By this time the Simon Commission was appointed. Like all-Nationalists, he was in favour of boycotting this all — white Simon Commission and it was under his lead that a resolution advocating its boycott was passed. The Congress and other political parties did not merely boycott this Commission which was appointed to explore further possibilities of political progress of India but also formed an All Parties Conference and produced what has passed in India's political history as the Nehru Report on political reform in India.

Simon Commission arrived at Lahore on October 30, 1928. Lajpat Rai was the head of a procession of people who demonstrated their discontentment against the Commission.

The procession was declared illegal and to disperse the crowds the police resorted to a *lathi* charge. Lajpat Rai was injured and as a consequence taken seriously ill. This assault was made on him by a British officer without any provocation whatsoever.

Men like Dr. Satyapal, Dr. Gopi Chand Bhargava, Raizada Hansraj, Dr. Mohammed Alam and Lala Jagannath tried to shield Lajpat Rai, but the British officer concentrated the attack on him. He never recovered from the illness that followed and passed away on November 17, 1928. Jawaharlal Nehru said in this connection. "National humiliation, involved in the assault on him, hastened his end."

Lala Jagan Nath explained the incident of assault on Lalaji. He said that Lalaji died a martyr's death. On the 30th October, 1928, there was a demonstration against the "Simon Commission outside the Lahore Railway Station. In spite of indisposition, Lalaji walked a long distance when the mammoth protest procession was proceeding though the streets of Lahore. When it reached the Lahore Railway Station, the number had swelled enormously. Many of us who were with Lalaji in the procession requested him to rest his weary limbs. But Lalaji somehow sensed that the British officers were bent on mischief and foul-play. Therefore, he said, that, even though his body was aching; he would not go away and leave us exposed to the wrath of the British officers. The crowd was perfectly peaceful. Lalaji's presence ensured that the crowd would remain perfectly non-violent. And so it did. But the British officers had pre-planned to teach Lalaji a lesson and, it possible to remove this thorn in their him without any provocation at all from Lalaji or from the crowd. There is absolutely no doubt in my mind that this was part of a plan to do away with Lalaji. Some of us, including other leaders of the demonstration, like Dr. Satyapal, Dr. Gopi Chand Bhargava, Raizade Hansraj and Dr. Mohammed Alam tried to shield Lalaji. But the British officer concentrated his attack on Lalaji. It was evident that he was inflicting blows on Lalaji not merely to cause him pain, but I to kill him."

Lala Lajpat Rai breathed his last on 17th November, 1928, just eighteen days after the brutal assault. Writing under the caption "Long live Lalaji", Mahatma Gandhi said, "Men like Lalaji cannot die so long as the sun shines in the Indian sky..." Madan Mohan Malviya said... I am too deeply distressed by the news of the death of Lala Lajpat Rai to be able properly to express the sense of loss the country has sustained by the passing away of a patriot, statesman, educationist and journalist of his calibre.

It is a misfortune to the country that a publicist so widely honoured, whose him in life was to serve the country and the community of which he was an ornament in the best possible ways, should have died just at a time when the need of his wise and sober guidance was the greatest. Lala Lajpat Rai loved his country intensely I and worked for it incessantly and unselfishly.

His pure patriotism, his robust independence, fearlessness, sincerity and earnestness, easily won for him the respect which he so widely enjoyed.

It is difficult to exaggerate the value of his services. It was needed at present to voice sound national opinion and to guide the country into the right path of national self-government. Lalaji's death has heavily added to the loss of many public men, which we have sustained during the last few years. While his passing away inflicts a heavy loss upon the country as a whole, it inflicts a special loss upon the Hindu community, the interest of which he had so much at heart and which he tried to protect without letting it stand in the way of the growth of sound national spirit, which was the very foundation upon which a national system of free government can be built up.

His works His main works are as under :

1. *The Problem of National Education in India.*
2. *Atmakatha.*
3. *The story of My Deportation.*
4. *The Arya Samaj.*
5. *England's Debt to India.*
6. *The Political Future of India.*
7. *Unhappy India.*
8. *The Fight for Crumbs.*
9. *A Call to Young India.*
10. *An open letter to Lloyd George.*
11. *The United States of America—A Hindu's Impressions and Study.*
12. *Self Determination for India.*
13. *Tawarikh-e-Hind.*
14. *Bandematram.*

Political Ideas

The political ideas of Lalji can be broken down as under :

His Views on Swaraj Lalaji demanded Swaraj for India. The Britisher talked of the blessings of the British rule in India. To this Lalaji replied that good government could never be a substitute for self-government, even assuming that the British did give good government. "Can it compensate for the loss of manhood which is involved in political bondage? Chains are chains, no matter if they are gilded. Can the wealth of the whole world be put in scales against liberty and honour? What would it avail of one were to get the sovereignty of the world, but lose his own soul? A subject people has no soul, just as a slave can have none."

Lalaji was a great nationalist. His concept of Swaraj was not something based on hatred for the Britishers. He said that what the nation wants is the power to appoint and dismiss its servants and not merely a change in the personnel of the services. For a long time to come, we may continue to employ British experts in the various departments of our government. We have (at least we ought to have) no prejudice against the British as such, What we object to is their mastery over us. As a friend, as a comrade, as an ally, even as a guide and adviser we may value the Englishmen's co-operation, but we do not want his "hakumat".

We must no longer be his subject. However, Lalaji made it clear that India should not depend upon anybody for long but should be self-reliant and self-dependent.

His View on Swadeshi Lalaji was a great advocate of Swadeshi. He looked upon Swadeshi as the remedy upon the right and continued use of which depended the alleviation of the sufferings of our country, or "the salvation of my country." He gave to the term a wider meaning, and included in it the ability. "To organise our capital, our resources, our labour, our, energies and our talents to the greatest good of all Indians. I want a better understanding of the economic needs and requirements of our country and a practical programme of industrial development based on scientific calculations."

He said a degenerate country, like ours, badly needs for her service such selfless workers as neither wealth nor power could buy. We had a large number of them in our glorious past when our country's towering moral and physical capabilities had elevated it to the lofty pinnacle of prosperity and happiness.

'**His Views on Communal Unity** According to Lalaji, "an intimate acquaintance with those who generally take a leading part in these communal conflicts inclines me to say that it is not religion that is responsible for them, but the lack of religion. Neither can it be traced to a keen sense of duty to the community. The latter is falsely stimulated by motives more or less personal. More often than not, personal ambition is the inspiring incentive. True religions as I have said, places duties before rights. True sociology emphasises co-operation as against competition."

He further said, "It is my conviction that the, best way to bring about true Hindu-Muslim unity is not by ignoring their differences, nor by emphasising them, nor by dividing the nation both longitudinally and latitudinally into so many compartments by communal and class representation in the councils, corporations and the services but by trying to make men truly religious and by asking each of them to undertake the responsibilities and duties of the whole.

What are the differences between these two communities? First there are the religious differences. Each party wants full religious freedom — freedom of belief, of worship, of association for religious purposes, and of expression and propaganda. Why should they not have it? To a large extent they have it now. Why should it not be guaranteed permanently in the future Indian state? This should be the first article of our future constitution. The clash which comes out of religious observances, festivals and celebrations, as well as from the proximity of place of worship — why is it not possible for a committee of Hindu and Mohammdan leaders to sit together and arrive at a full and thorough under standing with regard to such matters."

His Views on Untouchability Lalaji said, "Untouchability is the result of prejudice against certain kinds of labour. It may include certain elements of religious and social prejudices also. We have to remove both. Nor prejudice of any kind must be permitted to vitiate our future democracy. We do not propose to do it by a process of levelling down, but by that of levelling up. Our ideas of equality are not based on the theory of 'Natural rights' but on that of service. No form of labour is degrading which serves social ends which society needs. If there are any forms of labour which involve the degradation of the individual, or groups of individuals, they must be either abolished or the element of degradation must be removed from them. No one should suffer humiliation because of performing functions and doing services which serve social purposes, but these services have by a curious twist of human mind been made the reason of their performers and class being looked down upon by the rest of the society. It is useless to talk of a democratic state as long as this kind of prejudice sways our minds and influences our conduct towards those from whom we differ in religion, or whose forms of occupation we dislike."

His Faith in Passive Resistance Method of Gandhiji He was wholeheartedly in favour of the Gandhian policy of passive resistance. He said, "I am proud of the success you achieved in this first attempt at passive resistance in India. It is an achievement unique in our history, nay, in the history of the world. It has raised the political consciousness of the country by one big leap, and also raised the country in the estimation of the world."

His Views on India's Poverty Lala Lajpat Rai was of the opinion that India's poverty was mainly due to heavy drain which had been put on India's financial resources by the British Government. Lalaji said, "Our raw products find their way to England in order to develop her trade in manufactured articles, which are brought back and sold in India at enormous profits. They do not scruple to provide lucrative employment for their own men in this country and are always ready to do every thing that is calculated to promote their people's welfare. This genuine regard for providing for the good of their whole community is the secret of their prosperity and success all around." Lalaji was of the firm opinion that change in India's political set up was a must for change in our economic condition.

His Views on Co-operation According to Lalaji, co-operation of the people with the government is based on one of the two assumptions, either that the government represents them, or that the government is there to protect their interests. Now, in India, the first of these two assumptions cannot hold good. The second is unhappy in the course of being shattered to pieces, if not already gone. Co-operation with government, again is of two kinds : one enforceable by law and therefore, compulsory, for example, the payment of taxes, or serving the army under conscription; the other is voluntary, for example, accepting government service of joining the councils and so on. In the case of the former, every refusal is punishable. As for the later, there again you have to distinguish between co-operation which is obviously for the country's benefit and that which is not so. Co-operation, determined solely or mainly by economic consideration can only be refused, if we can find economic alternatives. Co-operation inspired by considerations of honour and dignity can be easily refused if the mentality of the people regarding honour and dignity can be changed. Last but not least, in the same class you may consider co-operation, which gives you opportunities of serving your country by attacking the citadels of power and privilege from the inside.

Lalaji said, "Co-operation which is immoral or which makes you a tool of a foreign bureaucracy or which leaves you no option but to give effect to their orders, stands on an entirely different footing from the one which is obviously for the benefit of the country; similarly, co-operation, which is inspired by economic necessity stands on a different footing from the one which is solely or mainly based on consideration of honour and dignity. Thpn again you must consider if your refusal of co-operation proceeds from the desire to make an immediate effective impression on the government of from the motive of habituating the people to take their destiny in their own hands."

Views on Socialism and Communism He defined Socialism as a "protest against degradation to which the working part of humanity has been reduced by the unproductive leisured class."

Regarding communism he wrote as under the 'Political Future of India' : "Nobody knows what Bolshevism represents. The socialist themselves are divided over it. The advanced wing is enthusiastic, the moderates are denouncing it... The only way to meet Bolshevism is to concede rights to the different people of the earth now being bled and exploited. Otherwise the discontented and exploited countries of the world will be the best breeding centres for it. India must come to her own soon, else not even the Himalayas can effectually bar the entry of Bolshevism into India."

His Ideas on Education The cause of education had always been close to Lalaji's heart. His association with the various educational institutions conducted by the Arya Samaj in the Punjab had offered him an opportunity to observe the shortcomings of an educational system whose avowed aim, in the words of Lord Macaulay was, 'to produce a class of persons, Indian in blood and colour but English in taste, in opinions, in morals and in intellect'. He outlines, his ideas on truly national education in *The problem of National Education in India.*

Writing about himself Lala Lajpat Rai says : 'Eversince I left school I have been actively associated with educational movements. The study of educational institutions, educational ideals and educational methods has been one of the passions of my life'. In foreign countries also I have devoted a substantial part of my time and energy to the study of educational questions always, with a view to their adaptation to the needs of India.

Lalaji's views on education can be broken down as under :

On National Education Giving the object and scope of national education, he himself says in the book *National Education* "What do we mean by national education. Do we want to distinguish it from local, provincial education, or from the denominational or sectarian education? How does education become nation? Is it the language which is the medium of instruction or the agency through which it is imparted or the agency which controls and regulates it or the books which are taught or the standards and ideals which underlie it?" Lalaji said, "It will be sheer folly to replace the modern treatises on Arithmetic, Geometry, Algebra, Trignometry and kindred subjects by Lilavati or other books on these subjects found in Sanskrit Language. Our Arthashastra may have been excellent in the good old time. It may do us good to study it for the purposes of comparison we will be cutting our nose to spite our faces if we fail to insist on the teaching of modern and up-to-date Arthashastra which controls and orders the economic life of the world." According to Lalaji, we may assume that the following general principles of national education are accepted all over the civilized world :

(1) That national education, being the surest and the most profitable national investment for gain, as well as the best and the most effectual insurance against loss, is as necessary for national safety as the military provision for its physical defence.

Economic and industrial efficiency does not mean the mere possession of gold and silver, but the brains and capacity of the whole nation to turn that gold and silver and other raw materials into modern arms and ammunitions —ships, submarines, aeroplanes, guns and bullets are only the concrete completed forms, containing numerous other parts, the manufacture of each of which requires technical skill of the highest order and last but not least, food and hospital necessities. Assuming, therefore, that security from without is the first duty of a state, popular, universal education alone can make it possible under modern conditions.

(2) The old ideas that the state was only concerned with making provision for elementary education is also gone. All over the world it is recognized that the duty of the state does not end with elementary education. The economic and industrial efficiency of the nation depends upon technical and industrial education, and that also must be provided by the state. Nor can the state ignore the necessity of higher education, for intelligent and efficient leadership depends on that.

(3) Education does not consist in imparting certain amounts of bookish knowledge and teaching the three R's, it includes provision for the physical development of the young. It embraces a provision for the general health of the child including feeding, if necessary, to such an extent as to ensure the fullest benefit to the child from the provision for his education made by the state.

(4) In short, the duty of bringing up the child with a view to helping him to become an efficient, intelligent and prudent citizen, rests with the state, and the state must be made to fulfil it. It no longer depends on the capacity or willingness of the parents.

At no times can or will private effort to further education be dispensed with. Pending the development of full national government private efforts must do a great deal of what the government fails to do. In short, private efforts should supplement the efforts of the government, without any pretence of supplanting it or doing what it is the latter's duty to do, and what it can : under the circumstances, be forced to do.

On Co-education Lalaji was in favour of co-education. Boys and girls should have every opportunity of seeing life, moving in life, experiencing shocks and reactions of life and of getting out of the holes into which their animal instincts and their youthful impulses thrust them.

Lalaji said that boys and girls must learn their social obligations when in their teens. To let boys and girls grow in isolation, ignorant of the conditions of actual life, innocent of its social amenities, with no experience of the sudden demands and emergencies of group life, is to deprive them of the most valuable element in their education. The aim of education is to fit men and women for the battle of life, we do not want to convert them to anchorities and ascetics.

Lalaji was of the view that our boys and girls must not be brought up in hot houses. They should be brought up in the midst of society of which they are the members. They should form habits and learn manners which will enable them to rise to every emergency. They should learns to rise above temptations and not shun them. The world is a temptation. It is a place to enjoy so long as by doing so one does not injure oneself and others. So long as one is loyal to the society in which his lot has been cast and towards which he has social obligations, one commits no sin by taking to the pleasures of life in a moderate degree.

Lalaji said that we should extend to them our fullest confidence, and encourage absolute frankness in them. Instead of keeping the sexes separate we should bring them together, "In my judgement greater harm is done by keeping them apart than by bringing them together. I know I am trading on delicate ground. Prejudice and sentiment, accumulated by centuries of restricted life, is all against it. The thing will come by degrees. But come it must and come it will."

On the role of Nationalism and Patriotism in Education No scheme of national education in India could be complete without including the active teaching of "partiotism" and "nationalism" as a regular subject of study. According to Lalaji, the teaching of patriotism in India and its place in the scheme of national education must revolve round the following points :

(1) Love of India as a whole, as distinguished from love of village, town, city or province.

I am sure Indian Nationalists do not want to set up an aggressive nationalism of the kind which will bread contempt or hatred of other nations. The idea that love of one's country necessarily involves hatred of others, or even indifference to the welfare of the rest or mankind, is absolutely fallacious and mischievous, and should be combated through and through.

Patriotism, however, does not include only the material and the physical aspects of a country. "It includes all that Renan has called, I am d'une nation, the more delicate shadings of feeling, such as piety for the past, admiration and love of the heroic figures in the history of the nation and its great achievements : love of language, community of tradition, laws and customs, and all that give individual character to the civilization of each nation."

This leads us to the second point around which our teaching of patriotism should revolve, *viz.* :

(2) The love of the nation as a whole, regardless of the various religious creeds and castes into which it is internally divided.

Every Indian child should be taught in so many words that every human being who is born in India, or of Indian parents, or who has made India his or her home is a compatriot, a brother or a sister, regardless of colour, creed, caste or vocation.

Lalaji said that the third part of our course for the teaching of patriotism must deal with our relations with the state. The promise of responsible self-government within the Empire makes us free to include our obligations to the State in this course. If the Empire, treats us on terms of equality, we shall be true and loyal to the Empire, and faithfully discharge our obligations towards it.

On Physical Education Lalaji also laid a great stress on physical education. He was of the view that students should be given an opportunity to improve their personality thought games. He believed in the dictum; a sound body has a sound mind. Lalaji said the education system should produce the students who are physically strong.

His Ideas on Nationalism Lajpat Rai's ideal was Indian Nationalism, writes Prof. P.N. Kirpal, and for this ideal he worked, suffered and ultimately laid down his life. He was not a mere worker in the cause of Nationalism. He gave the nationalist sentiment his own stamp and a new meaning. His thought coloured the Nationalist Movement and gave it a new turn. Exiled, and imprisonment afforded time for reflection and Lajpat Rai thought and wrote a good deal on India and her problems.

To him patriotism meant an intense love of liberty and justice and was a matter of self-respect. It was a powerful feeling which emanated from the heart and its intensity gave it the loftiness of a vision. This feeling was supported by a convincing theory of nationalism, deriving its inspiration from India's past'.

History Supports Nationalism Lalaji interpreted history to support nationalism. He said that British rule in India represented almost the only period of subjection to alien rule, and it was the most demoralising phase in the history of the country. In spite of the mystery and uncertainty which concealed the true picture of ancient India, it was clear that India then possessed, "a marvellous civilisation, a wonderful literature, a well-organised social system a conception of government based on law and on the legal rights of subject interest, as well as against the ruling monarch.

Lalaji said that history does not record a single instance of India being ruled from without, by a people of purely non-Indian blood and in the interests of another country and another people, before the British. India was always an empire by herself. She was never a part of another empire, much less a dependency. She had her own army, her own navy, her own flag. Her revenues were spent for her own benefit. She had her industries and manufactured the goods she consumed. Anyone wanting the privilege of trading with India under special terms had to obtain the sanction of her government, as the East India Company did. There was no Indian office in Arabia or in Persia or in Kabul, to which the people of India looked for initiative in the affairs of their native land.

India, writes Lalaji further, under the British is, however, entirely different. For the first time in history she becomes a part of another empire. India today is not empire by herself, but a part of the British Empire, as Britain once was a part of the Roman Empire. For the first time in history she has been reduced to the position of a dependency. For the first time in her history she is ruled from the outside. For the first time the Indians have been reduced to the position of a subject — people, governed by an alien race residing in a different and far — of country. For the first time she is ruled by a sovereign who does not live in India, who sends out every five years a Viceroy to administer the affairs of the country under the authority of a minister in a foreign land. For the first time her affairs are managed by people who come and go, under laws made outside of India. All the chief offices of state, the direction and control of armies, the administration of revenues, of divisions, of districts, the coining of money, the administration of justice, the imposing of taxes, etc. are generally in hands of foreigners who have absolutely no interest in the country, except as servants of the Crown, persons whose interests in the country, cease with the expiration of their terms of service.

Nationalism a Universal Cult According to Lalaji, nationalism is no longer confined to the classes. It promises to become a universal cult. It is permeating the masses. Only those Indians realise it who mix with the people and do not derive their knowledge from works written by Englishmen or by other arm-chair politicians. No foreigner, however, kind and sympathetic, however, great his knowledge of the language of the country, can ever realise it fully. Even the dancing girls are affected by it. They will sing political or national songs if you so wish. Even the wandering minstrel with his crude, one stringed instrument, knows the song that is likely to bring him help.

In Lalaji's view no amount of repression or espionage can stop it. No amount of official terrorism and no devices, invented or followed to inculcate loyalty, can stop or check the flow of the new feeling of patriotism and nationalism which is being constantly fed by the sentences of death and transportation that the British courts are passing on beardless youths. The Government cannot help it. They must punish the offender and the criminal. They must hunt up the seditionist. They would not be a government if they would do otherwise, but India is now at that stage, and Indian Nationalism is in that condition when repression, death sentences, and imprisonments are more beneficial to it than otherwise.

Lalaji said bluntly, "Rise up, young India, you are inferior to none. In our common men, in the men who till our fields and produce our food, in those men who do not get sufficient to eat twice a day, you have a wealth which no other country on the face of globe possesses. There are souls ready to redeem themselves and to be redeemed by those men who are ready to redeem them. Even though they will die even though they starve they will never dare to steal one mouthful of food from the house of the rich. Where on earth is that character to be found? If this state of things were to continue in any other country. I only admire the righteous phase of it; if in any other country the things were to happen, you will find all the capitalists concealing themselves in the wine cellars to protect themselves and their property. That is actually happening in Europe at present. I, therefore, beg of you, young men of India, your motherland is at the present moment lying prostrate; prostrate because of your lack of faith in yourselves, in your people and in your country; prostrate because of your weakness of mind and weakness of character. Raise up your minds, enthuse yourselves with electricity of self-confidence and self-reliance. And this race will rise phoenix-like and spread all over the world."

Lajpat Rai inspired the country with a new hope and faith. The struggle was likely to be long and hard but there was no doubt as to the ultimate victory. He said, "A movement of this nature never dies. The battle of freedom once begun is carried on from father to son, and it as good today as it ever was. Success may come at once, or be delayed, or the issue may be confused, according to the wisdom or the folly of its advocates, of the amount of earnestness they put into it, or the amount of influence they have over the masses, as well as by the wisdom or short-sightedness or cunning of those who oppose it. All the world over, progress of political movements had vicissitudes of fortune, stages of development, times of reactions, defeats and reverses. Governments always begin by ignoring such movements. Then comes a period of ridicule, followed by repression. But their efforts are futile. The food on which the tender plant of liberty thrives is the blood of the martyr. The rope of the hangman, the axe of the executioner, or the shot of the gunner, extinguishers individual life only to make the desire for corporate life keener and stronger. Banishments, deportation, imprisonments, tortures, and confiscations are the usual weapons of tyrants to strangle liberty to extirpate those that are after it, but they have so far proved ineffectual to kill it."

Estimate Men like Lalaji, writes Gandhi, cannot die so long as the sun shines in the Indian sky. Lalaji means an institution. From his youth he made of his country's service religion and his patriotism was no narrow creed. He loved his country because he loved the world. His nationalism was internationalism. Hence, he had a hold on the European mind. He claimed a large circle of friends in Europe and America. They loved him because they knew him.

His activities were multifarious. He was an ardent social and religious reformer. Like many of us he became a politician because his zeal for social and religious reform demanded participation in politics.

He observed at an early stage of his public career that not much reform of the type he wanted was possible until the country was freed from foreign domination. It appeared to him as to most of us a poison corrupting every department of life. It is impossible to think of a single public movement in which Lalaji was not to be found. His love of service was insatiable. He found educational institutions. He befriended the suppressed classes. Poverty where found, claimed his attention. He surrounded youngmen with extraordinary affection. No youngman appealed to him in vain for help.

According to Jawaharlal Nehru, "Lalaji was a strong man and a great nationalist. Sense of National humiliation involved in the assault on him hastened his end. He was truly a great son of the soil."

According to Prof. D.C. Sharma, "If one looks at all this critically, one finds a rich heritage for Lajpat Rai. The heroic way of life or the military attitude of the soul, as Emerson puts it, came to him from the soil where he was born. His interest in the reform of Hinduism and his enthusiasm for united Indian nationhood came to him from his father. In addition to these he got from him that burning desire for self-expression which was such a mighty weapon in his hands. All his genius for constructiveness and the basic spiritual quality of his nature were the gifts which he inherited from his mother. It is true his parents did not give him much in the way of worldly possessions, but surely from them he got much by way of intellectual, emotional and spiritual endowment."

Lajpat Rai inspired the country with a new hope and faith. The struggle was likely to be long and hard but there was no doubt as to the ultimate victory. He said, "A movement of this nature never dies. The battle of freedom once begun is carried on from father to son, is as good today as it ever was. Success may come at once, or be delayed, or the issue may be confused, according to the wisdom or the folly of its advocates, or the amount of earnestness they put into it or the amount of influence they have on the masses, as well as by the wisdom or short-sightedness or cunning of those who oppose it."

According to Annie Besant, "A grand merit he possessed was that when he led people into a position of danger, he shielded them and went himself along to take the brunt of the attack. He certainly carried out Charles Bradlaugh's words, when you advise an attack, do not say 'go' 'but' 'come'. At this special moment his loss is particularly great for although a few of his juniors have his courage, we have not yet his experience and confidence."

According to S. Sitaramayya, "to die in the battlefield is the longing of every hero. The Punjab is undoubtedly the most martial of Indian provinces. Of such a province Lala Lajpat Rai was the unchallenged leader, and had been so for the past quarter of a century. This patriot, this hero, this martyr, fell in the battle with the British bureaucracy carried on for over two decades on the economic, political, moral and finally the physical plane. There can be little doubt that the *lathi* blows dealt on this patriot of India by unthinking and heartless policemen has hastened the end of the revered Lala. If the end had come before the advent of the Simon Commission to Lahore, Lalaji's life would have been wanting in completeness. Like a veteran soldier that he was, he fought to the end, stood at his post of duty to lead the procession under the pressure of an unexpected situation and turned what would have been if he had been off his guard about in the first victory of the new era on the plane of non-violence in the battle for freedom."

Moti Lal Nehru paid a rich tribute to Lalaji when he said, "He was one of those outstanding personalities whose place it is impossible to fill. It would indeed be difficult to find another man with public activities, covering such a wide field as those of the remarkable man, whose loss India is mourning to-day. His earnest patriotism did not allow his inexhaustible energy to any particular channel, but found avenues for useful work in almost every department of life which goes to build up a nation. Politics and journalism may be taken to go hand in hand together and he was easily in the foremost ranks of both. But the useful, though silent work he did in the sphere of social reform, more specially among the untouchable and the suppressed classes, was not less valuable. At an early stage of his life, he devoted himself to the service of the land of his birth. His great sacrifices, his terrible suffering in the cause are well-known, but nothing deflected him from the path of duty."

To conclude we may say that to speak the truth, "he served his country at home as well as abroad, by his pen as well as with his tongue, through the legislature as well as outside. It is no wonder that his name will ever remain enshrined on the grateful hearts of his country men."

11

Shri Aurobindo Ghosh (1872-1950)

Life Sketch

When the Indian politics demanded the personalities sprang up. Maharishi Aurobindo Ghosh was like a sun amongst the stars. He was such a person that he was high above the calibre of Swami Vivekanand, Ramkrishna Paramhansa, and political thinkers like Mahatama Gandhi, Jawaharlal Nehru and the like. Aurobindo Ghosh renowned as the sage of Pondicherry discovered the soul of India. He thought of renaissance through the cultural and spiritual greatness of ancient heritage.

According to Romain Rolland, he was the prince among the Indian thinkers. He brought up his personality through the synthesis of Asian and European wisdom Dr. S. Radhakrishnan said of him to be "The most accomplished of Modern Indian Thinkers." So he was famous for his scholar and learned mind among the Indian thinkers. He was a great poet, master of metaphysics, a humanist, a seer, a devout patriot and a political philosopher. He had a spiritual message for the whole world humanity.

Rabindra Nath Tagore called him "The Messiah of Indian culture" and India will speak through his voice to the world. Fredrics, the American educationist of California called him "the guiding star of our earth and prophet of our age."

Dalip Kumar Roy speaks of him as a "Greatest living *yogi* of India."

Deshbandhu Chitranjan Das said in his address to the Aligarh Conspiracy 1909 said that "Long after he is dead and gone, Aurobindo will be looked upon as the poet of patriotism, as the prophet of nationalism and as the lover of humanity; his words will be echoed and re-echoed not only in India but across distant seas and lands."

Dr. Haridas Chaudhri described him as "amazingly creative personality, when a deep insight into the past, a firm hold upon the present and a prophetic vision of the future." He was a great poet, a great metaphysician, a great systematic thinker, a great seer and a great patriot. He had a message for the whole world.

Shri Aurobindo Ghosh was born on 15th August, 1872 in the city of Calcutta, a date which reminds us every year of the Independence. The day on which Napoleon Bonaparte was born on 15th August, 1769. His father Dr. Krishnandhan Ghosh, was a famous medical man of Calcutta. He was the third son. Hitler also fixed the date for the conquest of Europe on that date, *i.e.*, 15th August 1940. World War II ended on 15th August 1945. His father had spent some years at Aberdeen University in England, where he went for medical studies. He came to India with quite up to date Western styled civilization.

Hence, the atmosphere in the family was not in any way favouring nationalistic outlook. His father wanted all his children to grow under the westernized influence. Hence, he sent his three sons to Lorretto Convent School in Darjeeling. Aurobindo was of five years age. In the year of 1879 at his 7 years of age, his parents took him to England with other brothers. They were put under the English family to be brought up under the Western culture. He remained there for 14 years continuously and, took education at Manchester, London and Cambridge. He learnt with proficiency English and French; so also Latin and Greek with Knowledge of German, Italian and Spanish. He earned the scholarship of 80 pounds per year in 1890 and hence he continued his studies at Cambridge. He competed for I.C.S. with position. He disliked government service so he disqualified himself in the riding test. His life was completely changed in England. He was unaware of any Indian language but only he knew some Bengali. Thus, he was denationalized.

Dr. Karan Singh writes about Aurobindo in his book that he was hard up in England. His daily food consisted of one or two pieces of sandwiches or bread with butter and a cup of tea in morning and a penny worth of saveloy in the evening. Because he could get only meagre amount from his father irregularly and it was also stopped.

Although he was groomed to be moulded into an European gentleman yet deep at heart he had spiritual affinity for Indian culture. Certain other influences had to work on his life which were destined to transform him into great prophet of Indian Nationalism. While at his 11th year of age he had an intuition of being born with a mission. At the age of 14 he felt that mission of his life was to work for the liberation of Mother India. His father was also responsible for generating patriotism in him. His father was also dissatisfied with British sense of justice and fairplay. He was aware how badly Britishers had treated educated Indians. He sent the Bengali cuttings of papers to his sons for telling them of injustice done by Britishers in India. His spiritual thought also led to think of Indian emancipation. He wrote works of Mazinni and other Indian patriots who devoted themselves for Independence.

During his stay at Cambridge, he became an active member of Indian Majlis, a revolutionary organization for the liberation of India and as secretary served it. He organized a secret society called "Lotus and Dagger" wherein all pledged to work for the motherland. Thus, he came across the national zeal in England too. After his return from England he began his life in India.

At Baroda After his return from Britain commenced his life in the Indian field from the year of 1893 to 1906. He met Gaekwar of Baroda in London during the last days of his residence there. He gave him appointment and it was accepted by him. He was renationalized. Gaekwar was very much impressed by his personality and knowledge. He served the Maharaja of Baroda for thirteen years in various capacities. After the end of the service with Maharaja in 1906 he served as a lecturer of French and later on as Professor of English in Baroda College. He became the principal of the Baroda College. During this time he learnt Sanskrit, while under the state of Baroda, he served as Revenue Officer, Land Settlement Officer, Personal Secretary to the Maharaja. Thereafter in 1906 he joined National College, Calcutta as he resigned his post in the Baroda College. During these periods he took part in the service as well as the national activities. He studied the activities of Congress minutely and at times criticized Congress. He was overjoyed in reading and understanding *Ramayana, Maharbharata, Gita,* Kalidasa's poetry, masterpieces of Bankim Chandra Chatterjee and poetry of Madhusudan Dutta. In this way Indian culture paved a way for Aurobindo who was up to this time an intellectual soaked in western materialism. Spiritualism proved for him the eternal bliss. He gave politics a spiritual insight and he delivered it to the world.

He thought some day or the other India would be a spiritual and political Guru of the whole world humanity. Now Western philosophy became barren for him with dryness and purposelessness. Only spiritualism can save the Western world of humanity. This role would be played by India. He was an ardent believer of Sanatan Dharma.

About Congress he spoke "I say of the Congress then, this — its aims are mistaken that the spirit in which it proceeds towards their accomplishments is not a spirit of sincerity and whole-heartedness, and that the methods it has chosen are not the right methods, and the leaders, in whom it trusts are not the right sort of men to be leaders — in brief, that we are at present in the blind lead; if not by the blind, at any rate, by one eyed." In this way he criticised the Congress for its bias towards the Britishers.

He criticised the British Rule in India. Their conduct was illusory. He spoke that a self-respecting nation could not accept maltreatment like this. Again came the partition of Bengal. He accepted the editorship of "Bande Mataram" and he helped the national renaissance. He developed national spiritualism and spoke that motherland can also be served by spiritual perfection. To remove poverty spiritualism is required and for its independence only spiritualism could do. He spoke of the God's will to accomplish this task he had come and said, "I have the power to redeem this fallen race. It is not the physical power. I am not going to fight with swords or guns but the power of knowledge. The power of Kshatriya is not the only power there is another power, the fire power of Brahmin, which is founded on knowledge. This is not a new feeling. I have not imbibed it from modern culture — I was born with it. It is in the marrow of my bones. It is to accomplish this great mission that God has sent me to the earth."

Aurobindo was of the view for the attainment of complete freedom his view was that service of the country was the service of the Divine mother. Through Yoga India could achieve freedom. He said, "We believe that it is to make Yoga the ideal of human life that India rises today by the Yoga, she will get the strength to realise her freedom, unity and greatness, by the Yoga she will keep the strength to preserve it. It is a spiritual revolution we foresee and the material is only its shadow and reflex,"

At the same time Government had a close watch over his activities. He was designed to the "Alipore Conspiracy Case" and was jailed in Alipore. Bail was refused. Deshbandhu Das and C.R. Das advocated his case. In the end he was released and was acquitted of the charges. While in jail he studied Gita and developed power of *Sadhana* and Spiritual energies.

Aurobindo becomes a Yogi While at England he had no faith in Yoga. While taking education at Cambridge, his classmate Mr. Deshpande asked him to practise Yoga but he refused as it brought in action and distraction from the harsh realities of life. But while at Baroda he developed Yoga. He was in search of Guru. This he found in Vishnu Bhasker Lele. Thus, he became a perfect Yogi.

Politics at the backdoor In the service of Baroda's Gaekwar he was unable to take part in the active politics but indirectly he took the part. In Anglo-Marathi paper *Indu Prakash* published from Bombay he gave articles without name in the series of 'New Lamp for Old'. By this he criticized moderates dominating the Indian National Congress for policy of prayers and petitions and for their faith in the Britishers. He awakened the people being one against the tyranny of the British people. He hoped of the new leadership with dynamic and radical views. All methods possible — violent or non-violent — should be employed to liberate the country from Imperialism. Those article made a stir throughout the country. The paper management asked him to make his writings mild, but Aurobindo stopped writing to the paper.

Revountionary Aurobindo's urge for revolt became solid. While with Baroda service, he visited Bengal if political movement was possible. But seeing time as unfortunate and indifferent he came back to Baroda to resume his duties. Soon after, he sent Jatin Chatterjee, a soldier in the Baroda Army to organize a secret revolutionary party in Bengal and later he sent his younger brother for the same purpose to assist him, in the job of revolution throughout Bengal to organise cells which were kept under the control of devoted and dedicated revolutionaries who were expected to sacrifice their lives for the sake of motherland. The leaders of this movement worked under the grab of Yogis with purity and austerity. While in service of the Maharaja. Aurobindo attended the annual Congress Session held in the years 1902, 1904, and 1906. He persuaded Indian National Congress to declare complete independence.

Active Politics (1906-10) He was not satisfied with his acts. Patriotism was full to his head and heart. Hence, he left Baroda and took over the principalship at National College, Culcutta. Reaching Calcutta he called, the meeting of National leaders of Bengal and put forth his programme for liberation. He condemned the moderates for their policy of prayers and petitions. Complete Independence should be our aim of national struggle. Boycott, Swadeshi, National Education and passive resistance were the weapons for the Independence. He liked to oust the moderates and put the Congress in charge of Tilak.

He became Editor of *Bande Mataram,* a daily started by Bipin Chandra Pal. Educated mass of Bengal wefe aroused and revolutionary grounds were established. Government liked to take for conviction Aurobindo under sedition but it could not be done as his editorship was not established and proved. But the case brought him to the forefront in national field.

Alipore Jail Terrorism developed through his speeches. Two ladies were killed in a bomb outrage though it was for District Magistrate of Muzzaffarpore. Aurobindo and his brother Barinder Kumar Ghosh were arrested for criminal conspiracy. After the trial with imprisonment of one year in Alipore Jail, he was released as it was not proved due to pleadings of C.R. Das.

Departure for Pondicherry During April 1910 he came to Pondicherry to keep alone from the politics as he thought it unwise to do so. After his release from jail he started two magazines *Karmayogin* and *Dharma* which were non-political. It was heard that he would be deported. He did his Yoga and it was clear that he should go to Chandra Nagar and Pondicherry in French possession for spiritual attainment.

The Last Phase While at Pondicherry, Sri Aurobindo kept only indirect touch with Indian politics. He kept a close watch over all that was happening in the world and in Indian and intervened whenever necessary, but with silent spiritual action. He intervened in World War II. "At the beginning he did not actively concern himself with it, but when it appeared as if Hitler would crush all the forces opposed to him and Nazism dominate the world, he began to intervene... Inwardly he put spiritual force behind the Allies from the moment of Dunkirk when everybody was expecting the immediate downfall of England and the definite triumph of Hitler, and he had the satisfaction of seeing the rush of German victory almost immediately arrested and the tide of war began to turn in the opposite direction. This he did, because he saw that behind Hitler and Nazism were dark Asuric forces and their success would mean the enslavement of mankind to the tyranny of evil, and a setback to the cause of evolution and especially to the spiritual evolution of mankind..."

The retirement of Sri Aurobindo from active politics was not due to any feeling of helplessness of disappointment. He himself wrote as follows : came away because I did not want anything to interfere with my Yoga and because I got a very distinct Adesh in the matter. I have cut connection entirely with politics, but before I did so I know from within what the work I had begun there was destined to be carried forward, on lines I had foreseen by others, and that the ultimate triumph of the movement I had initiated was sure without any personal action or presence. There was not the least motive of despair or sense of futility behind my withdrawl."

The Writings of Sri Aurobindo

1. On Yoga— *The Synthesis of Yoga* (1965) (On Yoga I)
2. On Yoga II — *Tomes I and II* (1958)
3. *Speeches* (1942)
4. *Lights on Yoga* (1942)
5. *The Ideal of the Karmayogin* (1950)
6. *Sri Aurobindo on Himself and on the Mother* (1953)
7. *Bases of Yoga* (1949)

8. *Message of Sri Aurobindo* and *The Ashram* (1962)
9. *Message of Sri Aurobindo;* 15th August, 1947
10. *On The Veda* (1956)
11. *Essays; The Gita* (1966)
12. *The Human Cycle, Ideal of Human Unity and War and Self-Determination* (1962)
13. *The Foundations of Indian Culture* (1959)
14. *The Life Divine (American Edition)* (1965)
15. *Life-Literature-Yoga* (1967)
16. *The Mother* (1960)
17. *The Hour of God* (1964)
18. *The Problem of Rebirth* (1952)

Poems and Plays

19. *Savitri* (1954)
20. *Last Poems* (1953)
21. *The Future Poetry* (1953)
22. *Hymns to the Mystic Fire* (1952)
23. *Collected Poems and Plays* (2 Vols.) (1942)
24. *Perseus the Deliverer* (1955)
25. *Ilion* (1957)
26. *Vasavadatta* (1965)
27. *Vikramorvasie (The Hero and the Nymph)* a drama by Kalidasa translated from Sanskrit by Sri Aurobindo)

Newspapers, Journals, periodicals containing writings of Sri Aurobindo

1. *Bande Mataram* (1908)
2. *Arya* (1914)
3. *Indu Prakash* (1893/94)
4. *Jugantar* (1906)
5. *Karma Yogin* (1909)
6. *Dharma* (1909)

He died on 1950 and placed before the people of India, "Our ideal of patriotism proceeds from the basis of love and brotherhood and it looks beyond the unity of the nation and the ultimate unity. But it is a unity of brothers, close and free-men that we seek, not unity of masters and serfs of devourer an devoured."

His Political Philosophy Political philosophy can be described in the three stages of his career.

Firstly, he worked as a contributor of articles to the *Indu Prakash* an Anglo-Marathi paper edited by his Cambridge friend K.G. Despande under the caption of 'New Lamps for Old'. Here he criticised moderates, the dominating figures of the Congress during 1893-1906.

Secondly, he left Baroda for good and became the principal of the National College at Calcutta in 1906. After one year he became the Editor of *Bande Mataram,* a daily paper of Bipin Chandra Pal. He came in direct politics. He organized terrorist movement secretly in Bengal. His speeches and editorials under Bande Mataram spread nationalism and patriotism in the learned masses of Bengal. He became symbol of the new nationalist movement in Bengal and the country as a whole.

As for his third stage, it is concerned from 1910, when he retired form active politics and settled down at Pondicherry in French possessions. He dedicated his life to spiritual attainment and Yogic Sadhana.

The main political ideas can be summarised as below :

Criticism of the Moderates, dominating the Congress While at Gaekwar's service, he contributed articles to the Bombay paper *Indu Prakash* edited by his friend K.G. Despande. Here he criticised the ways and means adopted by Moderates who took to mild reforms in socio-political ways. They had faith in British rulers with co-operation. They tried persuations, prayers and petitions. They were weak, cowardly and hypocrites. The function of a nationalist was to revive in the minds of downtrodden Indians, a wave of patriotism based on self-respect and dignity of men. Aurobindo was of the view that till the old tempers and attitudes prevailed, it was not possible to inculcate the spirit of patriotism among the Indians. The demand of moderates regarding the participation of Indians in I.C.S. Government Services, Legislative Councils were all useless as it promoted for the interest of educated mass only. Hence, mass population was left uncared for. Again he said that foreign government was responsible for economic exploitation of the country.

He was the first nationalist who favoured complete Independence of India. To strive for anything less than a glorious freedom would be an insult of our past of greatness. In the "Doctrine of Passive Resistance", he said that we should not lower our demands less than a pin to Swaraj. Every nation had a divine mission free from external control. He disliked British forcing their culture on India. In the words of J.P. Suda "To have placed before the people of India, ideal of complete Independence and made them conscious of the moral degradation involved in the subjection to foreign rule was perhaps the greatest service rendered by him to Indian nationalism."

In *Bande Mataram,* he demanded full Swaraj. National development was not possible without self-government. Moral and spiritual evolution of nation was only possible in the atmosphere of freedom. India had to play a divine mission on Asia and it can be successful if India is free.

Criticism of the Moderates' Method of Struggle Moderates believed in the method of slow and steady struggle. Firstly, they believed in the sense of justice and fairplay of the British rulers. Secondly, they had faith in the constitutional methods. They accepted the reforms introduced by the British rulers as progressive steps towards the realization of their objectives. They wished to enter council chambers and bring about the constitutional changes Thirdly, they thought that the connections between India and England are providential.

Aurobindo was doubtful about their method of slavish mentality. He had no faith on the Britishers as they were only commercial men and came to India for trade purposes. They turned the Indian economic resources to their selfish motives. They had no interest in the welfare of the Indians.

Aurobindo ridiculed the idea of constitutional methods and reforms. In his opinion it was foolish to think that they will share power with the Indians. He thought their culture to be backward. He thought Britishers less cultured than the French people.

About moderates he was of the opinion that they thought foreign yoke easy to bear. Moderates never liked to throw away the foreign government. They had faith in British race and hence Aurobindo condemned them for praising if an Indian was appointed to high office. Whenever any Indian critic said against them, he was offered a good job. Such were the moderates, according to Aurobindo. They would sacrifice the interest of the country on such occasions.

According to Aurobindo, Indian National Congress was a body of middle class people who never cared for landless peasants and working classes. The country could not be uplifted without the peasants and workers. He was thinking of the spiritual elevation of the masses through proper education. He wished to enkindle the divine fire that lay dormant in them.

Criticism of the British Government Due to his residence in England, he knew the English people, their politics, their conduct customs, manners and baseless superstitions. He always regarded Britishers of base culture. British culture was less civilized to that of French people.

He criticised that British institutions in India as they were against the Indian spirit. The education introduced by them was also faulty. It had no spiritual nor ethical value.

Aurobindo's method of political struggle Aurobindo was in favour of complete Independence. Firstly, he rejected the methods adopted by moderates as prayers and petitions to be useless and unworthy of national dignity. He also condemned institutional methods like the election or nomination to the legislatures. Nation could not get freedom by stages. He suggested passive resistance as an appropriate method for compelling the Britishers to surrender power. His passive resistance movements included boycott, Swadeshi, non co-operation, national education and even non-payment of taxes Aurobindo's theory of passive resistance was not like Ahimsa. According to him, nation had right to attain Independence by whatever means possible — peaceful or violence. It may be said that it was violence or non-violence. He believed in Gita and Krishna's philosophy. He believed in ends and not in means. If the aim is noble, means may be of any kind and justifiable. Struggle for national emancipation was a *dharmayuddha.* Gandhi paid equal importance to both means and ends. He used right type of means for the achievement of noble ends. In his opinion Indian freedom was a noble cause and hence its means should also be noble and sublime. Hence, Gandhiji applied spirit of non-violence to the cause of freedom. On the other hand Aurobindo regarded armed revolt to be the "readiest and the swiftest, most thorough in results and demands the least powers of endurance and suffering, and the smallest and briefest sacrifices."

His views on passive Resistance Aurobindo was the propounder of the theory of Passive Resistance. Moderates and liberals were of the view of constitutional approach through prayers, petitions and protest which Aurobindo criticized. He gave positive mode of approach as passive resistance, In the year 1910, he put forward the theory in the paper *Bande Mataram* serially. As this method proved good to the Irish people to get their freedom from British rule. He spoke moderates as mendicants. It can only be done by self-help and self-realization. It meant that if a nation fails to achieve the Independence, there is no other way except violence. In essays on Gita he spoke of Dharmayuddha by which killing of national enemies is Dharmayuddha and it is our Dharma. He said "politics is the realm of Kshatriyas and the morality of Kshatriya ought to govern our political action. To impose in politics the Brahmanical duty of saintly sacrifice is to preach Varna-Samskar."

He defended aggression and armed revolt on the basis of the teaching of the Gita. He said in his article, "The morality of revolt" that "The Gita is the best answer to those who shrink from battle as a sin and aggression as alluring of morality."

He told of armed revolt as a political method. "The readiest and the swiftest, the most thorough in its results and demands the least powers of endurance and suffering and the smallest and the briefest sacrifices." He was not an armed revolutionary. But he was not opposed to the principle of violence.

The doctrine of passive resistance surrounded boycott which was a kind of non-co-operation with the English rulers and rejection of certain goods and ideas by which English people would be put to loss. At Aurobindo put it, "The aim of Passive Resistance was to make British administration impossible by an organized refusal to do anything which shall help the growth of British trade and commerce resulting in the exploitation of the country."

Obstructions may be put in the English rulers path, so that ruling of India would become hard for them as they were interested in trade and commerce. They made economic loss to India. By boycott their hold over India would become weak and their trade would suffer.

His doctrine of passive resistance was different from that advocated by Mahatma Gandhi.

Secondly, he asked people to boycott government schools and colleges. All schools started by English people produced clerks to run the administration. Boycott could hinder their idea of producing clerks. He attacked the education system as it was against Indian culture and national dignity.

Thirdly, British established courts should be boycott so that their disputes would be mutually settled through arbitration of Panchayats.

Lastly, no co-operation should be done with them and if any traitor did the co-operation, he may be boycotted also. In this way we find doctrine of Passive Resistance gave value to boycott much of British goods and use of Indian goods in their place, boycott of government schools and colleges and opening of National Schools, boycott of courts and establishment of arbitration courts, boycott of traitors. He also favoured non-payment of taxes, with direct conflict, mass arrests, imprisonment and fines. These boycotts did not come under legal infringement hence they could be adopted on mass scale. This boycott covered social, political economic and educational spheres of life. He was not based on theory but did it in practice.

We can say about Aurobindo that he was more extremist in his views and ideology than any other persons of that age of freedom fighters. He gave patriotic spirit to the public and prepared for effective action.

Passive Resistance meant active resistance with use of arms and all possible violent means to overthrow the government.

According to him, Passive Resistance only could build a strong nation when it became masculine, bold and ardent in spirit and ready at any moment at the bit notice to supplement itself with active resistance.

He said, "We do not want to develop a nation of women, who knows how to suffer and not how to strive."

Hence, we find that his method of Passive Resistance was quite different from Satyagraha of Mahatma Gandhi fundamentally who preached the complete pure and simple Satyagraha with non-violence. He was always carefully watching the terrorist movements of Bengal and other parts of India while he stayed at Baroda and till he reached Pondicherry.

Aurobindo's Theory of Nationalism and Human Unity "The ideal of human unity" the famous work defines the word nation as "a persistent psychological unity which nature has been busy developing into physical and political unity." To this he further added "political unity is not the essential factor, it may not yet be realized yet the nation persists and moves inevitably towards its realization." Again he said, "For what is a nation, what is our mother India. It is not a piece of earth, nor a figure of speech, nor a fiction of mind. It is a mighty composed of all the shakties of all the millions of units that make up the nation, just as Bhawani Mahisha Mardini sprang into being form the shakti of all the millions of gods assembled and in one mass of force and welded into unity. The Shakti we call in India, Bhawani Bharati, is the living unity of Shakties of 300 million people."

Aurobindo was a pioneer of neo-nationalism in India. This nationalism was not only patriotism. Indian leaders of late 19th century were no doubt patriots but all were not nationalists.

Dadabhai Naoroji, Ferozeshah Mehta, Gokhale, Surendranath Bnerjee and Tyabji were of moderate and liberal view of the time. According to Aurobindo, these were more patriotic than nationalists. They loved India but could not get the soul of India. They did not believe in spiritual greatness and basic genius of India and hence could give the people any spirit of national unity. They asked for political rights, administrative reforms as British subjects but not as proud citizens of India. They gave the inferiority complex to themselves. Aurobindo said "The nineteenth century leaders of national movement were imitative, self-forgetful and artificial. They aimed at reproduction of Europe in India." Imitation of British habits and behaviours by them was critized by him as India had a great spiritual, culture and intellectual heritage of her own.

India had a divine mission to lead the complete humanity by her great past. Psychological slavery, hypocrisy, cowardice and sentimentalism should be won. National renaissance can only take place if new spirit of naitonalism was given to the masses National awareness of the public was necessary for the liberation of the nation and to make the movement successful.

He said further quoting from Gita "Better the law of one's own being though it be badly done than an alien *dharma* well-followed, death in one's own *dharma* is better, it is a dangerous thing to follow the law of another's nature," .... "If we had succeeded in Europeanizing ourselves we would have lost for ever our spiritual capacity, our intellectual force, our national elasticity, and the power of self-renovation."

Thus, it is clear the nationalism of the previous Congress leaders was of a different kind with political concessions from the English people, while Aurobindo was quite different in his approach. He gave more value to the spiritual past by which awareness and pride can be revived so that nationalism may reach a hight which is clear from the following extract of his speech at Bombay on 19th January 1908, "Nationalism is not a mere political programme. Nationalism is a religion that has come from God. Nationalism is a creed which you shall have to live.... If you are going to be a nationalist, if you are going to assent to this religion of Nationalism, you must do it in the religious spirit. You must remember that you are the instruments of God.... Nationalism is not going to be crushed. Nationalism survives in the strength of God and it is not possible to crush it, whatever weapons are brought against it. Nationalism is immortal."

In *Bande Mataram* he said, "Nationalism is simply a passionate aspiration for the realization of Divine Unity in the nation. In the ideal of nationalism which India will set before the world, there will be an essential equality between man and man irrespective of caste, creed, religion or economic status. Nation is a Virat Purush or a magnified image of man and all the individuals are an integral part of that personality which is symbolized by the nation."

His nationalism was not chauvinism or narrow jingoism. He wished India to be free because she was a spiritual fountain head of humanity and the whole world looked at her to lead spiritually against materialistic principles of the west. In this way his nationalism took the roots of internationalism for human unity.

We find that nationalism with Aurobindo was not only a political bias but had also the religious view that came from God. Nationalism was immortal as it was a universal truth. He was in favour of spiritual society that will lead to rich and beautiful life. Political discords, conflicts, contradictions and struggle led to chaos and disharmony. In this way Aurobindo made nationalism a spiritual force and a stimulant religious sentiment. In "Ideal of Kormayogin" he has summarized his spiritual politics. We say to the individual and specially to the young who are now arising to do India's work, the world's work, the God's work — you cannot cherish these ideas, still less can you fulfil them if you subject your minds to European ideas or look at life from the material stand point. Materially, you are nothing, spiritually you are everything, dare everything, sacrifice everything : Firstly, therefore, become Indians. Recover the Aryan thought, the Aryan discipline, the Aryan character, the Aryan life. Recover the Vedanta, the Gita, the Yoga. Recover them not only in the intellect or sentiment but in your lives. Live them and you will be great and strong, mighty, invincible and fearless, neither life nor death will have any terrors for you. Difficulty and impossibility will vanish from your vocabularies. For, it is in the spirit that strength is eternal, and you must win back the kingdom of yourselves, the inner Swaraj before you can win back your outer empire. There the Mother dwells and she waits for worship that she may give strength. Believe in Her, serve Her, lose your wills in Her's your egoism in the greater ego of the country, your separate selfishness in the service of humanity. Recover the source of all strength in yourself and all else will be added to you, social soundness, intellectual pre-eminence, political freedom, the mastery of human thought, the hegemony of the world."

Aurobindo wished to raise an army of spiritually elevated political workers who would see after various aspects of social political and economic life.

Aurobindo's nationalism was not based on narrow regionalism. His spiritual bonds of unity comprised the world as a whole. He did not care for the restrictions of caste, creed, religion, territorial boundaries, colour, race or sex. He liked to free India so that she may became the spiritual leader of the whole world. As a nationalist leader, Aurobindo stood for inspired and exalted patriotism. Indian nation would stand for the manifestation of divinity. Mother India was not a division of a land or a geographical area but she was something more.

He said once, "Are we going to sacrifice our national destiny to the whims and interests of the foreigners or are we going to take ourselves seriously and struggle for the right to live that we may fulfil in this world our Heaven appointed mission."

Our existence depended on the Mother. Sanatan Dharma, stood for Indian nationalism. Till we have faith in Sanatan Dharma Indian nation would exist. The moment faith finished in the Sanatan Dharma, there would be no India at all. Sanatan Dharma stood for ancient Aryan religious philosophy.

The Ideal of Human Unity' is written by Aurobindo Ghosh. He was against the theory of Nation-State. Industrialization developed the powerful nation-states. Every nation liked to dominate the other and by this world-wars became necessary and it resulted in massacre and loss of property. Aurobindo was a student of world-history. Social evolution organized persons into groups as families, clans and villages. Inner social urge and outer compulsion were also responsible for organisation of bigger and bigger groups as kingdoms-states and empires.

Big empires were results of ruthless economic exploitation, and justified use of violence. The state is the highest and noblest organization during the process of social evolution. His ideas were similar to Aristotle and Hegal. But Aurobindo's ideas of state and nationalism were not narrow and fanantical but had cosmopolitan character. Nation was the necessary stage in the long process of social evolution. He gave the realization of brotherhood of mankind, foundation of which will be provided by religion of humanity and inner spiritual feeling of oneness.

About the state he said, "The State is a convenience and a rather clumsy convenience, for our common development, it ought never to be made an end in itself." He did not follow idealists. He believed in the limited functions of the state. He was not a socialist nor social democrat. He said, "It is the energy of the individual that really matters. The State sometimes comes to aid, if and when, if its aid does not mean undue control, it serves a positive end." Here he follows Individualists. He says, "The business of the State so long as it continuous to be a necessary element in human life and growth, is to provide all possible facilities for co-operative action to remove obstacles to prevent really all harmful waste and friction... and removing avoidable injustice to secure or every individual a just and equal change of self-development and satisfaction to the extent of his powers and in the line of his nature. To this extent the aim in Modern Socialism is right and good." Again ho said, "But all necessary interference with the freedom of Man's growth is to that extent harmful. Even co-operative action is injurious if instead of seeking the good of all it immolates the individual to a communal egoism and prevents so much freedom and initiative as is necessary for the flowering of a more perfectly developed humanity."

He wanted that all the nation-states of the world should be united in a common federation. Alternate proposal for Europe was to organize United States of Europe. To also United States of Asia, United States of

Africa and United States of North and South America. All these states again should combine and unite into a confederation. According to him, a time would come when all human races would give a single state and would be bound by spiritualism. In Ideal of Human Unity he said, "a world union will base on self-determination." Social ethnic groups would be separately organized. But no forceful or violent subjugation would be applied. Such union of world would not be dominated by pride, ego and selfishness of some nations but would be governed by humanity. A natural psychological unity would emerge among the humanity at large in the presence of such a psychological unity, the world union would become indestructible.

He further suggested that big empires would fall to pieces if they did not have any psychological unity. British empire would not subsist because of any idea of oneness among the subject-races. Political unity or administrative control would have no significance.

Thus, modern basis of nation-states would stumble as seen from the point of world union. At the same time the pride of such nations could be crushed by spiritual religion of humanity. Spiritual collectivism would subdue the spiritual claims of components. Spiritualized community would subdue social and political chaos of the modern period. Socialism or communism would lead to authoritarianism. Humanism could not be built by an imperfect man at the top. Religion also could not bind the society for lone as it would turn to dogmatism. Thus, only a spiritual society could build the future richness and good life. A sacred spirit and divine, reality existed all over. Human beings were the vehicles by which divine reality would be expressed. A time will show the kingdom of divine spirit on earth and other egoisms would disappear.

Metaphysics of Aurobindo Ghosh Aurobindo was brought up in England and was fully absorbed in western culture and philosophy. While in England he knew nothing of Indian culture but was completely westernized. While he arrived in India, he studied Sanskrit and Ancient Indian Literature. This ended his anglomania and he became complete Indian.

He reconciled the Indian spiritual idealism with the western secular materialism. Although some of the western philosophers believed in God but scientific techniques led them to the growth of materialism and secularism. Their aim was to conquer nature and retionalization of social life. Scientific reasoning developed scientific knowledge about natural and social environment with evolution. This gave birth to democracy, socialism and humanism. Man became the creator. Spirit or soul was thought to be a psychological process. Deep realization of divine life was not possible under the materialistic philosophy.

Aurobindo thought that west and east respectively gave value to matter and spirit. There must be a compromise between the two. He considered the middle path. He considered matter to be a veiled spirit. Europeans discovered the external freedom while India discovered the internal freedom. The best was to combine both and bring harmony among them.

Inadequacy of State According to Aurobindo, State is a collective ego of the people comprising the State. State looks to achieve collective aim, and ambitions imposed on a great mass of people by a handful of politicians, if the politicians were noble and good to exercise best interest of the people. But in modern democracies power politics was responsible for the rise of such people as were motivated by ignoble intentions. These politicians were morally degraded, selfish and timid. What they said and acted gave a great difference. Hence, state is nothing but political collective ego, without soul or spirit. While individual had soul and could rise above selfishness, individual could be spiritualized but State remained the same. Thus between them disharmony is seen. He said that "The State is a convenience, rather clumsy convenience in itself." Hence, he trusted in the limited functions of the State. He never opined for the State having absolutely sovereign with unlimited and indivisible power. He also discarded socialists who spoke of the state to be an agent of collective progress. According to him progress of a community depends on spiritual and moral dynamism of individuals. The chief function of the state was to remove obstruction from the path of good life of the public. All actions of State should being general good of all. Action should be justificable depending on moral and spiritual life of people. State should provide all possible facilities for co-operative action, to secure for all a just and equal chance for self-development. But unneccessary interference to human rights and freedom was harmful. He says further, "The individual does not owe his allegiance to the state which is a machine. His allegiance must be to the truth, the self and divine." But cannot reach the perfection unless they had spiritual and psychological transformation and shed off their ego. Hence, state is not the highest and noblest social organization. All human beings living in the world are one and the same. Efforts should be made for the spiritual elevation of humanity and organization of world union. The world-wide human unity can only be brought about by dissemination of spiritual knowledge.

Critical Estimate of Aurobindo's Philosophy Aurobindo was the pillar of extremist movement. He had given a new slogan to his contemporary national leaders. He gave new life to the nation. Pandit Jawaharlal Nehru said of him, "The whole career in active politics was a brief one from 1906 to 1910 when he retired to Pondicherry and devoted himself to spiritual and *yogi* exercises. During these five years he had shone like a brilliant meteor and created a powerful impression on the youth of India. The greater anti-partition movement in Bengal gained much of his philosophy from his and undoubtedly prepared the way for the great movement led by Mahatma Gandhi." Romain Rolland called him "The foremost of Indian Thinkers." He combined the materialism of west and spiritualism of India. He was a great *yogi,* a philosopher and intellectual. As a nationalist he was a great politician and raised the slogan of Swaraj. By his speeches he gave new hope and optimism among the demoralized people of India. He refused the supremacy of English people in culture and race. Passive Resistance and boycott were the effective instruments to finish the British interest in India. British thought him to be their political and economical enemy. Rabindranath Tagore, Bipin Chandra Pal, Gopal Krishna Gokhale and Lala Lajpat Rai paid him high tributes for his patriotism and intellectuality.

He preached human unity and one-world-theory which is needed most. Thus, he gave not only as a nationalist but as an internationalist a concept of'brotherhood of nations.

Dr. Karan Singh said of him, "Thus, with his inspiring articles in 'Bande Mataram' he became almost overnight a national hero, and the hole Bengal intelligentsia watched breathlessly for his inspiring pronouncements on events." Dr. Karan Singh also spoke of him, "He was largely responsible for imparting esoteric and spiritual significance to national movement, for placing before it the inspiring ideal of complete Independence, for invigorating the spirit of India by our association of the true basis of her cultural heritage, for expanding a practical system whereby the goal of Independence could be achieved and for placing the whole movement in the broader context of internationalism and the ideal of human unity."

Thus, he stands as one of the builders of Indian nation. He was the political-Lieutenant of Bal Gangadhar Tilak, Dr. Radhakrishnan called him, "The most accomplished of modern Indian Thinkers. Rabindranath Tagore regarded him as one of the "Messiah of Indian culture and civilization." In the words of Haridas Chaudhary he was "amazingly creative personality with a deep insight into the past a firm hold upon the present and prophetic vision of the future."

Views about Liberty Aurobindo was of the ideal of inner spiritual freedom. The idea of the attainment of spiritual freedom was not new as ancient Vadas put it. Aurobindo put it that the idea of freedom now to be got was from the West. But it was not new to India as past cultural heritage put it. He wanted that the individual should be loyal to the Truth, the Self, the Spirit and the Divine. By liberty he meant the "freedom to obey the law of our being, to grow our national fulfilment, to find out naturally and freely our harmony with the environment.

Thus, Aurbindo is known move as a Rishi or a spiritual leader than anything else.

12

Mahatma Gandhi (1869-1948)

(i) Introduction

Mohandas Karamchand Gandhi, the 'Father of the Nation' and the 'Architect of Modern India' respectfully, addressed and remembered as Mahatmaji, was born on the cross-roads of our history and gave it a purposeful direction. He made his mark as protestor, social worker, reformer, thinker and as the liberator. The political guise in which he appeared before the world he did not own. He was religious, humanist and the "practical idealist". He accepted life in all its comprehensiveness. A keen student of human affairs as he was, he expressed himself on problems that he and the contemporary society confronted the most. His 'thought' is, therefore, not academically cut and set. It is not free from inconsistency. In his postulations he has drawn upon the ancient heritage and philosophy. It has been to him, as to many others, the fountain of freshness and the ever bubbling source of ideas. To most of us, for our ignorance of our heritage, and for being conditioned by tire western political thought, his writings cause pouzzlement and contradiction. The effect, however, wears away, as deep in our mind, there is the ancient impact and our silent response to it. Our ancestors did not live only to die, or to be born again and again as the populist belief goes. They had developed the ideas suitable to their conditions. The Westernism, that has come between our heritage and ourselves makes often difficult for us, to make a rational and positive study of these ideas. Gandhi firmly believed that some of the ancient ideas can still be helpful in resolving some of our problems. The concepts and patterns that the terms like Varna, Karma, Satya, Ahimsa, Aparigraha, Samabhava, Sarvodaya and Dhama, etc., convey are interesting and refreshing. Gandhiji used these in positive and meaningful way; not necessarily as understood popularly.

Our 'literate' and 'expert' often take these words as of mere religious connotation having only the 'other world' business in view;

having no relation with this life of matter and money; social welfare and humanism. Yet he used these terms to indicate their deep relations with this life; here and now. He was not other worldly. The absurdity of it, he wished none to believe. Being an experimentalist, he had a mannerism of his own; and his ideas and work has a distinct dimension. He accepted challenge, worked out the solution, drew his conclusions and stood up to these. He did not claim perfection. He did not talk the language of last and final. Once he felt his mistake, he did not hesitate to reverse his opinion. He claimed for himself the humblest position; and yet exercised immense influence that ever a leader has. For all that he represented, he appears to have come from among the stock of ancient mythological personnel to awaken the soul of the nation. Proud of his heritage, he was as Jawaharlal described him, "Indian leadership, Indian style". He was a *rishi* in thought, word and deed. "Generations to come", said Albert Einstein "it may be, will scarce believe that such a one as this ever in flesh and blood walked upon this earth. He, for his belief in goodness, amity and peace came to be described as the "spokesman for the conscience of all mankind." Men of the type of Gandhi are born once in a millennium.

The personality of Gandhiji was built on the rock foundation of piety, truthfulness, service and sacrifice. The religious vows and fasts of his mother, her sense of service, the spirit of sacrifice and her simplicity influenced him the most. The domestic environment in which he sprang up was religious; the recitation of the religious texts, the piety and truthfulness had the ratifying effect on all and not less on the young Mohandas. Discipline was dominant in the family. This stimulated the inner motivation of the springing boy.

His sense of observation, analysis and experimentation even at a comparatively younger age gave him a distinct mental quality and approach to the matters that he confronted. For this the Ramcharitramanas, the Geeta and the Upanishads have new meaning for him. Being neither a determinist, nor a fanatic, bookish or dogmatist, he drew his own conclusions. In this spirit he received Tolstoy's Kingdom of God is Within You; Carlyle's Hero Worship; Ruskin's Unto This Last and Thoreau's Duty of Civil Disobedience. He was as Romain Rolland remarks "familiar with the best that Europe and America has produced. To him the Bible and the Quran was as familiar as to any other believer. He drew the best out of these yet, these did not sway him. He made something of these.

Gandhiji was contemplative and receptive, he reacted to the circumstances and situations in an uncommon way. Different factors, which are always present too influence, do not act the common way, Gandhi felt the impact of many a familiar situations, incidents and phenomena in an uncommon way. He experimented with his conditions, lived according to his light; looked for more. He did not challenge till he understood the object of challenge. And once he came to the decision, he pursued, executed and accepted its consequences in full measure. Understanding acting and living by the application of it and in devotion was the, Gandhian way. He lived by Gyana, Karma and in Bhakti — an ideal Karmyogi, he was.

(ii) His Early Life and Education

Mohandas was born of Putlibai and Karamchand, the Dewan of Porbander, a Kathiawar Gujarat State on October 2, 1869. Of his father, Gandhiji wrote; he was "truthful, brave and generous but short tempered". Being "incorruptible" he had "earned a name for strict impartiality in his family as well as outside". And, writing about his mother, he says, she "was deeply religious. She would not think of taking her meals without her daily prayer..." She was orthodox and believed in the current social taboos. Her illiteracy and ignorance of scripture, disabled her from clearing the doubts and misgivings of her introvert, brooding and thoughtful son, Mohandas, who could not reconcile with everything around. Her insistence for example, on him, not to touch Uka, the domestic sweeper, was so strange to the young boy. His deep sense of introspection troubled him most. For the wrongs and indiscretions he committed here and there he did not excuse himself.

Mohandas had his early education in Alfred High School, Rajkot. He was neither brilliant nor plodding. He had no demonstrative traits. "I had not any high regard for my ability. I was to be astonished whenever I won prizes and scholarships". He was meek. "I was even afraid lest anyone should poke fun at me." He finished his high school education at the age of eighteen. For further studies, he joined the college at Bhavnagar. The lectures, he felt were flowing over his head. He was disillusioned. His destiny, however, lay elsewhere. On the advice of a family friend, Mavgidave, it was decided at the family level that he should go to England, to be a barrister, for better prospects in life. The decision enthused youngman. It saved him immediately, from any further distress in the college and provided him the chance, as he felt, to see "the land of philosophers and poets, the very centre of civilization" as England was then in any one's imagination.

Mohandas was married, in his thirteenth year to Kasturbai of the same age, a daughter of Gokaldas Makani, a merchant of Porbander. The little couple, gradually came to know one another, developed intimacy and the husband in Mohandas, soon felt, the fondness for his wife. But, Sheikh Mehtab, his friend, fanned suspicion in him, against his wife, giving rise to the differences. This, however, proved to be a passing phenomenon. Between the chance differences and deepening affections, the Gandhis had a baby-son born to them.

He sailed from Bombay on September 4, 1888 to qualify at the bar. The voyage to England was hard and torturous for reasons more than one. His spoken English being weak, he had the difficulty in expressing himself; being a vegetarian, he had the food problem no less, to face. This apart the loneliness obssessed him. His mother, wife and the child claimed his thoughts and stole his sleep. These feelings he overcame, only after he landed in England. Here, he took interest "in fashion and frivolities than his studies. He showed himself as an English man". But soon, he overcame these detractions.

He was called to the bar on June 10, 1891. The years, he stayed in England, added to his experience. He became a reasoned vegetarian, after he had studied the Plea for Vegetarianism by Salt. The promise to remain a vegetarian, that he had given to his mother, was out of sentiment, but now it had become, a matter of faith. He moved a step further; he organized a vegetarian club in his locality and wrote several articles in support of his new faith. He was consequently, elected to the executive of the London Vegetarian Society.

Back home, life seemed difficulty. He failed to make a professional impact in Raj kot. It soon dawned upon him that he was completely ignorant of Indian law. He, therefore, went to Bombay to study law and to gain some experience at the High Court. Barrister Gandhi, contrary to the prevailing practice, considered it unprofessional to draw upon the touts to secure clients. The first brief he got, he found to be a real problem. The barrister failed to conduct the cross-examination. The profession, he flet would not secure him a living. He, therefore, took to a teaching job as well. Successively, he found his competence in drafting the petition and the memorials. It renewed his confience to follow his profession. He now went back to Rajkot, and took up this work. But, it was not that simple. The political agent whom, he went to see, in connection with the affairs of his brother, was rude to him. Gandhi felt humiliated. It was worse, as his work lay, in the court of the political agent, itself. He felt, that the stay in Rajkot would be uncongenial to, his work. He was unhappy. The luck, however, came to his rescue. He got a job, which took him to South Africa.

In May 1893, Gandhi reached Port Natal, in Durbart. He went, soon after, with his employer-client Abudulla, in the court, where the European magistrate, asked the barrister Gandhi to take off his turban, which according to the Indian practice was insulting. Gandhi refused to oblige. He further protested against it in the press. He had a similar humiliating experience, on his way to Pretoria, where he was asked to move from his first class carraige, to van compartment. This he refused. He was turned out. Feeling humiliated, he resolved to face the challenge. As if this was not enough, he was warned at Charles town not to sit with the Europeans inside the coach; he refused to move from his seat, dispite being belaboured. He had a similar experience at Johansburg. These indignities that Gandhiji suffered were the common lot of Indians. Therefore, on his arrived back at Pretoria, he orgnaized the Indians to resist this racial snoberry. Later, when he came to know, about the bill to disenfranchise the Indians, he explained to them its implications. They responded well, and requested him for guidance. But Gandhi's stay in South Africa was snearing the end, as the job with Abudulla had come to a happy end. Gandhi, in fact, was preparing to go back home. But, the appeals of the Indians touched the human in Gandhi. He responded; stayed with them, to fight for their rights. He settled at Natal as barrister, to practice in the Supreme Court. He made the Natal Congress to take up the political work. It also undertook the social and moral uplift of the community.

Gandhi had earned the gratitude of the Indians in South Africa. He had made a name. Since he had settled at Natal, he came to take his family to his place of settlement. Making use of this opportunity, he went out on a countrywide tour, to educate the people on the Indians problems in South Africa. He intimated about it to Sir Ferozshah Mehta in Bombay; and Balgangadhar Tilak and Gopalkrishnan Gokhle in Poona. In Madras, the Hindu, extended full welcome to him; and in Calcutta, the Statesman and the Englishman featured his interview. The cross-country tour came to a sudden end as the urgent call from Natal summoned him back. The Natal Europeans, as they had received the false, and exaggerated reports about his doings in India were up against Gandhi. They, therefore, demanded that the Indian should not be allowed to land. Their agitation kept the ship Gandhi was on board, and another, anchored for long. Finally, they landed, on January 13, 1897. The racist were unhappy at it. They subjected Gandhi, at West Street, Laughton, to a brutual attack. The timely help provided by a few good natured Europeans, here saved him. He was advised to take the legal actions against the ruffians. But as the entire community was involved in the race tyranny, he declined.

Despite all this, Gandhi was free from anger, malice or hate against the British in South Africa. He hated the wrong but not the wrong-doer. The Boer war 1899, which saw the British badly involved, made Gandhi come forward with his token help. He rendered full co-operation along with his 1100 men. It brought him gratitude and respect of all the Europeans and gave him the feeling, however, wrong that it would induce the government to give a better deal to the Indians. Under the assumption, he decided to come back to India. The people around him, felt most unhappy over his decisions. They finally secured a promise from him that if and when they needed his help, he would come back. Gandhi agreed.

Toward the close of the year 1901, he was in Bombay. He attended the session of the National Congress and piloted a resolution on the condition of Indians in South Africa. He also took to the country-wide travel. In the midst of this activity, he got a cable from the Indians in South Africa requesting him to come back. The condition of the Indians there had remained unimproved and unchanged. They, worked now to present their case, to the visiting Colonial Secretary, Mr. Chamberlain. Gandhi was thus back in Durban, in December 1902, The visiting dignity made no concession and held no hope.

The notion of simplicity and religiousness at this time had seized Gandhi. His belief in it was further strengthened by Ruskin's Unto This Last, which is a condemnation of the Industrial society, capitalist economy and pleads for attention to the poverty and injustice. He now conceived the idea of community living, and to experiment with it a hundred acres estate was purchased near Phoenix station. The settlers were given three acres of land each for use and if any one of them left, the land passed to a new settler. For himself, Gandhi made a small cottage. His room on Sundays was used as a community prayer hall. Here were recited the Geeta, Gujarati Bhajans, the Bible and the Christian hymns.

The problems of Indians had remained unresolved. The Government of South Africa was bent upon isolating them and also to discourage further immigration. To this effect, there had been introduced a bill requiring every Indian to register himself. It gave to the white police officers the authority to enter the house of Indians to check up their permits. Gandhi felt that this measure would wash down all that he had been doing for the last twelve years. Besides the measure was humiliating. He, therefore, organized the Indians to resist the move. He set up the Passive Resistance Association to carryout the campaign. There was enthusiastic response to his move against the Black Law. The government of Smuts deceived Gandhi, by telling him that if he agreed to the voluntary registrations, the Asiatic Registration Act, as the Black Law as called, would be rendered ineffective. On the contrary the government validated the voluntary registration of the Indians and thus carried out the purpose of the Black Act. This caused distress to the Indians. Gandhi now commenced a fresh struggle with a bonfire of the Registration Certificates, which they had received in consequence of the voluntary Registration. It had the mass appeal. People got greatly involved in it. The government adopted repressive measures. Many were deported. Gandhi was imprisoned. He was put with the Kaffir Criminals for the night. Successively, he was put to hard labour. The campaign was a long drawn one. The people suffered loss of business and privations. In face of the hard hitting policy of the government, the movement lost its force.

To house the families of the Satyagrahis and to provide them with some sustenance, there were established the Tolstoy Farm in Transval. The land for it was provided by a German architect, Kallenbach. Here all the residents undertook some sort of manual work, and made the colony self-sufficient.

In consequence of a settlement the Satyagrahis were released on 1st June 1911. But the government again went back on the given undertaking. The tax on the ex-indentured labourers and their families remained unbolished; the Supreme Court invalidated the marriages not solemnized according to the Christian rules and insisted on their registration. This rendered, in law, all marriages illegal and the children born illegitimate. It was the worse that the government could do.

Gandhi, therefore, initiated a new campaign on 23 September. It began with Kasturbai and sixteen others, crossing from Phoenix settlement in Natal to Transval in disregard of prohibitory law. They were arrested. With this began the new movement. It gained momentum, despite the harsh policy of the government. In support of the movement, Gopal Krishan Gokhle, who was in touch with Gandhi went out on a fund raising campaign in Bombay. Associations to raise funds were formed in various parts of the country as well. The Viceroy, Lord Hardinge too expressed sympathy for the Indian cause in South Africa. Finally, the settlement that followed provided some relief.

In the South Africa, Gandhi again and again rose against the self-indulgence, political bluff and the ricial snobbery of the white regime. He had the feel of the differences that were insisted upon between mea and man, black and white, poor and rich. The white civilization sustained all sorts of discriminations. Gandhi was unhappy over it. It was insensible to him. He believed in the basic unity of mankind. He was free from hate, and free from prejudice. During his South African tour, Gokhle had the feel of the work done by Gandhi. He recognized his work fully. Speaking of Gandhi he said that he is "made of the stuff of which heroes and martyrs are made. Nay, more, he has in him the marvellous spiritual power to turn ordinary men around him into heroes and martyrs". Gandhi emerged great from his South African experience though the experiments and the struggles, he remained involved did not bring forth the expected results.

All the same their importance cannot be under-valued. He finally decided to be back home. He chose to come via England as the possibility of war (1914-18) breaking out was imminent. He reached England on August 6 when that country had already declared war on August 4, 1914. He fully engaged himelf in helping to mobilize the resources for war. He wished the Indian residents there to co-operate with the British in their war efforts. He raised during his stay an ambulance unit as well. This he did despite the manner, the British had disowned their responsibility towards the Indian settlers in South Africa.

Thus, he rendered remarkable service in South Africa.

(iii) Gandhi in Action

The year nineteen fifteen was the year of beginnings and of endings. On January 9, Gandhi landed at the Appollo Bunder in Bombay to the warm welcome of the people. It was followed by a succession of receptions by the social organizations and the elite. At all these occasions his inner depths coupled with his modesty and simplicity left a deep impression on the people around. The imperial government taking him to be a safe politician of the moderate view invested him with the Kaiser-i-Hind gold medal. The Governor of Bombay Lord Willingdon, felt contrained to impress upon him his willingness to be available at anytime, he proposed to "take any step concerning the government". Gandhi soon got, busy in acquainting himself with the national politics. The moderates having lost their political appeal to the people, suffered further set back in the death of Gopal Krishan Gokhle in February. The Extremists were in dismay : Lajpat Rai was in exile : Aurobindo had renounced politics and Tilak had just been released. The political stage was thus vacant: the people were looking for a leader to appear. The activities of Home Rule League and of Mrs. Annie Besant had limited appeal. Gandhi did not show in the beginning the keenness to join the fray. He felt bound to the promise, he had given to Gokhale to study the national political scene for one year. He remained thus aloof. Besides, he was not willing to lend his support to any agitation against the British "during the war".

While Gandhi was on his way back from the South Africa, eighteen children along with Maganlal had come from Phoenix Farm. To house them, was established the Satyagaraha Ashram at Ahmedabad. Here were also housed the relatives and associates of those who had joined in the struggle in the South Africa. Later, due to inadequate accommodation and the out-break of plague, the Ashram was removed to the banks of river Sabarmati; hence the name. It came up as a self contained Ashram colony covering 150 acres.

The lot of indigo tenants of Champaran in Bihar was first to attract the attention of Gandhiji. The European Indigo planters and factory owners had imposed arrangements, extremely unjust on the tenants. Besides they were subjected to illegal exactions, racial discrimination and privations. Since the planters had links with the authorities they showed no care or concern for law and the humans. To make up their loss, which they were suffering now, due to the availability of the German synthetic indigo, they applied further squeezes on the tenants. The issue was taken up in 1916 session by the National Congress. At this time Gandhi did not feel interested. He was however, induced to visit Champaran by Raj Kumar Shukla, a peasant from that place. Gandhi studied the tenants problems and felt convinced of the wrong they were suffering. He look up their cause with the government. It finally felt constraint to take action, The relief it provided, was limited but they were relieved of the fear-grip that the European planters had instilled in them.

The textile indusry of Ahmedabad and the workers were looked in a Bonus dispute. The British collector of Ahmedabad induced Gandhi to resolve the conflict. After he hammered out a settlement the mill owners backed out. In protest Gandhi organized a strike on the principle of Satyagraha. Since the workers could not sustain the protest, there developed discontent amongst them. He went on fast to rally the workers. This brought pressure on the mill owners. They agreed to refer the issue to an arbitration; and the decision that followed went in favour of the workers.

The failure of crop caused distress to the peasants of Kheda district, in Bombay. They demanded total remisison of revenue. The local and the provincial government did not agree to their demand. Gandhi as the head of the Gujarat Sabha, took up the cause of the peasantry. He demanded the appointment of a committee to inquire in the whole affair but the authorities did not agree to it. Finally, Gandhi and Vallabhbhai Patel made the peasantry launch a Satyagraha. It began with the non-payment of revenue in the face of threats of confiscation of land and other property. Finally, the government declared that the land revenue should be charged only if a peasant is in a position to pay. In consequence, Gandhi withdrew the compaign. This Satyagraha had the effect of liberating the peasantry from the fear of officialdom.

(iv) Amritsar Tragedy

Gandhi exerted himself fully in securing for the government, the co-operation of the people, in their war efforts. In view of the growing

German thrust on the westen front, the viceroy in 1918 summoned a war conference to secure the co-operation of the leaders and of the people in their efforts. Gandhi too attended it. This all, he did with the expectation that the British would, once they were out of trouble, concede the self-government. But true to their exploitative colonial ways and to their imperialist overtaking mannerism, after their victory they forgot all about their secured co-operation. They instead brought forth the Rowlatt Bill (1919), curtailing the civil liberties of the people. It now obliterated the faith of the people in the Raj. Gandhi felt constrained to describe the Government in India as 'satanic'. He initiated Satyagraha to make the government to withdraw the bill. The movement was intended to be non-violent, but as violence broke at several places it was withdrawn. He resorted to a three days fast, to at one for it. In the already existing tense situatiuon, on the Baisakhi day (April 13) Brg. General Dyer carried out the brutalities in Jallianwalla Bagh. This massacre, the leaders and commons took to be the specimen of imperial rascality. The Congress appointed a fact finding committee with Gandhi as one of is members. This gave him the opportunity to see the wrong that the 'martial-law regime had caused to the people. He demanded, therefore, the recall of Dyer. He felt convinced that "the system of government which he had been trying to mend needed to be ended".

It goes without saying that this tragic incident created anger and animosity among the Indians.

(v) His Role in Freedom Struggle

Non-co-operation Movement

The publication of the Hunter Committee Report, on the Jallianwalla Bagh had neither a word of regret nor of repentence over the happenings. It was as such taken to be indicative of the temper of the government. This added intensity to the existing situation. Meanwhile, the orthodox among the Musalmans, at this time were unhappy with the British over the abolition of the Khilafat in Baghdad in consequence of the peace settlement with Turkey. This growing situation, Gandhiji used, to bring Hindus and Muslims together. He was now preparing to appear on the national stage to launch a fresh movement. Tilak had died in August 1920 and there was the need for national leadership. Thus, in September, Gandhi presented to the congress a non-cooperation programme, supported also by the Khilafat committee. It consisted of boycott of British established institutions such as the legislative councils, courts and schools; and of the British manufactured goods such as textiles. Gandhi held that with adequate response to programme, "Swaraj could be attained in one year". There was not less opposition to the programme. To Jawaharlal, Gandhi's definition of Swaraj was "delightfully vague", and Subhas Chandra Bose described the time limit of one year, to secure Swaraj "not only unwise but childish". Decision to this effect was taken at the special session at Calcutta and the same was confirmed at Nagpur session in December 1920. Gandhiji now emerged as the prime-mover on the national stage.

The movement gained stready momentum. The Prince of Wales, who was in the country on a royal visit felt the 'brooding silence' as he described it, wherever, he went. It caused him embarrassment. In November 1921 the provincial Congress committees were authorized to launch civil disobedience and to refuse the payment of taxes. Gandhi was now thinking of initiating mass civil disobedience in Bardoli. But, before, that could be initiated, there occurred the Chauri Chaura (a small village in Gorakhpur, U.P.) incident on February 3, 1922. Gandhi could not reconcile with the violence that broke out there. He felt that in miscalculating the preparedness of the nation for a non-violent movement, he had made a "Himalayan miscalculation". Thus, instinctively on February 24 he suspended the mass civil disobedience movement. He was soon arrested on the charge of sedition and imprisoned for six years.

The movement apparerntly sescured nothing. Many were left to suffer and many others thinking and guessing yet, it initiated the people to action, to self-denial and to self-sacrifice. The mass response to the new method was revealing of their dissillusionment of the Raj besides the might of collectivity was felt at all levels. With this ended finally the era of humble petitions and of requests. There was, hereafter, no drawing upon the mythical figures, historical heroes and on the religious beliefs. Gandhi set the people on the new political highway of secular politics.

The Hindu Muslim unity, during the period under study, had proved its vitality. The government was quick to note potentiality of its danger to their interest. It began to blook for the new avenues to work out divide et imperia. The elections and mistry making under the Act of 1919, provided it the opoportunity to exploit the situation. There was the Moplah riots in 1921 in Malabar which brought death and destruction to Hindus. In the Punjab, Fazli Hussain, a minister was keen at ousting Hindus and Sikhs "from positions of advantage held by them in the administration". Cow slaughter, the fanatics, again claimed to be their religious belief. The Congress-Khilafat committee honey-moon was thus rendered to be a short lived affair.

Meanwhile, also in consequence of elections C.R. Das, Motilal Nehru and V.J. Patel in disregard to the wishes of Gandhiji joined the council with the avowed object of "wrecking the legislature from within". They orgnaized the Swaraj Party (1923).

His Twenty-one Day Fast

Following an attack of appendicitis, Gandhi was released on February 5, 1924. The happenings outside the jail especially the communal riots, were most to his distaste. To help restore the communal peace he resorted to twenty-one day fast in September, in the house of Muhammad Ali. He now, took up the cause of communal harmony, removal of untouchability and the boycott of foreign goods as his immediate programme. He spoke of Charkha, as the remedy for the elimination of the dire poverty. Besides, to establish connect with the communality, he went on a cross-country tour. For the following few years, he tried to remain away from the politics.

Dandi March — Civil Disobedience Movement

The political lull that followed the non-political activity of Gandhi had for the time put the political issue in the background. The Congress factions, headed by Motilal Nehru, meanwhile, hammered out a compromise acceptable to Gandhi. It was agreed that if by December 31, 1929, the Dominion Status was not "granted the Congress, would demand complete independence." This compromise brought Gandhi back to politics. He was requested to be the president of the Congress; which he declined. He preferred to have some younger man to hold the office. He decided under the influence of Motilal for Jawaharlal.

At the Congress session, held at Lahore on December 31, 1929, Independence was declared to be the aim of the Congress, January 26, was declared to be the Independence Day. It was observed with great enthusiasm and the pledge : "it was crime against man and God to submit to British rule". Gandhi making the best of the psychological situation commenced the civil disobedience movement on March 11, at 6.30 a.m. when he began from Sabarmati the 24 mile march to Dandi on the sea coast, to break the salt law. He declared that he would not return to the Ashram, till the Salt Tax was repealed. The movement gained steady momentum. Gandhi was jailed on May 5, 1930, at Karadi a village near Dandi. This generated enthusiastic protest and stimulated the Satyagraha further more.

The Government met the situation with full might. With "the sternest repression which nationalism had known in India", it suppressed the movement. It was, however, realized that the repression alone would not do. The turmoil in which country was could not resolve the constitutional question. The government, therefore, settled on a policy of conciliation. Gandhi and the members of the working committee were released on January 25, 1931. There followed the negotiations and in consequence Gandhi agreed, to discontinue the civil disobedience and to participate in the Second Round Table Conference at London. The Delhi agreement or the Gandhi-Irwin Pact as it is called, left many issues connected with the Civil disobedience unresolved. This to Jawaharlal was a "tremendous shock". Others described it the "consolation prize". The people remained on the whole restive. Gandhi attended the Conference as the sole representative of the Congress.

Second Round Table Conference

The composition of the conference was an ordered arrangement. There were the princes and the big zamindars, investured persons and communal props-up, the spokesmen of the vested interests and the political expectants. They were there to nod their heads, to raise their hand and to speak in their master's voice; indeed in one voice. Gandhi found himself a stranger in this agglomeration of contradictory interests. He spoke at length and explained the representative and national character of the Congress. He demanded Purna Swaraj meaning "Complete Independence". He demanded for the country an esteemed partnership with Britain.

He did the plain speaking. He felt that in the unhopeful situation he had found himself, it was not worthwhile to stay further. He, therefore, left England and was back home on December 28, 1931. On his arrival, he was immediately arrested and lodged in the Yervada prison. There were protests and demonstration against it; the already existing tense situation, was thus rendered more tense. The government resorted to the repression and suppression. The governmental violence made a dent on the movement. By August 1932, it lost the momentum.

The Communal Award — Fast unto Death

While Gandhiji was in prison, Ramsay MacDonald, the British Prime Minister issued the Communal Award on August 17, 1932. While it affirmed the communal representation to the Muslims and the Christians, it conceded the same now to the Harijans. The country had, already suffered a lot due to the communal representation given to the Muslims. It had weakened the national at the root and harmed the political progress of the country. Here was now a sinister move to weakened the Hindu society, by compartmentalizing it. Gandhiji resented it. In protest, he decided to go on fast unto death, from September 20, unless the Award was withdrawn. This brought forth the Poona Pact, which undid the mischief. It provided for Joint constituencies with the reserved seats of the Harijans.

Gandhiji was against all social discrimination. He was a relentless fighter against the social discrimination of the Harijans, He now launched, from the prison, a relentless campaign against it through the Harijan and the Young India. In response to "a call from within" he went on a twenty-one day fast, from May 8, 1933. On the first day of his fast, he was released from the jail. He stayed to carry out his ordeal in 'Parnakule', the house of lady Thackery, in Poona. During this period, the civil disobedience movement remained suspended. He took an opportunity to write to the viceroy for an interview, but it was not conceded. In August, he was again arrested. He was released, three days later; was again arrested and sentenced to one year's imprisonment. This time, the facilities, he had earlier, to carry out his campaign against untouchability, were refused to him. He protested, and undertook on August 15 a fast. His health suffered deterioration and in consequence, he was released.

There was the growing feeling among his followers that non-co-operation, and the Charkha may not be the real weapons to liberate the country. Doubts were being raised and misgivings nursed in general about the effectiveness of this methodology. This whispering made Gandhi unhappy. He felt that his fifteen years teaching had not brought about the required response from his followers. In October, 1934, he, therefore, retired from the Congress. He decided to undertake social work and village unlift work. His friend and disciple, Jamnalal Bajaj, gave him a plot of land in Segaon, a village near Wardha. This settlement, developed into a colony and was named Sevagram. Here, he now, settled down, to conducted experiments for village uplift. The Sevagram, soon gained prominence.

The constitutional issue had remained unresolved all along. The appointment of the Simon Commission (1927) was followed by the publication of its Report (1930). The session of the Round-Table Conference (1930-31), the Gandhi Irwin Pact (1931) and the Communal Award and the Poona Pact (1932) were now followed by the publication of the White-Paper, and finally the Government of India Act 1935. This Act, according to the Manchester Guardian, as quoted by Dawan, seemed "like self-government in India, and "like British Raj", at Westminister. Here, doubts and misgivings were, raised about the several provisions of the Act. Gandhiji. however, supported it, as he said to "avoid a bloody revolution and a mass civil disobedience movement". The Congress, however, was assured by the viceroy that the governors would be keen to co-operate with the ministers and would not invoke unnecessarily the special provisions of the Act. The Congress finally accepted the provincial part, and rejected the Central part of the Act.

The Second World War 1939-45 broke out in Europe. On September 3, England joined the war and the Viceroy, Victor Alexander John Marquis of Linlithgow (1936-43), affirmed that the war had "broken out" and made the proclamation of the government's association with it. Gandhiji made known his willingness to provide the moral support to the government, if it would give a definite assurance of freedom after the war. The offer was not responded. Therefore, Gandhiji, to register his protest, decided to launch the individual Satyagraha. The individuals, to offer the Satyagraha, were selected by Gandhiji himself. It was a form of "Individual Civil Disobedience". The protest commenced on October 17, 1940. Apart from the arrests the government made, it was least influenced. This Individual, civil Disobedience, was now substituted by the "Representative Satyagraha". The Satyagrahis, now came, as the group representatives, representing the group like the Congress Working Committee, the Congress members of the legislatures, etc. This too proved ineffective.

The Cripps Mission

The war, meanwhile, had gained momentum. Japan rolled up the French, the Dutch and the British empires in the South-East Asia. The fall of Singapore, on February 15, 1942 at their hands, was sensational. It caused much uneasiness to the allies for its nearness to India. The President of U.S.A. is said to have influenced the British Prime Minister, Sir Winston Chruchill to attend to the Indian problem. For this, he is said to have sent Sir Stafford Cripps, a member of his Cabinet, with a draft proposal for the constitutional settlement. The proposals did not promise any immeidate change. These were for the future, to be implemented after the war. Gandhiji did not feel impressed by these. The mission was a failure. The political dead lock continued. And, for the time being, the possibility of any further negotiation on the issue looked a remote possibility.

The growing danger from Japan, the British disinterestedness to solve the constitutional issue, and the growing tense political situation made Gandhiji feel that the British should recognise India as an independent state and "then alone can there be irresistable opposition to Japanese aggression". Following this, he held "Whatever the consequences...to India her real safety and of Britain too lie in an orderly and timely British writhdrawâl from India". To this effect, he also wrote in the Harijan :

"Leave India in God's hands or in modern parlance, to anarchy. Then all parties will, fight one another, like dogs, or will, when real responsibility faces them, come to a reasonable agreement". The Congress working committee at Wardha, on July 14, 1942 took the decision that the "British Rule in India must end immediately". This resolution was adopted by the All India Congress Committee on the night of August 8, at its Bombay session. In the early hours of the morning of August 9, by a sudden and an unexpected move, Gandhiji and the members of the Working committee were arrested. It dazed the people. There followed protests all over the country. Violence erupted; post offices, police stations, railway tracts etc. were destroyed. The decisive move of the government, encouraged the police to violence; it in turn provoked more violence. The Viceroy, all the same, accused Gandhiji of supporting violence. It pained, the great apostle of peace, the most. He went on a twenty-one day fast from February 10, 1943, to seek 'a soothing balm'. The British ferosity, meanwhile, had succeeded in levelling down the agitation. The deadlock, however, continued.

During his arrest, Gandhiji had suffered personal loss in the death of Mahadev Desai, whom he described as his "Son, Secretary and lover rolled into one." So also, Kasturba his devoted wife, companion and friend died. She wished, that she 'should be cremated in a Sari made from yarn spun by him (Gandhiji)".

Gandhiji was released on May 6, 1944. On June 17, he wrote to Lord Wavell, the Viceroy (1943-47), appointed in place of Linlithgow who had since been recalled, for permission to meet the members of the Congress Working Committee. It was refused. He wrote to Churchill, to the same end. Nothing followed.

The Muslim League, in 1940 had declared, the establishment of Pakistan as its political aim. This, Gandhiji had described, as being neither in the interest of the Muslims nor in that of the country. He was against the two Nation theory, as postulated by the Muslim League. With this, the wedge between the Congress and the League went deeper. The British, exploiting the situation, attributed the failure to resolve the constitutional dead lock to the; Hindu-Muslim discord. Gandhiji, therefore, despite his reservations on Pakistan, addressed himself to Muhammad Ali Jinnah. The Gandhi-Jinnah talks, that followed, attracted much public interest. But Jinnah, never was less than adamant in his demand. He made, the partition of the country as the pre-condition for his co-operation for Independence. Gandhiji did not agree to it. The talks failed.

The international situation, meanwhile, had changed in favour of the allies. They had come out successful in the war. But, their apparent success and the peace that followed it was deceptive. They had now broken up into two ideological camps : The Capitalist, which included the Western countries headed by USA., and the Communist, the East-European countries leadered by USSR. The shooting war yielded place to the cold war between he one time allies even before all matter of peace had been settled. In England, the General Elections, that followed the peace brought the Socialist under Clement Attlee to form the govenment. Their assessment of the Indian stiuation was, as put forth by one of the members of the Cabinet Mr. Alexander as "Volcanic". "The Indian authorities were literally sitting on the top of Volcano and as a result the situation which has risen after the war, the out-break of revolution might be expected at any time". The Government, therefore, constituted a high powered Cabinet mission to hammer out the political solution. The mission reached here in March 1946. They took Gandhi in confidence formally and informally. He felt convinced of their intention to find out a settlement and the commended their efforts.

League and its Demand

The League to wrest Pakistan, the ethics of which, Jinnah was never inclined to discuss, declared August 16 as the Direct Action Day. It was declared a Public holiday, in Bengal, which was run by the League ministry. The day began with arson and plunder, murder of men and disparagement of women; desecretion of temples and all the unimagined of brutalities against the Hindu minority. The devil's dance, under the Government patronage went on unabated. The League, used this "forged weapon" in the Muslim majority Province of Punjab, which was under the Unionist Government. The air was full of anarchy. Destruction of human life and property that went on caused immense dismay to Gandhiji. It was repugnant to his nature, contrary to his ethics and in contradiction to his teaching. He, therefore, went out on a peace mission to provide the solace to the afflicted. He toured East Bengal, stayed in the villages and gave a word of consolation to the suffering. The people in Bihar reacted to the developments in Bengal, even though the government, effectively kept the situation under control. Gandhiji went there, came to seek protection of the Muslim minority. The killings in the Punjab were going on unchecked. It made Gandhiji more sad. "We are nearing a civil war", was his feeling. Central Government, as headed by Wavell, was inactive and ineffective. The Viceroy was recalled.

The Partition

The new Governor General, Lord Mountbatten reached here in March 1947. Quickly, he got down to the business; he had come to perform the final act. He did not accept the advice of Gandhi to invite Jinnah to form the Government. It was to him unpolitical. Jinnah, on his part, was in ordinately adamant on securing the Pakistan. The June 3, plan, finally conceded it to League. The Congress had to agree; and it accepted the unacceptable, the Two Nation theory and the consequent patrition. After the partition arrangements had been effected, India, minus the territory that came to be named Pakistan, became a Dominion on August 15, 1947.

Thus, with great efforts of Gandhiji India achieved its long pending Independence.

(vi) Martyrdom

What followed was tragic. The communal riots with all the diabolism, the mass movement of minorities across the newly demarcated frontiers; suspicions, doubts and misgivings against those not following the majority religion, characterized these agonizing days. It was unbearable to Gandhi. He resorted to fast on Ist September, so that the sanity may come those involved in these undoing acts. It caused immense anxiety to every one. The people, in Delhi, pledged to maitnain peace and he was made to give up his decision to go on fast. The happenings in the Punjab and Bengal; and the inexplicable sufferings of the involved made moments long and days endless. Again, this man of peace, on January 13, 1948 decided to go on fast so that the peace may come to the people. He yielded, this time too to the pressure; the people assured him that if they failed to keep their promise to maintain the communal harmony, he could resort to fast unto death. Such a situation did not arise. On January 30, 1948, when Gandhiji, was on his way to the prayer meeting, at the Birla House, New Delhi, with palms in namaskar to the assembled, he fell to the assassin's bullet, with 'He Ram' on his lips. The Hero, went bidding the farewell to the loved but now sobbing multitudes, everywhere, in the country leaving behind, the hallow to inspire, the generations to come.

(vii) Gandhian Thought

Mahatma Gandhi, an originator of a new era, was one of the greatest personalities of modern India. He was a deeply religious man. Gandhiji spiritualised politics and liberalised religion. He believed in the close relationship of religion and polities. He was a great political saint. The various sources of inspiration which moulded Gandhi's thought and philosophy are summarised as under :

(a) *Various Influences on Candhian thought and Philosophy.* Western *Influence on Gandhi's Thought and Philosophy*

Mahatma Gandhi was influenced not only by Western thinkers but also by Indian heritage. It is said that Gandhi's thought and philosophy was influenced by the three great personalities of the world...Tolstoy, Ruskin and Thoreau. He came in close contact with the literature of these personalities in South Africa. The study of this literature left a deep impression on his life. Gandhi's first biographer calls him a disciple of Tolstoy, a Russian novelist commonly known as Christian Anarchist. Gandhi also considered himself a devoted admirer of him. To quote him, "Tolstoy is one of the three moderns who have exerted the greatest spiritual influence on my life; the third being Ruskin." Gandhi made an intensive study of the works of Tolstoy, especially his *The Kingdom of God is Within You.* It had a profound influence on his thought and life. In his own words, 'Tolstoy's *Kingdom of God is Within You*' overwhelmed me. It left an abiding impression on me...Its readings turned me of my scepticism and made me a firm believer in *ahimsa.*" He again said, "I made too an intensive study of Tolstoy's books. *The Gospel in Brief What to do* and such other books made impressions on me." According to Tolstoy, Love is one of the adequate solutions for all humans problems. To quote him, "The renunciation of all opposition by force...means the law of love unperverted by sophistries. Love, or in other words the striving of men's souls towards unity and the submissive behaviour to one another that results therefrom, represents the highest and indeed the only law of life...any employment of force is incompatible with love as the highest law of life and...as soon as the use of force appears permissible even in a single case, the law itself is immediately negatived." Tolstoy condemned the state and its machinery, law courts, police and military, institution of private property capitalism, schools, etc. He also opposed the use of force, payment of taxes, compulsory military service, etc. He believed in informal co-operation instead of organised society. Tolstoy wanted to bring about such co-operation by method of love, non-resistance and non-co-operation. Like him, Gandhi too believed in non-violence. Both were, against the modern civilization as based on force and exploitation. Both laid stress on the reform of the individual for his inner self-perfection by love. Both believed in the purity of means and preached extreme simplicity of life, bread-labour celibacy, etc.

However, Gandhi was not a thorough-going Tolstoyan. In fact, as Dr. O.P. Goyal remarks, "it is doubtful whether Gandhi owes the origin of Satyagraha to Tolstoy or not, of course, it is obvious that he found in Tolstoy's views a Western confirmation of what he was doing in Transval". Even Gandhi himself admitted that one needs not accept all that Tolstoy says. Both differed in their methods. Tolstoy was a pacifist whereas Gandhiji was a Satyagrahi. Gandhi was more practical than Tolstoy.

Tolstoy was opposed to violence and force in all its forms whereas Gandhi followed the ideal of the Gita, action without attachment.

John Ruskin's *Unto This Last* also influenced Gandhi's thought and philosophy. In the words of Gandhi, "The one book that brought about an instantaneous and practical transformation in my life was Unto this Last. I translated it later into Gujarati entitling it Sarvodaya (The welfare of all). I believe that I discovered some of my deepest convictions reflected in this great book of Ruskin and that is why it so captured me and made me trans form my life." He read this book in South Africa and drew it three principles namely :

1. That the good of the individual is contained in the good of all.
2. That the lawyer's work has a same value as the barber's in as much as all have the same right of earning their livelihood from their work.
3. That a life of the labour, *i.e.*, the life of the tiller of the soil and the handicraftsman, is the life worth living.

Like Ruskin Gandhi preached the supremacy of the spirit and trust in the nobleness of human nature. Both regarded character as more important than intelligence. Both wanted to spiritualise politics : both distasted machinery. However, Gandhi differed from Ruskin in some spheres. They differed in their views on the natures and functions of the sate. Ruskin, like Gandhi did not accept non-violence in principle. Unlike Gandhi again, Ruskin believed in the extension of the sphere of state interference.

Another thinker who influenced the life and thought of Gandhi was Henry David Thoreau, the well known American anarchist who refused to pay his taxes as a protest against slavery system in America was the first to use the term 'Civil Disobedience'. However, Gandhi did not borrow his idea of Civil Disobedience from the works of Thoreau. However, it may be noted as Dr. O.P. Goyal remarks, "that Gandhi read this essay only when he was in jail as a result of his Satyagraha Campaign. Thus, the essay confirmed, elaborated and provided detailed suggestions for the conduct of his movements, but was not the source of his non-violent techniques." Gandhi was also impressed by Thoreau's ideas on the nature and functions of the state.

Indian Influences on Gandhi's Thought and Philosophy Thus, Tolstoy, Ruskin and Thoreau, were the three great influences on the making of Gandhi's thought and philosophy. He had many similarities with these great personalities. Gandhi himself admitted that these three great personalities had left a great impact on him. However, in spite of these western influences Gandhian thought is typically Indian. India is a land of great traditions, religions and great ideals. Gandhi being a typical Indian had inherited and also later on acquired his philosophy and way of life from some of these traditions. Thus, writings of Tolstoy, Ruskin and Thoreau only deepened and strengthened the convictions which had already gained a good place in the mind and heart of Gandhi.

Gandhi was born in Kathiawad (Porbander). He was greatly influenced by the way of life of that area. Gandhi inherited from his ancestors their uncompromsing sense of honour and their deep and profound faith in Vaishnavism. The atmosphere of his family was religious and people of different faiths were invited to discuss the religious matters from different angles. So Gandhi retained a firm and unshakable faith in his own religion but he always showed not only toleration but equal respect for their religions.

Of the books that have influenced the thought and philosophy of Gandhi, the Gita easily comes the first. He read the *Bhagavad Gita* in England in 1888-89 and began to regard it a spiritual book. For long, he read the Gita daily and derived inspiration and took guidance from it from time to time. In the words of Gandhi, ".... Hinduism as I know it entirely satisfies my soul, fills my whole being, and I find a solace in the *Bhagavad Gita* and the *Upanishads* that I miss even in the Sermon on the Mount....when doubt haunts, me, when disappointments stare me in the face, and when I see not one ray of light on the horizon, I turn to the *Bhagavad Gita,* and find a verse to comfort me, and I immediately begin to smile in the midst of overwhelming sorrow. My life has been full of external tragedies and if they have not left any visible and indelible effect on me, I owe it to the teachings of the *Bhagavad Gita*". The central theme of the Gita, according to Gandhi, regarding the way to self-realisation is the ideal of *nishkam karma i.e.,* action without desire for the result.

Gandhi inherited the idea of non-violence from Indian traditions. The tradition of non-violence is deeply rooted and continuous in our country. It is correctly regarded to be India's greatest contribution to the world thought. All religions in India preach non-violence as the highest moral duty. To quote Gandhi, "Non-violence is a universal law acting under all circumstances; disregard of it is the surest way to destruction". Similarly, Jainism and Buddhism had a great impact on Gandhi's thought and philosophy. Ahimsa or non-violence is the basic principle of the Jaina Philosophy. Gujarat is the strong hold of Jainism where Gandhi was born and brought up. But unlike Jaina Philosophy Gandhi laid emphasis on the positive aspect of *ahimsa. Buddism,* which believes in *ahimsa* both as love and avoidence of injury to self and others, influenced Gandhi.

Gandhi also had useful contacts with the top leaders of Indian Nationalist movement before he entered the scene of India's national struggle. His work in South Africa was appreciated by all the Indian nationalist leaders, which were divided into two schools of thought called — 'the Moderates' and the 'Extremists', Gandhi met different leaders in India in 1896. In his autobiography, he recorded his impressions. "Sir Pherozeshah had seemed to me like the Himalayas, the Lokmanya like the ocean. But Gokhale was as the Ganges. One could have a refreshing bath in the holy river. The Himalayas was unscalable and one could not easily launch forth on the sea, but the Ganges invited one to its bosom...." Gandhi regarded Gokhale as his political Guru. To quote him, "He was and remains for me the most perfect man on the political field. Not, therefore, that we had no differences...but that differences mattered neither to him nor to me. Nothing could part us asunder." Gandhi was greatly influenced by Gokhale's political ideas : his insistence on the purity of means and his spiritualisation of politics.

Another influence on Gandhi's thought and philosophy was that of Lokmanya Tilak. Prof. D.C. Sharma is of the view that it is Tilak's mantle that has failed on Mahatma Gandhi and not of Gokhale, though the Mahatma regards Gokhale as his political guru. For one thing, long before, Gandhiji preached his gospel of non-co-operation, Tilak... had set before the nation the whole, programme of non-co-operation". There were so many similarities between them. Both of them, Mr. T.L. Sahay remarks, "taught the classical message of 'perfect yourself to the highest aspiration of man, live in turth, live in pure nature, strive for the fulfilment of the purpose of life'. Their political philosophy was founded on this philosophy of life. Self-reliance, courage and willingness to sacrifice motivated each man and was a part of their message to all men." Above all these, 'Tilak had set before the nation the whole programme of non-co-operation which later on in the hands of Gandhi assumed the name of Satyagraha.

Conculsion Thus, Gandhi's thought and philosophy had a number of influences — Indian as well as Western. In spite of the impact of Western writings, Gandhi's ideas of the philosophy of life were deeply rooted in his mind, which had come to him....some by inheritance, some by tradition and some by his own experience which were typically Indian. Gita, Buddhism, Jainism and his own family background had produced a typically Indian saint. The writings of Tolstoy, Ruskin and Thoreau only deepened and strengthened his convictions, which had already gained a good place in the mind and heart of Gandhi.

(*b*) *Ideas on Religion and God*

Gandhiji was a firm believer in God and religion. He never separated religion from politics. He treated Truth as God. He said that religion is a part of politics as dimplomacy or any other institution. He also said that those who separated politics from religion were mistaken. However, his ideas on religion, God and separation of religion from politics can best be understood under the following headings.

Gandhi's belief in God was infinite. To him God was Truth and everything else flowed from that Truth. He wrote thus :

> "I am surer of His existence than of the fact that you and I are sitting in this room. Then I can also testify that I may live without air and water but not without Him. You pluck out my eyes, but that cannot kill me. You may chop off my nose but that will not kill me. But blast my belief in God and I am dead."

He says further that there is an indefinable mysterious power that pervades everything. "I feel it, though I do not see it." Gandhiji said, "it is this unseen power which makes itself felt and yet defies all proof, because it is so unlike all that he perceives through his senses. It is proved not by extraneous evidence but in the transformed conduct and character of those who have felt the real presence of God within. Such testimony is to be found in the experience of an unbroken line of prophets and sages of all countries and climes. To reject this evidence is to deny oneself."

'Well', said Gandhi, "it is beyond my power to induce in you a belief in God." There are some things which are self-proved, and some which are not proved at all. The existence of God is like a geometrical axiom. It may be beyond our heart-grasp. Gandhiji said that he would not talk of an intellectual grasp. Intellectual, attempts are more or less failures, as a' rational explanation cannot give you the faith in a living God. For, it is a thing beyond the grasp of reason. It transcends reason. There are numerous phenomena from which you can reason out the existence of God. Gandhiji said, "If I exist, God exists. With me it is a necessity of my being as it is with milliions. They may not be able to talk about it, but from their life you can see that it is part of their life. I am only asking you to restore the belief that has been undermined. In order to do so, you have to unlearn a lot that dazzles your intelligence and throws you off your feet. Start with the faith which is also a token of humility and an admission that we know nothing that we are less than atoms, I say atom, because the atom obeys the law of its being, whereas we in insolence of our ignorance deny the law of nature. But I have no intellectual argument to address to those who have no faith."

Gandhiji had complete faith in religion. He said, "I come forward saying that I have complete faith in religion and I do not conceal my deep faith in that." Gandhi said that Religion was essential for promoting morality. He used to say, "Most religious men I have met are politicians in disguise. I, however, wear the guise of a politician but am at heart a religious man." It was wrong to believe that the life of a man can be divided an one aspect separated from the other. Gandhiji, said that the whole gamut of man's activities constitutes an indivisible whole; you cannot divide social, economic political and purely religious work into water-tight compartments. There is religion apart from human activities. It provides a moral basis to all activities which they would otherwise lack reducing life to a maze of sound and fury signifying nothing.

Gandhiji was of the view that Religion, being the means of communion with God and the sustaining force, is the vital current that should pervade activity. He said that the root of religion is 'That which binds'. The root-meaning of its Sanskrit equivalent Dharma is 'That which holds'. It sustains a person, which nothing else does. It is reckbottom, fundamental morality. When morality becomes religion, because it binds, it holds, it sustains him in the hour of trial.

Man's ultimate aim is the realisation of God, and all his activities social, political and religious have to be guided by the ultimate aim of the vision of God. The immediate service of all human beings becomes a ncessary part of the endeavour, simply because the only way to find God is to see Him in His crtation and be one with it. This can only be done by service of all.

(c) Religion and Politics

Gandhiji did not conceive politics as divorced from religion. He said that religion should pervade everyone of our actions. Here religion does not mean sectarianism. It means a belief in ordered moral government of the Universe. It is not less real because it is unseen. This religion transcends Hinduism, Islam, Christianity, etc. It does not supersede them. It harmonises them and gives them reality.

He said, "There is no politics without religion, not the religion of the superstitious and the blind, the religion that hates and fights, but the universal religion of toleration, Politics without morality is a thing to be avoided."

Gandhi is of the view that politics bereft of religion is absolute dirt, ever to be to shunned. Politics concerns nations and that which concerns the welfare of nations must be one of the concerns of a man who is religiously inclined.

Gandhiji is of the firm view that religion cannot be separated from politics. He says that to see the universal and all pervading spirit of Truth

(God) face to face, one must be able to love the meanest of creation as one-self. And a man who aspires after that cannot afford to keep out of any field of life. That is why Gandhiji says, "Devotion to Truth has drawn me into the field of politics; and I can say without the slightest hesitation and yet in all humility that those who say that religion has nothing to do with politics, do not know what religion means".

Gandhiji remarks, "I could not be leading a religious life unless I identified myself with the whole mankind and that I could not do unless I take part in politics. The whole gamut of man's activities today constitutes an indivisible whole. You cannot divide social, economic, political and purely religious work into watertight compatments. I do not know religion apart from human activity. It provides a moral basis to all other activities which they would otherwise lack, reducing life to a maze of sound and fury signifying nothing."

(*d*) *His Concept of Satyagraha and Non-Violence*

Gandhiji attached too much importance to non-violence. He preached non-violent resistance, named Satyagraha to fight out British imperialism from India. Even when Czechoslovakia was invaded by Hitler, he advised Czechs to resort to non-violent resistance. He says : "We have to make Truth and non-violence not matters for mere individual practice, but for practice by groups, communities and nations. That, at any rate, is my dream. Ahimsa (non-violence) is the attribute of the soul, and, therefore, to be practised by everybody in all the affairs of life." He further says, "I swear by non-violence because I know that it alone conduces to the highest good of mankind, not merely in the next world but in this also. I object to violence because when it appears to do good, the good is only temporary, the evil it does is permanent."

Gandhiji attaches utmost importance to non-violence and says that the religon of non-violence is not meant merely for the Rishis and Saints. It is meant for the common people as well. Non-violence is the law of our species as violence is the law of the brute... . Non-violence in its dynamic condition means conscious suffering. It does not mean submission to the will of the evil doer, but it means the putting of one's whole soul against the will of the tyrant. The ideal society being based on non-violence, the control of the federation over the units will be purely moral and in no way coercive.

In fact, Gandhiji's philosophy of non-violence may be considered as the mightiest force at the disposal of mankind. Gandhiji says that non-violence does not admit of running away from danger and leaving dear ones unprotected. Not knowing the stuff of which non-violence is made, many have honestly believed that running away from danger every time was a virtue compared to offering resistance, especially when it was fraught with danger to one's life. As a teacher of non-violence, I must, as it is possible for me, guard against such an unmanly belief". He emphasises that unless the world adopts non-violence it will spell certain suicide for mankind. Gandhiji preaches non-violence of thought, belief and action. He says that the basic principle on which the practice of non-violence rests is that what holds good in respect of oneself, equally applies to the whole universe. Gandhiji points out the basic difference between non-violence and cowardice as follows : "If you believe that there is only a choice between cowardice and violence, I would advice violence."

Violence is a comprehensive category and is manifested both at the personal and the institutional levels. Evil thoughts, sentiments of revenge and brutality, verbal pugnacity and even accumulation of unnecessary things represent examples of personal violence. Falsehood, trickery, intrigues, chicanery and deceitfulness are also forms of violence, according to the comprehensive connotation given to the term by Gandhiji. Physical punishments, imprisionment, capital punishment and wars represent examples of violence committed by government. Economic exploitation and strangulation of others are also manifestations of violence. Even excess of emulation and competition can become species of violence. Non-violence or Ahimsa is, therefore, equally comprehensive and represents the total neutralization of violence in all forms.

His Concept on Satyagraha

Gandhiji in his autobiography explained the incidence of the birth of Satyagraha. He says, "The principle called Satyagraha came into being before that name was invented. Indeed when it was born, I could not myself say what it was. In Gujarati also we used the English phrase 'passive resistance' to describe it. When in a meeting of Europeans I found that the term 'passive resistance' was too narrowly construed, that it was supposed to be a weapon of the weak, that it could be characterised by hatred, and that it could finally manifest itself as violence, I had to demur all these statements and explain the real nature of the Indian movement. It was clear that a new word must be coined by the Indians to designate their struggle. But I could not for the life of me find out a new name, and therefore, offered nominal prize through 'Indian Opinion' to the reader who made the best suggestion on the subject. As a result, Magan Lal Gandhi coined the word 'Satagraha' (Sat-Truth, Agraha-firmness) and won the prize. But in order to make it clearer I changed the word to 'Satyagraha' which has since become current in Gujarati as a designation for the struggle".

To Gandhiji Satyagraha is literally holding on to Truth and it means, therefore, Truth-force. Truth is soul or spirit. It is, therefore, know as soul-force. It excludes the use of violence, because man is not capable of knowing the absolute truth and, therefore, not competent to punish. The word was coined in South Africa to distinguish the non-violent resistance of the Indians of South Africa from the contemporary resistance of the suffragettes and others. It is not conceived as a "passive weapon of the weak."

> "For the past thirty years I have been preaching and practising Satyagraha. The principles of Satyagraha, as I know it today, constitute gradual evolution".

Satyagraha (non-violent resistance) differs from Passive Resistance as the North Pole from the South. The latter has been conceived as a weapon of the weak and does not exclude the use of physical force of violence for the purpose of gaining one's end, whereas, the former has been conceived as a weapon of the strongest and excludes the use of violence in any shape or form.

Its root meaning is holding on to truth, hence, Truth-force. Gandhiji says, 'I have also called it Love-force or Soul — force. In the application of Satyagraha, I discovered in the earliest stages that pursuit of truth did not admit of violence being inflicted on one's opponent but that he must be weaned from error to the other. And patience means self-suffering. So the doctrine came to mean vindication of Truth not by infliction of suffering on the opponent but on one's self.'

In a Satyagrahi, there is no room for hatred or ill will. Mahadeo Desai has well said that Satyagraha is dynamic, passive resistance is static. Passive resistance acts negatively and suffers reluctantly. Satyagraha acts positively and suffers with cheerfulness because of love and makes the sufferings fruitful. Passive resistance is not by its very nature universal in its application. It cannot be directed against one's nearest relations as Satyagraha can be. Passive resistance offered in a spirit of weakness and despair weakness the resister psychologically and morally. Satyagraha emphasises all the time internal strength and actually develops the same. Satyagraha can offer more effective and determined opposition to injustice and tyranny than passive resistance.

Its Various Techniques

The technique of Satyagraha may take the following forms :

1. Non-co-operation.
2. Civil disobedience.
3. Hijrat.

4. Fasting.
5. Strike.

1. Non-co-operation India resorted to non-co-operation under Gandhi's guidance and leadership in 1931, in the famous 'Non-co-operation Movement.' To Gandhiji non-co-operation predominantly implies withdrawing of co-operation from the state that in the non-co-operator's view has become corrupt and excludes Civil Disobedience of the fierce type described above. By its very nature, non-co-operation is even open to children of understanding and can be safely practised by the masses. Civil Disobedience presupposes the habit of willing obedience to laws without fear of their sanctions. It can, therefore, be practised only as a last resort and by a select few in the first instance at any rate. Non-co-operation, too like Civil Disobedience is a branch of Satyagraha which includes all non-violent resistance for the vindication of Truth.

To Gandhiji non-co-operation is such a powerful and pure instrument, that if it is enforced in earnest, it will be like seeking first the kingdom of God, and everything else following as a matter of course. People will have then realised their true power. They would have learnt the value of discipline, self control, joint action, non-violence, organization and everything else that goes to make a nation great and good, and not merely great.

He said that non-co-operation is possible between a prince (State) and his people. In particular circumstances it may be the people's duty. Such circumstances can exist only where the lattter are by nature fearless and are lovers of liberty. They generally appreciate the laws of the State and obey them voluntarily without fear of punishment. Reasoned and willing obedience to the laws of the State is the first lesson in non-co-operation.

The second, is that of Tolerance we must tolerate many laws of State, even when they are inconvenient. It is only when they are unworthy of tolerance and immoral that we disobey them. When a people have proved their active loyalty by obeying many laws of State, they acquire the right of civil disobedience.

The third lesson, is that of suffering. He who has not the capacity of suffering cannot non-co-operate. He who has not learnt to sacrifice his property and even his family when necessary can never non-co-operate. It is possible that a prince (State) enraged by non-co-operation will inflict all manner of punishments. There lies the test of love, patience and strength. He who is not ready to undergo the fiery ordeal cannot non-co-operate.

2. Civil Disobedience In 1940, Gandhiji permitted 'Individuals to have recourse to Civil Disobedience.' It was then termed 'Individual Civil Disobedience.' In 1930 and 1932, it was 'Mass Civil Disobedience,' and finally in 'Quit India' movement of 1942 it was 'Complete Civil Disobedience.'

The doctrine of Civil Disobedience was elucidated by Gandhiji in *Young India* thus :

Civil Disobedience is civil breach of unmoral statutory enactments. The expression was, so far as I am aware, coined by Thoreau to signify his own resistance to the laws of Slave State. He has left a masterly treatise on the duty of Civil Disobedience. But Thoreau was not perhaps an out and out Champion of non-violence. Probably, also Thoreau limited his breach of statutory laws to the revenue law, *i.e.,* payment of taxes. Whereas the term Civil Disobedience as practised in 1919 covered breach of any statutory and unmoral law, it signified the resister's outlawry in a civil, *i.e.* non-violent manner. He invoked the sanctions of the law and cheerfully suffered imprisonment. It is a branch of Satyagraha.

Mass civil-disobedience stands on a different footing. It can only be tried in a calm atmosphere. It must be the calmness of strength not weakness of knowledge nor ignorance. Individual civil disobedience may be and often is vicarious. Mass civil disobedience may be and often is selfish in the sense that individuals expect personal gain from their disobedience. Thus, in South Africa, Kallenbach and Polak offered vicarious civil disobedience. They had nothing to gain. Thousands offered it because they expected personal gain also in the shape, say, of the removal of the annual poll-tax levied upon ex-indentured men and their wives and grown-up children. It is sufficient in mass civil-disobedience if the resisters understand the working of the doctrine.

Complete civil-disobedience is a state of peaceful rebellion, refusal to obey every single state-made law. It is certainly more dangerous than an armed rebellion. For it can never be put dowen it the civil resisters are prepared to face extreme hardships. It is based upon an implicit belief in the absolute efficiency of innocent suffering. By noiselessly going to prison a civil resister ensures a calm atmosphere. The wrong-doer wearies of wrong-doing in the absence of resistance. All pleasure is lost when the victim betrays no resistance. A full grasp of the conditions of successful civil resistance is necessary at least on the part of the representatives of the people before we can launch out an enterprise of such magnitude. The quickest remedies are always fraught with the greatest danger and require the utmost skill in handling them.

3. Hijrat Another form of Satyagraha recommended by Gandhiji was Hijrat which implied voluntary exile from the permanent place of residence. This was to be done by those "who feel oppressed and cannot live without loss of self-respect in a particular place and lack the strength that comes from true non-violence or the capacity to defend themselves violently". Hijrat was recommended by Gandhiji in 1928 to the people of Bardoli and in 1939 to those of Junagarh, Vithalgad and Limbdi.

4. Fasting When all other means fail, the votary of Ahimsa, takes to fasting. Gandhiji undertook fasting many a time as a last resort. He said that fast is the last weapon in the armoury of the votary of Ahimsa. When human ingenuity fails the votary fasts, his fasting quickens the spirit of prayer, that is to say, the fasting is a spiritual act and, therefore, addressed to God. The effect of such action on the life of the people is that when the person fasting is at all known to them their sleeping conscience is awakened. But there is the danger that the people through mistaken sympathy may act against their will in order to save the life of the loved one. This danger has got to be faced. One ought not to be deterred from right action when one is sure of rightness. It can but .promote circumstances. Such a fast is undertaken in obedience to the dictates of the inner voice, and therefore, prevents haste.

Fasting unto death is an integral part of Satyagraha programme, and, it is the greatest and most effective weapon in its armoury under given circumstances. Not every one is qualified for undertaking it without a proper course of training.

Gandhiji maintained, "Of course, it is not to be denied that fasts can be really coercive. Such fasts are to attain a selfish object. A fast undertaken to bring money from a person or fulfilling some such personal end would amount to exercise of coercion or undue influence." Gandhiji says, "I would unhesitatingly advocate resistance of such undue influence. I have myself successfully resisted it in the fasts that have been undertaken or threatened against me. And if it is argued that the dividing line between a selfish and unselfish end is often very thin, I would urge that a person who regards the end of a fast to be selfish or otherwise base should resolutely refuse to yield to it, even though the refusal may result in the death of the fasting person. If people will cultivate the habit of disregarding fasts which in their opinion are taken for unworthy ends, such fasts will be robbed of the taint of coercion and undue influence, Like all human institutions, fastings can be both legitimately and illegitimately used."

5. Strike Strike was another important method advocated by Gandhiji. According to him strike was a voluntary, purificatory suffering undertaken to convert the erring opponent. Gandhiji did not believe in the theory of class war. He did not subscribe to the proposition that labour and capital must remain in the opposite camps. His view was that industry was a joint enterprise of labour and capital, and both of them were trustees. The strikers were required to put forward their demands in very clear terms. The strikers were required to learn some manual craft so that during the strike period they may not have to depend upon the strike, fund.

Rules for Satyagraha According to Gandhiji, to make satyagraha effective certain psychological and sociological conditions are required. A Satyagrahi has to follow certain rules which are as under :

1. The Satyagrahi will not harbour any hatred within his heart against the opponent.
2. The issue for which Satyagraha is launched should be true and substantial.
3. The Satyagrahi should make himself ready to undergo all kinds of humiliation and suffering. He must prepare himself even to sacrifice his life if occasion demands. Gandhiji also gives some important rules for Satyagrahis :

1. A Satyagrahi will harbour no anger.
2. He will tolerate the anger of the opponent
3. In so doing he will put up with assault from the opponent, never retaliate, but he will never submit, out of fear of punishment to any order given in anger.
4. He should voluntarily submit to arrest if an order has been given by proper authority.
5. If a civil resister has any property in his possession as a trustee, he will refuse to surrender it, even though in defending it he may lose his life. He will, however, never retaliate.
6. Non-retaliation excludes swearing and crusing.
7. A civil resister will never insult his opponent and also not take part in any of the newly coined cries which are contrary to the spirit of Ahimsa.

No wonder it is a wonderful method.

(e) His Views on Communism

K.G. Mashruwala notes that it has been often said that Gandhiji was a communist minus violence. Indeed it is possible to quote Gandhiji himself in regard to this pro-position. Gandhiji was not in the habit of rejecting descriptions of him or his principles of they were meant as compliments, and if they helped his main mission. But in a careful examination of principles, such descriptions should not be regarded as very accurate and must not be used as handy definitions. The error of such descriptions lies in their capacity to conceal the full implications of the differential factor. When it is said that Gandhism in Communism minus violence, the impression created is that the minus violence factor in Communism is some small impurity the removal of which will make it the same as Gandhism. As a matter of fact even if it were possible to so equate Gandhism in terms of Communism, the 'minus violence' factor is a major factor of considerable value. The implications of 'minus violence' are so great as to make the equations as illusory as to say that red is green minus yellow and blue or a worm is a snake minus poison.

K.G. Mashruwala is of the opinion that the difference between the philosophies of Gandhiji and Marx manifests itself in their political and economic ideas. Marx puts forth thd theories of class war and its end through the dictatorship of the proletariat, exproprìtation of land, mines and other material and the regimentation of life and labour. As against this the Gandhian theories are those of Varnadharma, Satyagraha and arbitration, decentralisation, trusteeship and as much individual liberty and democratization is possible in social life.

However, we can discuss the difference between Gandhism and Communism under the following headings :

1. Interpretation of History Communism holds that the real cause of human conflict throughout history has been property. Engles stated that Marx maintained that every fundamental historical development, regardless of the character on the surface, was the result of changes in methods of production and property relations of the particular time and that the economic motive was the main, if not the sole, explanation of human behaviour.

Gandhi, on the other hand, was of the view that the main force which has built and pushed forward the human race was the instinct of love for fellow human beings. Conflicts had been generally resolved by this love-force. Non-violence was another name for love, and Gandhiji said that if we turn our eyes to the time of which history has any record down to our own time, we shall find that man has been steadily progressing towards Ahimsa (non-violence). If we believe that mankind has steadily progressed towards Ahimsa, it follows that it has to progress towards it still further.

Gandhi had implicit faith in God and believed that not a leaf could stir without His will. Rejecting the Marxist interpretation of history, Gandhi replied to a question put to him on the subject thus :

"No, not the economic factor alone. Ultimately it is the unseen power that governs the course of events even in the minds of men who make those events. Supposing Hitler were to die today, it would alter the whole course of current history. Similarly, supposing all capitalists were wiped out as a result of an earthquake or some other natural cataclysm, the history of class war would then be changed in a way least dreamt of by the exponents of economic interpretation of history. Would not the history of the present war have been different if instead of Chamberlain a more dynamic figure had been the Prime Minister of England? Or, if Chamberlain had not shown lack of political courage at the last moment?"

2. The State withers away The final aim of Communism was 'Stateless Society', Engels said that the proletariat seizes political power and turns the means of production into State Property. But in doing this, it abolishes itself as proletariat. It abolishes the State as State. Society thus far based on class antagonism had need of the State; when at last it becomes the real representative of the whole society, it renders itself unnecessary. As soon as there is no longer any social class to be held in subjections, nothing more remains to be repressed, and a special repressive state is no longer necessary. State interference is social relations becomes in one domain after another superfluous and then it dies out of itself. The State is not abolished, it dies out.

Gandhi, on the other hand, held that creation of a stateless society through violence is not possible. Such stateless society requires highly developed spiritual values.

Communism being built on violence was short-lived and bound to perish. Gandhiji held, "Bolshevism (Communism) does not preclude the use of force, but freely sanctions it for expropriation of private property and maintaining the collective state ownership of the same. And if that is so, the Bolshevik regime in its present from cannot last for long, for it is my firm conviction that nothing enduring can be built on violence."

3. Class war Another important assumption of Communism is the theory of 'Class War'. In the 'Communist Manifesto' (1848) Marx and Engels stated : "History hitherto existing is the history of class struggles and every form of society has been based on the antagonism of oppressive and oppressed classes."

Gandhiji considered 'Class War Theory' to be basically wrong. He said that class war was foreign to the essential genius of India; and that the idea of class war did not appeal to him. He said that Socialism and Communism of the West were based on certain conceptions which were fundamentally different from ours. One such conception was their belief in essential selfishness of human nature. He says, "I do not subscribe to it for I know that essential difference between man and the brute is that the former can respond to the call of the spirit in him, can rise superior to the passions that he owns in common with the brute and, therefore, superior to selfishness and violence, which belong to the brute nature and not to the immortal spirit of man. That is the fundamental conception of Hinduism, which has years of penance and austerity at the back of discovery of this truth. That is why, we have had saints who have worn out their bodies and laid down their lives in order to explore the secrets of the soul."

4. Violent revolution From 'Class War' Communism proceeds to violent 'Revolution'. Marx said that force was the midwife of every old society pregnant with a new one. According to him, revolution springs from a revolutionary situation. Chronic discontent, dissensions amongst the members of ruling class, recurrence of crisis, depression, strikes, riots, demonstrations and ultimate break down of the old order, create this situation. Mao preaches naked violence and war to establish Communism. He says, "Every communist must grasp the truth; political power grows out of the barrel of a gun, and according to the Marxist Theory of the State, army is the chief component of the political power of the State. Whoever wants to seize the political power of the State and to maintain it, must have a strong army. Some people have ridiculed us as advocates of 'Omnipotence of War,' yes we are, which is not bad at all, but is good, and is Marxist."

During his leadership of the Indian Liberation Movement, Gandhiji denounced the use of secret and violent means. He wrote, "So far as Bolshevism is based on violence and denial of God, it repels me. I do not believe in short, violent cuts to success. Those Bolshevik friends who are bestowing their attention on me should realize that, however, much I may sympathise with and admire worthy motives, I am an uncompromising opponent of violent methods even to serve the noblest of causes."

Gandhiji categorically stated :

"Communism of the Russian type, that is Communism, which is imposed on a people, would be repugnant to India".

5. Economic Order Prof. Dikshit has well summarised the difference of economic order between Communism and Gandhism. He states that in a Communist State, first there has to be socialisation of means of production, distribution and exchange. The State owns and controls all industry, agriculture, trade and commerce, citizen owns nothing and is a paid worker. By force of arms, the State seizes and retains total hold of economy and compels the individual to work to order. The Communist Party under the command of the economic life, as of political life, is limited to members of the Communist Party. The party members have a privileged position over the non-party masses. Secondly, a Communist State stands for centralised industrialism and materialism. The intellect and resources have to be polled for these achievements alone.

Regarding Gandhism, Dikshit says that Gandhian economic set up devises an order where individual ownership and individual management of economic means is maintained, with social restraint. This order nourishes individual initiative and enthusiasm for production, and yet empowers the State of checkmate misuse by an individual through legislation. The target is a balanced adjustment between spiritualism and materialism, craze for over production is deprecated, and centralised industrialism is rejected.

6. Religion The Communists don't believe in religion. Marx writes "Religion is the opium of the people."

Engels also says that all religion, however, is nothing but the fantastic reflection in men's minds of those external forces which control their daily life, a reflection in which the terrestial forces assume the form of supernatural forces.

However, atheism has become a dogma with the Communists and with the government manned by them.

To Gandhiji God is Truth and everything else flows from that Truth. He wrote thus:

> "I am surer of his existence than of the fact that you and I are sitting in this room. Then I can also testify that I may live without air and water. But not without Him. You may pluck out my eyes, but that cannot kill me. You may chop off my nose, but that will not kill me. But blast my belief in God that I am dead". "There is an indefinable mysterious power that pervades everything. I feel it, though I do not see it. It is this unseen power which makes itself felt and yet defies all proof, because it is so unlike all that I perceive through my senses. It is proved not by extraneous evidence but in the transformed conduct and character of those who have felt the real presence of God within. Such testimony is to be found in the experience of an unbroken line of prophets and sages of all countries and climes. To reject this evidence is to deny oneself."

Gandhiji says, "It is beyond my power to induce in you a belief in God. There are some things which are self-proved and some which are not proved at all. The existence of God is like a geometrical axiom. It may be beyond our heart-grasp. I shall not talk of an intellectual grasp. Intellectual attempts are more or less failures, as a rational explanation cannot give you the faith in a living God. For it is a thing beyond the grasp of reason. It transcends reason. There are numerous phenomena from which you can reason out the existence of God, but I shall not insult your intelligence by offering you a rational explanation of that type. I would have you brush aside all rational explanations and begin with a simple child-like faith in God. If I exist, God exists. With me it is a necessity of my being as it is with millions. They may be able to talk about it, but from their life you can see that it is a part of their life. I am only asking you to restore the belief that has been underminded. In order to do so, you have to unlearn a lot that dazzles your intelligence and throws you off your feet. Start with the faith which is also a token of humility and an admission that we know thing that we are less than atoms. I say atom, because the atom obeys the law of its being, whereas, we in the insolence of our ignorance deny the law of nature. But I have no intellectual argument to address to those who have no faith."

7. Materialism and Spiritualism Communism pinned faith in materialism alone and Gandhi stood by an adjustment of spiritualism and materialism. According to Engels, necessity of nature is primary, while human will and mind are secondary. The latter must adapt themselves to the former. According to Gandhi, on the other hand, spiritual happiness and growth of man is the essence, and 'necessity of nature' has to be adjusted to spiritual needs. Gandhi denounces Russian materalism. He says that Bolshevism is the necessary result of modern materialistic civilization. Its insenate worship of matter has given rise to a school which has been brought up to look upon material advancement as the goal and which has lost touch with the final things of life.

8. Individual Freedom According to Prof. Dikshit, 'Individual freedom is totally absent in a communist state. The state is totalitarian and authoritarian and the citizen is compulsorily to conform his conduct and expression to the dictates of the Communist Party. There is no freedom of expression, assembly, or of the press. The society is drilled and dragooned where only one opinion is allowed. Private property is non-existent, and the individual has to take up the work allotted to him by the party. As a citizen he cannot claim the right to enter the party. Recruitment to the party depends on the sweet will of the High Command'.

Gandhiji said that if individual liberty goes, then surely all is lost, for if the individual ceases to count, What is leaf to Society? Individual freedom alone can make a man voluntarily surrender himself completely to the service of the society. If it is wrested from him, he becomes an automaton and society is ruined. No society can positively be built on a denial of individual freedom, it is contrary to the very nature of man.

Gandhiji was of the firm view that every individual must have the fullest liberty to use talents consistently with equal use by his neighbours, but no one is entitled to the arbitrary use of the grains from the talents. He is part of the nation, or say, the social structure surrounding him. Therefore, he can use his talents not for self only but for the social structure of which he is a part and on whose sufferance he lives.

9. The Political Structure Prof. Dikshit says that in a communist state, admission to the party is a promise of better future, Candidates for membership are selected carefully. Only a portion of those desiring to join are admitted. After a candidate has served for one year, he enjoys a privileged position and belongs to a class that technically controls the destines of the overwhelming majority of the citizens. Within the party itself, it is a very small minority, sometimes one and sometimes a few, who define, formulate and ensure execution of the decisions of the party. The party organisation substitutes itself for the party as a whole.

Gandhiji, as Prof. Dikshit says, denounced Communist totalitarianism and also deprecated British pattern of democracy. True democracy of his conception has moral authority and not force as its basis. He has named it as 'Ram Raj' (Kingdom of God). He explains it thus :

> "By political independence I do not mean an imitation of the British House of Commons or the Soviet rule of Russia or the Fascist rule of Italy or their genius. We must have ours suited to ours. What that can be is more than I can tell. I have described it as Ram Raj, *i.e.*, sovereignty of the people based on pure moral authority."

> "Independence of my conception means nothing less than the realization of the 'Kindgom of God' within you and on this earth. I would rather work for and die in the pursuit of this dream, though it may never be realized. That means infinite patience and perseverance."

Conclusion We conclude with Dikshit who beautifully remarks that the theories of the two philosophies vitally differed from each other, because the fundamental premises of the two were basically different. The entire research of Marx was pin-pointed to economics alone, and that too to industrialism and capitalism. Everything else flowed from this research. To Gandhi, life could not be divided into compartments and was to be viewed as a whole. The needs of the spirit have to be kept in view along with the needs of the body, and a philosophy was bound to be fallacious, if it neglected ethics and founded itself on the one aspect of physical needs of the body alone.

(f) His Concept of Ideal State

According to Gandhiji, Sarvodya is the concept of ideal state. The ideal State of Gandhiji is a state of statelessness. He said that in such a state every one is his own ruler. He rules himself in such a manner that he is never a hindrance to his neighbour. In the ideal state, therefore, there is no political power because there is no state.

Gandhiji on present State Gandhiji greatly criticises the present state being greatly centralized. He says that the state represents violence in organized form. The individual has a soul but as the state is a soul-less machine, it can never be weaned from violence to which it owes its very existence. Gandhiji remarks, "It is my firm conviction that if the state suppresses capitalism by violence, it will be caught in the coils of violence itself and fail to develop non-violence at any time."

He wrote in *Young India,* "In truth a government that is ideal governs the least. It is no self-government that leaves nothing for the people to do. That is pupilage. But if we are to attain Swaraj, a large number of us must outgrow, enforce, manage and feel our adolescence. We must govern ourselves at least where there is no deadly opposition from armed authority."

Gandhiji looks upon an increase in the power of the state with greatest fear, because although while apparently doing good by minimising exploitation, it does the greatest harm to mankind by destroying individuality which lies at the root of all progress. We know of so many cases where men have adopted trusteeship but nowhere the state has really lived for the power. The State represents violence in a concentrated and organized form.

Gandhiji's ideal state He says that political power is not an end, but one of the means of enabling people to better their condition in every department of life. Political power means capacity to regulate national life through national representatives. If national life becomes so perfect as to become self-regulated, no representation becomes necessary. There is then a state of enlightened anarchy. In such a state, every one is his own ruler. He rules himself in such a manner that he is never a hindrance to his neighbour. In the ideal state therefore, there is no political power, because there is no state. But the ideal is never fully realized in life. Hence, the classical statement of Thoreau that "that Government is the best, which governs the least."

> 'As to whether in an ideal society, there should be any or no government, I do not think, we need worry about this at the moment. If we continue to work for such a society, it will slowly come into being to such an extent that the people can benefit by it.'

Gandhiji found communist process for achieving 'Stateless Society as impractical. He remarks that "unfortunately western socialists have a believed in the necessity of violence for enforcing socialist doctrines. Social justice, even up to the least and lowliest, is impossible of attainment by force." Gandhiji's ideal society will be based on democracy. He, however, had a different notion of democracy. The nearest approach to the purest anarchy would be democracy based on non-violence-in such a state everyone is his own ruler. He rules himself in such a manner that he is never a hindrance to his neighbour. In the ideal state, therefore, there is no political power because there is no state. He wrote about democracy "Popular state can never act in advance of public opinion. If it goes against it, it will be destroyed. Democracy disciplined and enlightened is the first thing in the world. A democracy, prejudiced, ignorant, superstitious, will land itself in chaos and may be self-destroyed."

In Sarvodaya society economy is decentralised, and each unit stands self-sufficient, so far as it goes. He says that you cannot build non-violence on a factory civilization but it can be built on a self-contained village. Rural economy eschews exploitation altogether, and exploitation is the essence of violence.

> "The end to be sought is human happiness combined with full mental and moral growth. I used the adjective moral as synonymous with spiritual. This end can be achieved under decentralisation. Centralization as a system is inconsistent with a non-violence structure of society."
>
> "Man is not born to live in isolation, but is essentially a social animal independent and interdependent. No one can or should ride on another's back. If we try to work out necessary conditions for such a life, we are forced to the conclusion that the unit of society should be a village or call it a manageable small group of people who would, in the ideal, be self-sufficient (in the matter or their vital requirements) as a unit and bound together in bonds of mutual co-operation and interdependence."

He repudiated the state on many grounds : ethical, historical and economic. The compulsive nature of state authority took away the moral of individual's action. A man is moral when he acts voluntarily. Gandhiji is of the view that the state represents violence in concentrated and organised form. The individual has a soul but as the state is a soulless machine, it can never be weaned from violence to which it owes its very existence.

The ideal of Mahatma Gandhi is stateless democracy where social life is self-regulated. He says that in such a state every one is his own ruler. He rules himself in such a manner that he is never a hindrance to his neighbour. In the ideal state, therefore, there is no political power because there is no state. The ideal democracy was to be federation of Satyagrahi village communities. "Society based on non-violence can only be of groups settled in villages in which voluntary co-operation is the condition of dignified and peaceful existence."

Gandhiji confesses that his ideal of society is not likely to be realised in its entirety. He says that a government cannot succeed in becoming entirely non-violence, because it represents all the people. To quote him, "I do not today conceive of such a golden age, but I do believe in the possibility of a predominantly non-violence society and I am working for it." The structure of the state is to emerge as a result of non-violent society and the facts of human nature. Gandhiji admitted to Lord Lothian that "democratic government was a distant dream so long as non-violence was not recognised as a living force, an inviolable creed, not a mere policy."

According to Gandhiji, the state was not an end in itself but "one of the means of enabling people to better their condition in every department of life." The state was only one of the means to secure the greatest good of all. In Gandhiji's own words, "Real Swaraj will come not by the acquisition of authority by a few but by acquisition of the capacity by all to resist authority when abused".

Gandhiji has endorsed the classical statement of Thoreau, "That Government is the best which governs the least." It provides, according to him, a stepping stone to the society where "there is no political power as there is no state". He wrote, "That state is perfect and non-violent where the people are governed the least. The nearest approach to purest anarchy would be a democracy based on non-violence".

Gandhiji says self-government means continuous effort, to be independent of government control, whether it is foreign government or whether it is national, Swaraj government will be a sorry affair if people look up to it for the regulation of every detail of life.

Gandhiji was of the view that true democracy could not bè established through violent means. He wrote thus :

> "I read Carlyle's History of the French Revolution, while I was in prison, and Pandit Jawaharlal has told me something about the Russian Revolution, but it is my conviction that in as much as these struggles were fought with the weapon of violence, they failed to realise the democratic ideal. In the democracy which I have envisaged, a democracy established by non-violence, there will be equal freedom for all. Every body will be his own master."

Gandhiji says that democracy and violence can ill go together. The states that are today nominally democratic have either to become frankly totalitarian, or if they are to become truly democratic, they must become courageously non-violent.

Regarding Election

Gandhiji advocated adult suffrage in electrons. He says, "I am I wedded to adult suffrage...adult suffrage is necessary for more reasons than one, and one of the decisive reasons to me is that it enables me to satisfy all the reasonable aspirations, not only of the Musalmans, but also of the so-called untouchables, of Cristians, of labourers and all kinds of classes."

By Swaraj Gandhiji means the government by the consent of the people as ascertained by the vote of the largest number of the adult population, male or female, native born or domiciled, who have contributed by manual labour to the service of the state and who have taken the trouble of having their names registered as voters.

Role of Legislation

A legislator in a true democracy has to conform his conduct to truth and non-violence. Gandhiji says that members of Assemblies, whether as members or ministers or speakers, have in every act of theirs to bear in mind the fact they have to conform to truth and non-violence. Thus, the conduct of a members of the Assembly would have to be that of strictest honesty and courtesy in dealing with his opponents. He will not resort to shabby politics, will not hit below the belt, will never take a mean advantage of his adversary. The greater his position in the Assembly, the greater his responsibility in these matters. A member in the Assembly no doubt represents his constituency and his party, but also represents the whole of his province. A minister no doubt advances his own party, but never at the expense of the nation as a whole.

> "If fighting for the legislatures meant a sacrifice of truth and non-violence, democracy would not be worth a moment's purchase. The voice of the people is the voice of God, and it is the voice of millions that we have to represent. It is not possible to do away with truth and non-violence."

People as Real Power

Gandhiji says that under a Free Government, the real power will be held by the people...The mightiest government, will be rendered absolutely impotent if the people realising their power use it in a disciplined manner and for the common good....It must be remembered that only an infinitesimal proportion of the people can hold positions of responsibility and power in a country's government. Experience all the world over shows that real power and wealth are possessed by people outside the group that holds the reigns of Government.

Gandhiji says that it is an illusion to think that M.L.As. are the guides of voters. Voters do not send representatives to the Assemblies in order to be guided by them. On the contrary, they are sent there loyally to carry out the people's wishes. The people are, therefore, the guides, not the M.L.As. The latter are servants, the former masters.

Gandhiji further remarks that if we look around, the world we shall find that the best guidance is given by those outside. If that were not so, a rot would set in all governments, because the field for guidance is vast and the Assembly is a very small thing. Parliaments are, after all, a mere drop in the ocean of national life.

Parliament — His Views

Gandhiji says that it is very difficult to get rid of our fondness for Parliament. It was no doubt barbarous when people tore off the skin, burned persons alive and cut off their ears or nose, but the tyranny of Parliament is much greater than that of Changiskhan, Tamerlane and others. Modern tyranny is a trap of temptation and, therefore, does great mischief. One can withstand strocities committed by one individual as such; but it is difficult to cope with the tyranny perpetrated upon a people in the name of the people. Even an extraordinarily intelligent man, caught in the meshes of this civilization, loses his sanity in Parliament

There is no human institution but has its danger. The greater the institution the greater are the chances of abuse. Democracy is a great institution and, therefore, it is liable to be greatly abused. The remedy, therefore, is not avoidance of democracy but reduction of abuse to a minimum.

His Views on Sphere of State

According to Gandhiji, the state was to perform its functions with the minimum use of coercion. It was to rule "through its moral authority based upon the greatest goodwill of the people".

Most of the functions of the state were to be transferred to the voluntary associations. Gandhiji says that self-government means continuous effort to be independent of Government control, whether it is foreign or whether it is national. Swaraj government will be a sorry affair if people look up to it for the regulation of every detail of life. He remarks, "I admit that there are certain things which cannot be done without political power, but there are numerous other things which do not at all depend upon political power. That is why a thinker like Thoreau says that government is the best which governs the least. This means that when people come into possession of political power, the interference with the freedom of the people is reduced to a minimum. In other words, a nation that runs its affairs smoothly and effectively without much state interference is truly democratic. Where such a condition is absent, the form of government is democratic in name."

Conclusion To those who reject the Gandhian way of life as utopian and impracticable we may say that Gandhiji always first put into practice what he preached to others. Tagore expressed this aspect of Gandhiji's life in the following words : If he (Gandhiji) proposes an experiment on society, he must first subject himself to its ordeal. If he calls for sacrifice, he must pay its price himself. While many socialists wait for all to be deprived of their privilege before they would part with theirs, this man first renounces before he ventures to make any claims on the renunciation of others. To put it in a nutshell he has given laudable *ideas* about state and its functions.

(g) His Views on Village Republics

Gandhiji's idea of village Swaraj is that it is complete republic, independent of its neighbours for its own vital wants and yet interdependent for many others in which dependence is necessary. Thus, every village's first concern will be to grow its own food and cotton. It should have a reserved piece of land for its cattle, and playgrounds for adults and children. Then, if there is more land available it should grow useful money crops, excluding ganja, tobacco, opium and the like.

Gandhiji said that the village will maintain a village theatre, school and public hall. It will have its own water works ensuring clean water supply. This can be done through controlled wells or tanks. Education will be compulsory up to the final Basic Courses. As far as possible, eyery activity will be conducted on co-operative basis.

Gandhiji says that non-violence with its technique of Satyagraha and non-co-operation will have the sanction of the village community. There will be a compulsory service of village guards who will be selected by rotation from the register maintained by the village. The Government of the village will be conducted by a Panchayat of five persons annually elected by the adult villagers, made and female possessing minimum prescribed qualifications. These will have all the authority and jurisdiction required. Since, there will be no system of punishments in the accepted sense, this Panchayat will be the legislature, judiciary and executive combined, to operate for its year of office.

Here is perfect democracy based upon individual freedom. The individual is the architect of his own government. The law of non-violence rules him. For the law governing every villager is that he will suffer death in the defence of his and his village's honour.

Gandhiji says that to model such a village may be the work of a life time. Any lover of democracy and village life can take up a village, treat it as his world and sole work, and he will find good results. He begins by being the village scavenger, spinner, watchman, medicine men and school master all at once. If nobody comes near him he will be satisfied with scavenging and spinning.

Gandhiji holds that Independence must begin at the bottom. Thus, every village will be a Republic or Panchayat having full powers. It follows, therefore, that every village has to be self-sustained and capable of managing its affairs even to the extent of defending itself against the whole world. It will be trained and prepared to perish in its attempt to defend itself against any onslaught from without. Thus, ultimately it is the individual who is the unit. This does not exclude dependence on and willing help from neighbours or from the world. It will be free and voluntary play of mutual forces. Such a society is necessarily highly cultured, in which every man and woman knows what he or she wants, and, what is more, knows that no one should want anything that others cannot have with equal labour.

> "In this structure composed of innumerable villages there will be ever-widening, never-ascending circles. Life will not be a pyramid with the apex sustained by the bottom. But it will be the individual always ready to perish for the village, the latter ready to perish for the circle of village, till at last the whole becomes one life composed of individuals, never aggressive in their arrogance but every humble, sharing the majesty of the oceanic circle of which they are integral units."

Therefore, the outermost circumference, Gandhiji writes, will not wield power to crush the inner circle but give strength to all within and derive its own from the centre. I may be taunted with the retort that this is all utopain, and therefore, not worth a single thought. If Euclid's point, though incapable of being drawn by human agency, has an imperishable value, my picture has its own for mankind to live. Let India live for this true picture, though never realisable in its completeness. We must have a proper picture of what we want before we can have something approaching it. If there is ever to be a republic of every village in India, then I claim verily for my picture in which the last is equal to the first, or in other words, none is to be first and none the last.

Gandhiji remarks that when Panchayat Raj is established, public opinion will do what violence can never do. The present power of the Zamindars, the capitalists and the Rajas can hold sway so long as the common people do not realise their own strength. If the people non-co-operate with the evil of Zamindari or capitalism, it must die of inanition. In Panchayat Raj only the Panchayat will be obeyed, and Panchayats can only work through the law of their making.

> "The greater the power of the Panchayats, the better for the people. Moreover, for Panchayats to be effective an efficient, the level of people's education has to be considerably raised. I do not conceive increase in the power of the people in military terms, but in moral realms."
>
> "The Panchayats should also see to an increase in quality of food stuffs grown in their village. That is to be accomplished by property manuring the soil. Then, they must see to the cleanliness of their village and its inhabitants."

(h) His Economic Ideas

Gandhian economic set up, writes Prof. Dikshit, devises on order where individual ownership and individual management of economic means is maintained with social restraint. This order nourishes individual initiative and enthusiasm for production, and yet empowers the state to checkmate misuse by an individual through legislation. The target being a balanced adjustment between spiritualism and materialism and materialism craze for over-production is deprecated, and centralised industrialism is rejected.

Gandhiji said that the economic constitution of India and for the matter of that the world should be such that no one under it should suffer from want of food and clothing. In other words, everybody should be able to get sufficient work to enable him to make the both ends meet. And this ideal can be universally realized only if the means of production of the elementary necessities of life remain in the control of the masses. These should be freely available to all as God's air and water are or ought to be; they should not be made vehicle of traffic for the exploitation of others, Their monopolization, by any country, nation or group of persons would be unjust. The neglect of this simple principle is the cause of the destitution that we witness today not only in this unhappy land but in other part of the world too.

Gandhiji's economic ideas can be broken down as under :

On Industrialisation Gandhiji opposed the craze for industralism and production, and stood for limiting human needs on the principle of 'plain living and high thinking'. Opposing craze for Industrialism and large scale production, he wrote thus : "Industrialism, is, I am afraid, going to be a curse for all time. Industrialism depends entirely on your capacity to exploit foreign markets open to you, and on the absence of competitors.

> "It has brought in its wake the recent world wars. This Second World War is not still over, and even if it comes to an end, we are hearing of a Third World War."

Gandhiji said that the mania for mass production is responsible for the world crisis. Granting for the moment that machinery may supply all the needs of humanity, still it would concentrate production in particular areas, so that you would have to go about in a round about way to regulate distribution, but in respective areas where things are required, it is automatically regulated, and there is less chance for fraud, none for speculation.

In his own words, "Dead machinery must not be pitted against the millions of living machines represented by the villagers scattered in the seven hundred thousand villages of India. Machinery to be well used is to help an easy human effort. The present use of machinery tends more and more concentrate within the hands of a few in total disregard of millions of men and women whose bread is snatched by it out of their mouths."

On Bread Labour In formulating 'Bread Labour' as philosophy of life, Gandhiji received inspiration from various sources. He wrote, "The law, that to live man must work, first came home to me from reading Tolstoy's writing on Bread Labour. But even before that I had begun to pay homage to it after reading Ruskin's *Unto this Last.* The divine law, that man must earn his bread by labouring with his own hands, was first stressed by a Russian writer named T.M. Bondaref. Tolstoy advertised it, and gave in wider publicity. In my view, the same principle has been set forth in the third chapter of the Gita, where we are told that he who eats without offering sacrifice, eats stolen food. Sacrifice here can only mean bread labour."

Sacrifices may be of many kinds. One of them may well be Bread Labour. If all laboured for their bread and no more, then there would be enough food and enough leisure for all. Then there would be no cry of over-population, no disease and no such misery as we see around. Such labour will be the highest form of sacrifice. Men will no doubt to may other things either through their bodies or through their minds but all this will be labour of love for the common good. There will then be no rich and no poor, none high and none low, no touchable and no untouchable. This may be an unattainable ideal. But we need not, therefore, crease to strive for it. Even if without fulfilling the whole law of sacrifice, that is, the law of our being, we performed physical labour enough for our daily bread, we should go a long way towards the ideal.

If we did so, our wants would be minimized, our food would be simple. We should then eat to live, not live to eat. Let anyone who doubts and accuracy of proposition try to sweat for his bread, he will drive the greatest relish from the productions of his labour, improve his health and discover that many things he took were superfluities.

Mere mental, that is, intellectual labour is for the soul and is its own satisfaction. It should never demand payment. In the ideal state, doctors, lawyers and the like will work solely for the benefit of society, not for self. Obedience to law of bread labour will bring about a silent revolution in the structure of society. Men's triumph will consist in substituting the struggle for existence by the struggle for mutual service. The law of the brute will be replaced by the law of man."

On Khadi According to Gandhiji, Khadi (hand-spun and hand-woven cloth) marks the beginning of economic freedom and equality, Khadi is the symbol of unity of Indian humanity, of its economic freedom and, therefore, ultimately in the poetic expression of Jawaharlal Nehru, "the livery of Indian's freedom". Moreover, Khadi mentality needs decentralization of production and distribution of necessaries of life.

Gandhiji holds that the message of the spinning wheel is much wider than its circumference. Its message is one of simplicity, service of mankind, living so as not to hate others, creating an indissoluble bond between the rich and the poor, capital and labour, the prince and the peasant.

"I can only think, writes Gandhiji, of spinning at the fittest and most acceptable sacrificial body-labour. I cannot imagine anything nobler or more national than that, for say one hour in the day, we should all do the labour that the poor must do, and thus identify ourselves with them and through them with all mankind. I cannot imagine better worship of God than the labour done in His name. I should labour for the poor even as they do. The spinning wheel spells a more equitable distribution of the riches of the earth."

In his opinion, Swadeshi, without Khaddar, was a body without life. Swadeshi is like the air we breathe. The test of Swadeshi is not the universality of the use of an article which goes under the name of Swadeshi, but the universality of participation in the production or manufacturing of such an article. Thus, considered mill-made cloth is Swadeshi only in a restricted sense for in its manufacturing only an infinitesimal number of Indian millions can take part, but in the manufacture of Khaddar millions can take part.

According to Gandhiji, Khadi must have an important place in free India in so far as it represents a way of life based on non-violence. In *the Harijan,* dated 21-12-1947, he wrote as under :

> "I have no doubt that spinning and weaving of Khadi are more important than ever if we are to have freedom that is to be instinctively felt by the masses of the villages of India. That is the kingdom of God on earth. Through Khadi we are striving for equality of all men and women in the place of the gross inequality to be witnessed today. We are striving to attain subservience of capital under labour in the place of the insolent triumph of capital over labour. Unless, therefore, all the effort made during the past thirty years in India was a retrograde step, hand-spinning and all it implies must be prosecuted with much greater vigour and far greater intelligence than hitherto."

On Capital Labour Relations Prof. Dikshit writes : Gandhiji believed in resolving conflicts between industrialists and labour by way of settlement with a view to achieving co-operation between the two. When persuasion failed, he advised resource to the technique of non-violent and non-co-operation.

Gandhiji remarked, "By the non-violence methods we seek not to destroy the capitalist, we seek to destroy capitalism. We invite the capitalist, to regard himself as a trustee for those on whom he depends for the making, the retention and the increase of his capital. Nor need the worker wait for his conversion. If capital is power, so is work. Either power can be used destructively or creatively. Either is dependent on the other. Immediately the worker realises his strength, he is in a position to become a co-sharer of the capitalist instead of remaining his slave. If he aims at becoming the sole owner, he will most likely be killing the goose that lays the golden eggs. Inequalities in intelligence and even opportunity will last till the end of time."

Gandhiji further holds, "if inequalities stare us in the face, the essential quality too is not to be missed. Every man has an equal right for the necessaries of life, even as birds and beasts have. And since every right carries with it a corresponding duty and the corresponding remedy for resisting any attack upon it, it is merely a matter of finding out the corresponding duties and remedies to vindicate the fundamental elementary equality. The corresponding remedy is to non-co-operate with him who deprives me of the fruit of my labour. And if I would recognise the fundamental equality, as I must, of the capitalist and the labourer, I must not aim at his destruction I must strive for his conversion. My non-co-operation with him will open his eye to the wrong he may be doing. No need I be afraid of someone else taking my place when I have non-co-operated, for I except to influence my co-workers so as not to help the wrong doing of my employer. This kind of education of the mass of workers is no doubt a low process, but as also the surest, it is necessarily the quickest. It can be easily demonstrated that destruction of the capitalist must mean destruction in the end of the worker, as no human being is so perfect as to warrant his destroying him whom he wrongly considers to be wholly evil."

On Swadeshi In *the Harijan* Gandhiji defines Swadeshi as, the spirit which dictates man to serve his next door neighbour to the exclusion of any other.

According to Gandhiji, one who serves his immediate neighbour serves the world as a whole. He says that our capacity for service has obvious limits. We can serve even our neighbours with some difficulty. If everyone of us duly performs his duty to his neighbour, no one in the world who needs assistance will be left unattended to. Therefore, one who serves his neighbours serves the world. As a matter of fact, there is in Swadeshi, no room for distinction between one's own and other people. To serve one's neighbour is to serve the world.

As Such Gandhiji firmly believes that Swadeshi should be accepted as a creed.

Nationalization of Industries Gandhiji never recommended total nationalization of industries. He said that private individuals could run and manage large scale industries to a limited degree only if they accepted the principles of trusteeship, but not otherwise, He replied to the question put to him whether or not he would like to have a factory for the manufacture of sewing machines :

> "I am socialist enough to say that such factories should be nationalised or state controlled. They ought to be working under the most attractive and ideal conditions, not for profit, but for the benefit of humanity, love taking the place of greed as the motive. It is an alteration in the conditions of labour that I want. This mad rush for wealth must cease, and the labour must be assured, not only a living wage but a daily task that is not a mere drudgery."

On Socialism Socialism was not born with the discovery of the misuse of capital by capitalists. As I have contended that socialism, even communism, is explicit in the first verse of the ishopanishad. What is true is that when some reformers lost faith in the method of conversion, the technique of what is known as scientific socialism was born.

Gandhiji writes, "My socialism means 'Unto This Last'. I read Ruskin's *Unto This Last* during a train journey to Durban and it gripped me immediately. I saw clearly that, if mankind was to progress and to realise the ideal of quality and brotherhood, it must adopt and act on the principle of 'Unto this last'. It must take along with it even the dumb, the blind and the lame."

> "My socialism was natural to me and not adopted from any books. It came out of my unshakable belief in non-violence. No man could be activity non-violent and not rise against social injustice, no matter where it occurred. I have always held that social justice, even up to the least and the lowliest, is impossible of attainment by force. I have further believed that it is possible by proper training of the lowliest by non-violent means to secure redress of the wrongs suffered by them. That means non-violent non-co-operation. At times non-co-operation becomes as much a duty as co-operation".

To Gandhiji the basis of socialism is economic equality. There can be no Ramrajaya in the present state of iniquitous inequalities in which a few roll in riches and the masses do not get even enough to eat.

In Socialism all the members of society are equal — none low, none high. In the individual body, the head is not high, because it is the top of the body, nor are the soles of the feed low because they touch the earth. Even as members of the individual body are equal, so are the members of society. This is socialism.

On Communism Theoretically, as Prof. Dikshit writes, Gandhi was akin to communism in which economic equality and total employment are assured, and "to each according to need" is the rule followed. In practise, however, Gandhiji found communist methods of achieving that objective as faulty, unendourable and reactionary.

Addressing the young communists some of whom were disturbing the labour meeting at which he was speaking, he said, "I may tell you that I have been trying my best to live up to the ideal communism in the best sense of the term."

Gandhiji denounced communism and propounded his own theory of non-violent socialism.

Conclusion To conclude we may say that Gandhiji's economic ideas are developed in the social and economic background of India. His ideas are really great. In the words of Allen, it was the merit of Gandhiji that while revealing to us the potentiality of the single human being in an age of organization and machinery and the masses, he put those powers to the highest use. In him we saw what can be accomplished, not by the self-assertive will, but by the will wholly dedicated to God and the good of man. He possessed the only valid kind of authority not that which depresses others that it may rise, but that which lifts others to its own level. He had the rare capacity to make others what he was himself an independent centre of spiritual life. So doing he gave us a new faith in man as the bearer of the inner light and heartened us in our turn to attempt the task of living in freedom and confidence in God's will for us.

(i) His Social Ideas

Gandhi's social ideas constitute a challenge to the main currents of present civilization. According to Lord Boyd Orr, "Is it possible that these great principles, these wonderful ideas, could be applied on a world-wide scale? I think the time has come when they can be applied, they must be applied, and they will be applied, because people realise, that there is no other hope, with modern science and the abnormal powers which the scientists have let loose for destruction, and which cannot be bottled up again."

His social ideals can be broken down as under :

Untouchability : Gandhiji regarded untouchability as the greatest blot on Hinduism.

Regarding untouchability Gandhiji said, "To remove untouchability is a penance that caste Hindus owe to Hinduism and to themselves. The purification required is not 'untouchables' but of the so called superior castes. There is no vice that is special to the untouchables not even dirt and insanitation. It is our arrogance which blinds us, superior Hindus, to our own blemishes and which magnifies those of our down trodden brethren who we have suppressed and whom we keep under suppression. Religions like nations are being weighed in the balance. God's grace and revelation are the monopoly of no race or nation. They descend equally upon all who wait upon God. That religion and that nation will be blotted out from the face of the earth which pins its faith on injustice, untruth or violence."

Gandhiji said : "I do not want to be reborn. But if I have to be reborn, I should be boru an untouchable, so that I may share their sorrows, sufferings and the affronts levelled at them, in order that I may endeavour to free myself and them from that miserable condition. I, therefore, pray that if I should be born again, I should do so not as a Brahmin, Kshatriya, Vaishya or Shudra but as an Atishudra."

Gandhiji claimed for the untouchables in Hindu society the right to enter Hindu temples. About this Gandhiji says : "Temple entry is the one spiritual act that would constitute the message of freedom to the 'untouchables' and assure them that they are not outcastes before God."

It is not a question of Harijans asserting their right of temple-entry or claiming it. They may or may not want to enter that temple even when it is declared open to them. But it is the bounden duty of 'every caste Hindu to secure that opening for Harijans.

Gandhiji says that there is none that is high and none that is low, all the absolutely equal, equal because all are the creatures of that Creator. And this is not a philosophical thing to be dished out to Brahmanas as Kshatriyas, but it enunciates an eternal truth which admits of no reduction, on palliation. And if that is so, how can anyone here dare to arrogate superiority to himself or herself over any other human being?

As a results of Gandhi's efforts, India after Independence abolished by law the evil of untouchability.

Women Uplift Gandhiji wrote in the *Young India* dated 17, October 1929 as follows : "I am uncompromising in the matter of women's rights. In my opinion she should labour under no legal disability not suffered by man, I should treat the daughters and sons on a footing of perfect equality." In another issue of the same weekly he remarked that to call woman the weaker sex is a libel; it is man's injustice, to woman. If by strength is meant'brute strength then indeed is woman less brute than man. If by strength is meant power, then women is immeasurably man's superior. Has she not greater intuition, is she not more self-sacrificing, has she not greater power of endurance, has she not greater courage? Without her man could not be. If non-violence is the law of our being, the future is with women. In Vedic times men and women were equal in all walks of life, including the religious and the intellectual. Therefore, Gandhiji claims that he was following the more ancient authorities than of the later law-givers, Manu and others. About this Gandhiji says, "The saying attributed to Manu that for women there can be no freedom is not to be sacrosanct. It only shows that probably, at the time when it was promulgated, women were kept in a state of subjection. Tire epithets used in our literature to describe a wife are 'Ardhangani', the better half and 'Sahadharmini', the helpmate. The husband addressing the wife as 'devi' or goddess does not show any disparagement. But unfortunately, a time came when the woman was divested of many other rights and privileges and was reduced to a status of inferiority."

Widow Remarriage A child-widow, according to Gandhiji was not in reality a widow but a maiden, and must be treated as such. He says that we cry out for cow-protection in the name of religion, but we refuse protection to the human cow in the shape of a girl-widow. We would resent force in religion. But in the name of religion we force widowhood upon our girl-widows who could not understand the import of the marriage ceremony. To force widow-hood upon little girls is a trutal crime for which we Hindus are daily paying dearly. If our conscience was truly awakened, there would be no marriage before 15, let alone widowhood, and we would declare that these girls were never religiously married. There is no warrant in any Shastra for such widowhood.

Gandhiji holds that so long as we have thousands of widows in our midst, we are sitting on a mine which may explode at any moment. If we would be pure, if we would save Hinduism, we must ridourselves of this poison of enforced widowhood. The reform must begin by those who have girl-widows taking courage in both their hands and seeing that the child-widows in their charge are duty and well married. They were never really married.

On Dowry System Gandhiji was against the dowry system. For the middle and poor classes it was a nightmare. It was also on this account that while there was joy on the birth of the male child, there was expressed a silent mourning on the birth of a female child. Gandhiji remarks that discrimination against the female sex is an anachronism. Both are God's gifts. They have an equal right to live, and are equally necessary to keep the world going.

Addressing a women's meeting, he said, "If I was born a woman, I would rise in rebellion against any pretension on the part of man that woman is born to be his plaything. I have mentally become a woman in order to steal into her heart. I could not steal into my wife's heart until I decided to treat her differently than I used to do, and so I restored to her all her rights by dispossessing myself of all my co called rights as her husband. Any you see her today as simple as myself. You find no necklaces, no fineries on her. I want you to be like that. Refuse to be the slaves of your own whims and fancies, and the slaves of men. Refuse to decorate yourselves, and don't go in for scents and lavender waters. If you (women) want to give out the proper scent, it must come out of your heart, and then you will captivate not man, but humanity. It is your birth-right."

On Prohibition According to Kirplani, in consonance with his idea about the simplification of life through the limitation of wants, necessary for a healthy, cultural and moral life, Gandhiji wanted India to be free from the evil of the use of intoxicating drinks and drugs.

Gandhiji says, "Having identified myself with labour. I know what ruin drink has brought to the homes of labourers given to drink. I know that they will not touch liquor if it was not within (their) reach. We have contemporaneous evidence that drinkers themselves are in many cases asking for prohibition."

It was said as to why did Gandhiji insist on prohibition by law, when he knew that the law in this respect was said to have failed in America. Gandhiji says that India is not America. The American example is a hindrance rather than a help to us. In America drinking carries no shame with it. It is the fashion there to drink. It reflects the greatest credit on the determined minority in America that by sheer force of its moral weight it was able to carry through the prohibition measure, however short-lived it was. I do not regard that experiment to have been failure.

Gandhiji further says, "In no part of the world is prohibition as easy to carry out as in India, for with us it is only a minority that drinks. Drinking is generally considered disrespectable. And there are millions, I believe, who have never known what drink is."

In giving up liquor revenue, the State Governments would lose little of their income, Gandhiji says, "Let it be remembered that this drink and drugs revenue is a form of extremely degrading taxation. All taxation to be healthy must return ten fold to the tax-paper in the form on necessary services. Excise makes people pay for their own corruption, moral, mental and physical. It falls like a dead weight on those who are least able to bear it." He further says that the loss of revenue is only apparent. Removal of this degrading tax enables the drinker, *i.e.*, the tax-payer, to earn and spend better. Apart, therefore, from this tremendous gain, it means a substantial economic grain to the nation.

On Varna (caste) According to Gandhiji, the Law of Varna prescribes that a person should for his living follow the lawful occupation of his forefathers. Gandhiji holds this to be a universal law governing the human family. Its breach entails, as it has entailed, serious consequences for us. But the vast majority of men unwittingly follow the hereditary occupation of their forefathers. Hinduism rendered a great service to mankind by discovery of, and conscious obedience to, this law, If man's, as distinguished from lower animals, function is to know God, it follows that he must not devote chief part of his life to making experiments in finding out what occupation will best suit him for earning his livelihood. On the contrary he will recognise that it is best for him to follow his father's occupation and devote his spare time and talent to qualifying himself for the task to which mankind is called.

In this conception of the law of Varna no one is superior to any other. All occupations are equal and honourable insofar as they are not in conflict with morals, private or public. A scavenger has the same status as a Brahman.

Let us not say against this law of Varna that is makes life dull and robs it of all ambition. In Gandhiji's opinion the law of Varna alone makes life liveable by all and restores to ambition the only object worthy of it, namely, self-realization. Today we seem to think of and strive for material pursuits which are in their vary nature transitory, and we do this almost to the exclusion of the one thing needful.

On Idol worship He said that an idol worshipper sees God even in a stone, and therefore, takes the help of an idol to establish, his union with God. In 1942 he wrote in his *Young India,* Churches, mosques and temples, which cover so much hypocrisy and humbug and shut the poorest out of them, seem but a mockery of God and His worship when one sees the eternally renewed temple of worship under the vast blue canopy inviting every one of us to real worship, instead of abusing his name by quarrelling in the name of religion.

In the *Young India* dated 28th August, 1924, he wrote as follows : "I value the spirit behind idol-worship. It plays a most important part in the uplift of the human race. And I would like to possess, the ability to defend with my life the thousands of holy temples which sanctify this land of ours."

On Cow protection Cow worship, he said, was a unique contribution of Hinduism to the evolution of humanitarianism. It is a practical application of the belief in the oneness, and therefore, sacredness of all life. The great belief in transmigration is a direct consequence of that belief.

In his own words, "Out mother gives us milk for a couple of years and then expects us to serve her when we grow up. Mother cow expects from us nothing but grass and grain. Our mother often falls ill and expects service from us. Mother cow rarely falls ill.

On Education By education Gandhiji means an all round drawing out to the best in child and man-body, mind and spirit. Literacy according to Gandhi is not the end of education nor even the beginning. It is only one of the means whereby man and women can be educated. Literacy in itself is no education. Gandhiji, therefore, begins in child's education by teaching it a useful handicraft and enabling it to produce from the moment it begins its training. Thus, every school can be made self-supporting the condition being that the state takes over the manufactures of these schools.

The following are the fundamentals of Basic Education as stated by Gandhiji himself :

1. All education to be true must be self-supporting, that is to say, in the end it will pay for itself, except the capital which will remain intact.
2. Manual skill will be utilized up to the final stage. The hands of the pupil will be working skilfully at some industry for some periods during the day.

3. All education must be imparted through the medium of the provincial language.
4. There is no room for giving sectional religious training. Fundamental universal ethics will have full scope.
5. This education, where it is confined to children or adults, male or female, will find its way into the homes of the pupils.
6. Since millions of students receiving this education will consider themselves as the whole of India, they must learn an inter-provincial language. This common-inter-provincial language and this common inter-provincial speech can only be Hindustani written in Nagri or Urdu script.

Conclusion We conclude our study of social ideas of Gandhiji with Kriplani who has nicely remarked that Gandhiji's contribution in the field of social reform was important for the reconstruction of the life of the nation. In its wide sweep it embraced almost all its aspects. It can be said that the whole of his constructive programme was devoted to social reform.

(j) His Concept of Trusteeship

Gandhiji was against centralization of economic power in the hands of the state. Also he was very anxious to prevent misuse of property of private owners. For a solution of this he evolved the theory of Trusteeship. He said, "What I would personally perfer, would be, not a centralization of power in the hands of the state but an extension of the sense of trusteeship; as in my opinion, the violence of private ownership is less injurious than the violence of the state. However, if it is unavoidable, I would support a minimum of state ownership."

Gandhiji said that if the State suppressed capitalism by violence, it will be caught in the evils of violence itself and fail to develop non-violence at any time. The state represents violence in a concentrated and organised form. The individual has a soul, but as the state is a soul-less machine, it can never be weaned from violence to which it owes its very existence. Hence, Gandhiji prefers the doctrine of trusteeship.

Foundation of Trusteeship Gandhiji evolved his theory of trusteeship in 1903, while in South Africa.

The basis of the theory is the 1st verse of Ishopanishad. English rendering where of is as under :

> "Whatever is there in this universe is the abode of God. Utilise it without attachment. Do not covet another's property".

In the words of Gandhi, "When an individual has more than his proportionate portion, he becomes trustee for that portion for God's people."

Gandhi elaborated the theory thus. "Supposing I have come by a fair amount of wealth either by way of legacy, or by means of trade and industry, I must know that all that wealth does not belongs to me what belongs to me is the right to an honourable livelihood, no better than that enjoyed by millions of others. The rest of my wealth belongs to the community and must be used for the welfare of the community. Gandhiji said that he enunciated this theory when the socialist theory was placed before the country in respect to the possessions held by zamindars and ruling chiefs. They would do away with these privileged classes. Gandhiji wants them to out grow there greed and sense of possession, and to come down in spite of their wealth to the level of those who earn their bread by labour."

Gandhiji remarks that in the nature of things, some will have ability to earn more and others less. People with talents will have more and they will utilize their talents kindly, they will be performing the work of the State. Such people exist as trustees, on no other terms. Gandhi is of the view that the bulk of his greater earnings must be used for the good of the state, just as the income of all earning sons of the fathers goes to the common family funds. They would have their earnings only as trustees.

Gandhiji clearly states that everything belongs to God and was got from God. Therefore, it was for His people as a whole, not for a particular individual. When an individual had more than his portion he became trustee of that portion for his God's people. God who was all-powerful had no need to store. He created from day-to day, hence men also should in theory live from day-today and not stock things. If this truth was imbibed by the people generally, it would become legalised and trusteeship would become a legalised institution. As to the successor, the trustee in office would have the right to nominate his successor subject to legal sanction.

Some aspects of Gandhiji's theory as explained by him can be given as under :

1. The present owners of wealth will be allowed to retain the stewardship of their possessions and to use their talent to increase the wealth, not for their own sake, but for the sake of the nation and, therefore, without exploitation.
2. The state would regulate the rate of commission which they will get commensurate with the service rendered and its value to society. Their children will inherit the stewardship only if they prove their fitness for it.
3. All the capitalists will have an opportunity of becoming statutory trustees. But such a statute will not be imposed from above. It will have to come from below.

4. When the people understand the implications of trusteeship and the atmosphere is ripe for it, the people themselves, beginning with Gram Panchayats, will begin to introduce such states. Such a thing coming from below is easy to swallow. Coming from above, it is liable to provide a dead weight.
5. A trustee has no heir but the public. In a state built on the basis of non-violence, the commission of trustees will be regulated. Princes and Zamindars will be on a par with the other men of wealth.
6. How would the successor of a trustee be determined, the right of finalization being vested in the state? Gandhiji said that choice should be given to the original owner who became the first trustee, but the choice must be finalised by the state, Such arrangement puts a check on the state as well as the Individual.

Implementation of Trusteeship According to Gandhiji, the theory can be implemented by way of persuasion and non-violent co-operation. He said, "We must appeal to the good in human beings of society that response. It is conducive to the well-being of society that every member uses all his talents, not only for personal aggrandizement but for the good of all." Gandhiji says that we do not want to produce a dead quality where every person becomes or is rendered incapable of using his ability to the utmost possible extent. Such a society must ultimately perish. Gandhiji, therefore, suggests that moneyed men earn their crores (honestly only, of course) but so to dedicate them to the service of all is perfectly sound. 'Ten Tyakten Bhunjeetha' is a *mantra* based on uncommon knowledge. It is the surest method to evolve a new order of life of universal benefit in the place of the present one where each one lives for himself without regard to what happens to his neighbour. Gandhiji says, "I will bring about trusteeship not merely be verbal persuasion. I will concentrate on my means. Some have called me the greatest revolutionary of all time a non-violent revoluntionary. My means are non co-operation willing of forced of the people concerned."

According to Gandhiji that his theory of "Trusteeship is no camouflage. It will survive all other theories. It has the sanction of philosophy and religion behind it. No other theory is compatible with non-violence. In the non-violent method the wrong doer compasses his own end, if he does not unto the wrong. For either through non-violent non-co-operation he is made to see his error, or he finds himself completely isolated.

"According to the doctrine of trusteeship, the rich may not possess a rupee more than their neighbours. How is this to be brought about? Non-violently? Or should the wealthy be

> dispossessed of their possessions? To do this we would naturally have to resort to violence. This violent action cannot benefit-society. Society will be the poorer, for it will lose the gifts of a man who knows how to accumulate wealth. Therefore, the non-violent was is evidently superior. The rich man will be left in possession of his wealth, of which he wall use what he reasonably requires for the personal needs and will act as a trustee for the remainder to be used for society. In this argument, honesty on the part of the trustee is assumed."

(k) Gokhale and Gandhi

Gandhi visited India in 1896, to seek this help of the people for the South African problem. For this, he met different national leaders, Tilak, Sir Pherozeshah Mehta, Prof. Bhandarkar, Justice M.G. Ranade and Gokhale. But he was so much impressed by the ideals and personality of Gokhale that he accepted him as his political guru Gokhale was also impressed by the personality of Gandhi. He said, "In all my life I have known only two men who have affected me spiritually in the manner that Gandhi does — one great patriarch, Mr. Dadabhai Naoroji, and my late master, Mr. Ranade. About Gandhi, Gokhale said, "I think this personality is going to play a great part in the future history of India. Mark my words, you are much younger than I am. I may not live to see the day, but I visualise it clearly before me that Gandhiji is going to be in the vanguard of a great movement when some of us are gone." After the Gandhi-Smults agreement of 1914, Gokhale instructed Gandhi to return home. Gandhi followed Gokhale's instructions like a disciple. When he reached Poona, he was very keen to join the Servants of India Society. Gokhale also wanted and possibly looked upon him as his successor. But the other members of the Society had doubts that his ideals and methods of work might later on be the cause of differences in the society. Therefore, Gandhiji was not allowed to become the member of the society. Srinivasa Sastri later explained the reason why Gandhi was not allowed to join the society. To quote him, Mr. Gandhi having completed the year of travel prescribed by Gokhale knocked at our door for admission... . We saw deep differences between him and us and felt though none of us could have given clear expression to it, that his political evolution would take him further from us. Still our hearts trembled as well as grieved when we told him that it was best for both of us to remain apart and pursue our several courses — still so curious and contradictory is human relationship that sharply contrasted as Mr. Gandhi and the society are in outward action, they would be found near him where motives were weighed and the spirit were taken into account'. However, Gokhale told

Gandhi, whether you are formally admitted as a member or not, I am going to look upon you as one.

There were some differences too in Gandhi and Gokhale. They differed in 1901 on the question of social ideas *e.g.*, widow remarriage. They differed even in their approach to western culture and civilisation.

Gokhale was an adopted child of the Western traditions. He was of the opinion that the history of India had nothing to offer in so far as the political and social ideas were concerned. He wanted to reform Indian social and political institutions in the image of the west. But Gandhi, on the other hand was the hero of non-co-operation. Gokhale also differed from Gandhi in his extreme views on non-violence. On the basis of these differences, it has been pointed out by Prof. D.S. Sharma and Prof. T.L. Sahay that Gandhi was wrong in considering himself a political disciple of Gokhale. It has been said that Gandhi was more akin to Tilak's political weapons. But Gandhi made it clear and said, I cannot claim the honour of being a follower of the late Lokmanya. I admire him like millions of his countrymen for his indomitable will, his vast learning, his love of that country and above all the purity of his private life and great sacrifice of all the men of modern times, he captivated the imagination of the people. He breathed into us the spirit of Swarajya. No one perhaps realised the evils of the existing system as Tilak did. And in all humility I claim to deliver his message to the country as truly as the best of his disciples. But I am conscious that my method is not his method. Gandhi admired Tilak but was and continued to be a political disciple of Gokhale. He said, He (Gokhale) was and remains for me the most perfect man on the political field. Not, therefore, that we had no differences ... But these differences mattered neither to him nor to me. Nothing could part us asunder. It were blasphemous to conjecture what would have happened if he were alive today. I know, that I would have been working under him. In fact, Gandhi derived his basic principle of purity of means for Gokhale's spiritualisation of public life. It was as Dr. Goyal remarks because Gokhale believed in the 'Spiritualisation of Public Life' that he adhered to the principle of constitutionalism and did not subscribe to the method of passive resistance of the extremist type. He believed that political activities could lead to salvation and freedom only when they were based on religion or in other words "spiritualised".

Conclusion In fact, Mahatma Gandhi's appearance on the Indian political scene was a phenomenon. His thought and personality was a moment in itself. This movement was different both in from and in content from that of the moderates and the extremists. In fact the differences between the moderates and the extremists were narrowed and were later bridged with the appearance of Gandhi on Indian Political scene. Gandhi preached and practised the essential points of both the schools of thought in modern India.

(viii) Estimate

Mahatma Gandhi, the Father of the Indian Nation was known all over the world and no wonder glowing tributes were paid to the greatness of the Saint of Sabarmati. Rev. Dr. J.H. Homes, an American missionary described Mahatma Gandhi "as the greatest Indian since Gautama Buddha and the greatest man of the World has been since Jesus Christ."

According to Edward Thompson, "He is a superb judge of other men. His humanity is one of the profoundest at things that history has seen: He has pity and love for every race and most of all for the poor and oppressed."

According to Halifax, "I suppose there can be few men in all history who by their personal character and example have been able deeply to influence the thought of their generation."

According to Romain Rolland, "Mahatma Gandhi has raised up three hundred millions of his fellowmen, shaken the British Empire and inaugurated in human politics the most powerful movement that the whole world has been for nearly two thousand years."

According to Sir Stafford Cripps, "There has been no greater spiritual leader in the world in our own times than Mahatma Gandhi."

According to Louis Fischer, "The symbol of India's unanimous wish for freedom is Mahatma Gandhi. He does not represent all of India, but he does reflect the will of all-India for national liberation. A great man is like good sculpture, made of one piece. A great man lives a single tracked life. Lincoln was great, he lived for the Union. Lenin was great, he lived in order to raise Russia out of feudal mire. Churchill is great because of all of his acts have been directed towards the preservation of England as a first class power. And at the same way, Gandhi is great because every single act that he performed was calculated to promote the one goal of his life — the liberation of India. He is not the man, he has no intention and never had to rule India or administer India. His function ends when he frees India. Again Gandhi is the Father of India's defiance and its symbol. Gandhi walks to sea to make salt in definance of the British. It becomes a popular pilgrimage. The idealism of the youth spills into it. So does the leaderless nation's yearning for a leader. Gandhi has given his followers the elation of standing up to a foreigner who is the master in their house.

On the eve of Independence, a Press Correspondent told Gandhiji, "Independence is your crown", for which Gandhi replied, "But, partition is my cross". From this it is very obvious how he takes the partition of India with great sufferings in his mind.

According to Prof. Percival Spear, "For nearly thirty years Congress was dominated by Gandhi, and India influenced more by him than by any other single man. It is not too much to say that the destiny of India was modified and the world itself influenced by this single personality. An unimpressive figure with a reedy voice, an ingratiating manner, and an astute expression concealed a character of great charm and baffling complexity. Gandhi was one of those men who concealed thought in the volume of his speech and meaning in the wealth of explanation. He was always explaining himself and was never understood. He convinced those whose attention was caught by one facet or other of his character in turn that he was a fanatic, a visionary, a consummate tactician, a saint, a prophet, or a trickster. To this day he remains an enigma; the only fact of which we can be quite certain is the magnitude of his influence upon the people and events of his time and afterwards."

According to Acharya Kirplani, "The Mahatma is more right when he is wrong than we are when we are right." Again, "many of us are correct in our little correctness and are small in the process. But the Mahatma was incorrect in many things and yet correct in the sum-total and big in the very inconsistenses. In the end, he seldom or never came out of the wrong place."

According to Nagendranath Gupta, "Is it not strange that although Mahatma Gandhi is the leader of a movement of political freedom, he has never been compared to such great national leaders as Rienze, Mirabeau, Washington, Hampden, Mazzini, Sun-Yat-Sen or Zaghlul Pasha? Yet he has been repeatedly and widely compared to great teachers like Zoroaster, Buddha and Christ, or a saint like St. Francis or Assisi. What political leader has observed fast for twenty one days to do penance for his country and the warring factions of his countrymen?"

According to Dr. Rajendra Prasad, former President of India, "Mahatma Gandhi's contribution to Indian politics has been immense. The Indian National Congress had been in existence for thirty years when he returned to India finally from South Africa in 1915. The Congress had aroused and organised national consciousness to certain extent, but the awakening was confined largely to the English educated middle classes and had not panetrated the masses. He carried it to the masses and made it a mass movement. Mahatma Gandhi's movement operated both horizontally and vertically. He took up the causes which were not entirely political but which touched very intimately the life of large masses of people." Again, "Mahatma Gandhi's greatest contribution, however does not consist in making the masses of India politically self-conscious and organising them on a scale they had never before been organised. To my mind his greatest contribution to Indian politics and perhaps to suffering humanity in the world at large lies in the unique method which he had prescribed and employed for fighting wrongs. He has taught us how it is possible for us to successfully fight the mighty British Empire without arms, he has given us and the world a moral substitute for war..."

Gandhiji has placed truth on its pedestal of glory even in politics, no matter how harmful its effect appears to' be at the moment. He himself firmly and strongly stated that "he is ready to sacrifice Ahimsa for the sake of Truth and not *vice versa*." Thus, he laid more stress on Truth than Ahimsa from the beginning of his career till he was shot dead by a cruel Hindu fanatic.

Gandhi has given more importance to non-violence during his struggle for India's Independence. This policy has been recognised not only the straightest course but also the widest policy. When we were feeling utterly helpless, Gandhi made us realise our own strength through Truth and Non-violence.

When the Communal Award was announced by Ramsay Mac Donold (1932) for separate electorate to the depressed classes, Gandhiji strongly resented it and went on fast for protesting against it. From this it is very clear how he tried to preserve the unity of the Hindus. Moreover, he tried to preserve the Hindu-Muslim unity by avoiding partition of India. But nature took a different turn. However, he gave his approval unwillingly.

Gandhiji's life was example io other people. If we go through his autobiography *My Experiments with Truth*, we are able to know the various facts in his life which raised him to the status of a superman in the world.

Since Gandhiji had all the fine qualities, he has been styled as the Knower, the Doer and the Sayer by the people of the world.

Mahatma Gandhi had renounced everything for the sake of the country. Now he had to sacrifice his life as well. His life was a sacrificial offer. Many memorials of brick and stone and metal have been raised to perpetuate his memory. But these memorials fall short of what he deserved. The greatest memorial to Mahatma Gandhi is the Independence that we enjoy.

To put it in a nutshell Mahatma Gandhi thought like a saint, spoke like a saint and lived like a saint. He was a saint strayed into politics.

13

Vinoba Bhave (1895-1988)

His Life Sketch

Vinoba Bhave was born on the 11th September, 1895 in Gagode, a village of Colaba District in Maharastra. His full name is Vinayak Narhari Bhave. Vinoba Bhave is the eldest of the five children of his father. His father Shri Narhari Shambhurao, was a textile technologist. He commanded sufficient social respect. Vinoba's family was religious-minded and had faith in religious toleration. It is said, 'Vinoba was brought up in an atmosphere of natural conscience and voluntary observance of social obligations even in small matters'.

Vinoba Bhave received his early education at home. At the age of 15, he joined a school at Baroda.

During his educational career, he took keen interest in extra-curricular activities especially reading the biographies and autobiographies of national heroes and saints. He Matriculated in November 1, 1913 and joined a college for higher studies. Vinoba disliked the educational system of Indian Universities as it was based on bookish knowledge rather than on practical life and decided to discontinue his study. He got so much disillusioned that he even burnt his Matriculation Certificate.

In 1916, Vinoba Bhave left Baroda for Banaras to study the scriptures of the Hindu religion. At Banaras, he also came in contact with the political workers of those days. During this period he read Mahatma Gandhi's thrilling and inspring speech delivered in Banaras Hindu University. He was so much impressed by Gandhi's speech that he decided to give up all his plans of joining the terrorists of Bengal.

For some time, Vinoba corresponded with Mahatma Gandhi and later joined his Sabarmati Ashram. In the Ashram, he worked hard and greatly impressed Gandhi who wrote to his father: Your son Vinoba is with me. At a tender age he has acquired a degree of spirituality and asceticism that took me years of patient labour to attain'. Vinoba became the ful-fledged member of the Ashram and he did all kinds of work like cooking, spinning, scavenging, etc. In the Ashram, he worked day and night with the result that his health broke down and he was asked to leave the Ashram on a year's leave and to come back after one year. In the leave period, Vinoba observed the rules of the Ashram. In a letter Gandhi wrote to him, "I do not know what epithet to use in respect of you. Your love and character overwhelm me. I am not competent to judge you. You have tried yourself and I accept your judgment as mine. I accept the position of father you have asked me to. You come very near fulfilling my expectation of you.... you have scrupulously kept the Ashram observances even out of it... May God give you long life! May he make of you an instrument of service to Hind! That is my prayer." On the expiry of exactly one year, Vinoba again returned to the Ashram. After sometime, he got the news that his whole family was sick and was in the hospital. Vinoba refused to see his ailing family on the plea that he had renuciated the world. But on Gandhi's insistence he went to see his family. In 1921, Shri Jamna Lal Bajaj decided to open a branch of Sabarmati Ashram at Wardha and requested Gandhiji to send one of his devoted disciples who could preach Gandhian ideals there in the true sense. Mahatma Gandhi selected Vinoba Bhave. Accordingly, Vinoba reached the new Ashram on 8th April, 1921. He created still greater impression on Gandhiji who declared Vinoba as the "Jewel of his disciples".

It was in the year 1940 that Vinoba Bhave came to limelight on the national scene when Gandhiji selected him for the individual Satyagraha for civil disobedience movement. In his *Harijan* of 20th October, 1940, Gandhiji introduced Vinoba to the Nation in the following words : He is an undergraduate having left college after my return to India in 1916. He is a Sanskrit scholar. He joined the Ashram almost at its inception. He was among the first members. He has made scoffers realise that spinning is the handicraft par excellence which lends itself to being effectively used for basic education. He has revolutionalized takli-spinning and drawn out its hitherto unknown possibilities. For perfect spinning probably he has no rival in all-India. He has abolished every trace of untouchability from his heart. He believes in communal unity with the same passion that I have. In order to know the best mind of Islam, he gave one year to the study of Kuran in original. He has, therefore, leamt Arabic. He found this study necessary for cultivating a contact with the Muslims living in his neighbourhood. He is responsible for producing the youngmen who have dedicated themselves to the service of lepers... He believes in the necessity of political independence of India. He is an accurate student of history, but he believes that real independence of villages is impossible without the constructive programme of which Khadi is the centre. He believes that the Charkha is the most equitable outward symbol of non-violence which has become an integral part of his life.... With many co-workers he believes that silent constructive work with civil disobedience in the background is far more effective than the already heavily-crowded political platform. And already he thoroughly believes that non-violent resistance is impossible without a hearty, belief in and practice of constructive work. For offering individual Satyagraha, Vinoba Bhave was imprisoned for three months and later on for six months and then for one year. On the second and third occasion respectively. This brought him to great prominence throughout the world. He was jailed for three years without trial in connection with the historic movement of August 1942. In his detention period he learnt the four languages of Andhra, Karnataka, Tamilnadu and Kerala. Vinoba Bhave knows several Indian languages.

After Mahatma Gandhi's death in 1948, the task of bringing about peaceful social and economic revolution fell on Vinoba's shoulders. Since then he has devoted himself to the task through his philosophy of Bhoodan. On the 8th March 1951 he started moving on foot from village to village to have first hand knowledge of the people. He is preaching the message of Bhoodan. Vinoba commands great respect from the people. In the words of Shri Jawaharlal Nehru, 'In the troubled but dynamic scene that is India today the frail figure of Vinobaji stands like a rock of strength, modest and gentle.... He represents, as none else does the spirit and tradition of Gandhiji and of India'.

His works Acharya Vinoba Bhave has written a large number of important and interesting books, which reveal his basic ideas and the principles of his philosophy. He also writes articles which are published in various journals from time to time. His important works are as under:

1. *Madukar*
2. *Thoughts on Education*
3. *Geeta*
4. *Talks on Geeta*
5. *Satchitaprajna Darshan*
6. *Geetai Chintanika*
7. *Upanishadacha Abhyas*
8. *Ishavasyavritti*
9. *Vicharpothi*
10. *Swarajya Sastra*
11. *Jeevan Drishti*
12. *Simhavalokna*
13. *Philosophy of man of steadfast wisdom, etc.*

His Political Ideas

Vinoba Bhave's political ideas are to be found mainly in his book *Swarajya Shastra* and in his introduction to Mashruwala's *Gandhi and Marx* besides his various speeches and articles published in different journals from time to time. The main elements of his political thought are mentioned as under :

On Democracy : Vinoba Bhave begins with Lincoln's definition of democracy as 'government of the people, by the people, and for the people', *i.e.*, government in which the people govern themselves. In monarchy, there is government by one, in aristocracy, government by few and in democracy government by all. But Vinoba is opposed to the retention of democracy in its present form as the ideal one. According to him, the government by all is only an appearance but not the reality; the concept of 'majority rule' makes it impossible for the 'government by all' to be realised anywhere. Not to talk of rule by all, the present type of democracy does not ensure even the majority rule by a small minority. The ruling party assumes to itself the role of the totalitarian state. In the words of Barkar, 'It is perhaps the exaltation of party and of the disciplines and loyalties of party which has been the greatest of the internal difficulties of democracy, at any rate in the field of pure politics, during the present century'.

The part has made three successive and increasing encroachments :

First, it has made itself an organ of state, entrenched within the state either by legal right or by the *de facto* power exercised by party conferences in the country or party meetings in the legislature.

Secondly, it has made itself a state within the state, an imperium in imperio, with a totalitarian claim on its members and a totalitarian apparatus of action.

And finally, some one victorious party, disdaining to be an imperium in imperio by the side of the other and rival imperial, has ejected the other imperial and become the one and only imperium.

In this consummation, party ceases to be a part of the state, and the state be part or an expression of the life of party.

Today, the politics has become a sort of profession and it is dangerous to the growth of democracy.

In democracy, government tries to do each and everything and to decide about political, economic, social, religious, educational and cultural policies for the country. According to Vinoba Bhave, it is basically wrong.

The Government of the people, by the people, for the people for the people is actually run by a few people. The representatives have failed completely to represent the will of the voters.

According to Vinoba, there is not much difference between monarchical rule in ancient times and democratic government in modern times.

Another argument which Vinoba Bhave gives against democracy is the problem of large electorate. It is impossible for all the voters to participate effectively in the affairs of the government. Moreover, all the voters do not participate in the general elections. In India sixty to seventy per cent voters only go to the polls. It is very rare that the ruling party obtains an absolute majority of the votes polled; sometimes the party in power has the support of not more then 35 to 40 per cent of the total electorate. Even the leader of majority party who is elected as Prime Minister is seldom of unanimous choice. According to Vinoba Bhave, there are other faults in the prevalent form of democratic government like the distorting influence of money in elections, propaganda and canvassing, the spirit of casteism and communalism, etc. The candidates use cheap means to win elections. The method of choosing candidates for parliamentary elections is also-wrong. The general practice is that the party boss selects candidates for the various constituencies; the voters play no role in their primary choice. This makes the party bosses very powerful.

In the words of Vasant Nargolkar, "....the trend in modern civilized life is to eliminate the middle-man whether in the field of religion or of economic activities. We do not want the priest to pray for us, we say we would like to do it ourselves. We do not now very much need an intermediary between God and ourselves, as in olden times. We consider it a progressive stamp if we can do away with commission agents or middlemen in selling or buying and replace them by 'producers or consumers' co-operative societies. Similarly, Vinobaji, would like to ask why we should not relieve the middleman in the business of government and revert to governing ourselves in, small, compact, decentralised communities."

Vinoba Bhave points out other drawbacks of modern democracies which arise from the highly centralised character of their administration. The individual is no longer self-reliant and self-governing; he now depends upon the government for each and everything. We expect everything to be got done by the government. The result is the state has assumed large number of functions, *i.e.*, the state has become a welfare state. But to Vinoba Bhave, the idea of a welfare state appears to be very frightful; if the government has to do everything, the people are bound to become passive, 'nothing but a flock of sheep'. In the words of Vinoba himself, 'Before Independence we used to get things done by ourselves. When an earthquake took place in Bihar, Jamna Lal Bajaj was there at once, and relief work was organised by the people themselves. When there were floods in Gujarat, Vallabhbhai took the lead in the rescue work, and the people did so much that the British government was shamed into helping. But nowadays people do not try to help one another when flood occurs; they expect the government to give what is needed.' It is clear, that Vinobaji is against the concept of a welfare state, he wants all welfare work to be done by the people themselves. He is also critical of the Five Year Plans launched by the Government of India. In connection with the welfare state Vinoba says, "Normally, I do not strongly raise my voice against the government but on proper occasions, I do speak to persons in authority resides in the hands of the Central Government I would not be prepared to call such a state a welfare state, but an ill fare state. It is no welfare whatsoever to let the political power concentrate in the hands of a few persons. The ideology of non-violence gains currency only when political power is distributed in each and every village. Does it means that power and authority should be conferred on every village? No, power and authority is not acquired through someone bestowing it. It has to be deserved and exercised."

On Lok-niti : Like Gandhiji, Vinoba Bhave also wants to establish a stateless society. He wants to replace the present Power-Politics or *Rajniti* by Lokniti; in which the real power and authority will be in the hands of the people. The people will do each and everything themselves by unanimous decisions or by 'sarvasmmati' and thus there will be no interference of political leaders in the elections. According to Vinoba Bhave there is a vital difference between *Lokniti* and *Rajniti*. In his preface to Vinoba Bhave's book 'Democratic Values'. Dada Dharmadhikari explains the difference between *raj-niti* or politics, of power and *lok-niti* in the following words :

1. *Raj-niti* strengthens authoritarianism. *Lok-niti* develops the potential powers of the citizens.
2. *Raj-niti* regards political power as the chief tool of public welfare and renders people more and more dependent on the date. It increases reliance on coercive political power. *Lok-niti* regards personal freedom expressed in a sense of mutual responsibility as the vital breadth of all corporate life. It therefore encourages voluntary activities among the people and gets them to take the initiative in establishing independent popular institutions for public welfare.
3. *Raj-niti* relies on compulsion and control. It has constantly to devise ways and means of enforcing the decrees of the state. In *Lok-niti* self-discipline or self-control is the key-stone.

4. In *Raj-niti* there is ceaseless rivalry for power and a constant struggle for positions of authority. Each and all are standing candidates for political power. In *Lok-niti* there is no candidature and contest for power. Every citizen is anxious to work for the development of public spirit and civil consciousness; electioneering has no place.
5. In *Raj-niti* every citizen watches jealously over his own rights and interests and is indifferent to the right and interests of his neighbour. In *Lok-niti,* he is alert to his own duty and obligations, and jealous of the rights of others. According to Vinobaji, the Ethics of *Lok-niti* can be established if the people become aware of their inner strength and base their life and conduct on Truth and Non-Violence.

His Views on an Ideal form of Government : In his book *Swaraj Shastra* Vinoba Bhave has expounded his principles of a non-violent political order. Like Mahatma Gandhi he believes in non-violent self-government. In his own words, let us strive, for self-government, I do not desire to govern. 'This ideal of self-government of Lok-Swaraj,' as Dr. Goyal remarks, is the only way towards the attainment of a Sarvodays Society. To Vinoba, an ideal government is one which is based on non-violence and governs the least. It will emerge when the people join together and of their free will, and after due deliberations, invest with power one or more of themselves, whom they know to be free from attachment and hatred, devoted to the welfare of all and wise and capable, than though that Government may in form, be the 'rule by one' or 'rule by more than one', still if it is based on non-violence it should in reality be regarded as 'rule by all'. Vinoba in his 'Swaraj-Shastra' mentions certain principles which are to constitute the criterion for testing whether a particular form of government is an ideal one or not and also to point the direction in which a government should move. These principles are :

1. International brotherhood;
2. Co-operation of all the elements of a nation; co-operation being willing and active rather than mere acquiescence;
3. Unity of interests as between the capable few and the masses;
4. Regard for all-sided and equal development of every member of society;
5. The most extensive distribution of governmental power;
6. The least amount of governing;
7. The simplest government machinery;
8. The lowest administrative expenditure;
9. The smallest organisation for defence;

10. Spread of knowledge uninterrupted, unbiased and free.

Vinoba Bhave also mentions four conditions for a faultless form of government. These are :

1. Capable individuals will direct their capacity to the service of the people;
2. The people will be fully self-dependent and co-operate with each other;
3. Non-violence will be the basis of their continual co-operation, and of occasional non-co-operation or resistance;
4. Honest work on the part of any one will be considered to be of equal value.

Vinoba Bhave believes in the principle of equality in respect of citizen's rights and liberty.

His Views about Village Autonomy : Acharya Vinoba Bhave has travelled on foot from village to village throughout the country. As such he knows the real problems of the Indian villages. He, therefore, believes that the country cannot go a head as long as the villages are backward. According to him, the country's advancement and development cannot be judged from the cities, it is the villages which can indicate the real progress. To Vinoba, if India is to develop and rise in the real sense, it is only by way of village autonomy or 'Gram Swarajya'. In his own words, Rajya or Government is one thing *Swarajya* or self-government is another. Government can be had through violence. Self government is impossible without non-violence. So the thoughtful gentleman desire self government. They urge the people to strive for self-government. Vasant Nagolkar defines Gram Swarajya as direct government of the local community by the whole Community itself, without, as far as possible, any unwarranted outside interference, in the affairs of the village. The concept of Gram Swarajya emphasises the political ideal under Sarvodaya. Vinoba Bhave wants perfect village autonomy, each village having sufficient resources to produce for its consumption. Every village should have its own economic and political systems suited to its own conditions. Each village should have an elected council consisting of one representative at least, from each family. The council should meet at least once a month and should also have a smaller body to solve day-to day problems of the village. Internally, each village should be autonomous, but it will not be isolated from neighbouring village. Vinoba Bhave says, that which brings together self-governing village units is the nominal provincial political organisation. That which brings together such provinces normally is the national organisation and that which brings about mutual co-operation between such self-governments is the nominal political organisation of all humanity. In this political organisation there will be a parliament of individuals, wise representatives and the impartial, drawn from all over the world. This parliament will have no power of punishment or physical force, but it will have obtained power or restraint or moral force. To Vinoba there is always some interdependence. There is to be mutual co-operation between such self-governing villages. Vinoba Bhave also believes in cottage industries, but he is not against large scale industry or the introduction of machinery. In fact, he is opposed to the craze for machinery.

His Concept of Bhoodan Acharya Vinoba Bhave wants to bring about a new social and economic order in the country through non-violent and peaceful means. The basic principle of his philosophy is that the people should themselves give up their sense of ownership and should realise the need and necessity of sharing their surplus wealth with those who need it the most. According to him, this could be done easily through legislation but such a step would not achieve the basic end of withdrawing ownership voluntarily. He wants to implement this through his concept of Bhoodan. Vinoba Bhave believes that a man's mind could be changed, if the man who wants to change the same, possesses a high moral character. If the preacher touches the inner core of the listener, the latter can be changed, provided the approach of the preacher should be sincere, selfless and in the interest of common good. The idea of Bhoodan had its origin in Telangana. It was during his tour from village that he learnt of the communist sponsored disturbances in Telengana. He found that these disturbances were due to the pitiable economic conditions of the landless people. On the 15th April 1951, Vinoba Bhave entered Telangana as a Shanti Sainik to solve the problem of the landless peasants of that area. On the 18th April 1951 he addressed a meeting at Pochampalli in Telangana and demanded some land from land-owners for their starving Harijan brethem so that they could cultivate and save themselves from starvation. On his appeal, a big landlord Shri Ram Chandra Reddy stood up and said, I offer one hundred acres of land as a gift' and thus the Bhoodan movement started. Thereafter, he visited the next village and informed the people of the land donation of Shri Ram Chandra Reddy. There, too, a donor came forward and donated his land to Vinobaji for the poor. It confirmed Vinoba's faith in conversion of ones mind through love and persuasion. Then he started his Padayatra from place to place for his Bhoodan mission. His argument is that land belongs to all, like air and water. To give land to the landless is just like a dan, Vinoba says to the land owners, 'You think me one of your sons and distribute your land in a way that I too, get my share'.

The Bhoodan Movement is not to be regarded only as a project of just receiving land and then distributing it among the landless. Its scope is much wider. According to Jai Prakash Narayan, 'It is the Gandhian way of bringing about economic and social revolution, the theory and practice of a new way of life, a new social philosophy. It is the initiation of a new humanity and a new civilisation'. Its aim is to purify the hearts and minds of the people. The land can be distributed to the landless through legislation but as Vinobaji said, the law would no doubt take away surplus lands, but would it release you of the bond of attachment, a sense of possession and pride? Can we enact and enforce a law to compel people to give up all pride, to discard all feelings of superiority to take to the life of sacrifice and case away greed? Can this be achieved by legislation? Surely these are things which one must do oneself of one's free will. Vinobaji explained the main object of the movement in the words'. Let us be very clear about the main object of our movement. Redistribution of land in a village is only the first step. Our movement aims at creating a new man, not only in India but also all over the world. It is world wide in its implication. We are restricting the scope of our activities only to our are country just now because we feel that if we could show results here, it is bound to affect the world. Land distribution in India is only the first step of the movement when we say that land belongs to God, it really means that it should be free for use by all the men in the world. It should be open for the beast and the birds also. Some states in India are very densely populated.

Similarly, in Australia, there is plenty of unoccupied space. If immigration is free, five times the present population can live there but the Australians do not desire that outsiders should come there and disturb their security and their culture. In this age of science such parochialism can have no place. We must have large minds and hearts to think of the whole world as one. That is the only way to peace.

In the words of Radhakrishnan, "The Bhoodan movement acquires great significance in this context of urgent change. It underlines traditions that are implicit in the Indian way of life. It re-captures the idea of the social order as the family writ large.... The movement started by Acharya Vinoba Bhave is potentially revolutionary in character.... Even if it does not by itself bring about an agrarian revolution, it prepares for it by producing a climate of opinion in which courageous methods of land reform can be put through."

His Concept of Gramdan After Bhoodan Vinoba Bhave moves to Gramdan, another significant stage in his Sarvodaya Movement. The idea of Gramdan was originated in Bihar and was started when the Village Mangrota in Hamirpur District (U.P.) was donated as Gramdan by its owner in May 1952. Gramdan means that the whole village is given in dan as a gift to the community. All the individual owners in the village surrender their entire holdings to the village community. According to Vasant Nargolkar. It means voluntary abolition of private property and investing it in the community as a whole as represented by the village. Private ownership of land comes to an end : ownership stands vested in the village community as a whole. For purposes of cultivation, entire land of the village is distributed among all the families living in the village, irrespective of the fact whether any family had land previously or not. The land is to be distributed according to the size and need of each family; the larger families receiving more and the smaller ones receiving less. Each family tills the land allotted to it but there is no private ownership. The entire land of the village belongs to the village community. The villagers are to do work like the members of a joint family. Thus, the people of the *gramdan* live a common life and share their joys and sorrows together. Even the land revenue is paid collectively in the name of the village. The teacher, the carpenter, the potter, the washerman, the ironsmith, etc., each man of profession works for the community as a whole. Village shops are to be managed by the village community. Since, there is no private ownership in land, nobody can sell or mortgage the land assigned. Out of the yield from the soil, some amount is to be spent for communal purposes; *e.g.*, education of the children, marriage, etc. In the words of Vinoba Bhave, a teacher, a singer, a craftsman, a farmer, each will follow his own vocation. The village will give each a share from the annual harvest. All will feel as one and share a common life. Such *gramdan* will also have its own cottage industries to make it self-sufficient. It should not look to the Central Government for various measures like improving agricultural production; construction of dams or the sinking of wells for irrigation purposes, etc. It should be self-sufficient as far as possible.

To manage the affairs of the village, Vinoba Bhave suggests that there should be a village council consisting of at least one member from each family. *Raj-niti* is to be replaced by *Lok-niti*. In the words of Vinoba, 'Let it be understood clearly that increasing agricultural production is not the aim and object of Bhoodan and Gramdan. That would be only incidental. Its main object is to widen man's loyalty to the entire society. It helps to create a climate where man will have the same solicitude for the society as he feels for his own children. *Gramdan* will end duality between individual and social life'.

His Concept of *Sampatidan* In the beginning Acharya Vinoba Bhave was not in favour of accepting money from the people; as it gives birth to frictions and disputes. In the words of Vasant Nargolkar, 'Accumulation of wealth not only within individual persons but also within an institution does not, according to him, lead to economic or social health. He holds firmly to an old doctrine that miserliness breeds covetousness'. But later on, Vinobaji felt the need to collecting money for accomplishing his mission. *Sampatidan* means that one can donate a definite fraction of one's net annual income for' rehabilitating the landless labourers. Vinoba Bhave regards miserliness as much actionable as theft. In his own words, 'Today public opinion has no respect for a thief. The same should be its attitude to the miser or the holder. That is, just as a thief is liable to be brought under law, so public opinion should regard a miser as actionable under the law. Just as cultured parents teach their children even from childhood that to take anything without asking is a great wrong, educational science should help that not to give to one who asks it in need is a moral wrong. This idea is not new but it has not yet been given effect to as a general principle'.

His Concept of *Budhidan* *Budhidan* means that a talented person can also contribute in the Sarvodaya movement, by way of conducting study circles for the youth, delivering lectures, contributing articles, dedicating his intellectual capacity to the promotion of some sacred cause, etc. The concept of *Budhidan* is meant for those persons who are engaged in liberal professions and cannot devote whole of their time to the movement. Through Budhidan, they can serve the community. To Vinoba, the educated and intelligent people can provide very useful and significant contribution for the welfare of the community.

His Concept of *Shramdan* In addition to *Bhoodan, Sampaitidan* and *Budhidan,* Vinoba Bhave lays emphasis on *Shramdan* in physical labour also. The people should not only contribute their land or property or intelligence, but should also participate in the movement by giving free physical labour (Sewa) for the completion of projects of public utility. In this way, Vinoba Bhave wants to save money to be spent on payments of wages for completion of projects and there will be real devotion to the work which will produce better quality. He wants the people to donate free labour willingly. He advises the workers that they should not depend on finances from outside for running Bhoodan Movement but they should depend upon the dignity of labour. According to Vinoba, the concept of *Shramdan* can also help in the establishment of Gramdan and *Gramraj.* In the words of Vasant Nargolkar, 'Gram Raj coming as it does after the laying of the foundation in the form of Gramdan emphasises the economic reconstruction of the villages. It includes measures to improve agricultural production such as bunding of fields, use of better seeds, better implements and local organic manures in preference to costly inorganic manures, preservation of forests, if any, or constructing small dams or irrigation channels. Gram Raj also means encouragement of the principle of Swadeshi and, therefore, residents of a Gramdan village would do everything in their power to receive or promote as many village and cottage industries as possible with a view to dealing with the problem of local unemployment.'

His Concept of *Jeevandan* *Jeevandan* means when a person donates his whole life for the Sarvodaya Movement, he places his services at the disposal of the movement for his entire life. In other words, *Jeevandani* dedicates his entire life for the service of the society through the membership of the *Sarvodaya Samaj*. At present, Shri Jai Prakash Narayan is a *Jeevandani* under Vinoba Bhave's Sarvodaya Movement.

On International Problems According to Vinoba Bhave, it is the most essential duty of a country to defend and protect its national borders. A country which fails to defend and protect its territories is not only criminal before the people but also a culprit for the posterity. Vinoba Bhave is not in favour of wars. He Was shocked to know when China invaded India. He wants that all international disputes should be settled through peaceful methods. In this connection, he says, 'If necessary the matter should be referred to an arbitrator and a settlement reached. When even such a proposal is not accepted it affects a neutral person like me and one is bound to believe that this war is being thrust on India. It is not an age of wars this is likely to lead to dangerous consequences. I would, therefore, pray to God that he should induce wisdom in them to accept this proposal that has been put forward. If there is any alternative plan, it may also be suggested and considered'. He is against territorial expansion and regards it as a curse. The nations which encourage imperialism and colonialism are inflaming war and as such are enemies of humanity. Vinoba Bhave also believes in disarmament and is against resorting to arms.

On Communism Vinoba Bhave is a great critic of communism. In his book *Introduction to Gandhi and Marx* he has pointed out various weaknesses of communism. To quote him. 'Within the short space of 20 years the Russian Revolution has become so colourless that it has almost lost its original attraction. The reason for the same it that of the four aspects of capitalism namely, centralism, worship of large scale machinery, faith in violence and exploitation, scientific socialism seeks to retain the first-three and avoid the last but this is impossible. It is a delusive labyrinth. It should not be difficult to see that in spite of all efforce, it will be necessary to accompany the other three. The infatuation for efficiency resulting for centralisation, for the leisure and comfort securable through worship of large scale industries and for the promise of defence and security held out by faith in arms, is so great that people lost it in a labyrinth of delusions and accustomed to save life are unable to do without even one of three in order to put an end to exploitation.' Vinoba also opposes communism as it uses force. He rejects the concept of historical materialism too. According to Vasant Nargolkar, 'He shows scant respect for one of the doctrines of historical matrialism, of the inevitability of the socialistic revolution as expounded by Marx, Engels and Lenin. He, therefore, condemns rigid, schooling, regimentation of thought or in doctrination of both the young and the old. Again, Vinobaji makes a decisive reference to another famous doctrine of Marxism, of struggle or conflict being a fundamental element in nature and a necessary part of any progress. Dialectics, according to Lenin, is a study of contradictions with in the essence of things while development is the struggle of opposites. Vinobaji, however, disagrees'. In spite of his criticism, Vinoba Bhave is also alive to the merits of communism. He praises communism so far as it pleads the cause of the poor and the downtrodden, but also for its scientific approach to every problem of life.

His Religious Ideas Acharya Vinoba Bhave is a deeply religious man. He has deep faith in the existence of God. In his book *Random Reflection* Vinoba asks the question : 'Are you quite sure of God's existence as you are quite sure of the presence of this lamp in front of us?' He answers himself: 'I have an unshakable faith in God's existence. I cannot guarantee that this lamp in front of us does in fact exist'. His faith in God is regarded as the corner-stone of his philosophy of life. According to Vinoba, the inner experience which reveals the reality of God is infallible. He believes that one can feel the existence of God in the state of Samadhi. Vinoba Bhave loves all religions and feels at home in a temple or in a church or in a mosque. To quote him, 'I have been welcomed with visible affection in mosques, Sikh temples and churches by numbers of those faiths. Ajmer is considered to be the Mecca of India. I visited that place in 1948 and I recited one usual prayer from the Gita before a gathering of about 10,000 Muslims. I also participated there after in their Namaz. At the end of the Namaz all those who were present kissed my hand as is their custom. They have thus, showered their love on me. Who will not love a person whose heart is brimful with love.' According to Vinoba, all religious lead to achieve the same spiritual goal, *i.e.*, the purification of soul. To him, religion also means service to humanity.

Acharya Vinoba Bhave is not against idol-worship because he considers idol as a channel for concentration, but it should not be considered as on end in itself. He said, 'It is a fact that I believe in the worship of an idol, that I am a devotes of Deity in the temple. But I have also cultivated the habit of seeing God every where.' According to Vasant

Nargolkar, 'Vinobaji believes along with Shri Aurobindo that the mind with all its intellectual or emotional faculties and its innate egoism is the highest form of matter that has evolved in the vital body'.

Vinoba Bhave as Gandhian Anarchist

After the study of the political philosophy of Acharya Vinoba Bhave it is clear that there is a great element of a philosophical anarchist in his thought. Like an anarchist, he is against the state, its structure, government, political parties, etc. Like Gandhi he wants to establish a stateless society. From these views he comes very near to anarchism but this does not mean that he is an anarchist. In fact, Vinoba Bhave is an anarchist of the Gandhian type. There are various points of difference between Sarvodaya and Anarchism. Almost all the anarchists oppose the machinery of the state and regard it as an evil. But vinoba Bhave does not want the absence of government, but freedom from government. He would not object to authority which sticks to *Jana Shakti.* In fact, he wants to have the government of the politicians. Sarvodays lays stress on the duty of the individual and his devotion to the common good. The anarchism is opposed to Church but Vinobaji has deep faith in all the religions. The anarchists also condemn the institution of property and want to abolish it by forceful methods. Vinobaji, like Gandhiji, believes in a peaceful revolution for having a social and economic change. He is a staunch follower of Mahatma Gandhi and seeks solution of his problems in the Gandhian Philosophy.

Criticism of his Philosophy Acharya Vinoba Bhave is trying to bring about a social and economic revolution in the country through non-violent and peaceful means. It is quite praise worthy. But his *Bhoodan Movement* has come under severe criticism by the critics on the plea that the performance has not reached the expectations raised nor does it raise our expectations for the future.

One of the main criticisms advanced against Vinoba's *Bhoodan Movement* is the problem of fragmentation of land into small pieces. There is already a serious problem of fragmentation of land in the country. According to critics. Vinoba Bhave's acceptance of small donations of land and then distribution of the same to the landless is nothing else but fragmentation of land further. Such a policy is not applicable to our economy. The government policy and programme is to encourage consolidation of land and to introduce co-operative system in agriculture. But Vinoba Bhave's programme of distributing land to the landless, is bound to lead to so many complications.

Another argument against Vinoba's movement is that there is no proper system of distribution of land. About 75 per cent of the land still remains to be distributed. After donating the land, the donor does not take keen interest in cultivation unless the donated land is given to the landless. This results in low production and loss to the nation.

The critics have also pointed out that accepting land from small landowners and giving that to the landless is of no practical utility as the cultivation requires technique and skill.

Some of the critics have condemned Vinoba's *Bhoodan Movement* on the ground that the land donated to him is almost as is not cultivable. The landowners relieve themselves of the difficulty. There is no use of such land to the landless. Vinoba Bhave regards the donation of land to the landless as a matter of gratitude, but this is against human psychology.

Another argument advanced by the critics is that Vinoba Bhave has not been in a position to convince the landlords and propertied people.

In spite of this there was servere criticism against Vinobaji's *Bhoodan Movement.* We cannot underestimate his contribution. His efforts to bring about a peaceful social and economic revolution is very creditable. In the words of Dr. Radhakrishnan, "The Bhoodan Movement acquires great significance in this context of urgent change. It underlines traditions that are implicit in the Indian way of life. It recaptures the ideas of the social order as the family writ large.... The movement started by Acharya Vinnoba Bhave is potentially revolutionary in character.... Even if it does not by itself bring about an agrarian revolution, it prepares for it by producing a climate of opinion in which courageous methods of land reform can be put through."

14

Jaya Prakash Narayan (1902-1979)

His Life Sketch

Jaya Prakash Narayan was born in 1902 and received his education in the U.S.A. While studying there he came in contact with many socialists and practically went under the influence of Marxism. He also studied the writings of Manavendra Nath Roy, one of the Indian revolutionaries, who had fled to the U.S.A. to save himself from arrest. It further confirmed Narayan's faith in the Marxist Philosophy. But as time passed, he began to lose faith in the Marxist Philosophy because it denied individual liberty.

In 1929, he returned to India to participate in India's struggle for Swaraj. In the Civil Disobedience Movement, he supported Mahatma Gandhi. He was of the opinion that the nationalist leaders and the leftist forces in India should work in collaboration. So he founded the Congress Socialist Party in 1934 and also admitted the Communists. But the communists admitted were not sincere to the socialist doctrines, and Narayan turned them ouf.

In 1940, he openly denounced the Popular Front of the communists and since then he is a great critic of communism.

In 1942, Jaya Prakash Narayan actively participated in *Quit India Movement* and won name and fame. He was arrested and imprisoned for four years.

After his release, he planned along with other socialists for a mass revolution. His name was also proposed by Mahatma Gandhi for the Congress Presidentship but it was not accepted by the Congress Working Committee.

In 1953, he had talks with late Shri Jawaharlal Nehru to have more co-operation between the Congress and the Socialists, but he could not succeed. In 1954, Narayan resigned from his Socialist Party and became Jeevandani under Vinoba Bhave's Sarvodaya Movement. He tried to reform the Indian Society through non-violent and peaceful methods.

Philosophy of Sarvodaya

The term Sarvodaya is composed of two words, 'Sarva' and 'Udaya', meaning the 'Rise of all' or 'Uplift of all'. This term was used first by Mahatma Gandhi in 1904 as the title of his Gujarati translation of Ruskin's *Unto This Last.* The words 'Unto this Last' meant the uplift of the last or 'Good of all' or 'Service to all' or welfare of all, etc. The term Sarvodaya meaning the 'welfare of all' is quite different from the welfare of the last. Gandhi modified Ruskin.

To Gandhi, the ideal of Sarvodaya is that good of every individual is contained in collective welfare.

According to Vinoba Bhave, 'Self-sacrifice is the very foundation of the Sarvodaya which preaches the emerging of oneself in the good of all'. He believes that Sarvodaya is a moral concept.

Vinoba Bhave along with Jaya Prakash Narayan wants to bring about political revolution through the Sarvodaya Society.

After the death of Mahatma Gandhi, his disciples met at Sevagram March 1948 to discuss the methods to implement his last will. Gandhi in his 'Will and Testament' wrote : 'India still has to attain social, moral and economic independence in terms of its seven hundred thousand villages as distinguished from its cities and towns. The struggle for the ascendency of civil over military power is bound to take place in India's progress towards its democratic goal. It must be kept out of unhealthy competition with political parties and communal bodies'. To attain this goal, a Sarvodaya Samaj was established. Non-violence and truth are the two fundamental principles of the Sarvodaya Samaj.

The term Sarvodaya is to be distinguished from the utilitarian doctrine of the 'Greatest Happiness of the Greatest Number.' It is not concerned with the rise of many or the greatest number only but with the good of one and all. In the words of Vinoba, 'We can be satisfied only with the good of one and all, of the high and the low, of the strong and the weak, the intelligent as well as the dull. Only then will we all be satisfied.' The word 'Sarvodaya' expresses this lofty and all embracing sentiment. Its motto is far higher than 'live and let others live', it is 'Live for the sake of others'. It is the practical application of the Vedanta Philosophy. He further writes, 'In this unhappy world every body requires to be uplifted, for everyone has fallen long since, and the poor have never risen at all. The result is that both need to be uplifted' : the poor materially and the rich spiritually. Hence, Sarvodays advocates welfare of all.

As Gandhi remarked, 'A votary of Ahimsa will strive for the greatest good of all and die in the attempt to realise the ideal. He will, therefore, be willing to die so that others may live. He will serve himself with the rest by himself dying'. Thus, Sarvodaya implies service and self-suffering, the utilitarian doctrime, the concept of hedonistic pleasure. Here the term happiness is to be understood by goodness or perfection and not by pleasure. Perfection means not only the perfection of the body but of the soul also.

As R.R. Diwakar in his *Education and Sarvodaya* wrote, 'The body is but an instrument and a house, a tabernacle of the spirit. We are not mere bodies ensouled, we are rather souls embodied. We have to take note of this important fact. Man can be said to live a full life and be a perfect being only when his body and his life of the senses lead him to the higher and nobler spheres of consciousness. Man's life can be said to be perfect and integrated only when his body is healthy and shining; his mind is clear and penetrating; his emotions are pure and rich with truth, love, goodness and beauty; his ethical being is sensitive and respondent to the claims and needs of others; and his personality is ever widening and broadening till it reaches the very confines of universality. This is the attainment of Sarvodaya, total progress by the individual.'

Sarvodaya puts emphasis on village autonomy. The people in the villages are to be uplifted. They should have Village Panchayats on non-party basis. In the words of Gandhi, 'Society based on non-violence can only consist of groups settled in villages in which voluntary co-operation is the condition of dignified and peaceful existence. 'In Sarvodaya society there would be partyless democracy and as such the evil inferences of the present party system would be eliminated'. Sarvodaya also stands for Decentralisation of Authority in the economic and political spheres. Its main object is to replace the *Raj-niti* (the politics of power) by *Lok-niti* (the politics of co-operation).

Sarvodaya Samaj In Vinoba or Narayan's philosophy, the Sarvodaya Samaj would be Shasan Mukta or free from coercive centralised authority. It will be more or less a loose federation of a number of small self-governing villages of about three to four thousand population each. Each unit will be self-sufficient and self-governing as far as possible and will try to attain the highest degree of decentralisation in the political and economic spheres. In Sarvodaya Samaj, there should be absolutely no need of a large and powerful Parliament elected on the basis of adult franchise and making laws and administering national affairs on the principle of majority rule. The politics of such a Samaj will be those of service and not of power; *Lok-niti* would take the plae of *Raj-niti*. In the words of Dharmad-hikari, *Raj-niti* strengthens authoritarianism; Lok-niti relies on compulsion and control; in *Lok-niti*, self-discipline or self-control is the key stone. In *Raj-niti*, there is ceaseless rivalry for power and a constant struggle for positions of authority. In *Lok-niti* there is no candidates and contest for power'. In Sarvodaya society, there is no place for government, its aim is to free the people from the oppressive rule of the government.

Truth and non-violence are the two fundamental principle of the Sarvodaya Samaj. In the words of Vinoba Bhave, 'We want to overhaul the entire social structure without recourse to violence that is, we want both peace and revolution. Revolution is indispensable. Now if we want peace also, then we have to prove that peace too has the power to revolutionise society — not gradually but with the speed of revolution. This is what we call a peaceful revolution or Sarvodaya. In the Sarvodaya Samaj there will be no exploitation of man by man. There will be no gambling, immorality or class-hatred. Every member of the Samaj is to live a life of virtue. Each member is also to contribute to the welfare of the society. There will be no distinction between the rich or the poor, the high or the low, the priviliged or un-priviliged. Self control and self-suffering form one the basic requisites, for realising Sarvodaya.'

The Governor of the state must live in a cottage accesible to all. His motto must be plain living and high thinking. Being a citizen of India, he must be a citizen of the world. All the people are to contribute to the service of the state. The people will have individual freedom. In the Sarvodaya Samaj, the rights of the minority are not to be exploited by the majority. In the words of Adi H. Doctor, 'Sarvodaya begins with the family as the primary social unity. It is here that the individual learns the values of co-operation, mutual adjustment and self-sacrifice values which every good and wise society must do all in its powers to preserve and develop. The individual is so much a part of the family that it is impossible to conceive of the one without the other'. In the Sarvodaya Samaj the village will manage all its problems. We may conclude in the words of Adi H. Doctor, 'The ideal Sarvodaya Society may be described in general terms as made up of numerous self-sufficient autonomous villages with no coercive authority above these, the villages themselves having as their sovereign, moral authority with rules and administration being confined, only over things not persons; with complete freedom from police, army, law courts, taxes and centralized production.'

Qualifications of Sarvodaya Workers The following are some qualifications prescribed by Vinoba Bhave for a Sarvodaya worker :

1. A Sarvodaya worker must be a habitual Khadi-worker and spinner. He must patronise and use goods produced by the cottage and small scale industries.
2. He must clean latrines and other places in the village at least once a month.

3. He is required to work for the introduction of a basic educational system. He must also learn at least one regional language of the country in addition to his mother tongue.
4. He must have a living faith in God. He should have faith in religious coexistence and try to promote unity amongst various religions.
5. He must be ready and willing to give up his life and his possessions for the sake of a good cause.
6. He must be a teetotaller and be free from the use of other intoxicants.
7. He must believe in truth and non-violence as his creed and have faith in the inherent goodness of human nature.
8. He must have faith in the principles of equality in all the spheres of life. He should discard caste system.
9. He is required to work for the unity of workers and for the uplift of the poor.

Political Implications of Sarvodaya The main object of the Sarvodaya movement is the realisation of the happiness and elevation of all. It attacks the Marxist theory of class struggle. According to Sarvodaya thought, there is no struggle between the various classes. It believes in the brotherhood of all the classes. In the Sarvodaya society, all the classes live as brothers, they share their wealth, land, property and intellect. In the true Sarvodaya Samaj there is no possibility of class-struggle. Service, dedication and realisation of common good are basic elements of Sarvodaya. Sarvodaya is also opposed to the use of violence. It believes in the rational theory of social good and harmony. It wants to bring about dynamic change through love and non-violence. Sarvodaya also advocates the rights of the minority. It repudietes the concepts of majoritarianism, *i.e.*, the element of superior virtue supposed to be present in the judgment of a majority. To Gandhi in matters of conscience the law of majority has no place. Minority also has a perfect right to act differently from the majority. Hence, the Sarvodayists want to replace the concept of majoritarianism by the concept of consensus. Sarvodaya also lays emphasis on Bhoodan and Satyagraha. Vinoba Bhave regards Bhoodan movement as Satyagraha. He says, 'The work I have undertaken, is not merely a land problem. Land is a mere pretext. My main aim is to unite hearts — for this purpose I have taken in hand the problem of landless labour, the solution of which is noble and the crying need of the age. If I merely preached love and unity the people would merely brand it as saintly talk. That is why I do not merely ask them to love each other but also to give proof of this love by giving land.'

His Political Ideas *As a Democrat* : As mentioned earlier, Jaya Prakash Narayan has been a passionate lover of individual liberty all through his life. This makes him a great democrat. He wants to build up a new democratic set up in India according to the Sarvodaya thought. He is a great critic of the present democratic set up in India and in other western countries. He advocates democratic institutions. To him, democracy is both a creed as well as a way of life. Moreover, Narayan believes in moral values of democracy. He says, 'First of all, let it be pointed out that the problem of democracy is basically, and above all, a moral problem. Constitutions, systems of governments, parties and elections — all these are relevant to the business of democracy. But unless the moral and spiritual qualities of the people are appropriate the best constitutions and political systems would not make democracy work'.

Jaya Prakash Narayan suggests the following qualities for the proper working of democracy :

(i) concern, for truth;
(ii) aversion to violence;
(iii) love of liberty and the courage to resist oppression;
(iv) the spirit of co-operation;
(v) toleration for the opinion of others;
(vi) the sense of duty or responsibility;
(vii) belief in human equality and
(viii) ability to lead a simple life.

Like Gandhi, Narayan believes in the concept of the inner Swaraj. It means the capacity of a person to control his desires and impulses in the light of an ideal; it implies the ability of the individual to sacrifice his personal good for the sake of the common good. Narayan is also against the growth of centralisation in the political and economic spheres.

Jaya Prakash Narayan has been always a socialist throughout his life. He advocates the socialist principles in democracy. In the initial stage, he had faith in Marxian socialism, but gradually he began to realise the India must evolve a type of socialism suited to her needs and conditions and should be brought about through the use of non-violent method. He wants to establish both political and economic democracy in India. He is of the opinion that there can be no socialism without democracy. To quote him, 'In this democracy man will neither be a slave to capitalism nor to a party or the state. Man will be free.' As a socialist, Narayan believes in the urgency of solving economic problems of the country. According to Dr. Vishwanath Prasad Verma, 'Jaya Prakash Narayan is the most well-known and recongnised personality in the field of Indian socialism. It was his important contribution to have joined the Socialist Movement in India to help the great struggle for national freedom that was being fought under the banner of the Indian National Congress..... In the context of immense poverty and decadent agricultural society of India. Narayan has stressed the elimination of the restraints, both mechanical and social that hamper agricultural productivity.'

As a Critic of Indian Democracy Jaya Prakash Narayan is a great critic of democracy in its present form. He has pointed out various weaknesses in the working of parliamentary democracy in India and suggests ways and means to remove them.

According to Narayan, the most serious drawback of the present democratic set up is its highly centralised character. The central government has become very strong. The government, according to Narayan, oppresses through the public, law-courts and majority rule. This has reduced the individual to the position of helplessness. He cannot take a more active part in the working of democracy than to cast his vote at the time of general elections. Narayan has no faith in written constitution, division of powers, etc. To him, it will hardly be able to guarantee liberty to the people because 'the economic and political bureaucracy would be so strong and in occupation of such vantage points that the liberties and rights of the people as well as their bread would be entirely at its mercy. 'If the individual ceases to count, what is left of society? Individual freedom alone can make a man voluntarily surrender himself completely to the service of society. If it is wrested from him, he becomes an automation and society is ruined.' In the words of Gandhi, 'I look upon an increase in the power of the state with the greatest fear, because although while apparently doing good by minimising exploitation, it does greater harm to mankind by destroying individuality, which lies at the root of all progress'. In the present parliamentary democracy bureaucracy has grown very powerful; a cabinet being overburdened with work is compelled to leave more work to the permanent officials. Due to the emergence of welfare state too, the number of government officials has increased the power of bureaucracy. The people, in actual practice, do not take active part in the working of democracy. Jaya Prakash Narayan is of the view that the people are ruled much in the same manner and by the same kind of people as during British rule. They find that not even in local affairs have they a hand and that not even the humblest civil servant is in any manner accountable to them; on the contrary, they find that he lords it over them and even exacts illegal gratification much as in the old days. Narayan sees oppression in every form of bureaucratic administration. In the words of Vinoba, Administration oppreses by snatching away individual freedom. That is why a society to be free from oppression must necessarily be administration — free (Shasan-mukta).

The second drawback, according to Narayan, in our democratic set up is its very narrow base. He says that it is like an inverted pyramid that stands on its head, and wants that it should be made to stand on its base. This charge is not so obvious and self-evident as the first one; it is not easy to understand how a system built on adult franchise and the responsibility of the executive to the popular branch of the legislature can be criticised as resting on a narrow base, as an inverted pyramid standing on its head. Jaya Prakash Narayan, as mentioned earlier, has no faith in written constitution. He points out defects in our legislative assemblies which lead, in fact, to minority governments. Instead of the majority, it is the minority that rules. In general elections, so many candidates contest for one seat and the candidate who secures more votes than his other rivals, gets elected even though he secures less than fifty per cent votes. The second general election resulted in the setting up of minority governments in a majority of states, seven out of thirteen. It is clear from the following statistics; Bihar, Congress 44.7 per cent; Bombay, Congress 48.66 per cent; Kerala, Communists 37.48 per cent; Madras, Congress 46.52 per cent; U.P. Congress 46.29 per cent; Orissa, Congress 40.01 per cent; West Bengal, Congress 49.29 per cent. The plea that elections enable the people to participate in the working of government, is according to Narayan, myth and an eye-wash. Only rich people can contest elections. In such a situation, as Vinoba says, how can the poor and the dumb raise their voice? The people are to vote only once in five years. Narayan points out other evils of the election system. According to him, the election system encourages damagogues. The real interests of the people are ignored and the demagogue triumphs.

Another grave defect of the election system, Narayan emphasises, is its natural tendency to create rifts within the ranks of political parties. Those who fail to get the party ticket, often play a negative role.The political parties also play an undemocratic role at the time of general elections. They hire 'goondas' to threaten those who don't vote for the party and to offer others the temptation of loaves and fishes. In this way, Dada Dharmadhikari writes, every election is characterised by the triple evils of misuse of power, bossism or goondalism and corruption. The main object of the political parties is to capture power and then to retain it by all means rather than to serve the people. It leads to a game of seeking and retaining political power. In the words of Vinoba : If this virus continues for another 10 to 20 years, it is likely to poison our mutual relations and public life beyond redemption. All progress and planning will come to a standstill and evils like dacoity, slaughter, prostitution, smoking and drinking will further gain the day. It will tear our villages as under; social and economic freedom will become a distant dream. Nay even our political freedom may be reduced to a myth? Jaya Prakash Narayan suggests ways and means to remove all the above mentioned defects in parliamentary democracy. He suggests partyless democracy, decentralisation of power and introduction of participating type of democracy in India.

His Concept of Partyless Democracy Jaya Prakash Narayan was influenced not only by the writings of Gandhi and Vinoba, but also by those of M.N. Roy, in his views on partyless democracy. In fact, as Dr. Goyal writes, 'the contents of their programmes indicate clear ideological affinities... both M.N. Roy and Jaya Prakash had the common Marxist experience and both of them were disillusioned with the theory find practice of communism. Both of them had the experience of elections and political parties as they operated in the Indian situation : both of them find that the general direct elections do not lead to choice of capable and wise candidates and that rationality has a very little role to play in election politics'. To quote Jaya Prakash Narayan, "Parties backed by financial organisations and the means of propaganda could impose themselves on the people, how people's rule became in effect party rule, how party rule in turn, became the rule of a caucus of coterie; how democracy was reduced to mere casting of votes; how even this right of vote was restricted severely by the system of powerful parties, setting up their candidates from whom alone, for all practical purposes the voters had to make their choice; how even this limited choice, was made unreal by the fact that the issues posed before the electorate were by and large incomprehensible to it." Thus, according to Narayan, there is no use of elections. In the elections, political parties play a divisive role and corrupt politics. Therefore. Narayan advocates the concept of partyless or powerless democracy. He believes in the introduction of 'participating democracy' in India. This is possible as Narayan puts it, through only partyless democracy and decentralisation of authority. He got the idea of an administration — free and power — free society specially from the experiments that are being carried on in Yugoslavia. In April 1958, Narayan toured various European countries like England, France, Germany, Switzerland, Holland, Denmark, Belgium, Norway, Sweden, Austria, Italy, Greece, Poland and Yugoslavia. In Yugoslavia, the people's committees, manage the local affairs and enjoy vast powers inclusive those of police and running factories. To Narayan, it is the only country in Europe, which has the maximum participating democracy and maximum participating socialism. In 1959, he prepared his thesis 'Reconstruction of Indian Polity' in which he explained his concept of partyless or powerless democracy on the lines of Yugoslavia.

According to Narayan, the concept of partyless democracy can be realised through the Bhoodan Movement. He mentions four ways to introduce partyless or powerless democracy:

First, in each village, the people should by consensus nominate the workers whom they consider to be their best servants. The people will choose their best servants through the techniques of *Bhoodan, Gramdan, Sampattidan*, etc. These representatives will form a Mandal or a Panchayat of the members of the village. There will be no election. In the selection of the members of Gram Mandal, ordinarily one member will be chosen from each family of the village. It will meet once a month to decide all the village issues. The Gram Mandal will choose the members of 'Thana Panchayat'. Then the members of Thana-Panchayat will choose the members of 'District-Panchayats'. 'Provincial Panchayat' and the 'Central Panchayat' will be chosen on the similar pattern. In this way, the concept of partyless democracy will start from the bottom. It will be based on two principles. First, the replacement of the party-politics and elections by community consensus and secondly replacement of the principle of majority by unanimity. But in actual practice, it is very difficult to realise.

The second method to operate party less democracy is, according to Narayan, to establish a Sarvodaya society first, which should be free from party politics. To quote Narayan, 'The aim of Sarvodaya is to establish a society, which will be free from the malady of political parties. We in India have decided not to fight village elections on party lines and what is right for a village is also right for the nation'. The workers in Sarvodaya Samaj will not contest election and for life they will dedicate themselves to the service of the movement. This Sarvodaya Samaj, free from all types of party-politics, will best serve the interests of the people.

The third method for the realisation of powerless democracy, according to Narayan, is to invite all the political parties to co-operate in Sarvodaya work. These parties may have their own ideologies but they should help in the establishment of Sarvodaya Samaj. With concentrated efforts made by all the political parties the ideal of Sarvodaya can be realised. To quote Vinoba Bhave, 'As regards the related question of our policy towards the different political parties, I am inclined to take the view that they should cease as different parties and combine to form a united front made up of all good and honest people in the country carrying out commonly agreed programmes. And to that end I try to put before the people a programme of work which may be acceptable to all and in which all can join forgetting their differences. This will tend to draw the parties nearer one another with the result that their differences will gradually shrink and the points of agreement increase. Now, we have such a programme in *Bhoodan* which is acceptable to all, which helps the country go forward and withal makes for the growth of *Jana-Shakti* — the inherent strength of the people.'

The fourth method for the realisation of partyless democracy, according to Jaya Prakash Narayan, is the neutralisation of all the political parties in the legislatures. The people may fight election on party lines, but after election, the element of party-belongingness of the representatives should cease. Instead of the party whips, the members should vote according to their conscience. In this system, the ministers will be chosen not on party-lines but on the basis of highest preferences a member obtains. But it is very difficult to operate this method.

Estimate of the practicability of Partyless Democracy Jaya Prakash Narayan's concept of partyless or powerless democracy is based on misconceived assumptions regarding the parties, elections and the like; while the suggestions he gives, may not prove workable. It looks good on paper but it lacks practicability.

First, it is not possible to hold elections without political parties at the provincial and central levels; it may be feasible at the village level. In the words of Hoeber Rudolph, 'To many Indians, finding a consensus appears, to sustain and foster community solidarity and mutual accommodation, while adversary proceedings appear to sacrifice community harmony because they establish only partial sentiments of community purpose and interest. This is too extreme a juxtaposition, because adversary proceedings usually rest upon substantial if latent community agreement, on values and procedure, while finding a consensus often involves latent partiality and coercion. But the matter of appearance is important, for it reflects the moral standard by which the processes are judged; many Indians see the traditional way as moral and the modern as evil'. The method of indirect nomination for choosing the members of provincial and central legislatures is unworkable.

Secondly, it is very difficult to persuade all the political parties with different ideologies to work together in the establishment of the Sarvodaya Samaj. If they organise themselves into one single unit, there will be no end to their differences, rather it will increase the number of factions within the same party.

Thirdly, under this scheme, there will be no contract between the voter and the members of the provincial or central legislatures.

Fourthly, the method of neutralisation of the political parties in the legislature after election seems to be unconvincing and unworkable. So far as the selection of ministers is concerned, it is also unworkable. It will not abolish party spirit. Hence, it is not possible to establish the partyless or powerless democracy as J.P. Narayan envisages.

Panchayati Raj In place of the ever-growing centralisation of power, Jaya Prakash Narayan pleads for decentralisation of authority. He wants to evolve a participating democracy, which is possible only through decentralisation of authority. Jaya Prakash Narayan writes in his book *Swaraj for the People* : 'What I have in mind is what Gandhiji often used to emphasize namely, that as you proceed from the bottom level of government to the top each higher level should have less and less functions and powers, the broad upper level of present day democracy must be drastically sawn off and large portions of the vast upper floors brought down to earth, so that the pyramid of democracy could become a real pyramid narrow at the top and broad at the bottom'. To Narayan, Panchayati Raj is the way to evolve a participating democracy. He lays down certain conditions in his book 'Socialism, Sarvodaya and Democracy', which must be fulfilled before 'Panchayati Raj' can really lead to the evolution of a participating democracy in India. These conditions are summarised

1. There should be promotion of education and research in the desirability and techniques of Panchayati Raj. Narayan suggests to form a non-party 'All India Voters Association' to render educative service to the people.
2. There should be no interference by political parties in the various institutions of Panchayati Raj.
3. At each level of Panchayati Raj, there should be a real and adequate devolution of power.
4. At each level of Panchayati Raj, there should be a provision of their own resources. Narayan suggests that land-revenue should be placed at the disposal of the village Panchayat and Panchayat Samiti.
5. Panchayati Raj should have real control over the civil servants who work in their jurisdiction.
6. There should be a statutory collective body at each level of the Panchyati Raj.
7. In the selection of the Village Panchayats, unanimity should be encouraged.
8. The Urban Communities should also be integrated in the same pattern as Panchayati Raj.
9. The job of assisting, guiding and supervising the establishment, working and development of Panchayati Raj should be entrusted to a non-political autonomous body headed by a person who does not belong to the civil service.

According to Jaya Prakash Narayan, there is need of the economic pyramid along with political decentralisation, otherwise it remains ineffective. Therefore, he suggests certain condition for the economic pyramid also. These conditions are :

1. The economy must be a small-machine and labour-intensive economy.
2. A decentralised economy must aim at relating full utilization of local and regional resources, human and material to the satisfaction of local and regional units.
3. Village industries must be integrated with village agriculture, the aim being to develop small group of villages as an agro-industrial economy.
4. The organisational pattern of the decentralised economy must be the owner-worker or co-operative type.
5. Political institutions of Panchayati Raj will have to play an important role in this economic development.

Jaya Prakash Narayan suggests that the Panchayati Raj should not stop at the district level but should extend right up to the level of the top structure.

15

Manavendra Nath Roy (1886-1954)

Manavendra Nath Roy was one of the learned thinkers of modern , India. He was one of the Extremists in India's struggle for Independence. In the beginning, he came under the influence of Marxism but later on he changed his ideology. He struggled for attaning national freedom even from the platform of Indian National Congress. He believed in the rational approach to judge every problem of life. He was a great rationalist and judged everything by the critierion of reason and rationality. He was also great lover of individual freedom. In his opinion, the individual should come first and everything afterwards.

After 1946, M.N. Roy lost faith in Marxian Philosophy and expounded his theory of 'Radical Humanism' or 'New Humanism' or 'Scientific Humanism. Even Roy became a staunch critic of Marx. He challenged his basic concepts of Dialectical Materialism and Theory of Surplus Value. M.N. Roy was also a critic of Parliamentary Democracy in its present form.

Like Jaya Prakash Narayan, he, believed in the concept of Partyless democracy or organised democracy. His contribution to the Indian Political Thought is commendable.

His Life Sketch Manavendra Nath Roy was born on February 6, 1886 in 24-Parganas District of Bengal. His first name was Narendra Nath Bhattacharya. He got his early education in Calcutta. From his very childhood, he was a revolutionary. He was also influenced by Swami Vivekananda, Swami Ramatirth and Swami Dayananda Saraswati.

After the partition of Bengal in 1905, he started his revolutionary activities. In 1907, he was arrested for the first time when he was hardly 14 on a charge of a political dacoity in Calcutta. He was, however, acquited because the judge could not be convinced by the idea of a boy of 14 participating in a political dacoity. M.N. Roy received his early political training in the course of the Swadeshi Movement of Bengal. He was highly influenced by the political ideas of Bipin Chandra Pal. Aurobindo Ghosh and Surendra Nath Banerjee.

He also got inspiration from the life of sacrifice and sufferings of V.D. Savarkar.

In 1910, Roy was imprisoned in connection with the Howrah Conspiracy Case. His revolutionary activities came to prominence during the period of the First World War. During the course of the war, the Indian revolutionaries in Berlin organised an Indian Independence Committee there. They were to smuggle arms and amunitions from Germany to India. M.N. Roy was given this responsible task of receiving arms in Java from a ship which was to come there from the United States. But Roy came back disappointed and frustrated because the ship did not reach Java.

In 1915, he again went to Java in search of arms and amunitions for Indian revolutionaries but returned disappointed. Again, he was arrested in 1915 in connection with another political dacoity in Calcutta. In the same year, he fled to Dutch Indies. He also visited Japan, China, U.S.A., Mexico, Germany and Russia. He reached San Francisco in late 1915. It was here that he came in contact with the Indian revolutionaries and Indian students who were working for the national struggle. Roy also tried to organise them to provide a forum for the Indian National Struggle. He also worked for some time here in collaboration with Lala Lajpat Rai. At the same time, he changed his name from Narendra Nath Bhattacharya to Manovendra Nath Roy.

From the U.S.A., M.N. Roy went to Mexico. Here, he contributed several articles about India's poverty and the method in which the Britishers were exploiting Indian resources. In Mexico. Roy founded the first Communist Party outside the U.S.S.R. and became its Secretary-General. While he was in Mexico, he was called by V.I. Lenin after the Bolshevik Revolution to Russia. Roy reached Russia in the beginning of 1920 and became an advisor of the Bolshevik Party on colonial questions. Here, he also attended the second Congress of the Communist International. He put forward his own thesis and even pointed out the defects of resolutions sponsored by Lenin. He had a difference of opinion with Lenin.

To quote Overstreet and Miller, "Lenin believed that Bourgeios Nationalist Movements were characteristically revolutionary and the Communists should support them. Roy believed that they were not revolutionaries, and therefore, were unworthy of support."

In fact, Roy's views were more realistic and Lenin was impressed by his thesis. M.N. Roy was also elected as the member of the Central Asiatic Board by the Communist Party to propagate the cause of Communism in India.

In the year 1922, M.N. Roy went to Berlin to organise the Indian National revolutionaries there and also started a Journal, *The Vangaurd of Indian Independence.* He was named a member of the Presidium of the Comintern at its fourth Congress International.

M.N. Roy pleaded for a separate Communist Party in India to spread Communism there in a better way. He also suggested the formation of People's Party with a revolutionary programme. He was then sent to China to propagate Communism there. But he was not successful in his mission.

In 1922, Roy published his book, *India's Problem and Its Solution* in which he condemned the Gandhian Social Ideology as it did not contain any revolutionary programme. Gradually, he got dissatisfied with the Communist Organisation and began to differ from its members. Therefore, in 1928, he even did not attend the Sixth Congress of the Communist International.

On account of his differences with the Communist Organisation, Roy came back to India in December 1930. Here, he soon contacted the Indian revolutionaries. For some time, he could not be detected by the Indian Police Personnel and thus could consolidate his position.

On the invitation of Pandit Jawaharlal Nehru, M.N. Roy, attended the Karachi Session of the Indian National Congress. In July 1931 he was however arrested and imprisoned for six years. After his release in 1936, he became a member of the Indian National Congress which he wished to organise on a revolutionary basis.

In April 1937, he started his weekly, *Independent India.* Later on it was named as *Radical Humanist.* He also formed a league of radical congressmen.

During the 2nd World War, Roy developed differences with the Congress. The dominant group in the Indian National Congress wanted to boycott war efforts by Indians in favour of the Britishers. But Roy held the opinion that England was fighting war against Fascism and Nazism. So every Indian should contribute with money and material to avoid the spread of Nazism in the world. He even criticised the movments of Mahatma Gandhi.

In 1940, Roy founded 'Radical Democratic Party' separate from Indian National Congress.

In l944, he founded 'Indian Federation of Labour'.

After Independence, in 1948, Roy dissolved his Radical Democratic Party and established 'Indian Renaissance Movement' in its place.

In 1952, he was elected Vice-President of 'International Humanist and Ethical Association' in Amsterdam. He died on January 25, 1954, probably unknown.

His Works M.N. Roy was a prolofic writer. Some of his important works are as under :

1. *India in Transition.*
2. *Revolution and Counter-revolution in China.*
3. *Our Differences.*
4. *Materialism.*
5. *Science and Philosophy.*
6. *People's Plan.*
7. *On the Congress Constitution.*
8. *National Government or People's Government.*
9. *Rise, Romanticism and Revolution, etc.*

He also contributed several articles in various papers and established his own journals to propagate his ideas.

Humanism Manavendra Nath Roy was a born revolutionary. As mentioned earlier, he came under the influence of Marxism while in the U.S.A. He was one of the most learned persons of the Marxist world and had a safe chance to secure a top position in the Communist world. But later on differences arose between M.N. Roy and Stalin, and Roy was condemned as a revisionist and a pronounced critic of communist theory and practice. As time passed. M.N. Roy became a great critic of Marxism and came to the conclusion that Communism provided no solution to worldly problems. After 1955, he changed over from Marxism to what he called 'Radical Humanism', 'New Humanism'. It is a great contribution of M.N. Roy to Modern Indian Political Thought.

M.N. Roy termed his Humanism as rational, radical or new with a view to distinguishing it from the humanist versions of other thinkers. The term 'Humanism' is not new and the same can be traced in the writings of Protagoras, Erasmus, More, Herder, Jacques Maritain, etc. Roy himself admitted that humanism 'is an old and venerable tradition in the history of human thought'. The 19th Century humanists attached great importance to man and individual liberty but Roy believed that they could not 'get away from the fallacy of subordinating man to some super-human and super-natural agencies. To Roy, man is the centre of that Humanism which banishes every type of supernatural agency from the human world. The Indian humanists like Raja Ram Mohan Roy, Rabindranath Tagore, Sri Aurobindo, Gandhiji and Pt. Jawaharlal Nehru also attached the greatest importance to man and individual liberty. But according to Roy, none of them can be called a true humanist. M.N. Roy explained 'Radical Humanism' as a 'Philosophy of freedom based on modern scientific knowledge'. The fundamental principles of his philosophy are summarised as under :

Nature of Man According to M.N. Roy, man is a part of physical nature on account of his biological descent and there is nothing extra-natural in man. Man is the product of biological evolution and grows out of the back-ground of inaminate nature. Everything in man which deals with biological evolution is thus traceable. Soul or atman which is beyond and mind cannot be thus traced, hence, to radical humanist, there is no soul or atman. The theory of soul and God had no place in the philosophy of radical humanism. Another consequence is that, man himself must be law — governed like physical nature. Man is an integral part of the physical universe; which is a moral order governed by laws inherent in it. M.N. Roy named these laws as natural laws and are derived from experience. The regularity of nature is a fact of man's experience. It is the rational nature of man which discovers these laws by establishing casual relations in nature. Man's reason is nothing but he has power to become familiar with the law-governed character of this universe. Man's reason helps him to make an effort to understand the law of gravitation.

According to M.N. Roy, reason or brain has grown as a result of man's link with physical universe and the stimulus provided by it after the growth of nervous systems in man. Hence, reason results 'from the consciousness of man's being an integral part of law governed physical nature'. Man is rational by instinct, therefore, to a radical humanist, all super-human, religious and super-natural powers are meaningless. To Roy, a religious man is a symptom of a bad case of hysteria. There is no place of supernatural things and factors like the Divine will or a soul distinct from human consciousness whose existence cannot be scientifically prayed. A radical humanist is interested only in those things which can be shown to affect human life. A person who believes that God has created the world and that the destiny of an individual is determinated by his fate or will of God can never become a humanist. Hence, a radical humanist has no faith in any mystic or transcendental entity called God, Providence, Brahman or the Absolute.

Materialism Another fundamental principle of M.N. Roy's Philosophy of Radical Humanism is materialism. He was a thorough going Marxist but he differed from Karl Marx in details. He continued to be a materialist, but believed that marxian doctrine of Materialism was dogmatic and unscientific. Roy interpreted the term materialism in a different way. He wrote in an introduction to *Scientific Politics,* "Our approach to the problems of political theory and practice claimed to be free from any dogmatic pre-supposition. Otherwise, we could not pretend to be advocates of Scientific Politics. Freedom from dogma is the specific feature of thought. Those who regard Marxism as such a closed system of thought, cannot also pretend to subscribe to the iconoclastic principles of Radicalism which knows no dogma and respects no authority". Thus, he took the scientific method of Marx in his new philosophy of Radical Humanism. M.N. Roy regarded matter as real and independent. Mind is the outcome of matter. In Roy's view there was no difference between the organic and in-organic matter. All living bodies were created out of certain chemical matters. Roy believed that mind was the product of matter at a high stage of development. In the words of Dr. Sharma, 'The term matter, however, has not been used in the old classical sense, *i.e.*, in terms of its ultimate constituents, called atoms, existing in space and time. In the light of modern scientific knowledge, matter has been identified with energy. According to this view, the mass and motion of a thing are simply due to electrical charge. Space and time, too, are derivative categories representing respectively the geometrical and chronological functions of material existence'.

On the basis of matter, M.N. Roy explained the origin of life and mind. Biological evolution takes place from physical universe. In the words of Roy, 'For, it represents the knowledge of nature as it really exists. Knowledge acquired through the contemplation, observation and investigation of the phenomenon of nature itself.... It simply maintain that the origin of everything that really exists is matter, that there does not exist anything but matter, all other appearances being transformations of matter, and these transformations are governed necessarily by laws inherent in nature.... our bodies, our organs of sensation..... the nervous system, the brain, the entire cognitive apparatus have grown out of the background of inanimate matter'. All living bodies are formed out of such chemical elements as, carbon, oxygen hydrogen, nitrogen, sulphur, potassium, sodium, etc. Hence, to Roy, there is a close relationship between mind and matter. Every living body is the product of matter. M.N. Roy corroborated his materialistic philosophy wih the latest scientific knowledge.

Individual Freedom Next fundamental concept of the Radical Humanists is concerning the relation between the individual and society. Of the two they gave primacy to the individual. According to M.N. Roy, individual was an end in itself and society was simply a means to an end. He subordinated everthing to individual freedom. According to Roy, man created society for certain objects. It meant that all social relations, political, economic, social and ethical must be adjusted to the fundamental requirement of promoting the freedom or liberty of the individual. Roy even subordinated religion and morality or any other supernatural power to individual freedom. In the words of Ellen and Roy, 'The purpose of all rational human endeavour, individual as well as collective, is attainment of freedom in an ever-increasing measure. Freedom is progressive disappearance of all restrictions or the unfolding of the potentialities of individuals as human beings, and not as cogs in the wheels of a Mechanised social organism.' The position of the individual therefore, is the measure of the progressive and liberating influence of any collective effort or social organisation. The success of any collective endeavour is to be measured by the actual benefit for its constituent units.' The main object of radical humanist is to ensure the freedom of the individual.

M. N. Roy held that the slogan of individual liberty was empty in the 19th century liberalism. He wanted to revive the liberty of the individual. He used the word 'Radical' before Humanism. Roy's humanism included radicalism. To him, the greater the rationalism of the individuals composing a society, the larger would be the measure of freedom enjoyed by them. The object of radical humanists was to organise society in a rational manner. The more rationality, the greater would be the freedom. According to Roy, the individual will not be fully free unless the society is organised on rational basis.

According to M.N. Roy, the state and the society have been established to maintain individual liberty. But unfortunately, some devices are trying to dominate man and are suppressing his freedom. Religion or morality is also destroying individual liberty imposing on human mind the chains of superstition and supernatural beliefs. Roy regarded marriage, family and class as the hindrances to human development and freedom. He also regarded society and class as the greatest obstacles to individual freedom. Roy wanted that society should be understood as means to an end and not end in itself.

Views about History M.N. Roy rejected Karl Marx's view point about history as a dialectical process governed by the economic forces alone. According to him, there were many forces and factors which determined the course of history. Even the economic factor, to Roy, was not the most important; cultural and ideological factors played a more important role in the process of history. Thus, Roy said, 'History, therefore, does not follow the Marxian pattern of dialectics, but is a movement from homogeneous masses to the evolution of distinct individualistic experimenting in various forms of harmonisation between themselves.' M.N. Roy regarded history as a record of struggle for freedom. It was the story of man's quest for freedom. Roy was of the opinion that the people had always fought for their political or social or economic freedom. The struggle for freedom did not come to an end.

Criticism M.N. Roy's philosophy of radical humanism has been criticised on so many grounds.

According to Roy, all living bodies originated out of the matter. Even the mind is the product of matter. But Roy has failed to give logical and adequate reasons as to how the living bodies are created out of matter. He builds his theory on the presumption that man is essentially a rational being. Everything is to be decided by reason. Reason plays a very important role in the life of an individual. But unfortunately Roy has failed to explain clearly the term 'reason'.

Similarly, Roy has also condemned religion as a hindrance in the development of freedom. But his opinion about religion is wrong. In fact, religion plays a very significant role in our cultural and intellectual development. Religion is a part of human life. It is quite undesirable to condemn the institution of religion, which plays a very important role in human life.

Another presumption of Roy is that physical and social beings are governed by the same laws but such an analogy is not correct. M.N. Roy's concept of individual freedom is also misleading.

To quote Dr. Goyal, "A political philosophy or a scheme of social reconstruction is useless unless it provides the concrete contents of individual freedom. Roy regarded the institution of marriage and family as obstacles in the development of freedom. But who can deny that marriage and family satisfy the sex and parental instincts? So it is undesirable to denounce the institution of marriage and family."

Views on Modern Democracy Manavendra Nath Roy was a great lover of individual freedom. The most remarkable feature of his philosophy of 'Radical Humanism' was considering relations between the individual and the society. Of the two Roy gave primacy to the individual. He should be regarded as an end in itself and society as a means to an end. He subordinated everything to individual freedom. Roy emphasised the importance of the individual and his liberty. He was of the opinion that man had always fought with his environment for freedom. Roy regarded history as a record of human struggle for freedom. Man created society to attain freedom. He entered a state for peace and security. According to Roy, the main function of the state should be 'to regulate public relations in such a manner as to promote the general welfare without any prejudice to the freedom of the individual'. To quote him, "Freedom is a human urge, an instinct for whose satisfaction he fought against physical nature." Roy wanted the individual in society to be able to enjoy economic sufficiency and security but live in a social psychological atmosphere free from cultural regimentation and helpful to the development of his intellectual and other human potentialities. According to him, individual liberty was possible only in a proper democratic set up.

Criticism According to M.N. Roy, there is no individual freedom in the present form of democratic institutions, not even to speak of collectivist and regimental states. So Roy criticises the institutions of modern democracy.

According to him, the modern democratic states accept the ideal of individual freedom only in theory, but in actual practice the individual is suppressed under collective control in the name of collective welfare.

Democracy ensures neither better government nor greater liberty. Indeed, some of the strongest democratic tendencies are adverse to liberty. On the contrary strong arguments may be adduced both from history and from the nature of things to show that modern democracy may often prove the direct opposite of liberty.

Roy was of the opinion that in the past the political power was concentrated in the hands of a few persons. Even in the modern democratic states we find the rule of the elite or of a few persons. The masses are controlled in the name of 'Popular Governments' and the ideal of popular sovereignty. Masses have no control over the affairs of the state. There is no link between the people and their elected representatives. The introduction of representative institutions has also paralysed initiative among the people.

Another defect of modern democracy is that it lacks responsibility in the elected representatives of the people. The system of representation in a modern democratic state is, based on false presumption and that leads to the rule of demagogues who are experts in the art of manipulating elections.

According to M.N. Roy, the emergence of political parties in the working of democracy has brought in its wake all the evils of party politics. To quote him, 'With the rise of party system, the idea of popular sovereignty became a constitutional fiction. The political parties encourage hollowness and insincerity, lead to spoils system and debase moral standards. In the modern democratic states, there is rule by a party which constitutes only a small fraction of the people, in fact, a rule by minority over majority.'

According to Roy, the system of party-politics leads to bribery and corruption. The main object of political parties is to capture political power by all means. They do not hesitate to retain power with the unscruplous and corrupt means. Money plays a very important role in politics. In the struggle for power, political parties ignore the principles of morality and public welfare.

Roy was of the opinion that the people above corruption stay out of the scramble for power because it might corrupt even the best of men. He held the view that in the name of welfare state, the party in power restricts freedom of the people. He, therefore, suggested the system of organised democracy for establishing the real freedom of the individual.

His concept of organised democracy M.N. Roy's concept of organised democracy was based on decentralization and partyless democracy. Like Jaya Prakash Narayan, he also opposed the system of Party-Politics. In his organised democracy, there was no place of political parties and the power was to be vested in the hands of the people themselves. The people will be sovereign in this new social order. Roy wanted that his concept of organised democracy should be put in practice. In his own words, 'Even in large political units and highly complex social organisations of the modern world, direct democracy will be possible in the form of a network of small co-operative common wealths which will replace the helpless atomised voter of formal parliamentary democracy. Under this new system, the principle of popular sovereignty will be real and effective. The whole structure of the system will be based on local democracies'. Roy, however, laid down some basic conditions for the success of his organised democracy. One such condition was that the people should be of sufficiently high general cultural level. The power should be vested only in those persons who have high moral charcter and high standard of intelligence. Otherwise, they will be duped by clever demagogues. In the words of M.N. Roy, "Until the intellectual level of the entire community is raised considerably, election alone cannot possibly bring its best elements to the forfront and unless the available intellectual detachment and moral integrity are brought to bear upon the situation, democracy cannot come to her own". He also observed that the people had not as yet attained high intellectual and moral standards, so, he suggested that in the initial stages there should be elective and selective democracy both. Roy drafted a model Constitution 'Constitution of Free India' on this basis which was to be a model of his organised democracy.

Constitution of Free India As mentioned earlier, Roy drafted a model Constitution of India on the basis of his organised democracy. Part I of the constitution deals with the declaration of rights and fundamental principles, according to which supreme sovereignty is vested in the people who have absolute right to change or modify any political unit. The people will exercise their soverign power through People's Committees in villages, towns and cities. A bill of rights containing not only political and social, but economic rights also is incorporated in the Constitution.

The method of proportional representation has been also incorporated in the constitution to protect the rights of minorities. According to Roy, all the provinces in India, will be formed on the basis of linguistic and cultural homogeneity. He suggested a federal type of government and the institutions of referendum, initiative and recall. The following institutions have been suggested by Roy in his model Constitution for free India :

People's Committees M.N. Roy suggested the system of direct democracy where the power flows from the people. The people will exercise their sovereign power through the local people's committees.

The main object of Roy to suggest People's Committees was to purify politics and to eliminate the party system.

According to him, 'Political ends can be achieved with out capuring power. Politics can be practised without a party organisation'. There will be a people's committee in each village, city or town, elected annually on the basis of adult suffrage (18 years or of above age). The total number of each people's committee will be l/5th of the total number of voters in the locality. Roy suggested that larger and larger powers of managing local affairs should be entrusted to these committees.

In the words of Ellen and Roy, these institutions shall be the effective centres of organised democracy, bringing in the process of their growth and development the existing gap between state and society. Growing out of the co-operation of discriminate individuals, and drawing in more and more local people into its functioning, these committees shall simultaneously be the units of the state and central social institutions of the local people. They shall also be the media through which experiments in co-operation between the educated few and the common people shall have to be made. And as in the process, more and more people shall develop ability and desire for administration of social life, the danger of state becoming omnipotent at the expense of individual liberty shall be greatly reduced.

The other functions of these committees shall be to nominate candidates for seeking election to the provincial council and to the Federal Assembly; to recommend the recall of elected representatives of the respective constituency either in the Federal Assembly or in the Provincial People's Council and to recommend the recall of the Governor General or the Governor of the respective province. The people's committees shall also initiate legislation and could demand a referendum on any legislative or executive measure. In short, the People's Committees shall become the political schools to train the people in intelligent citizenship.

Provincial People's Councils Each province shall have a Provincial Peoples Council consisting of the Governor and Deputies of the people. The Governor shall be elected directly by the people of the province for the term of five years. The Deputies of the people will also be elected directly by the people of the province for a period of four years. This council shall meet once in three months to legislate on all matters except those reserved for the Federal Assembly. It will also form a Provincial Council of Ministers to perform the executive functions of the province. The Council of Ministers will be collectively responsible to the council. The provincial People's Council shall also supervise and control the working of various departments in the province.

Supreme People's Council Roy suggested Federal Union for free India which will include both the British India and the Indian provinces. According to him, all the provinces in India will be formed on the basis of linguistic and cultural homogeneity. The provinces shall have the right to secede from the Federal Union Roy suggested that the Federation of India shall be a member of British Commonwealth. He also suggested the system of refendum. At the central level, there shall be a Supreme People's Council consisting of the Governor-General, Council of State and the Federal Assembly. The Governor-General shall be elected by the entire electorate of the Federal Union for a period of five years. He shall preside over the joint sessions of the Council of the State and Federal Assembly.

Federal Assembly It will consist of elected representatives of the Federal Union, each representative for every five lakh people. They shall be elected for four years on the basis of adult franchise in a manner specially devised for the election. It will meet at least quarterly and could he dissolved by the Governor-General before the tarm on the recommendation of the Prime Minister. The Federal Assembly will legislate on the subjects other than assigned to the Provincial Councils. It will form a Federal Council of Ministers to perform the administrative duties. The Council of Ministers shall be responsible to the Supreme People's Council. The Federal Assembly shall also supervise and control the working of various departments.'

Council of State It will consist of intelligent people, appointed by the Provincial Government for the period of six years, and its numbers shall be equal for all the Provinces. The members will be nominated from the various professions — Engineers, Economists, Scientists, Medical Men, Jurists and Historians, the persons who have made outstanding contribution to modern throught in Philosophy or the Social Sciences and the three civil servants from each province. The Council of State will be an advisory body, to guide and advise the assembly. It will also supervise planning and other branches of society, economic, health, education, culture, etc.

In addition to this, Roy also suggested the organisation of judiciary to deal with cases brought before it both by citizens and the provinces. He also mentioned the various institutions to perform the functions of local self-government in their respective areas. These institutions will be responsible for maintaining sanitation, public health, education — primary and secondary — building and maintenance of roads and public parks, etc.

Criticism M.N. Roy's concept of organised democracy has been condemned on so many grounds. His views on Partyless and Powerless democracy are very interesting. Neither they are useful nor original. Mahatma Gandhi preached the concept of Powerless democracy, in India. At present the Sarvodaya School of thought is preaching the same ideas.

The critics point out that Roy's views about organised democracy have no mass appeal. His views could not get popularity and had not gone beyond the circle of a few intelligent persons.

Secondly, Roy could not properly understand the relation between the individual and society. He laid too much stress on the importance of individual liberty. Roy was of the opinion that man created society and had to accept the bondages of society to become the member of the state. But he forgot that 'man is a social animal' and society is essential for man for his proper development and also very existence. In fact, Roy failed to understand the importance of society.

Thirdly, he laid too much stress on the role of People's Committees. It needs a high degree of character and public spiritendness among the people.

Fourthly, M.N. Roy had condemned and discarded the institution of religion. Religion had played a very important role in preserving our culture and civilisation. Roy had failed to understand the significance of relation. It should not be regarded as irrational.

Lastly, Roy like Jaya Prakash Narayan advocated Powerless and Partyless democracy. Nobody can deny the evils of Party-politics. But the democratic institutions cannot function without the existence of the political parties. Both go together. It is impossible to eliminate political parties. Even Roy's concept of organised democracy is not possible without political parties. In the elections, party system will emerge in one form or the other. It is very difficult to organise the electorate in such a big country like India without the party system. Infact, democracy cannot exist without political parties.

Manavendra Nath Roy's concept of organised democracy is impracticable. It can work successfully only in small countries where the people are very intelligent and have high moral character cannot exist. So it is very much doubtful that Roy's concept of organised democracy is practicable.

His Views on Marxism Manavendra Nath Roy has been described as the most colourful of all non-Russian Communists in the era of Lenin and Stalin. He was a born revolutionary. Like other revolutionaries, he was receptive of Marxism. His love for Marxian Philosophy was so deep that under his arrangement, the only solution to existing Indian problems lay in Marxism. M.N. Roy regarded Marx as a merciless critic of social injustice in the traditions of the great Jewish Prophets. Like Marx. Roy was a staunch materialist. He continued to be a materialist, "for, it represents the knowledge of nature as it really exists, knowledge acquired through the contemplation, observation and investigation of the phenomenon of nature itself... It simply maintain that the origin of everything that really exists is matter, that there does not exist anything but matter, all other appearances being transformations of matter, and these transformation are governed necessarily by laws inherent in nature." Roy was one of the most learned persons of the Marxist world and had a safe chance to secure a top position in the Communist world. But later on differences arose between Roy and Stalin. As time passed, he became a great critic of Marxism and came to the conclusion that Communism provided no solution to wordly problems. After 1946, he changed over from Marxism to Radical Humanism.

Manavendra Nath Roy accepted, however, even in his humanist phase some of the principles of Marxian thought. First, he continued to be a staunch materialist. In this sense Roy was a thorough-going Marxist. Like Karl Marx, he regarded matter as real and independent. According to him, even mind was the product of matter at a high stage of development. Roy also studied the latest scientific theories. Materialist philosophy, according to Roy, was corroborated by the latest scientific knowledge. Secondly, like Karl Marx, Roy regarded the capitalist system of economy most rotten and out dated. He was of the opinion that industry should be controlled by the people themselves. Like Marx, he worked on the essential principle that there should be no exploitation of the poor by the rich. Thirdly, Roy was in agreement with Marx that any action, to be successful, must be in consonance with a clear thought and plan. But any plan, to be effective, should also be based on the existing structure of things. Fourthly, like Marx, Roy believed that all knowledge has its roots in the physical universe. To quote him, 'To seek the knowledge of the phenomenon of nature in a hypothetical supernatural sense, is logically absurd and philosophically in admissible.' He regarded sensations and perceptions as the sources of knowledge.

Criticism As mentioned earlier, M.N. Roy became a great critic of Marxian philosophy later on. So far as Marx's teachings are concerned, either he repudiated them or made substantial modifications in them. Roy provided a detailed criticism of Marxism. First, Roy was a staunch materialist but he believed that Marxian doctrine of materialism was dogmatic and unscientific. Roy interpreted the term materialism in a different way. He wrote in an introduction to *Scientific Politics*, "Our approach to he problems of political theory and practice is claimed to be free from any dogmatic pre-supposition. Otherwise, we could not pretend to be advocates of scientific politics, Freedom from dogma is the specific feature of scientific thought. Those who regard Marxism as such a closed system of thought, cannot also pretend to subscribe to the iconoclastic principles of radicalism which knows to dogma and respects no authority." According to Roy, Marx under the influence of Hegelian dialectics had rejected the 18th century materialism of Ludwing Feuerback. He held the view that it was quite unfortunate on the part of Marx.

Secondly, according to M.N. Roy, the principal defect of Marxism is its denial of individual liberty. In his opinion, there was complete regimentation in Marxism, no place for individual freedom and the individual was a slave in the name of freedom. To quote him, "History is made by the operation of the productive forces; there is little man can do about it, he must recognise necessity and then he is free, once you realise that you cannot be free that you are bound hand and foot to some mysterious forces of production, then you are free". Marx did not pay adequate attention to the worth and significance of the empirical individual.

Thirdly, Roy was highly critical of Marxian theory of dialectical materialism. To quote him, "the dialectic process does not leave any room for the greatest of revolutionaries, armed with the philosophy of Marxism, to change the world. The irreconcilable contradiction between dialectic materialism and the programme of a revolutionary reconstruction of society is the basic fallacy of Marxism." He did not agree with the historical interpretation given by Marx. Roy had doubts on the sociology of class-struggle. There have been so many different social classes in history. Besides the forces of social tensions and struggles there had also been operative a social cohesive bond. Further, the failure of contemporary society to get divided into antisectors as prophesied by Marx adds additional material for doubts upon the Marxist thesis.

Fourthly, Marx had been proved to be a false prophet in his statement regarding the disappearance of the middle classes. Instead, the middle classes emerged as a powerful and forceful factor that influenced in moulding national policies and programmes. In fact, the expansion of the economic process also leads to the increase in the numbers of middle class.

Fifthly, Roy was critical of Marx's rejection of the liberal concept of individualism. This he did under the influence of Hegel's theory of moral positivism. According to Roy, moral positivism resulted in the minimization of the role of the individual. In his neglect of the value of the individual autonomy, by rejecting the liberal concept of the individual Marx virtually betrayed his earlier humanism.

Sixthly, Roy also condemned Karl Marxs economic interpretation of history. He was of the opinion that biology and not economics dictated the early activities of mankind. The theory of historical materialism was faulty as it did not seek to explain and analyse the primitive history of the human species. Even in later history of man we find that there were diverse types of activities wherein mankind found satisfaction without economic factor. Thus, economic determinism did not necessarily follow as a logical corollary from the philosophy of materialism. Hence, Roy concludes that there is not inevitable connection between the philosophical materialism and economic interpretation of history.

Lastly, Roy felt that the ethical foundations of Marxism were weak because of their relativistic and dogmatic nature. Marx expounded the radical behaviouristic concept that in the process of struggles with nature, man changes his own nature. There is nothing stable in human nature. According to Roy, the psychological foundations of Marxian philosophy were also weak. In opposition to Marx Roy accepted that there is something stable and permanent in human nature which is the basis of our duties and rights. According to him, the subordination of man to the dominance of the forces of production was a neutralisation of his autonomy and creativity. Morality was not the product of economic forces. In opposition to Marxian Ethics, Roy presented humanist ethics, which exalts the sovereignty of the individual and beliefs in freedom and justice. To Roy there was something permanent in the ethical values.

Thus, Roy had only discussed the drawbacks of Marxist Philosophy and the sociology of historical materialism. But he did not enter into the technicalities of Marxian economics.

16

Jawaharlal Nehru (1889-1964)

(1) Introduction

Pandit Jawaharlal Nehru dominated the Indian political science for about half a century. Together with Gandhiji, he fought and struggled hard for the freedom of India. In fact, he dedicated his life to the cause of his country. After Independence, he remained the Prime Minister of his country for 17 years till his death. During this period, he raised India to an important position among nations of the world. It was sincere work for peaceful coexistence and faith in democratic socialism which made him popular not only in India but throughout the world. Perhaps this is the reason that he is called by Lord Boyd Orr as the ablest and most highly respected leader among what should rightly be termed as the free nations... Stalin called him 'the Man of Peace' Even Chou-En-Lai called him as 'A great gentleman'.

In Gandhiji's words, "He is fearless, yet gentle, being a stranger to weakness and weakening diffidence, detects weakness in a flash; having no diplomacy about him, hates diplomatic language and insists upon going straight to the compliment by dismissing my claim. I honour him."

Rabindra Nath Tagore, too, testified to his straight-forwardness when he said : "He never fought shy of truth when it was dangerous, nor made alliance with falsehood when it would be convenient."

According to Dr. S. Radhakrishan, "As a man, Nehru combined a fine sensitivity of mind, a rate delicacy of feeling, with large and generous impulses. To the weak and the frustrated, his heart went out in profound sympathy. He was an author of distinction. His *Autobiography*, which tells the story of his life and struggle, without a touch of self-pity or moral superiority, is one of the most remarkable books of our time.

Life and Works

(a) *Various Influences on Pandit Nehru*

The factors that constitute personality are difficult to explain. All explanations are conditional. The inherent traits, family environment, social background apart, motivation, education, and associations are some of its highly significant constituents. Panditji had the economic security and the cultured environment to stimulate his motivations and to prop his efforts. Very much also, he has been influenced by Mahatma Gandhi, the cultural heritage, Marxist dialectics and by the jail going ordeals.

Impact of Gandhiji

Mahatma Gandhi, the selfless man, that he was, had established complete identity, with the political problem, which he was determined to resolve; equally, he was one with the men who were involved with this work. Pandit Nehru, amongst them, invited his deep attention. And, no less, to Nehru, Gandhiji was the model, whom he described the "Indian leadership, Indian style." This deep understanding of Gandhi, gave great strength to Nehru. Gandhi had perfected his character. He was a man of action. He believed in truth; and, was an experimentalist. His commitment to Swaraj, which Nehru described, "delightfully vague," was uncompromisable. Gandhiji did not, however, allow it to stand in the way of Nehru's aim of complete Independence. The two had ultimately the common aim the honesty of purpose. They acted, the selfless way. This kept them honour bound one to other, even when, at times they did not see eye to eye. Nehru had complete communion with Gandhi. His deep impact, his illustrious example, and the faith in his leadership made Nehru say on the death of Gandhiji "the light has gone out of our lives and there is darkness everywhere..." Gandhi during his life charmed Nehru and after his death remained an inspiration to him.

Influence of Ancient Heritage

Being deeply cultured and highly educated, Jawaharlal got attracted to heritage, despite all the Westernism attributed to him. He was intelligent enough to be attracted by its eternal appeal. Its quiet impact, on him is for anybody to see. His rationalism, made him see in it, the compelling force and the guiding principle. The birds eye view of these readings and of the conclusions he has given in the *Discovery of India*, is rewarding to any reader. It is no less his confession of indebtedness to it.

> "The roots of that present lay in the past and so I made voyages of discovery into the past, ever seeking clue in it, if any such

existed, to the understanding of the present. The domination of the present never left me even when I lost myself in musings of past events and of persons far away and long ago, forgetting where or what I was. If felt occasionally that I belonged to the past, I felt also that the past belonged to me in the present. Past history merged into contemporary history; It became a living reality tied up with sensations of pain and pleasure."

The strength of Indian culture and its continuity is simply amazing. It is to many, and it was so no less to Nehru. "If her basic culture survived these contacts there must have been something in that culture itself which gave it the dynamic strength to do so, some inner vitality and understanding of life. For this three or four thousand years of cultural growth and continuity is remarkable." To make his point clear, he quotes, the words of Max Muller "There is, in fact, an unbroken continuity between the most modern and the most ancient phases of Hindu thought, extending over more than three thousand years." And further he refers to his famous words : "If we were to look over the whole world to find out the country most richly endowed with all the wealth, power, and beauty that nature can bestow — in some parts a very paradise on earth — I should point to India. If I were asked under what sky the human mind has most fully developed some of its choicest gifts, has most deeply pondered over the greatest problems of life and has found solutions of some of them which well deserve the attention even of those who have studied Plato and Kant-I should point to India. And if I were to ask myself from what literature we here in Europe, we who have been nurtured almost exclusively on the thoughts of Greeks and Romans, and of one Semitic race, the Jewish, may draw the corrective which is most wanted in order to make our inner life more perfect, more comprehensive, more universal, in fact more truly human a life, not for this life only, but a transfightured and eternal life-again I should point to India". He adds further : "Nearly half a century later Romain Rolland wrote in the same strain; 'If there is one place on the face of the earth where all the dreams of living men have found a home from the very earliest days when man began the dream of existence, it is India." This heritage has its own attraction. He drew solace out of it; it was to him the source of constant inspiration. The small size copy of the Bhagaved Geeta, that he always kept with him, bears full testimony to it.

"It is the thought of this particular heritage and its application to the present that has long filled my mind, and it is about this that I should like to write, though the difficulty and complexity of the subject appeal me and I can only touch the surface of it. I cannot do justice to it, but in attempting it I might be able to do some justice to myself by clearing my own mind and preparing it for the next stages of thought and action". His appreciation of the heritage and his effort to understand it, is clear. Its application in the present conditions did engage his mind.

Marx and Socialism

The recent past, had no less meaning for him. "A study of Marx and Lenin produced a powerful effect on my mind and helped me to see history and current affairs in a new light. The long chain of history and of social development appeared to have some meaning, some sequence, and the future lost some of its obscurity. The practical achievements of the Soviet Union were also tremendously impressive." Yet the "over much regimentation", it envisaged did not appeal him. He did not overlook the contradictions in it. He however, did not bother to attend to these. His feeling, was that the "lesser liberties may often need limitatiohs in the interest of the larger freedom."

He claimed to be, and truly, he was heir, "To all this and much more, in common with all men. But there is a special heritage for those of us of India, not an exclusive one, for none is exclusive and all are common to the race of man, one more especially applicable to us, something that is in our flesh and blood and bones, that has gone to make us what we are and what we are likely to be."

Jail going

Jail going was an experience to him. It gave him time to study and meditate to find answer to his question. "Long after, looking back on these fallow years, he remarked that it was the acceptance of Gandhi's leadership, and the civil disobedience and jail-going which had followed, that had made a man of him. Life now had meaning in the service of a cause". His complete identity with man in the street, coupled with his socialist democratic aspirations gave to Jawaharlal, a matter of fact approach. His clarity of mind, sweeping imagination and cultivated mannerism made him a rare finished product of a long cultural heritage.

(b) Early Life and Education

Jawaharlal was born on November, 14, 1889, in the midst of affluence and luxury that had come to the family, due to the newly acquired fortune by his father Motilal Nehru. Being the first living son of his father, from his second wife Swaruparani (both the first born son and the first wife of Motilal had died earlier); the new born was the total attraction of his parents. He was brought up with extra care and emotion charged affection.

Nothing, they felt was too much for and nothing they keep away from him. After, the Nehrus shifted to their newly purchased house, which is now known as the Swaraj Bhawan, the springing lad was provided with all the best that wealth could secure for him. They remained, till 1929, in this house.

Motilal, was keen to provide his son, the education as best as his wealth could procure. The learned Sanskrit scholar, Pandit Ganganath Jha was fixed to teach him Sanskrit; and on the recommendation of Mrs. Annie Besant, F.T. Brooks, was appointed to teach him English. The young boy did not respond to the Sanskrit learning, but he did well in learning English. Mr. Brooks, is said to have also induced him to read the *Upanishads* and the *Bhagwad Geeta.* Jawaharlal, from his parents, got the nice upbringing, good education, cultured living and economic security, all in full measure. These, though great assets, do not explain, the true, the guiding and the deep abiding impact if any, of his parents on him.

In his fifteenth year, Motilal got Jawaharlal admitted to him the Harrow Public School, in England. Here, he showed, himself a hard working student. The headmaster, reporting, his progress to his father, noted; "Progress good — has brains." But, the youngman, during his stay, at the school, never felt happy. He did not, however, fell homesick. In 1907, he joined the Cambridge. He was associated formally with several student bodies, but he remained on the whole a quiet scholar. After his Tripos, he joined the Inner Temple for his professional degree, in law. The formal education in England did not enamour him. He liked, however, the British environment. It left a deep impact on him.

A distinctive feature of this period was that he showed interest in the political development at home. He wrote to his father for a regular supply of newspapers. He was back home in August 1912.

While, Jawaharlal was in England, his father was looking for a girl, here to be married to him. After a long search he picked up Kamala, a girl of thirteen from a middle class Kashmere family of Delhi. The engagement over, she was brought to Allahabad and moulded to fit, the Nehru family. Subsequently, the marriage solemnised on Fabruary 8, 1916, at Delhi, Nehru was then ten years senior to his spouse. They had their first child Indira, in November.

Jawaharlal joined his father's Chambers in Allahabad. But the profession of law did not attract him. He, instead got involved in the public activity of a sort : served as one of the secretaries of St. John Ambulance Association; associated for himself actively with the U.P. South African Committee for the collection of funds for the passive resisters in the

South Africa. He also helped his father, to run the 'Independent' which he had started in February 1919.

(c) His Role in Politics

The Jalianwala Bagh tragedy shook the contemporary society and Jawaharlal was no exception to it. For the Amritsar victims, he organized relief. He went, with his father, on a fact finding mission to Amritsar. This work and the connected developments brought him in contact with Gandhiji. In consequence, he was one of the first to sign the Satyagraha pledge which Gandhiji initiated soon after. He, thus was coming to politics, the phantasm, that is was at that time.

In the summer of 1920, he was with his family at Mussorie staying in a Hotel, where also stagyed an Afghan delegation, presumed to have come to support the Khilafat movement. The government felt that the members of the delegation might be used as contact men with Indians in Afghanistan and Russia, therefore, the local police was asked to secure from Jawaharlal an undertaking, not to get in touch with the delegation. To this Jawaharlal did not agree. He yielded to the expulsion order, moved out of the hill station and came back to Allahabad.

Here, as one may say, the stage had come to be set for him. A delegation of peasants, from Pratapgarh, to seek the redressal of their grievances, had come, to meet Gandhiji, who was then supposed to be in Allahabad. Instead, they met Jawaharlal who had just arrived. He thus, got introduced to the Kisan problems. He felt so much influenced that he wished to link up the Kisan movement with the non-co-operation movement.

In Allahabad, the non-co-operation movement was guided by him. He organized the volunteer squads to make the *hartal* a success and to effectively picket the shops selling the foreign goods. This, and the writings in the 'Independent', brought the son and the father on December 5, 1921 to the jail. While the movement was gaining popular support, Gandhiji, called it off, due to the *Chauri-Chaura* incident (1922). It caused surprise to flie people to the political workers and to the leader, Jawaharlal felt no less. On his release from prison, on March 10, 1922, to whisper new confidence among his followers, he issued a message, at the first available opportunity. It said; "I have only to say this, keep fighting, continue to work for independent India and do not stop. Do not abandon your creed. Do not accept false compromises. Continue to follow your great leader Mahatma Gandhi and remain true to Congress. Be efficient, be well organised and above all remember of *charkha* and *ahimsa*."

In consequence of the political activities in which he got engaged subsequently, he was again, arrested on May 12. He, did not, as a non-cooperator, put up any defence, when he was brought to trial. He, however, made a statement which revealed the dedicated and proud patriot he had come to be. "I marvel at my good fortune. To serve India in the battle of freedom is honour enough. To serve her under a leader like Mahatma Gandhi is doubly fortunate. But to suffer for the dear country: what greater good fortune could be fall an Indian, unless it be death for the cause or the full realisation of our glorious dream."

This brought him to the national stage. "Motilal was delighted, when he was on an all-India tour later in the year, that his son's influence was widespread; and he was much moved when a large crowd in Delhi cheered him and his wife as the father and mother of Jawaharlal." Jawaharlal was not a supporter of the Act of 1919. Unlike his father, he did not support the Council entry. Therefore, when on his release in January 1923, a hint was thrown to him, if he would like to be a minister, he declined. In April, however, he was elected to the office of the Chairman of Allahabad Municipal Board. During his tenure, he introduced new ideas in the administration and added zeal to it. He gave due recognition to the competent subordinates. He gave equally, a good demonstration of his integrity and of his high character. All the same, working in the office, he found to be a hindrance in his political work.

The efficient organizing skill, he had exhibited, during the non-co-operation movement had made deep impression on the leadership. In recognition to this, he was made one of the three general secretaries of the Congress. He made use of this opportunity to bring about numerous procedural changes in the administration of the Congress organization.

These years in his family life, were disturbing. His wife, Kamala, after a premature delivery in 1924, lost her new born son. She also began in to show the signs of tuberculosis. Himself too, Jawaharlal, the following year, underwent a minor operation.

To get the ailment of his wife cured, Jawaharlal along with her, on March 1, 1926 sailed to Geneva, Switzerland. Their daughter Indira also accompanied them. Here, he nursed his wife, attended to his daughter and devoted himself to reading. He found also time to move out to several European Capitals to contact political workers and the Indian exiles. He thus, got introduced to the broader aspects of the contemporary politics.

Here, as the representative of Indian National Congress, he got an invitation to help in organizing the International Congress against colonial oppression and Imperialism which was to meet at Brussels in February 1927. He accepted the invitation. Here, on the appointed day, he met the communists from the European countries, the nationalists from Latin America, Africa and Asia and also the trade Unionists. Russia was conspicuous by its absence; yet her influence was too dominant to be missed. The Congress was against imperialism, especially, the British.

Nehru participated in all the discussions. He made out that the Indian poverty was due to the British exploitation. From "their Capitalist and Imperialist points of view they wanted to do everything in their power to hold on to India." He emphasised that, the British created differences among the people, and intensified wherever these existed.

The Brussels Conference ended with the hope to organise co-operation between nationalist movements and the anti-imperialist movement in the colonies. Jawaharlal was made an executive member of the league and also its honorary president.

The deliberations at Brussels, induced him to read about the revolutionary change that had seized the Soviet Union since 1917. Just then, he got a welcome invitation from Soviet Union ambassador in Berlin, to visit his country. In Russia, he was impressed, by the progress, the country had made in agriculture, in the removal of illiteracy and in liberating women. All the same, he was conscious of the fact that his tour was a conducted one.

The stay of the year and a half in Switzerland, did not prove for much advantage to kamala. Jawaharlal was also keen to attend the Congress Session in Madras (December 1927) so he came back along with his family.

In Madras, with the active support of Mrs. Annie Besant, Jawaharlal, pushed through the committee stage a resolution on the independence to the dismay of a many and to the pleasure of some. Gandhiji, who had not come to attend the session, later chided him for the move he had initiated. But, the idea of Independence had now fully seized his mind. He got engaged with the work of propagating his belief and set up the Independence League, to achieve this end.

The appointment of the Simon Commission, in which no Indian was included, was announced in 1927. Its terms of reference were ill defined. The Congress opposed it for its composition and ill defined aims. Jawaharlal opposing it, observed "our aim is completely free India and we have nothing to discuss except on this basis." As the General Secretary of the Congress, he organized nation-wide strike against the Commission. During the time, the Commission was touring the country, he got organized demonstrations against it wherever, it went with the slogan : "Go back Simon, go back Simon". In Lucknow, Jawaharlal was one among the demonstrators who were *lathi*-charged. The news of it shook the people all over the country.

The year 1929, Jawaharlal spent in revitalizing the Congress Organization and in preparing the nation for the coming struggle for Independence. Earlier Motilal had impressed upon Gandhiji, the desirability of making, Jawaharlal the President of the Congress. This suggestion had not been accepted by Gandhiji in 1927. But now, he agreed and Jawaharlal was elected to the high office. He presided over the Lahore Session, of December 1929. Here, January 26, of the new year was announced to be the Independence Day and it was observed, as such, all over the country.

The Civil Disobedience movement was initiated by Gandhiji, when on April 6, 1930, he made salt from the sea water at Dandi, which was against the Law. The movement had the impact all over the country. In Allahabad, Jawaharlal was incharge of the movement. He got the full support of his wife. They were arrested. Jawaharlal was lodged in a barrack reserved for the hardened persons. The time he had now available, he utilized in reading and writing. Here, he wrote The *Glimpses of World History.* Kamala Nehru, on her arrest felt the satisfaction of following "the foot steps" of her husband. Motilal too was imprisionsed on June 30, and was lodged in the same jail, in which was Jawaharlal. The son attended well upon his father.

Motilal had not joined politics for his inner compulsion. He was neither impelled by hate imperialism nor love India emotion. He neither agreed to non-co-operation, nor even to the idea to boycott the council elections. He was, in the words of Jawaharlal, "immoderately moderate". With doubts and misgivings, Motilal all the same got gravitated to the views of his son who was committed to Gandhiji and to non-co-operation. The father supported the council entry and the Dominion status but the son opposed both. This apart, the father and son on personal level, has deep bonds of mutuality and understanding. At the death of Motilal, on February 6, 1931, Jawaharlal felt the deep void. The feeling of emptiness troubled him. He writes, "If father had been alive! How my mind wanders unconsiously and dwells on him and how empty I feel at the thought that he is not there. For months and years we lived far from each other — when I was in Europe — but it did not matter so much. Always one had the feeling that he was there and one could always, go to him for help and counsel. Now there is an emptiness..." At another occasion, when he read in the paper, about the unveiling ceremony of Motilal's staute he had, his eyes "full of tears."

The health of Kamala Nehru had been deteriorating. No treatment cured her. When Jawaharlal was in jail, in May 1935, she had to be sent to a clinic in Baden Weiler in the Black Forests, Germany with an attendant doctor and her daughter, Indira. Her condition did not improve. Therefore, on an urgent call from the doctor Jawaharlal was permitted to go to Germany to visit her. Reaching, there, he removed her to Lausane for better treatment. But her condition remained fluctuating with no hope of recovery. She died on February 28, 1936, in her thirty seventh year. Jawaharlal came back and brought her ashes for the immersion in the holy Sangam, a part of it he retained to be immerse with his own after his death.

Kamla Nehru was charming and upright; clear headed and devoted wife. The growing comradeship between her and Jawaharlal is testified by an entry in his diary which reads : "I am much fond of her". She gave full moral support to her husband and was to him "vital, so bright and so full of life". She was not a more appendix to him. "My wife influenced me considerably in many ways, though unobtrusively." In her death, Jawaharlal suffered no ordinary loss as it testified by his retaining part of her ashes to be mixed with his own when such time came.

(d) Towards Independence

The late twenties saw Jawaharlal a mellowing politician. The decade that followed caused him disenchantments both, personal and political and, the forties were full of anxiety. The sweeping German victory over Europe in the early years of this decade caused him distress. He was no supporter of dictatorship. He was keen to co-operate with the allies. To this effect, the AICC met at Poona and adopted a resolution. The Government declined the offer. Soon after Jawaharlal, on October 30, 1940, was arrested. The prison life, this time, was made severe for him. He accepted it, as a truly dedicated man. Here, his sole companion was the Bhagvad Geeta, which had deeply now influenced him. "All we can do", he wrote to his daughter "is to face our job and do it well as we can and to remain tranquil inspite of shock and disaster." He was released, however, on December 4, 1941.

The failure of Cripps Mission, put to an end, for the time being, the possibility of any further negotiation. Gandhi was keen to start a civil disobedience movement; Jawaharlal did not favour it. At Bombay, the AICC finally appealed the British, to end their hegemony. This resolution, was confirmed at Poona. Before anything followed, the Government acted swiftly, and put the leaders under arrest at 5 a.m. on August 9, 1942. Jawaharlal was one among the arrested.

After, people awoke to the reality of what had happened, leaderless, they acted and sharply too. It delighted Nehru. But the district level leadership, and that too, in the face of the tremendous Government ferocity, could not be expected to guide the movement. It thus by October 1943, lost its momentum.

The international situation became complex, despite the allied victory. They were now involved in the cold war. England had emerged exhausted. The people were keen on domestic reconstruction and elected labour to form the government. At home, the situation continued to be tense. The economic recession, demobilization, and the unemployment, that followed the end of the war coupled with growing labour unrest, the I.N.A. episode and the pending trial of their leaders and the unresolved constitutional problem, demanded solution at the earliest. In this developing situation, the leaders were released. Jawaharlal was out of the prison on June 15, 1945, after the term of thirty four months, the longest he had ever served.

The I.N.A. which generated great emotion demanded immediate attention. Nehru, organized relief for the families of the arrested members. To boost the moral of the I.N.A. men, he went to Malaya where he first met Mountbatten who was then the Supreme Allied Naval Commander in the South-East Asia. Back home he joined the panel of lawyers, set up for the legal defence of such of the I.N.A. personnel who were brought before the military court.

The Imperialist were keen to revive their hold on the territories from where, the Japanese had earlier thrown them out. The French in Indo-China, Dutch in Indonesia and the British in Malaya were all working to this end. They were hot willing to concede, to the change. It caused anguish to Jawaharlal. He, therefore, on the suggestion of Aung San of Burma, took steps to organise the Asian Conference. It met, successively under the auspicious of the Indian Council of World Affairs, between March 23 and April 1947.

The mutiny in the Royal Indian Navy that broke out on February 18, 1946, added a new dimension to the existing tense situation. The British government in England, saw in it the disastrous possibilities. They felt now impelled to attend to the constitutional issue with a new determination to avoid an irremediable situation from developing. The government, therefore, commissioned three members of the Cabinet — the Cabinet Mission — to bring about a final settlement.

On the manner, the settlement should follow, Nehru had his own ideas. He believed that, the only issue to be discussed is the manner of transforming the power and everything else, besides that, could be settled by the Constituent Assembly.

The Mission, while rejecting the idea of Pakistan as a sovereign state, conceded to the League, a "Grouping Arrangement". It was a compromise arrangement. It remained, a matter of discussion and observation. The Cabinet Mission on its part, was satisfied with the arrangement it has evolved, and with the degree of its acceptance by the concerned parties. They now wished the Governor General to constitute the Interim Government, and to execute the plan. The Mission left on June 29.

Incidental to these development, Nehru was elected (1946) to the Congress Presidency. Few days later, at a Press Conference, he referred among other things to the Grouping Arrangement as well. In this connection, he observed, "we are not bound by a single thing except that we have decided to go into the Constituent Assembly". This statement, Jinnah pounded upon, and exploited to explain what, he considered the truth and reality in his arguments for Pakistan. He declared the withdrawal of his acceptance of the Cabinet Mission Plan. This, rendered, the political situation, once again fluid and uncertain.

The Interim Government, meanwhile was formed on September 2, 1946. Nehru held the foreign affairs. The League members of the Government opposed and criticised his policy. In Bengal, the Muslim League being in power, resorted to the Direct Action, the slaughter of the Hindus and the Sikhs, arson and destruction of property and of the desecration of the religious places. The government abetted in this. The policy stood helpless witness to it. The League members in the Interim Government being non-co-operative and acrimonious, the Governor-General did not act in the fulfilment of his supreme duty; to enforce law, to ensure security and to punish the guilty. It appeared too as if the link between the Governor General and the Provincial Governor did not exist.

The British government in London, had much to feel concerned about. They summoned the political leaders including Nehru and Jinnah for consultations. The Conference in London, was a failure. It served no purpose. The ending year was out, as much in the gory conditions as the new creeped in.

The Partition

Jawaharlal, now demanded that as the League had withdrawn its support to the Cabinet Mission Plan, its nominee should quit the Interim Government. The parting of the ways, which was already in the air, now, secured a positive form. The partition whatever, it meant, was in everybody's mind. The new Viceroy, Mountbatten, as the instrument of the destiny hastened the process and there followed the partition.

On the midnight of August 14, 1947, the Indian community left behind the age of religious recrimination, communal eruptions, patchwork social order, unassimilated interests and the never-ending stagnation. India, now arose, out of its eternal past, proud of its continuity, and to the immensity of future. Now on the threshold of the era of purposeful activity, with belief in charge and faith in the destiny, the following morning, Jawaharlal Nehru, one of the authors of this revolution was sworn in as the Prime Minister of Free India. He remained at the helm of affairs to the end of his life — May 27, 1964. Here the old ended and the new began.

His Writings

1. *Soviet Russia* (1929).
2. *Letters from Father to his Daughter* (1930).
3. *Recent Essays and Writings* (1934).
4. *Autobiography* (1936).
5. *India and the World* (1936).
6. *Eighteen Months in India* (1936).
7. *Glimpses of World History* (1939).
8. *The Unity of India* (1944).
9. *The Discovery of India* (1946).
10. *Independence and After* (1949).
11. *Nehru on Gandhi* (1949).
12. *A Bunch of Old Letters* (1958).

(2) Nehru's Political Ideas

Pt. Jawaharlal Nehru was a great architect of India. He devoted his life to the cause of national struggle. To *Pearl Buck*, 'Nehru is unforgettable because he has made free India pivot between the East and the West speaking the language of both". *Lord Bertrand Russell,* the noted British philosopher says in an article on Jawaharlal Nehru that it was he who made democracy safe in India and thereby, made it a real possibility in other parts of Asia and Africa.

According to Walter Crocker, Nehru's achievements may be summarised as under :

1. He held India together. He gave a sense of unity to Indians.
2. To encourage the growth of parliamentary and cabinet system which the British started in India.

3. The modernisation of India..... through 3 Five Year Plans. His political ideas can be broken down as under:

His Views about Nationalism

To him, nationalism is indeed a noble phase of self-magnification. He said, "nationalism is essentially a group memory of past achievements, traditions, and nationalism is stronger today than it has ever been... Whenever a crisis has arisen nationalism has emerged again and dominated the seene, and people have sought comfort and strength in their old traditions. One of the remarkable developments of the present age has been the rediscovery of the past and of the nation".

In fact, Nehru was a great nationalist leader who loved India's freedom above everything. He himself once said in the *Discovery of India*, 'India was in my blood and there was much in her that instinctively thrilled me. And yet I approached her as an alien critic, full of dislike for the present as well as for many of the relics of the past that I saw'. He farther said, "I shall have no real respect for India if it followed blindly the American pattern or the Russian pattern or the Chinese or the British."

Then it would not be India but a pale imitation of somebody else. That it does not mean I do not respects the American, British or other patterns. What I say is that we shall have to function according to our thinking. What is the good of an individual who does not have an integrated personality who merely copies something or somebody else, much more so a nations, which just copies.

He further said in the Constituent Assembly, "Every Indian person can see that if you have a narrow national policy, it may enthuse the multitude for the moment, but it is bad for the nation and it is bad internationally because you lose sight of the ultimate goal and thereby endanger our own good."

Her views about Internationalism Nehru was a great internationalist. He was a great spokesman of Asian and African aspirations for complete freedom. He was an exponent of Panchsheel. In June 1954, the fundamental concepts of Panchsheel were laid down in the course of a joint declaration by Nehru and Chou-En-Lai. They are:

(i) Mutual respect for each other's territorial integrity and sovereignty;
(ii) Non-aggression;
(iii) Non-interference in each other's internal affairs;
(iv) Equality and mutual advantage and
(v) Peaceful coexistence and economic co-operation.

Nehru said, 'I have no doubt that these principles of international behaviour, if accepted and acted upon by all countries of the world, would go a long way to put an end to the fears and apprehensions which cast dark shadows over the world." Nehru was in favour of one world federation. He said that world government must and will come, for there is no remedy for the world's sickness. The machinery for it is difficult to devise. It can be an extension of the federal principle, a growth of the idea underlying the United Nations, giving each national unit freedom to fashion its destiny according to its genius, but subject always to the basic covenant of the world Government. Nehru held that we have arrived at a stage in human affairs when the ideal of the one world and kind of world federation seems to be essential though there are many dangers and obstacles in the way..... We, therefore, support United Nations structure which is painfully emerging from its infancy."

Explaining these principles he said that it is in recognition of the right of each country to fashion its own destiny that the Indian Government and the People's Government of China agreed to the five principles to govern their relations with each other. These principles were respect for each other's territorial integrity and sovereignty, non-aggression; non-interference in each other's internal affairs, equality and mutual benefit and peaceful coexistence. Subsequently these principles were accepted by Burma, Yugoslavia and the Soviet Government has also expressed its approval of them.

By thinking of Panchsheel and peaceful coexistence in this wide warring world, we have gained a measure of respect and attention. We have been able to gain this respect because our thinking has been correct and based on principles which are not opportunist and also because the broad policies we laid down have not been very divergent from the action we have taken; that is there has been an approximation between our ideals and action in our foreign policy.

Nehru held that history has proved that in spite of mutual rivalries, the world was coming nearer and nearer. He said, "In respect of our past history of conflict we hope that independent India will have friendly and co-operative relations with England and countries of British Commonwealth. But it is well to remember what is happening in one part of the Commonwealth today. In South Africa racialism is state doctrine and our people are putting up a heroic struggle against the tyranny of national minority. The world in spite of its rivalries and hatreds and inner conflicts, moves inevitably towards closer co-operation and the building up of a world commonwealth. It is for this one world that free India will work, a world in which there is the free co-operation of free peoples and no class or group exploits another."

His Views on Non-alignment

Nehru was a firm believer in the policy of non-alignment. On October 17, 1949 during the course of his speech at Columbia University he said, "I am asked frequently why India does not align herself with a particular nation or a group of nations and told that because we have refrained from doing so, we are involved in it deeply to regard calm objectivity in others irrational, short sighted, negative, unreal or even unmanly. But I should like to make it clear that the policy India has sought to pursue is not a negative and neutral policy. It is positive and vital policy that flows from our struggle for freedom and from the teachings of Mahatma Gandhi."

Nehru held that India should as far as possible keep away from the power politics of group, aligned against one another which have led in the past to world wars and which may again lead to disasters on an even vaster scale. The world, in spite of its rivalries and hatreds and inner conflicts, moves inevitably towards closer co-operation and the building up of a world commonwealth. It is for this One World that free India will work.

He said that non-alignment had become a summary description of the policy of friendship towards all nations, uncompromised by adhering to any military pacts. This was not due to any indifference to issues that arose, but rather to desire to judge them ourselves in full freedom and without any preconceived partisan bias. It implied basically a conviction that good and evil are mixed up in this world, that a nation cannot be divided into sheep and goats to be condemned or approved accordingly and that if we were to join one military camp rather than the other, it was liable to increase and not diminish the risk of major clash between them.

His Views on Commonwealth

Since Indian Independence, Nehru made clear his idea of joining the British Commonwealth of nations. Nehru held the view that our association with the Commonwealth is remarkable in that it does not bind us down in any way whatsoever. Being in the Commonwealth means a meeting once or twice a year and occasional consultations and references, surely that is not too great a price to pay for the advantages we get. He said, "If the Commonwealth had the right to interfere with any constituent country then I should certainly cease to be in the Commonwealth. If any honourable member thinks that the nations of the Commonwealth have common war or defence policies, allow me to assure them that they are completely mistaken. We have never discussed defence policies in the Commonwealth either jointly or separately".

Commonwealth makes coexistence possible. He said, "We have to face tremendous strains all the time. In the past we have faced them and we have survived them as a Commonwealth. We may have to face them in the future because the world is full of strain and trouble and conflict accompanied by fear and apprehension and it is not an easy matter to maintain the temper of democracy. Democracy, in other words is peaceful coexistence not only between those who are like each other but also between those who are unlike each other. It is easy to coexist when you are like each other. It involves no problems, no effort. But when you differ in opinion, in way of life, even in objectives and yet forbear and try to understand the other, that is peaceful coexistence."

His Views on the U.N.O.

Being a great supporter of world peace, Nehru believed in the nobility of the charter of the world. He said that in spite of its faults, the United Nations serves an essential purpose. Nehru wanted that China be represented in the U.N.O. Any proposal to exclude any independent country from the United Nations is unwise and harmful. Nehru held the view that disappearance of U.N.O. would mean a great tragedy for the world. He shys, "I have believed and I do believe that the United nations in spite of its many faults, in spite of its having deviated from its aims somewhat is, nevertheless, a basic and fundamental thing in the structure of the world today. Not to have it or to do away with it would be a tragedy for the world."

Nehru asserts that first of all, "We find that the principle of Universality with which the United Nations started has been departed from. A great country like China is not given recognition at the United Nations. Whether we like or dislike the present government in China or whether we approve or disapprove of China's revolution is not at all relevant to the patent fact. The basic principle of universality has been abandoned by the United Nations. This is a return to the attitude that caused the League of Nations to fail. The matter does not end with expressing an academic opinion; the failure of the United Nations to give recognition to a country which is obviously stable and strong has given rise to fresh problems of a universal character."

His View of Religion

Nehru denounced superstition and rediculed fanaticism in religion. Once he even remarked that religion was an affair of women. But he was not an irreligious man what he did not like in religion was its dogma and ritual. He said :

"It was closely associated with superstitious practices and dogmatic beliefs and behind it lay a method of approach to life's problems, which was not certainly that of science. There was an element of magic about it, an uncritical credulousness, a reliance on the supernatural."

Yet he recognized that it was obvious that religion had supplied some deeply felt inner need of human nature, and that the vast majority of people all over the world could not do without some form of religious belief.

He could not tolerate the so called 'Mahatmas' and 'yogis'. He said :

> "Where a long thread of a tuft of hair on the crown of the head or along mark on the forehead of a *fakir's* dress or a sannyasis's yellow of ochre garb is a passport to holiness, it is not difficult to impose on the public. In most countries, religion has become one of the biggest and the most paying businesses-almost a big industry."

Gandhiji felt that despite the facts Nehru disclaimed any faith in religion, he was a religious man. Gandhiji wrote, "While Jawaharlal always says that he does not believe in God, he is nearer to God than many who profess to be his worshippers. His idea of religion was service of humanity and he was truly devoted to his duty of working for the betterment of humanity. In Sanskrit, there is one world both for religion and duty-Dharma. He was truly a *dharmik* man in that sense."

His Views on Democracy There was a considerable influence on him of western democratic traditions yet he was committed socialism. He says that democracy means equality and democracy can only flourish in an equal society....it means equality not merely the equality of possessing vote but economic and social equality.

To him, "democracy is a dynamic, not a static thing and as it changes it may be that its domain will become wider and wider. Ultimately, it is a mental approach applied to our political and economic problems."

Nehru said, "One has to find equilibrium among the various forces at work. In finding this equilibrium in a democratic country, one has produced a sensation in them that they are partners in the vast undertaking of running a nation, partners in government, partners in industry. That is the essence of democracy." To Nehru, democracy is not only the expression of the sovereign will of the people through their votes, it is not only political, not only economic, but something of the mind as everything is ultimately something of the mind. It involves equality of opportunity to all people, as far as possible, in the political and economic domain. It involves the freedom of the individual to now and to make to best of his capacities and ability. It involves a certain tolerance of others and even of other's opinions when they differ from yours. It involves a certain contemplative tendency and a certain inquisitive search for truth."

Nehru held the view that political democracy by itself is not enough except that it may be used to obtain a gradually increasing measure of economic democracy. Parliamentary democracy is inevitably going in the direction, everywhere, of that might be called economic democracy. It may take different forms, but only in the measure that it solves the economic problems. Does it succeed even in the political field? If the economic problems are non-solved then the political structure tends to weaken and crack up."

His Views on Local Self-Government He wanted Local self-Government to be introduced in villages. He said that a village can no longer be a self-contained economic unit (though it may often be intimately connected with a collective or co-operative farm), but it can very well be a governmental and electoral unit, each such unit functioning as a self-governing community within the larger political framework, and looking after the essential need of the village. If it is treated to some extent as an electoral unit, it will simplify provincial and All India election considerably by reducing the number of direct electors. The village council, itself chosen by all the adult men and women of the village could form these electors for the bigger elections Indirect elections may have some disadvantages but, having regard to the background in India, the village should be treated as a unit. This will give a true and more responsible representation.

His Views on Peace and War

He said once, "Peace and freedom have become indivisible and the world cannot continue for long partly free and partly subject. In this atomic age, peace has also become a test of human survival."

Nehru was ardently dedicated to peace and peaceful methods. He realized that in thermo-nuclear age, war would mean the extinction of all civilized values. That is why he was convinced that the true role of a statesman in this distracted world lay in the way of lessening (tensions and conflicts and bringing about a climate of understanding and mutual accommodation, with a view to the settlement of international differences without resort to the horrors of war. On several international questions, such as, Korea, Laos, Congo and Vietnam. He was the voice of peace and friendship and his voice was always heard with respect. In short he was a great apostle of peace.

World peace was his most cherished objective and that was true victory that left neither party to dispute with the feeling being either victor or vanquished.

This translation of respect of the other man's dignity gave to international dialogue and intercourse a new quality that worked against war and strengthened the forces of peace.

Nehru said that the lesson of history, the long course of history, and more especially the lesson of last two great wars which have devasted humanity has been that out of hatred and violence only hatred and violence will come. We have got into a cycle of harted and violence and not the most brilliant debates will get you out of it, unless you look some other way and find some other means. It is obvious that if we continue in this cycle and have wars, the result will not only be tremendous devastation all over the world, but the non-achievement by any individual or power group of its objective.

His Views on One-World

Nehru believed in one-world. He was of the opinion that the day is not far when there will be one world. He said in his speech delivered in New Delhi on March, 1947 on the eve of Asian Conference, "We have arrived at a stage in human affairs when the ideal of one world and some kind of world federation seems to be essential, though there are many dangers and obstacles in the way. We should work for that ideal, not for any grouping which comes in the way of this larger world group. We, therefore, support the United Nations structure which is painfully marching from its infancy. But is order to have one world, we must also in Asia think of all countries of Asia co-operating to that larger ideal."

He said in his 'Discovery of India', "We March to the one world up tomorrow where national cultures will be intermingled with the international calverts of the human ways. We shall, therefore, seek wisdom and knowledge and friendship and comradeship wherever we can find them, and co-operate with others in common tasks, but we are no suppliants for other's favour and patronage."

His Views on Science and Technology

Dr. Rajender Prashad remarked about Nehru that he was "essentially a man of science and technology with undoubted faith in their progress and achievements." "It is now patent", he said, "that without science and technology we cannot progress." So great was his zeal for science and for the scientific approach to life that he missed no opportunity of imparting his views to others. To quote him "You know that whenever the chance offers itself. I say something about the importance of science and its off-shoot, technology. It think, we should realize how modern life is an offspring of science and technology."

> "After all", he said, "how has agriculture grown in many other countries greatly? It is because of the application of science and technology. If modern life depends so much on science and technology, then we must seize hold of them, understand them and apply them."

"What is science?" He asked and replied that it is the research for truth, truth of the physical world....truth arrived at by a process of trial and error, by experiment, not taking something for granted until it is proved, and rejecting everything that is disproved or does not fit in with the facts before us. It not only gives us a greater understanding of the world as it is, but creates ultimately a temper, an objective temper, a dispassionate scientific temper which should help its in dealing with other problems. All the problems that come up in Parliament or elsewhere, or whatever they may be, could be dealt with better if we approach them in a scientific frame of mind. If was the scientific temper which he cherished, which he wished to inculcate in the Indian people.

He said, "Science has developed at an ever-increasing pace since the beginning of the century, so that the gap between the advanced and backward countries has widened more and more. It is only by adopting the most vigorous measures and by putting for ward our utmost effort into the development of science that we can bridge the gap. It is an inherent obligation of a great country like India, with its traditions of scholarship and original thinking and its great cultural heritage, to participate fully in the march of science, which is probably mankind's greatest enterprise today."

Nehru was a man of the future. He always looked ahead. Once he said, "If man was meant to go back or always took back, he would have had his eyes at the back of his head." His contempt for the static was best brought out when he said, "India must break with much of her past and not allow it to dominate the present. Our lives are encumbered with the dead wood of this past; and that is dead and has served its purpose has to go."

Shrimati Aruna Asaf Ali an old and intimate colleague of Nehru, spoke for millions when she said: "Every aspect of Jawaharlal Nehru's personality fasciented us. He was our faultless and flawless idol, ideally perfect."

(4) Nehru's Economic Ideas

Nehru said that great as was the success of India in evolving a stable society, she failed in a vital particular and because she failed in this, she fell and remains fallen. No solution was found for the problem of equality. India deliberately ignored this and built up her social structure on inequality and we have the tragic consequences of this policy in the millions of our people who till yesterday were suppressed and had little opportunity for growth. His economic ideas can be broken down as under :

His Ideas on Planned Economy

According to Nehru, "Excessive economic power in a relatively few hands and the uses to which it may be put disturb the balance of power in a democracy and expose the social structure to new strains and tensions and come in the way of diffusion of economic opportunity. Proper planning is meant to prevent it." Nehru said, "We have achieved political freedom, but our revolution is not yet complete and it is still in progress, for political freedom without the assurance of the right to live and pursue happiness, which economic progress alone can bring, can never satisfy the people. Therefore, our immediate task is to raise the living standard of our people to remove all that comes in the way of economic growth of the nation."

To achieve the talk, according to Nehru, we must have planning. In his opinion planning is a continuous process and cannot be isolated for short periods. Planning is continuous movement towards desired goals and, because of this, all major decisions have to be made by agencies informed of these goals and the social purpose behind them. Even in considering a five year period, forward and long-term planning has always to be kept in view. Indeed, perspective planning is the essence of the planning process. As this process develops there is a certain rhythm of expansion in the development comes to them. They people of India today, with all this burdens and problems, live on the frontier of a new world which they are helping to build. In order to cross this frontier they have to possess courage and enterprise, the spirit of endurance and capacity for hardwork, and the vision of the future.'

His Ideas on Socialistic Pattern of Society

Nehru's idea of socialistic pattern of society is one in which there is equality of opportunity. Nehru says that we lay great stress on equality on the removal of disparties and it has to be remembered always that socialism is not spreading out of poverty. There must be wealth and production.

To him, fulfilment of a socialist society was possible by a widely diffused small sector consisting of ancillary and cottage industries adopting latest scientific methods of production and organised and run progressively by co-operatives. "It is quite evident", he once remarked, "the small enterpreneur cannot succeed against the competition of large-scale sector unless he can develop industries through co-operatives."

He was convinced that socialism above could solve India's economic problems. The only key to solve the problems is socialism according to him. Nehru said that there was no way of ending the poverty, the unemployment, the degradation and the subjection of the Indian people except through socialism. He declared in the Lahore Congress, I must frankly fonfess that I am a socialist and a Republican and am no believer in kings and princes, or in the order which produces the modern kings of industry, who have greater power over the lives and fortunes of men than the kings of old and whose methods are as perdatory as those of the old feudal Aristocracy."

Nehru wanted to establish a truly democratic socialist state in India. He was in favour of abolition of Zamindari institution in India. Nehru spoke in Lok Sabha, "That the pattern of society which we look forward is the socialistic pattern of society which is classless and casteless."

Sardar K.M. Panikkar evaluating Mr. Nehru said that Nehru frankly admired the achievement of communism in many fields. He accepted from communism many ideas-specially the idea of planned economy. He worked in friendly co-operation with the Soviet Union on many issues. But he was essentially democrat who worked through democratic processes and without the forcible liquidation of classes. The result of the last fifteen years of his administration has been, therefore, to endow India with the framework of a society based on democratic socialism. If India follows broadly the policy of Nehru, the prospects of the Communist Party achieving power in India would cease to be a matter of practical concern. Jawaharlal Nehru was the lover for ideals of socialism and wanted to build India of his dreams of a socialistic basis. Socialism appealed to him as a philosophy of life and was in his estimation, the only key to the solution of world's problem and of India's problems.

His Views on Equitable Industrial Production and Equitable Distribution of the National Wealth

Nehru wanted greater and equitable industrial production and equitable distribution of the national wealth. He says that the aim should be the expansion of the productive capacity of the nation in every possible way at the same time absorbing the labour power of the nation is some activity or other and preventing unemployment. As far as possible there should be freedom to choose one's occupation. An equalisation of income will not result from all this, but there will be far more equitable sharing and a progressive tendency towards equalisation. In any event, the vast differences that exist today will disappear completely and class distinctions which are essentially based on differences in income, will begin to fade out.

The Views on Social Ownership

The basic philosophy of "social ownership" according to Nehru means public ownership of the basic and major industries. It means the co-operative or collective control of land. Such a system of democracy and democratic collectivism will need of careful and continuous planning and adaptation to the changing need of people. He said that the state may be organized on semi-specialistic lines for the benefit of the owning classes. A state socialism and state capitalism are much the samething; the real question is who is in command in the State, and also profits by it, the whole community or a particular possessing class.

His Views on Nationalisation of Industries Regarding nationalisation of industries, Nehru laid that state should nationalise only key industries. Subject to this, Nehru believed, there should be every opportunity and freedom for private enterprize to grow. He was of the view that state should increase and encourage every element to produce and help nation building. However, Nehru held that public sector should be given much greater scope.

To conclude Nehru's economic ideas, we can say that Nehru wanted Indian society based on a socialistic pattern. As Kurbeddy said, in order to create an Indian society based on equality, social justice and security, he sought to develop a social philosophy which seeks a fundamental transformation of the structure which is not dominated by the urge for private profit and by individual greed and in which there is a fair distribution of political and economic power.

In fact, Nehru found the solution of Indian problems and world problems in socialism. For him, socialism was something even more than an economic doctrine. He wrote, "I see no way of ending the poverty, the vast unemployment, the degradation and the subjection of the Indian people except through socialism." He considered socialism necessary not only for India but for the entire world. About the inevitability of socialm Nehru stated : "Inevitably we are led to the only possible solution —

the establishment of a socialist order, which national boundaries, and eventually in distribution on wealth for the public good.

(5) Nehru and Gandhi

"For nearly fifty years", writes Frank Moraes, "India has lived in the shadow of two extraordinary men-Gandhi and Nehru. In this period, the pattern of her thought and action was moulded by these two men, in many ways dissimilar and in many respects strongly alike. India's good fortune lay in the fact that Nehru was not a conflicting but a complementary element in the amalgam which made the Mahatma's political magic. Together they represented India. They were India."

About Nehru and Gandhiji, everybody has formed his own estimate of their personalities, their political ideas and their contribution to the nation and humanity.

That is the reason why some have seen in Gandhi the world's greatest pacifist and the others, a saint and the founder of a new doctrine of religion. Nehru was similarly judged by some as pro British, and more international than nationalist, and others have regarded him as a neutralist, unrealist and narcissist.

As a matter of fact, there are certain, similarities and dissimilarities between the two. For our conveniences, we shall first deal with similarities and then dissimilarities between the two.

Similarities

According to Frank Moraes, there are two similarities between Nehru and Gandhi. He said that two qualities were foremost in both of them their sense of service and sacrifice. The rebel in Gandhi, a man who hated injustice and cruelty, who refused to be content with the mere enunciation of lofty principles but insisted on action, drew Jawaharlal to the Mahatma. "Behind all his courteous interest," Nehru wrote of the Mahatma, "one has the impression that one is addressing a closed door, "how true it was of both men. In both was an implacably stubborn streak deriving its strength in the case of one from first principles and in the other from elemental loyalties.

Nehru was greatly influenced by Gandhiji, 'Apart from' his international aspect of leadership, great contribution made by him to our national struggle was his attitude to the gospel of non-violence. He was the friend of Afro-Asian Unity. Before freedom Gandhiji was not very much interested in international politics. Nehru who was always passionately interested in what was happening in the world outside India and in the struggle for liberation of dependent countries was the conscience keeper of Gandhiji as far as external affairs were concerned. He was considerably influenced in laying down the foreign policy of India by Gandhi and his philosophy."

Other points of Similarity can be stated as under :

1. Both Gandhiji and Nehru hated untouchability from the core of their heart.
2. Regarding war, both Gandhiji and Nehru were of the opinion that national and international problems could not be solved by war. Both felt necessity of understanding about difference among nations.
3. Regarding role of morality in politics, both had the same approach. Both believed between the close relationship between morality and politics. They believed that morality and politics could not be separated from each other.
4. We also find that both Gandhiji and Nehru agreed that good means should be adopted for getting good results. Both were of the opinion that means should justify ends.
5. Both believed in upliftment and reconstruction of villages in India. Both were of the opinion that majority of Indian population lived in villages. So real advancement of India lay in the advancement of villages.
6. Both had great love and affection with their country and were willing to devote their lives for the sake of the nation.
7. Both believed in self-reliance in national struggle.
8. Like Gandhiji, Nehru believed that state should not hold more and more powers, but should leave much to the care of individuals.
9. As a great Gandhian, Nehru pleaded for integration between thought and action.

Dissimilarities

The gulf between Gandhi and Nehru became apparent with Independence. Nehru was left alone to pursue his ideas and plans. Many have interpreted his seventeen years as free India's first Prime Minister as representing a break with Gandhian traditions.

In spite of many similarities between the two, we also find some differences. These can be enumerated as under :

Frank Moraes pointed out the following points of difference :

1. Nehru differed from Gandhi both in tactics and strategy. He always liked to have the ultimate objective clear and well-defined where as Mahatma whose approach was pragmatic was content to feel his way step by step. For instance, while condemning untouchability as a blot on Hinduism, Gandhi condoned the cast system describing it, in a typical effort to sublimate it, as a functional system based on division of labour. I once remarked on this contradiction to Nehru.
2. The sense of hustle and history which infused Nehru and Gandhi which often precipitated him on impulsive courses was wholly absent in Gandhi.
3. Both on the economic and political planes Gandhi preferred to build up-ward from the people. The close association of the government with the people at every level of the political pyramid was the distinctive mark of Gandhism. The Mahatma was more concerned with individuals than with causes, society signifying to him individuals and not, as with Nehru's Congress Party, group. Gandhi saw India as much in the face of a peasant or a landlord as in the eyes of a teacher or a child.
4. While approving of Nehru's foreign policy of non-alignment Gandhi would, one feels, have scrupulously insisted that it should not be neutral "on one side." Himself an upholder of absolute principles he would never have compromised with any appeasement of wrong."

Other points of differences are :

5. Nehru was a great politician and a statesman, but Gandhiji was both a saint and a politician.
6. Nehru was an internationalist and had deep knowledge of Western political philosophy. But Gandhiji was indifferent to international politics.
7. Nehru was a progressive thinker and emphasised the progress of science and technology. But Gandhi was a conservative thinker and hated the impact of science on human life.
8. According to Dr. Mookerjee, the characteristics which were common between Mahatma Gandhi and Subhash Chandra Bose, were, first, their ability to "transform ideas into facts" and secondly, both of them were more practical idealists and less dreamers and theoreticians. Jawaharlal, on the other hand, was always richer in ideas, but he was so because of the abundance

of ideas which swarmed in his head, in spite of the fact that he was never so successful in realising them. That was why in a great many ways Bose came nearer to Gandhi than Nehru.

9. Another characteristic which comes out well in cantrast is that Nehru never had the same talent for organisation as his two contemporaries. Mahatma Gandhi was really gifted with remarkable capacities for making men and women do things in a disciplined manner and shape them into real human beings. At the same time, when Mahatma Gandhi began to organise the masses of the India people, the idea of national independence was still incohate and in its infancy and was considered by many as a dream.
10. Compared to the uncompromising attitudes of Gandhi, Nehru was more forgiving, more easily given to pardon and forget which according to one of his biographers, bordered on the tolerance of inefficiency and incapacity often with grave political consequences. Gandhi, on the other hand, did not even spare Kasturba, his much suffering wife, and those who have read the famous article in *Young India* know how much Mahatma Gandhi embarrassed her by fasting, for the failure to adhere strictly to the disciplines of the Ashram, by acquiring, I think, a few rupees in order to make a modest present to her grand-child.
11. Both Nehru and Gandhi differed in their views regarding religion. Nehru was a secularist. He did not lay great stress on religion as Gandhiji did. Gandhiji said that he was first a religious man and then politician.
12. Nehru had not that much regard for ancient Indian culture and civilization as Gandhiji had.

To conclude we may say that there are many differences between Gandhiji and Nehru but there are agreements on different matters of political thought between the two.

Nehru wrote in his *Autobiography* : Indeologically he was sometimes amazingly backward, and yet in action he had been the greatest revolutionary of recent times in India. He was a unique personality, and it was impossible to judge him by the usual standards or even to apply the ordinary cannons of logic to him. But because he was a revolutionary at bottom and was pledged to political independence for India, he was bound to play an uncompromising role till that independence was achieved. And in this very process he would release tremendous energies and would himself, I have hoped, advance-step by step towards the social goal.

(6) Estimate

In his long public life of nearly half a century, Jawaharlal Nehru achieved great distinction in many ways. He was the leader of the front rank in India's struggle for freedom.

It was Nehru who taught India how to face hardships and keep up courage even in the midst of all the pains and penalties that fell to her lot as a British dependency. Furthermore, it was his emotional identification with human suffering and his great spirit of sacrifice that made Jawaharlal sympathetic not only to the needs and aspirations of his own people but to those of the people in the countries similarly situated, whether in Asia, Africa or even in Europe. To Nehru's credit, it may be said that he not only understood their problems and sympathised with their lot but generated among his own people a similar reaction.

Ashok Mehta well remarked that Pandit Nehru combined in himself three qualities that have rarely gone together. First, he had a passion for knowledge; no sphere of it was alien to him. He roamed over the world of knowledge with the same zest and communion with which he moved in the world of men. Secondly, he had the insight of historian. Behind the ebb and flow of events he sought the patterns and purposes of men. He was able to bring simultaneously both commitment and objectivity because he could set events in the background as wall as the perspective of history. Again, he was proudly concerned about the dignity of the lowliest of men. To help every person to discover and realize his full stature was his fundamental quest.

To evaluate the contribution of Pt. Nehru, it is imperative to see his many sided personality.

Nehru as a Historian His contribution to Indian historical literature has been notable. His *Discovery of India* is in every sense a major work on Indian history, though it would not be so classified by textbook writers. It does not bring to light any new fact; nor does , it unearth new dynasties, fill up any of the gaps in our knowledge, or settle the controversies that add to the complications which students of Indian history face. Its significance lies in the fact that it is the first attempt to write a story of the Indian people to give a picture of the evolution of India from the earliest days to our own time, It was thus a history in the proper sense of the word and not an assemblage of facts and details, a wearying narrative of local wars and struggles without any central purpose.

Anyone who studies his work as the Prime Minister of India can easily see that not only in his internal politics but in the formulation of his external policy he is dominated by a sense of history. The sense of urgency in dealing with India's social, economic and political problems arises from his knowledge of India's past failures, due to her social backwardness, her undeveloped economic life and her lack of unity.

Every country and people in the East and the West has had an individuality, a message, and has attempted to solve life's problems in its own way. Greece is something, definite superb in its own a way so is India, so is China, so is Iran, Ancient India and ancient Greece were different from each other, and yet they were akin, just ancient India and ancient China had kinship in thought, in spite of great differences. They all had the same broad the tolerant, pagan outlook joy in life and in the surprising beauty, and infinite variety of nature, love of art, and the wisdom that comes from the accumulated experience of an old race.

Nehru as an Internationalist He was a great internationalist. Pandit Nehru's greatest contribution lay in defining certain principles of international behaviour. He calls them as Panchsheela or five principles of peaceful coexistence. Explaining these he says, It is in recognition of the right of each country to fashion its own destiny that the Indian government and the People's Government of China agreed to the five principles to govern their relations with each other. These principles were respect for each other's territorial integrity and sovereignty, non-aggression, non-interference in each other's internal affairs, equality and mutual benefit and peaceful coexistence. Subsequently these principles were accepted by Burma and Yugoslavia, and the Sovit Union has also expressed its approval of them.

Nehru as a Nationalist India was most dear to him. With his internationalism he believed in nationalism. About India he said, "India was in my blood and there was much in her that instinctively thrilled me."

In his wellknown book 'Unity of India' he says that India will be a land, and in the past, of many faiths equally honoured and respected, of one national outlook, not a narrow nationalism living in its own shell but rather the tolerant creative nationalism, which believing in itself and genius of its people takes, full part in the establishment of an international order.

Nehru as a Socialist He was a great socialist. In order to create an Indian society based on equality social justice and security, he thought of developing a social philosophy which seeks a fundamental transformation of the social structure which is not dominated by the urge of private profit and by individual greed and in which there is a fair distribution of political and economic power.

Nehru as a Humanist Nehru's three ultimate objectives were as under :

(a) Every man, woman and child is to have a decent material standard of living. His goal is to wipe out poverty and misery from the face of his earth.

(b) He wants a world in which every individual, race and nation will have an equal opportunity to develop a good life.

(c) He wants a world in which every individual will be able to enjoy the basic human freedoms, especially the freedom of self-expression and self-development.

Nehru as Futurist Nehru was a man of the future. He always looked ahead. He said, "If man was meant go back or always look back, he would have had his eyes at the back of his head". His contempt for the static was best brought out when he said, "India must break with much of her past and not allow it to dominate the present. Our lives are encumbered with the dead wood of this past : all that is dead and has served its propose has to go".

Nehru as a Statesman and Idealist While all these many aspects and versatile activities deserve full recognition, the unique features which will ensure him a place among the great men of history were his statesmanship and idealism. This is a rare and at times an embarrassing accommodation. Statesmanship has to be essentially I pragmatic, intent on attaining practical ends through available means. A statesman has always to be ready for reasonable compromise not inconsistent with fundamental principles and policies. He has to manage colleagues and subordinates of widely different outlooks and temperaments. Lastly, he has to reconcile the needs of the present with the claims of the future.

Nehru as a Man "If any people choose to think of me" wrote Jawaharlal Nehru, "I should like to say : This was a man, who with all his mind and heart loved India and the Indian people. And they, in turn, were indulgent to him and of their love most abundantly and extravagant." Nehru was the darling of all young or old, man or woman. He used to draw his inspiration from the crowds of people.

Nehru once said, "I have received so much love from the Indian people that nothing than I can do, can repay even a small fraction of it, and indeed there can be no repayment of so precious a thing as affection."

Nehru as a Through Democrat There was considerable influence on him of Western democratic traditions yet he was committed to socialism. He says, "democracy means equality and democracy can only flourish in an equal society...it means equality, not merely the equality of possessing vote but economic and social equality." Jawaharlal Nehru may justly be regarded as the foremost interpreter of liberal democracy that Asia has produced.

He had great faith in democracy, freedom and equality. Nehru is not a political philosopher in the conventional sense, he is a political leader, a politician, who has read widely and thought deeply upon the problems of democracy. His philosophical bent of mind has enabled him to interpret day today problems with a certain theoretical perspective. His political theory is essentially eclectic, drawn from diverse intellectual currents of the nineteenth and twentieth centuries. A map of grat sensitivity, Nehru has absorbed and combined in himself many of the dominant impulses and ideas of modern democratic thought.

Nehru as a Secular Philosopher Another distinct contribution of Jawaharlal Nehru to modern India political thought is his philosophy of secularism. 'Nehru's theory of secular state becomes a twentieth century interpretation of the concept of the Indian state and society. The theory of secular state in India raises many problems unknown to western political experience.' 'Jawaharlal Nehru may be regarded as the foremost interpreter of liberal democracy that Asia has produced. Other Indian writers such as Vivekanand, Tagore and Aurobindo gave relatively little attention to political subjects and none of them grappled with the problems of democracy in independent India, Gandhi did not claim to believe in Western democracy and was thus in no position to interpret it to India.' Nehru's secular state may be defined in terms of:

(a) state policy of neutrality towards all religions and
(b) a state in which all citizens enjoy equal rights irrespective of religion.

Nehru as a Karmayogi Nehru was a Karmayogi and believed more in practice than in theory. His important contribution to political philosophy was his application of democratic principles of Indian conditions. To Nehru, "Democracy is a dynamic, not static thing and as it changes it may be that its domain will become wider and wider, ultimately it is a mental approach applied to our political and economic problems".

His Place in the Indian Political Thought To estimate Nehru's place in the Indian political thought, it is worthwhile to note down the remarks of great authors about Nehru.

According to Walter Crocker, Nehru's achievements may be summarised as under :

1. He was to hold India together. He gave a sense of unity to Indians.
2. To encourage the growth of parliamentary and cabinet system which the British started in India.
3. The modernisation of India...through Three Five Year Plans.

Lord Bertrand Russell, the noted British philosopher, says in an article on Jawaharlal Nehru that it was he who made democracy a safe in India and thereby, made it a real possibility in other parts of Asia and Africa.

He adds : "I do not believe Nehru's greatness is fully appreciated, but...if mankind is allowed to survive, he will be recognized in a manner adequate to his stature. Nehru's absence will teach us how much we owe him."

According to Pearl Buck, "Nehru is unforgettable because he made free India a pivot between the east and the west speaking the language of both."

According to Dr. Zakir Hussain (President of India) : "Central to his philosophy was his deep-rooted sense of secularism. This was not a matter of mere attitude or empty slogan of him but a positive and profound proportionate blend of thought and action."

According to H.N. Kunzru (President of the Indian Council of World Affairs) "He was able to impart continuing stability to our political life. Secondly, his ability to look forward beyond the current disputes and immediately pressing problems, enables him to be the country's philosopher and guide. Thirdly, he was one man who emphasised again and again the importance of the concept to a single citizenship for all Indians irrespective of diversity of religion, speech, culture, colour or sex, and largely succeeded in impressing it on the attention of his countrymen. Fourthly, the driving passion of his life was the desire to improve the material conditions of life for the common man.

To M.C. Chagla, "He was deeply interested in culture even in its narrow sense. He had a deep historical and wise thinking of future of India and its great cultural legacy we have inherited from our forefather."

V.K.R.V. Rao says, "Perhaps the greatest contribution of Nehru to India's renovating culture is his emphasis on science and what he calls the scientific temper."

K. Gupta says, "I will certainly say in very unspectacular but in a sure way, Mr. Nehru had helped to break the centuries old stagation of India's social life. In regard to foreign policy, I really think, he correctly estimated the factors which transcended the cold war and necessitated peaceful coexistence among great powers of the world."

Dr. S.D. Sen remarks, "The years between 1947 and 1964 really constituted the Nehru era. In these years Nehru put India on the political map of the world and by his dynamic personality and idealism projected to the world the image of a new, youthful, vigourous India. Although Mr. Nehru was like a colossus over the party, he failed to discipline the heterogeneous elements. The Congress gradually became a shabby and degenerate party of tin gods with little fresh blood to revive its energies."

Pandit Jawaharlal Nehru was really foremost disciple of the great apostle of Indian freedom, wise counsellor and moulder of policies of a reborn nation, renowned interpreter of the aspirations of a great race, his intellectual leadership has combined the profound knowledge of the West with the great heritage and enduring traditions of the East, a champion of under-privileged people, his devotion to the people, ideas of universal peace and understanding have won for him the respect and claim of all mankind.

In Gandhiji's word, "He is fearless, yet gentle, being a strange to weakness and weakening difference, detects weakness in a flash; having diplomacy about him, hates diplomatic language and insists upon going straight to the point. As I consider myself to be in advance of him, he returns the compliment by dismissing my claim. I honour him."

Rabindranath Tagore, too, testified to his straight forwardness when he said : "He never fought shy of truth when it was dangerous, nor mere allinance with falsehood when would be convenient."

To conclude we may say that he was the man of vision and wisdom, a lover of nature and out door life. Nehru had a vision of India in which getting the British out of it was merely the preliminary stage.

We conclude with Shrimati Aruna Asaf Ali, an old and intimate colleague of Nehru, who spoke for millions when she said : "Every aspect of Jawaharlal Nehru's personality fascinated us. He was our faultless and flawless idol, ideally perfect."

17

Acharya Narendra Dev (1889-1956)

Acharya Narendra Dev was the most remarkable man. 'He was a perfect combination', as Shri Prakasha writes, of genuine greatness and true goodness, difficult, almost impossible, to find in the limitations of the world in which our lives are cast. His learning knew no bounds. He was equally at home in the history of many lands and many ages, well versed in the philosophies of many faiths, master of many languages which he could use to good purposes. He was certainly the finest speaker on the Indian platform, and spoke with great force and eloquence in Hindi, Urdu and English alike. When he used a language for his public speeches, he spoke in that language alone: he never mixed up words of different languages. When he spoke on politics, he was full of fire and when he spoke on philosophy, the audience found how deep and profound his erudition was!

His Life Acharya Narendra Dev was born at Sitapur on October 30, 1889. From his childhood he was keenly interested in religious books. At a young age he recited *Gita* and *Amarkosh*. As Narendra Dev himself said, "I read at home the *Ramayana* composed by Tulsidas and the translation of the *Mahabharata*. I also read *Baital Pachchisi, Sinmhasan Battisi, Sur Sagar*, etc. *Chandrakanta* was the most popular novel of that time. I must have read it not less than sixteen times. I went through *Chandra Santati* which is in twenty-four volumes once. Perhaps, many people learnt Hindi only to go through *Chandrakanta*. In those days, books of that type were generally the rare. My thread ceremony was performed when I was ten. I used to perform my evening prayers with my father and read the *Bhagvadgita* daily. A Maharashtrian Brahman taught me to chant, with proper accent, the Vedas and there was a time when I had memorized the entire *Gita Rudra*. I had also read *Amarkosh* and *Loghu Kaumudi*."

The Acharya was sent to school in 1902. In 1904 and 1905 he learnt Bengali. His career was greatly influenced by his father. Narendra Dev was always a good student. Books like *Memoirs of a Revolutionary, Mutual Aid* by Kropotkin, *Essays in Nationalism, Idealism* by A.K.

Coomaraswamy, writings of Aurobindo Ghosh and Hardayal, stories of Turgeneve, Life of Garibardi, writings of Mazzini, books on the stories of the *French Revolution.* Bluntschelli's *Theory of the State* and a lot of Nihilist literature from Russia, were thoroughly studied by him.

He studied at Central College and after completing his education up to law, he practised at Fyzabad. He could hardly practise law for about five years when he plunged into non-co-operation movement and since then had been to jail several times. In 1942, hewas in Ahmednagar Fort along with the members of Congress Working Committee, where he wrote a few scholarly books. In 1921, under the pressure of friends, particularly of Jawaharlal Nehru, he joined Kashi Vidyapith, a national institution with patriotic traditions. After five years, he became its principal and was called "Acharya".

"Acharyaji is one of the greatest orators in India. It is not easy to think even a few names, who combine his great learning and his stately eloquence. And yet, so shy is his nature, that he did not even speak in the Congress till 1934, though he had been a member of the A.I.C.C. from 1917. In 1934, also it was the strong insistence of his socialist friends that got him on to the platform.

According to Sri Prakasha, his nature was very child-like and his life was simple to a fault. He was a person of rare courage, and had most sensitive nature. He would brook no insult, and the only occasion when he suspected that any reflection was being cast on his honour and integrity or his motives were suspected. He was a most lovable personality hence people were attracted to him almost unconsciously, and came to have great respect for him after even casual contacts. He carried his learning very lightly, and it was almost impossible to make him talk about himself. Unfortunately, he kept very bad health, and in the latter half of his life suffered grievously from asthma. He bore his physical sufferings with remarkable patience and never allowed them to interfere with his work.

He was a great writer also. He translated into Hindi Poussin's French version of the *Abidharma Kosha,* one of the most important works of Sarvastivada or the realistic theory that everything exists. Besides his translation of the *Abhidharma Kosha,* he studies and summarised many other original works on Buddhist Philosophy in Ahmednagar.

He wrote the Hindi book entitled *Rashtriyata Our Samajavada* (Nationalism and socialism) This is a collection of speeches, addresses and articles and runs into 714 pages. It is divided into 8 sections.

1. History of the Nationalist Movement;
2. The struggle for Freedom;
3. Towards Socialism;

4. Socialism;
5. Education;
6. Culture;
7. International Affairs and
8. Miscellaneous.

His Political Ideas Acharya Narendra Dev, as Ashok Mehta writes, was at once a magnificent expression and respected spokes man of the best political trends of his time. He was cradled in the freedom struggle. His genius, perhaps the ethos of his time also permitted him to combine in himself diverse possibilities that do not seem to recur now.

He was an intellectual and a politician. He combined intense absorption in political work with unswerving adherence to moral principles. He was firm and always principled, but he never aroused unfriendliness. He could weave into current activities his clear vision of the future.

He was scholar-politician. His devotion to scholarship was wellknown. His varied intellectual counted him among our savants. His ideas had such clarity and incandescence that his expression had chasteness and beauty rarely met since; he was an orator whose speeches were rich with ideas, insights and analytical as well as intuitive perceptions. His scholarship is enshrined in the studies on Buddhism that he carried out. His tenures as Vice-Chancellor of Lucknow University and later of the Banaras Hindu University were among memorable once for those distinguished institutions of learning. His academic colleagues were proud to accept his leadership, the students revered him as their *guru.* A whole generation of young people were inspired by Acharyaji, not only in their intellectual pursuits but also in their devotion to national liberation and social transformation.

His Social Ideas : On Socialism

He was a great socialist leader. 'Narendra Dev had a much wider concept of socialism than most other socialist leaders in India. He had realised that a caste ridden people steeped in superstition had to be lifted out of their backwardness by a sustained programme of cultural re-education. He started the Samajwadi Yuwak Sabha with the object of instilling new social values among youth'.

In May 1934, Acharya Narendra Dev presided over the Socialist Convention in Patna. This convention laid the foundation of an all-India socialist movement. "It was intended to fulfil the tasks of two eras, the task of the era of nationalism and that of socialism. It aimed at national freedom conjointly with other democratic forces for "the eradication of imperialism, racialism, colonialism and other forms of oppression and economic inequality among nations and the creation of a democratic socialist world". For more than twenty years he worked as its philosopher and guide. To him no sacrifice was too great for socialism, which he regarded as "the gospel of the new age".

Narendra Dev is claimed to be a Marxist and as such held that the "historical necessity of a basic change in a social order can be realised only through a revolution". Besides Marx and Engles, Karl Kautsky, Rosa Luxenburg and Lenin exercised their influence over him.

For him the socialist movement has never been purely an economic movement. It has also been an ethical and cultural movement. He, therefore, constantly laid stress on ethical and cultural values of socialism and strove for their creative realisation in society. He was considerably inspired by certain enduring human values enshrined in Indian culture of which he was a great scholar and wished them to be vitalised and preserved in socialist culture. The task before us, he felt was "the presentation of its vital elements and their synthesis with modern thought".

Dealing with the right to property, he said that the fundamental right with regard to property should be so revised that it may be possible for the legislative authority of both the Union and States to acquire property for public purposes, to sanction its redistribution on equitable basis and to socialise public management of private property undertakings in the general interest of the community or workers concerned. The legislative authority alone should have the power to determine it and what compensation is to be paid in aforesaid cases.

He asked the socialist workers to educate the peasants in the art of co-operatives and to inculcate in them the spirit of co-operation, the sense of social responsibility and the feeling of sanctity for social property.

In the Gaya thesis, Acharya Narendra Dev dealt with this problem. He said that Society is part of every individual and added that it is just as real as any or all of its members. Although it does not exist apart from the individuals who constitute it, it cannot be completely reduced to them. It is an order out or which individuals acquire their very individuality.

Thus, accusing the present individualist social structure of having distorted a human personality into self-seeking machine, Narendra Dev argues in favour of a socialistic approach. This does not mean, he writes, "the disregard by the individual of his personality. It only means that individualism, narrowly egoistic, retards the growth of personality and that individuality can attain its supreme development only in the highest common social effort".

M. N. Rai said that the one great quality of a true Marxist was that he was not dogmatic or sectarian in his attitude. The dialectical method was a living method of grat elasticity and one who followed it had to adapt himself to the changing situation. It did not mean that the Marxist was an opportunist or that he was ready to compromise his principles. He knew the limitations and the possibilities of a particular situation and he would not sacrifice the gains from it merely for the sake of a doctrine or a dogma. Narendra Dev had no doubt that socialism was certain to come in this country and that its critics were wrong.

Socialism, he said, could not be established overnight and it was a growing thing. "The truth is that were always willing to each the masses, but never to learn from them", he said.

As a member of the legislature. Narendra Dev mostly confined himself to land reform, labour welfare, abolition of casteism and communalism, civil liberties and education, and about each of these he was in dead earnest.

On Democracy Democracy, said Narendra Dev, is not only a form of government but also a way of life and therefore, the ideal of democracy' is not to be confined to the political sphere only, but has to be extended to every other sphere of human activity. Newly-born nations that borrow foreign democratic constitutions only in limitation or simply in the belief that this a sign of being regarded as progressive cannot succeed in establishing a truly democratic form of government if they have not developed democratic sentiments in them. Democracy is a matter of habit and is the tradition and is the result of a long and painful effort. The democratic tradition has to be built up and the democratic sentiment cultivated. A people who are torn by castes and creeds and who recognise privilege built on birth or wealth, race or creed will have to make conscious efforts in all possible ways to achieve the democratic way of life. Democracy must be become a creed and govern their entire life and behaviour.

It is a truism that unless we develop the social and political consciousness of the people, we cannot make democracy function successfully. Democracy means an intelligent and active participation, of all the sections of the people in the political life of the country.

On Education Narendra Dev said that our educational system needs overhauling. It needs a new orientation and a new philosophy to secure international peace and co-operation for the promotion of human welfare. Coming nearer home the education for the masses should be planned as to developing in them a healthy, non-communal out-look on life, new democratic and human values have to be emphasized. Moreover, education, should not stop, at a particular age but should be a continuous process. We are living in an ever-changing world, therefore, our education needs reconditioning from to time. Apart from imparting literary education, an effort should be made on behalf of the state to educate the people from time to time on important public issues.

Acharyaji further emphasised that the State should, therefore, aim at imparting basic education to the people so that they may develop their faculties and acquire a capacity for self-direction. Civic education which does not stop at the nation but is comprehensive enough to include international obligations must receive a high priority. We should not forget that we are moving towards a world community and, therefore, all our educational projects should be prepared from that point of view. We cannot be indifferent to what is going on in other parts of the world and live in isolation. Our education should be such as may ehable us to live happily and securely in the world of today, We must cultivate international goodwill and fellowship and should always be prepared to work for peace and to fulfil our international obligations.

As Ganga Saran Sinha said as an educationist Acharyaji was highly respected all over the country by all educationists. In the post-Independence period he was pressed to assume responsibilities as Vice-Chancellor of the Lucknow University and then that of the Banaras Hindu University. In both these universities he endeared himself to students and considerably toned up their discipline and morale. The educational ideals which he placed before University Teachers Conference as their president and in various committee reports deserved to be carefully studied.

On Communal Unity Narendra Dev said that the system of caste is an antithesis to democracy. It has also lost its vitality and is not serving any useful purpose. That is why Hindu social polity is collapsing and deteriorating. In the interest of both Hindu society and national solidarity, it is necessary that we should remodel our society on a new basis which accepts the principle of democracy and which may unite the different religious communities and weld them into a nation. Unity can be forged only if we strive together to achieve a common destiny. Nationalism transcends differences in language and religion and acts as a uniting force. There is no reason to despair. What has been possible else where can be made possible here as well, only if we have the right understanding and the vision to do the right thing.

On Gandhism Acharya Narendra Dev, as G.S. Sinha writes, had profound respects for Gandhiji whose dynamic personality and ideas had their deep impress on him almost imperceptibly. But he differed from him in many matters such as the boycott of the legislatures, the idea of the conversion of heart of the imperial rulers, the theory of trusteeship, self-sufficiency in education and anti-intellectual approach to several questions. He valued Satyagraha as a technique of organised mass pressure, respected Gandhiji as a great national leader who realised the importance of the masses for a national struggle and who alone could start a "nation wide" struggle against foreign domination. Gandhiji's leadership was, therefore, regarded by him as most valuable for national freedom, and consequently he supported it till the last struggle for freedom.

Estimate As an educationist Acharyaji was highly respected all over the country by all educationists. In the post-Independence period he was pressed to assume responsibilities as Vice-Chancellor of the Lucknow University and then that of the Banaras Hindu University.

> 'Like all greatmen, Acharya Narendra Dev was a representative of his age. Both his life and thought represented the deep sorrows and urges of his people as well as the cultural and ideological currents of his time. But he was also a prophet and builder of a new age'.

He was deeply interested in the youth movement and urged the youths to have "deep faith in democratic ideals" to cultivate, "self-discipline" and democratic ways of life, to shun power-politics, to develop capacity for hard constructive work.

According to Achyut Patwardhan, Narendra Dev belongs to the select band of intellectuals who have helped to shape the political outlook and perspective of modern India.

B.V. Keskar says, 'There is no doubt that he was one of the very really great men that this country produced in modern; times. His example is such that younger people should copy at least some of his great qualities and thus show that he did not pass away unhonoured and unsung. To those like me who were attached to him by an indissoluble bond of a regard and affection, it was an irreparable loss like an elder of the family passing away".

As a matter of fact, as Surendra Nath Dwivedy says : "It is not easy to write about Acharya Narendra Dev. He was a full personality. No man is infallible and no one can claim to have attained perfection. But Acharyaji was an embodiment of all that is good, noble, honest and desirable. He was a revolutionary in thought and action; amiable and considerate in his behaviour; and had full knowledge and study of the development of human society. He was a learned scholar and educationist, a versatile genius who had a thorough grasp of our ancient culture and civilisation; and with a modern and scientific mind and approach he became a true interpreter and real representative of our country. His unassuming nature and constant illness prevented him from rising to that high place in Indian political and cultural life as would have unfolded to a wider sphere the greatness of his life and character".

According to Ashok Mehta, "He was a scholar who was a man of the masses...Among the common folk and average political workers, his association ignited love for ideas and understanding of principles. He was never pulled down to the level of mass politics, he lifted the people to a higher level of understanding and to the widening of their horizon. If he knelt, he knelt only to raise."

> "He was among those whose personality had a liberating effect on other persons, whose contact uplifted, whose achievement spread an aroma of idealism. He fought for liberty, he cherished equality but loved fraternity. To have known him was to have gathered richness in one's life'.

Yusuf Meherally writes that his captivating manners, his assuming, but gigantic scholarship, his gifts of character and intellect have endeared him to hundreds of thousands. His is the typical case of a man who lives for an ideal and a faith the ideal of a new classless society, where poverty, ignorance and exploitation are banished and faith in the common man and his revolutionary ability to create a new world is there. And he lives his life with so much purity of purpose and dignity of spirit that it ennobles all who come into contact with him and imparts a new tone to public life.

18

Dr. Ram Manohar Lohia (1910-67)

Dr. Ram Manohar Lohia is the founder leader of the Socialist Party of India. He was a great freedom-fighter and has imprisoned several times for taking part in India's independence struggle. He was opposed to the use of English in India. He had several compaigns for the removal of British statutes from India. He was a great critic of the Congress.

His Life Dr. Ram Manohar Lohia was born on March 23, 1910 in a Marwari family in a village in U.P. He was educated at Bombay and Calcutta. He went to Germany after graduation and got Ph.D. from there. Lohia took keen interest even when he was a college student.

In 1928, he led the college students to boycott the Simon Commission. In this very year, he came very close to Pt. Nehru. He also left a great impression on Subhash Chandra Bose.

Due to Pt. Nehru's recommendation he became the secretary of the foreign department of the Congress. In 1938, he was included in the Executive Committee of the Congress Socialist Party.

Dr. Lohia took active part in the freedom struggle of India from 1938 to 1946. During this period, he was arrested several times.

In February 1947, the Congress Socialist Party held its session at Kanpur under the chairmanship of Dr. Lohia. At this session, the party dropped the word 'Congress' before its name and became the independent Socialist Party.

In 1952, there was a merger of Kisan Mazdoor Praja Party with the Socialist Party. As a result of it, a new party named as Praja Socialist Party came into being. Dr. Lohia became its President. He died in 1967.

His works Dr. Lohia has written many standard works. Some of his significant works are as under :

1. *Wheel of History* (1950)
2. *The Will to Power* (1963)
3. *History of Socialist Movement* (1969)
4. *Aspects of Socialist Party* (1952)

5. *On the Move*
6. *Fragments of World Mind.*

Political Ideas

His Views on Capitalism and Communism Dr. Lohia was against both capitalism and communism. He treated both these systems, as wasteful and unsuitable for India. He pleaded that Gandhiji's ideas and actions may act as a filter through which socialist ideas would flow and get rid of their dress. Dr. Lohia remarks, "Nobody would be happier then I if Gandhi's ideas were also to influence the other two systems, capitalism and communism, but one may reasonably doubt that this can be done."

Lohia said that the world today was in the grip of two system and the third was coming up. He remarks that capitalism and communism are almost fully elaborated systems and the whole world in their grip, and the result is poverty and war and fear. The third idea is also making itself felt on the world stage. It is still inadequate, and it has not been fully elaborated, but it is open Lohia called this third idea as the true socialist idea based on Gandhi's ideas of decentralized economy and village government.

His Concept of Four Pillar State Lohia firmly believed in four pillar state. In this state, Dr. Lohia synthesized the two opposite concepts of centralization and decentralization. According to Lohia, this state, there will be functional federalism at four levels namely, the village, the Mandal (district), the province and the central government. In this system, the district magistracy would be abolished. Also in the Four Pillar State, the village, the city and the district Panchayats are to take charge of making policies and take over the welfare functions.

The main features of this, according to Lohia, will be :

1. One fourth of all governmental and plan expenditure shall be through village, district and city Panchayats.
2. Police shall remain subordinate to village, city and district Panchayats.
3. The post of collector shall be abolished and all his functions will be distributed among various bodies in the district.
4. Agriculture, industry and other property, which is nationalized, will as far as possible, be owned and administered by village city and district Panchayats.
5. Economic decentralization, corresponding to political and administrative decentralization, will have to be brought about through maximum utilization of small machines.

His Views About Cyclical Theory

Lohia believed that history moves in a cyclic order. In his most famous work *Wheel of History* Lohia said that history moved without emotion. He rejected Hegelian as well as Marxian's interpretation of History. He remarks that for those, who profess to give us a law or even some inkling of a process as to how man has developed through various periods must be able to indicate why peoples and classes have risen and fallen. If there is no answer to that, it would be futile to speak of a law of history. To describe symptoms is not to indicate causes. Lohia argued that no law can be fixed about the purpose of design in history.

Lohia's notion of cyclical theory corresponds to Aristotelian cyclic theory. He agreed with Spengler, Northtrop Sorokin and Toynbee that the rise and fall of people and civilization have ever taken place and, as students of history, we must have all concerned ourselves with the rise of the British Empire, the fall of Pharoah Empire, the rise of the Gupta Kingdom and the fall of the Roman Empire and so forth...

Dr. Lohia was in favour of a world union. He urged the socialist parties of the world to think in terms of a world union. He said that no true internationalism can arise unless its votaries realize that the present crisis of foreign policy is a crisis of human civilization and that it can be overcome only by a union of minds all over the world that cuts across national frontiers and interests and is prepared to hold general principles even when they operate against one's own system of national or world alliances.

According to Dr. Lohia, Asian politics have some special problems. He said that in Asia, a European type of socialist democracy is of little use. Also the method used by European countries for economic and political reconstruction were not suitable to Indian way of life. So Lohia felt that new methods must be sought. He said that the peasant must learn intensive agriculture and he must be persuaded to enter into co-operative farming of one type or another. Such machines should be made available to him as do not cost much capital. He must develop initiative and, therefore, maximum state power, both legislative and administrative, should belong to him in his village community. Communist re-division of land is a hoax to begin with and a futile cruelty in the end. Socialist re-division of land, because it is coupled with decentralization of power, will produce good economic results as well as a new way of living.

Dr. Lohia felt that traditional and organized socialism was a dead doctrine and a dying organization. So Lohia urged for a new socialism. He said that equality, democracy, non-violence, decentralization and socialism are the main five principles found not only in India's politics, but also in that of all many other countries. He said that new socialism must attain these principles.

Lohia said that seven revolutions are taking place everywhere in the world. These revolutions are :

1. For equality between man and woman;
2. against political, economic and spiritual inequality based on skin, colour;
3. against inequality of backward and high groups or castes based on long tradition, and for giving special opportunities to the backward;
4. against foreign enslavement;
5. for equality and planned production and against the existence of and attachment for private capital;
6. against unjust encroachments on private life and for democratic methods;
7. against weapons and for Satyagraha.

According to Dr. Lohia, the attainment of 'New Socialism' all over the world depends upon the success of these seven revolutions.

According to Lohia, all human history has become internal movement between castes and classes. He writes, "Caste represents conservative forces of stagnation, inertia and prescriptive right, while classes stand for a dynamic force of social mobilization". Dr. Lohia said that a struggle between castes and classes would go on in the history till the evil in man and society was not prevented from breeding. Lohia hoped that "the world might, through intelligent design, try to achieve a multi-coloured harmony of human race".

Dr. Lohia was a great critic of Nehru's policy of non-alignment. He wanted the foreign policy of India to be reoriented. Lohia suggested that socialist foreign policy based on socialistic principles should be adopted. He said that U.N.O. and its agencies should be strengthened. He wanted that friendly relations with all world governments and the people be developed. Also, support should be given to all socialist movements. There should be a World Parliament.

To conclude, we may say that Dr. Lohia was a great intellectual. He always stressed the need of original thinking. He was a world-minded person and aspired for true international unity. He advocated the creation of an intellectual pool that would combine spirit and matter into an autonomous relationship.

19

Ashok Mehta

His Life Ashok Mehta was the founder member of the Socialist Party and was Chairman of Praja Socialist Party. In 1957 he was a chairman of Foodgrains Inquiry Committee and had recommended state trading in foodgrains. He took active part in freedom struggle of India and was imprisoned several times in this connection. He became Member of Parliament in 1954. During freedom struggle, he edited the *Congress Socialist Weekly.*

He was appointed Deputy Chairman of the Planning Commission. At the time of split in Congress in 1969, Mehta joined Congress (O). Ashok Mehta has written some standard works like :

1. *Indian Shipping,*
2. *Communal Triangle in India,*
3. *The Great Rebellion of 1857,*
4. *Who Owns India*? and
5. *Democratic Socialism.*

Ashok Mehta was in favour of democratic socialism and opposed the authoritarian socialism an expounded by Marx, Lenin and Stalin. He was a great critic of Marxism. He said that the Marxists have never been happy with democracy. To deny it and, where necessary to disrupt it, becomes their instinctive approach. In Asian countries, where democracy is struggling for strength, it is easy to adopt the traditional Marxist stance, but it is far more necessary to explore revisionist re-statement where socialism becomes integral to democracy. Mehta pleaded for Asian socialism which would be revisionist, democratic and pacific. He said "Somerset Maugham has said somewhere : Prose is rococo art: poetry is baroque. One might say likewise that revolutionary socialism which is elemental, massive, mystical; tragic is baroque;, revisionist socialism, which, as it were, prefers accomplishment to power, stability to intransigence, vigour to grandeur, is rococo. In the free countries of Asia, a shift is desired from the baroque to the rococo".

Apart from proclaiming his faith in democracy, Ashok Mehta has often expressed to the thought that in India, with its poverty and ever-growing population, the problem of production is no less, if not more, important than the problem of distribution. Ashok Mehta said that the main aim of Indian socialism should be to complete or telescope in India within a short period the economic progress made in industrially advanced European countries over a long period. He wanted that the poor would not be satisfied with political democracy for long, unless such a democracy could act fast enough and plan sufficiently well and raise production adequately in order to cope with the problem of poverty. It is, therefore, clear, writes Ashok Mehta, that unless development gathers speed early enough, growing population can retard further development. Again, if after thirty years' development efforts, the preconsumer income remains virtually unchanged, can stability be maintained? Only a rapid tempo of development can maintain an accelerating momentum, check fertility, raise level of living and uphold democracy.

He wanted the Indian socialists to devise ways and means to enhance agriculture production. He was in favour of mixed economy. Also, he suggested that Indian handicrafts and cottage industries should be developed in India to absorb the growing population. He wanted that the private sector should be controlled in such a manner in which fair distribution of goods under a system of price-fixation can be ensured.

Ashok Mehta was in favour of co-operative farming. He said that land should go to actual tillers. The government should provide better seeds, fertilizers and better techniques of agriculture. So he suggested various land reforms.

Besides land reforms, Ashok Mehta also suggested certain social reforms. He said that untouchability should be removed. He was in favour of uplift of the womenfolk. He said that social evils should be removed by imparting proper knowledge to the people.

To conclude, we may say that Ashok Mehta was a great socialist and a defender of existing socio-economic order. He occupied an eminent position amongst Indian socialists. He led vigorous political activities during the period of national struggle for freedom.

20

Dutt, Dange and Ranadive

Rajni Palme Dutt

Rajni Palme Dutt was born in 1896 in England. His father was a medical practitioner. His mother was of a Swedish nationality. He got his education in England and was brought up there.

R.P. Dutt founded the British Communist Party in 1920. He was elected to the Central Committee and Politbureau and was also a member of the Executive Committee of the London India League. Being an Indian by descent and being most popular in the British Communist Party, Dutt acted as a co-ordinator between the Communist Party of India and the Communist International. He was a great architect of the Communist policy and programme in India.

In 1926, R.P. Dutt wrote a book *Modern India* in which he explained the methods and tectics that the Communists in India should adopt.

Dutt's thesis, as Prof. Sankar Ghose writes, was that the Indian I bourgeoisie were co-operating with the British capitalists and were penetrating into the Indian economy so that it was a dangerous delusion to think that the capitalist development in India was a national development. The interest of the Indian bourgeoisie and, therefore, the Indian national struggle had to be struggle of the working masses against the political and economic exploitation of the British capitalists as also of the Indian bourgeoisie, who had entered into a partnership with the former, that is to say, "the struggle of the Indian people must be ultimately a struggle for social liberation".

Dutt acknowledged contribution of Mahatma Gandhi to the national movement. He agrees that Gandhi brought before the masses a policy of action... Non-co-operation is the attempt to force the government to submit by the use of the power of the united action of the masses.

There is no question of gentle, persuasive spiritual argument. Besides this, Dutt has no faith either in non-violence or in the spirituality of Gandhi. He said, "There is no question of a gentle persuasive power".

Dutt also attacked Gandhiji for his belief that in the nationalist movement there could be a reconciliation of the interests of the bourgeoisie on the one hand and the workers and peasants on the other, or that they could combine in a movement of non-violent non-co-operation. Dutt said that all parasific and propertied classes have to weave around themselves a fog of confused language, superstition, traditions, religion, reverence, etc. in order to hide from the masses the fact of their exploitation... From this class alignment inevitably follows his (Gandhi's) co-operation with the imperialist Government.

Swaraj or liberation, as defined by R.P. Dutt, was economic Swaraj which would usher in a classless society. Dutt pleaded for paying greater attention to the workers and peasants. He said the Swaraj was not to be treated as an .'indefinable mystery' but as meaning liberation from imperialistic dominion. Such liberation was to be not merely political but also social and economic, that is to say, a liberation which was to end class divisions and exploitation by the common entry of the whole people into the possession of their country... (and) into the wealth and means of livelihood, into the common sharing of work and the return on work."

Also for Dutt Independence is not an end in itself because 'Real liberation is social — that is the ending of class divisions and exploitation by the common entry of the whole people into the possession of their country (ultimately in a world scale) into the wealth and means of likelihood, into the common sharing of work and the return on work.'

Dutt criticised the western form of parliamentary democracy as a 'mockery of popular representation and whose so called liberties are an obvious sham'. However, he insist on 'a fight for the winning of the elementary civil rights of free speech, press, meeting and combination'.

S.A. Dange

S.A. Dange was born on 10 October 1899. He is one of the founding members of the Communist Party of India. He became a member of the central executive. He was also elected as a Vice-President of World Federation of Trade Unions. He was imprisoned several times for his involvement in strikes. He was elected to the Lok Sabha in 1957 and again in 1967.

In 1921 S.A. Dange published a small book *Gandhi and Lenin*. He had the support of Lotwala, a richman. With his help Dange organised a library of Marxist literature, published translations of Marxist classics and circulated Marxist interpretation of Indian affairs. Dange also established a publishing house, 'Indu Parkash' and 'Socialist'.

He leads a moderate wing within the Communist Party. At the time of the Chinese aggression on India in Octoher 1962. There appeared a rift between the Communist Party.

The National Council of the Communist Party passed a resolution to condemn the Chinese aggression on India under the influence of S.A. Dange. The pro-Chinese group with the party was annoyed with such a resolution. However, the left wing formed another party called the CPM in 1964. The right wing under the leadership of S.A. Dange followed the Soviet line and remained with the official party of the CPI.

After the rift in the Communist Party, Dange holds that India is not fit for revolution. He expresses the view that change can be brought in India by peaceful means. He says that Parliament can play an important role for bringing about social, political and economic changes.

In the field of foreign affairs, S.A. Dange believes in the policy of non-alignment. He wanted that India should have friendly relations with her neighbours including China and Pakistan.

In India's international affairs, Dange feels that the monopoly houses should be brought under governmental control, banks should be nationalised, the current tax system should be overhauled. In short the policies and programmes as advocated by the CPI were strongly supported by S.A. Dange.

B.T. Ranadive

B.T. Ranadive came into prominence after India became independent. He forwarded his thesis regarding the future role of the Indian Communists. He expressed leftist views. He favoured violence for the quick achievement of required results. His thesis found favourable consideration with a number of Communists in India. His policy of revolution, subversion and violence was followed by many Communists in South, West Bengal and other parts of the country.

Ranadive was closer to Chinese philosophy. He said, "Our revolution in many respects differs from the classical Russian Revolution; and is to a great extent similar to that of the Chinese Revolution."

Ranadive supported the demand for Pakistan and formulated a multi-national theory. He wrote in the *People's Age,* 'What is the progressive essence of the Pakistan demand? The application of the principle of self-determination to certain nationalities in India. Muslims in certain areas do form a distinct nationality bound together by common culture, history and tradition. In consonance with the demands of justice and fair play, they must have the completest liberty to built their own life and liberty sanctioned by the right to form a separate state if and when they choose.'

Ranadive considered that Pandit Nehru's government was tied to the apron-strings of Anglo-American imperialists. He said that Nehru government had to be overthrown by violence and revolution. In October 1949 as a secretary of the CPI, he wrote to Mao-Tse-Tung... "I wish to assure you and through you the people of China that the Communist Party of India will unmask all the anti-Chinese intrigues that the Nehru Government might hatch under the dictates of the American imperialists and really the people to defeat them." Soon after the preaching the violence by Ranadive, some elements within the CPI began to realise the mistake of Ranadive.

21

Sayyid Ahmad Khan (1817-1898)

In the words of K.A. Nizami "Sayyid Ahmad Khan is one of the most dynamic and resplendent personalities of the 19th century. At once a theologian, scholar, social reformer, educationist, politician, author and journalist, he contributed many essential elements to the resurgence of modern India".

He further adds 'In the history to India's transition from medievalism to modernism, Sayyid Ahmad Khan stands out prominently as a dynamic force pitted against conservatism, superstition, inertia and ignorance. He contributed many of the essential elements to the development of modern India and paved the way for the growth of a healthy scientific attitude of mind which is a *sine qua* non for advancement, both material and intellectual.'

His Life Sayyid Ahmad Khan was born in 1817 and died in 1898. These 81 years were a most momentous period in India's history, a period characterized by transition in almost every sphere of life, political, social and economic.

Sayyid Ahmad Khan spent his early youth in the aristocratic atmosphere of the house of his maternal grandfather, Khawaja Fariduddin.

Recalling in his old age the incidents of his early life, he said, my maternal grandfather used to take his lunch in the female apartment. A large 'dastarkhawan' was spread out and all his sons, daughters, grandsons, grand-daughters and wives of sons joined the lunch. Empty dishes were placed before the children. My grandfather used to ask every child : "What dish would you like to have? Whatever the child indicated he himself put with a spoon in his plate. The children partook of their food with great decorum. Everyone took care that nothing dropped on the carpet and that his hands were not soiled and that no chewing sound was produced. He used to take dinner in the male apartment. It was temporarily converted into Zenana and my mother and my aunt came out to serve dinner to him. All the boys used to sit there. We were particularly careful about the clearliness of our feet because if anybody's feet left some mark on the chandni, he was reprimanded. If any child had ink sports on his clothes, he was displeased with him also. In the evening, when it was time for lighting the candles, all his grand children who read in the maktabs, and of whom I was one, went to him to read out their lessons. Whoever had studied his lesson well, was given some good sweets; whoever did not remember his lesson well, was admonished".

The most powerful single factor in shaping the character of Sayyid Ahmad Khan was the influence of his mother, Aziz-un-nisa Begum.

When Sayyid Ahmad Khan was a Munsif at Delhi, he always used to go out in a carriage. His mother advised him, "Wherever you have to go regularly, sometimes go on foot and sometimes in a carriage. Who knows, tomorrow you may not be in a position to afford a carriage. Cultivate habits which you can continue even in adverse circumstances".

Sayyid Ahmad Khan inherited from his mother her generosity and large heartedness. Sayyid Ahmad Khan's formal education ended when he was 18 years old, but his interest in books continued.

On December 24, 1841, Sayyid Ahmad Khan was appointed Munsif of Mainpuri. However, within two weeks he was transferred to Fatehput Sikri.

After his transfer to Fatehpur Sikri, Sayyid Ahmad Khan came to Delhi for a brief holiday.

On February 18, 1846, Sayyid Ahmad was transferred to Delhi at his own request. During his stay at Delhi, Sayyid Ahmad Khan spent most of his time in the study of traditional subjects like Muslim jurisdiction.

So long as Sayyid Ahmad Khan was Munsif at Delhi, he used to give his entire salary of Rs. 100 p.m. to his mother. She would give him five rupees for pocket expenses and spend the rest on the household. "Whatever clothes she got prepared for me, I gladly wore; and whatever food she gave to me, I gladly took". Sayyid Ahmad Khan used to say.

In 1855 he accepted the job of Amin at Bijnor. In the 'Loyal Muhammedans of India' he gives the following account of his activity during this period :

> "In the early part of the year 1857, I held the office of Sudder Ammen at Bijnore, and when the first stunning news of the mutiny at Meerut arrived, I disbelieved it entirely, but when at length all doubts on the subject were painfully dispelled, I at once made up my mind as to my own conduct, and firmly resolved to stand by the Government at all hazards.... In pursuance of this determination, I attached myself to the person of Mr. Alexander Shakespeare, Magistrate and Collector of Bijnore, and was beside that gentleman on every occasion of emergency that

> arose in that perilous time. In fact, I forsook my own dwelling place, and was ever present night and day, at Mr. Shakespeare's, residence feeling myself impelled to do utmost to guard the lives of the ladies and children and I don't recollect that at any time in the day I put off from my person the weapons with which I had armed myself.

In April 1858, Sayyid Ahmad Khan was transferred to Moradabad as Sad rus Sudur.

In 1860, a severe famine broke out in the North Western Province. J. Statchey, the Collector of Moradabad, entrusted him with the work of organizing relief.

Raja Jai Kishan Das is reported to have said : "When Sir Sayyid started his journal, *The Loyal Muhammedans of India*, some of its sentences gave the impression that Sayyid Ahmad Khan was a fanatic who had no sympathy for Hindus. At that time I had also thought of bringing out a similar journal containing accounts of Hindus who had supported the British Government. In the meantime I happened to visit Moradabad. I went to the relief centre and met Sir Sayyid Ahmad whom I had not seen before. I referred to sentences which had given me the impression of his being a fanatic. He apologized and confessed that it was due to slip of pen. This was, however, a polite reply. But the affection and sympathy with which he was behaving with men of all religions and all castes made my heart absolutely clean towards him. I was, in fact, struck with wonder when I found what a noble soul he was. It was on that day that I established friendship with him, which went on increasing every day".

In 1861, Sayyid Ahmad Khan's wife died at Moradabad.

On May 12, 1862, Sayyid Ahmad Khan reached Ghazipur. Here, he compiled Tabyin-ul-Kalam and thought of measures to improve the condition of the people.

On August 15, 1867, Sayyid Ahmad Khan was promoted as a judge of the small cause court and was transferred to Banares.

In, a number of letters written to his friends in India he has given his impressions of the: new world.

In a letter addressed to Raja Jai Kishan Das, he wrote, "What I have seen and seen daily, is utterly beyond the imagination of a native of India. If any of my countrymen does not believe what I say, you may certainly put them down as frogs and fishes. There was once a living fish that fell from a fisherman's net into a well in which were a number of frogs. When they saw a new traveller, white in colour, and glittering like silver, they behaved very kindly to him, and asked where he came from. The fish said that he was a native of the Ganges. The frogs asked the fish if his watery country was similar to theirs; to which the fish answered in the affirmative, adding that it was a bright, good country, swept by a fine wind, which raised waves in which fishes were rocked as in a swing, and disported themselves, and that it was broad and long. On learning this a frog came out a foot from the side of the well, and said. What 'as long and as broad as the distance I have come from the well?' The fish said, 'Much greater'. The frog came another foot out, and again put his question to the fish, which said, 'Much greater'. The frog went on, getting the same answer the further he went, until he got to the opposite side of the well, asked the same question the fish gave the same reply. The frog said, 'You lie; it cannot be larger than this moment a man let down a bucket and drew water thus causing small waves on the surface.' The frog asked the fish if his country's waves were as large, on which the fish laughed, saying, those things that you have never seen, and which it is impossible for you to imagine, cannot be thought of by you without seeing, why therefore, do you ask about them?"

He was impressed by the literary interests and activities of the women of England. Is it not a matter for astonishment that a women when ill, should read with the object of improving her mind? Have you ever seen such a custom in India in the family of any noble, *nawab, raja* or man of high family? If our women in India were to frequent the bazars with faces uncovered, how astonished and alarmed would not their husbands be? It is undoubtedly a fact that the women here, when they hear that the women of India are unable to read or write, are ignorant of education or instructions, are equally astonished, and are displeased with and despise them.

Looking critically at the conditions prevailing in India, he remarked "I am extremely pleased that my Bengali and Parsi brethren have begun, to some extent, to promote civilization but their pace is so fast that there is danger of their falling. The fatal should of complacent self-esteem is wrapt around the Mahommendan community; they remember the old tales of their ancestors, and think that there are none like themselves".

In a letter to Raja Jai Kishan Das, he wrote : "O well-wishers of Hindustan : Do not place your dependence on any one spread abroad, relying on yourselves and your subscriptions, translate works of arts and sciences; and when you have mastered these and attained to civilization, you will think very little of going into Government serive. 'I hope and trust that such a day may soon come".

After coming from England he formed Scientific Society and devoted much of his time in social service.

His works He has written very widely on different subjects. His books on historical subjects include :

1. *Jam-i-jum;*
2. *Asar-us-Sanadid;*
3. *Silsilatul-Muluk;*
4. *History of Bijnor:*
5. *Edition of Ain-in-Akbari;*
6. *Edition of Tarikh-i-Firoz Shahi;* and
7. *Edition of Tuzuki-i-Jehangiri.*

He wrote some books on law and translated some Acts into Urdu.

1. They are *Intikhab-al-Akhwain* published in 1846.
2. Urdu translation of all cases decided between 1810-72 in three volumes.
3. Acts No. 10, 14 and 16.

Apart from these books and brochures, Sayyid Ahmad Khan wrote innumerable articles on different subjects : legal, religious social, political, literary, etc. A collection of all these articles would run into several volumes.

His Political Ideas Sayyid Ahmad's political thought, writes Nizami, was the outcome of his political experience and was based on a careful and realistic appraisal of the contemporary Indian life and its problems.

He was incomparably the noblest man, remarked, Beck "whom it has been my fortune to have ever met intimately". He would forgive and forget his enemies and advise his friends to do the same. "Bhai Sirajuddin", he writes to a friend. "God has created us in this world to wish well to all and sundry. What have we got to do with the vices of those who commit wrongs? We should keep our heart, our tongue-everything clean. We should be sorry for the wicked and for those who do not wish well to us. But doing any thing more, is to place oneself in the category of those who commit wrongs. We should be patient and enduring towards those who speak ill of us".

Factors Contributing to His Political Ideas

Prof. N.A. Nizami has pointed out the following factors, contributed to the formulation of his political ideas :

(1) The failure of Sayyid Ahmad Shahid's movement (1831) to regain political power made it abundantly clear to him that without knowledge of modern scientific developments, which had revolutionized every sphere of human life and thought, no attempt at political regeneration could fructify.

(2) The miserable plight of the Indian people after 1857 convinced him that unless the people moved with the times and adopted Western science and learning, they could not get rid of their backwardness, ignorance and inertia.

(3) Since the Indians did not possess the requisite resources, organization, discipline and above all the determination to wrest power through force, he was convinced of the utter futility of the use of force for regaining political power and prestige.

In a speech, he said : "The people of Ireland are carrying on. I their struggle for Independence. Where are the men who can launch such a struggle in India?"

(4) Sayyid Ahmad thought that education was more urgently required than political freedom. Without education, political freedom, even if obtained,' could not be retained; but education could be instrumental in winning back the lost political power and prestige.

On Indian Revolt In the causes of the Indian Revolt, Sayyid Ahmad gives a careful and thought — provoking exposition of the principles of revolutions. Universal rebellion might arise, he remarks, from the universal grounds, from discontent of, from streams deriving from many different sources but finally merging in one wide-spreading turbulent water. Elaborating his point further, he said that a very important cause of the conflagration of 1857 was the non-representation of Indians in the Governor-General's Legislative Council. He insisted that it was in the interest of the Government that people should have a voice in its councils.

On Education Sayyid Ahmad found in education the panacea to all ills-social, political and economic — of the contemporary Indian , society.

Addressing a public meeting at Amritsar, on January 29, 1884, he said : "If the Government has not given some of our rights to us as yet for which we may have a grudge, higher education is a thing, which, willy-nilly, would oblige them to give (those rights) us".

On August 1, 1867, Sayyid Ahmad sent a memorandum to the Viceroy in which he particularly asked for the following :

(a) Arrangements for higher learning in different arts and sciences through Indian languages;

(b) Examination in Indian languages;

(c) No discrimination ingranting degrees to those who pass their examinations in English and

(d) The establishment of a faculty of Urdu at the Calcutta University or a separate university for imparting instruction in Indian languages in the North-Western Provinces.

He said that instead of increasing the number of schools, it was necessary to improve the standard of instruction. Quality, he observed, was more important than quantity.

It would be more beneficial to the country if Government should leave the entire management of education to the people, and desist from interference, he remarked.

Sayyid Ahmad refuted the idea that Muslim women of respectable families were ignorant. "A sort of indigenous education of a moderate degree, prevails among them and they study religious and moral books in Urdu and Persian, and in some instances in Arabic," he said.

The state of female education was satisfactory. "Any endeavours on the part of the Government", he remarked, "to introduce female education among Muhammedans will, under the present social circumstances, prove a complete failure".

On the question of the medium of instruction, he said that in the vernacular and primary schools, it was better to provide instruction in the vernacular languages, but in English schools it was essential to use English as the medium of instruction.

On Social Reforms According to K.A. Nizami, Sayyid Ahmad's task in the sphere of social reforms was two-fold; first he had to persuade people to give up habits and practices which stood in the way of social advancement, and secondly, he had to persuade them to accept the new scientific approach in all matters. He advised the Muslims:

1. to develop freedom of thought and get out of the rut of custom and tradition. "So long as freedom of thought is not developed, there can be no civilized life," he declared;
2. to get rid of those religious beliefs which had no real religious sanction behind them, but stood as an obstacle to the growth of culture;
3. to get rid of all religious and other superstitions;
4. to educate children, for no real progress was possible with out literacy on a wide scale;
5. to educate women and to teach them handicrafts etc.;
6. to make collective efforts for providing educational facilities and
7. to develop various arts and industries.

He emphasised self-help, "He was the first Indian", writes the author of the Sayyid's life in the Natesan series, "who taught the principle of self-help. When his prophetic vision recognized the needs of his people, he did not resign himself to Fate or appeal helplessly to Government for aid. He knew that the reforms he aimed at, if they were to be accomplished at all, must be accomplished by the people themselves".

Sayyid Ahmad was critical of social vices such as selfishness, lack of self-respect, habits of wasting time and indulging in loose talk and the waste of money on ceremonies as the causes of social backwardness and decay.

He condemned polygamy outright and said that it brought disgrace and slur on Muslims.

On Indian Muslims 'In us Mussalmans, a very serious defect has developed,' he writes, 'and it is this that sometimes by a mistaken sense of goodness, we consider fanaticism as something good and whoever displays great fanaticism in religion and looks down upon followers of other religions and decries their arts and sciences is considered a praiseworthy person who is firm and orthodox in following his religion. But thinking in this way is a great mistake. In fact, such an attitude has ruined the Mussalmans'.

On Religion To Sayyid, religion was neither static nor an irrational attitude of mind. To him religion was a dynamic force, which could serve the needs of the people. According to K.A. Nizami, Sayyid Ahmad's religious thought and activity was conditioned by two factors: the activities of the Christian missionaries in India and the naturalistic trends of thought in the West. He appeared as a Muslim scholastic to meet the first and as a Muslim Rationalist to meet the second situation. He reacted sharply to the activities of the Christians. In 'Causes of the Indian Revolt', he indignantly refers to the activities of Christian missionaries in India. His remarks deserve to be quoted in full :

> 'There is not the smallest doubt that all men, whether ignorant or well-informed, whether high or low, felt a firm conviction that the English Government was bent on interfering with their religion, and with their old-established customs. They believed that the Government intended to force the Christian religion and foreign customs upon Hindus and Mussalmans alike. This was the chief among the secondary causes of the rebellion. It was believed by everyone that the Government was slowly but surely developing its plans. Every step, it was thought, was being taken with the most extreme caution. Hence, it is that men said that the Government does not speak of proselytising Mohammedans summarily and by force; but it will throw off the veil as it feels itself stronger and will act with greater decision. Events increased and strengthened this conviction. Men never thought that our Government would openly compel them to

> change their religion. The idea was, that indirect steps would be taken. It was supposed that Government would, by making the people devoid of a knowledge of their own faith, work on the cupidity and poverty of its subjects, and, on condition of their abjuring their faith, offer them employment in its own service'.

Sayyid Ahmad believed in *ijtihad* (re-interpretation of religious concepts according to the needs of the time). In a letter, he wrote to Nawab Mohsin-ul-Mulk : "Listen, dear brother, this is not the time that I should conceal my conscience from you. I tell you frankly that if people will not give up blind adherence and will not search out that particular light which can be had from the Quran and the reliable traditions of the prophet and will not compare (reconcile) religion with modern sciences, the religion of Islam would disappear from India. This anxiety for the well-being of Islam has forced me to carry on all these researches and I do not care for the traditional rut. Otherwise you know well that in my view, to remain a Muslim and to be entitled for Paradise, it is enough to follow Maulvi Habbu, not to speak of the great jurists of Islam".

On Hindu-Muslim Unity Sayyid Ahmad was in favour of Hindu-Muslim Unity. In a speech delivered at Patna on January 27, 1883, he said that just as the high-caste Hindus came and settled down in this land once, forgot where their earlier home was and considered India to be their own country, the Muslims also did exactly the same thing — they also left their climes hundreds of years ago and they also regarded this land of India as their very own. Both my Hindu brethem and my Muslim co-religionists breathe the same air, drink the water of the sacred Ganga and the Jamuna, eat the products of the earth which God has given to this country, live and die together. Both of us have shed off our former dress and habits, and while Muslims have adopted numerous customs belonging to the Hindus, the Hindus have been vastly influenced by Muslim manners and customs. I say with conviction that if we were to disregard for a moment our conception of God head, then in all matters of everyday like Hindus and Muslims really belong to one nation (Qaum)... and the progress of the country is possible only if we have a union of hearts, mutual sympathy and love.... I have always said that our land of India is like a newly — wedded bridge whose two beautiful and luscious eyes are the Hindus and Musalmans; if the two exist in mutual concord the bride will remain for ever resplendent and becoming, while if they make up their mind to see in different directions, the bride is bound to become squinted and even partially blind.

In a speech delivered at Gurdaspur on January 27, 1884, he said that we (Hindus and Muslims) should try to become one heart and soul and act in unison; if united, we can support each other. If not, the effect of one against the other would tend to the destruction and downfall of both.

Distrust in National Congress To start with, Sayyid Ahmad Khan did not express any views about the Indian National Congress, but later on he entered the field as one of its critics.

He said: "Gentlemen, I am not given to speaking on politics, and I do not recollect having ever previously given a political lecture. My attention has always been directed towards the education of my brethren Mohammedans; for from education I anticipate benefit for my people, for Hindustan, and for the Government. But at the present time, circumstances have arisen which make it necessary for me, I think, to tell my brethren Mussalmans clearly what my opinions are."

Estimate Hali once said : "My heart used to fly even from the bewitching young beauties, but this old man capture it in a single glance." Indians apart, even Europeans felt the magnetic pull of his personality.

Addressing a condolence meeting on his death, Theodore Beck remarked : "His talents were very great, but his character was greater still. I have never in England or India been brought into contact with a man who roused in me such feelings of respect and admiration".

The Indian Association of Lahore paid tribute to him in the following words :

> "Not the least remarkable feature of your public career has been the breadth of your views and your liberal attitude towards sections of the community other than your co-religionists. Your conduct throughout has been stainless of bias or bigotry. The benefits of the noble educational institution you have established at Aligarh are open alike to Hindus as well as Mohammedans. Our unhappy country is so split up with petty religious and sectarian jealousies and had suffered so much in the past from sectarian and religious dissensions, that the advent of a man of your large-hearted and liberal views is a matter of your peculiar congratulation at this time. Long may you be spread to inculcate knowledge among Mohammedans and Hindus alike, and by eradicating prejudice and bigotry from their minds, to unite them in the firm bonds of fraternal union".

According to K.A. Nizani, he was the first Muslim in modern india to catch a glimpse of the dynamic character of the coming age and he dedicated his whole life to what he thought to be the supreme need of the hour — the uplift of Indians by apprising them of the problems of the modern world. He ignored all hurdles in his way and strove, patiently and incessantly; to bring about a reorientation in the outlook and behaviour of the Indians, particularly the Muslims, who were more backward in education and learning than any other Indian community. He thus became a social and a moral force which accelerated the processes of transition from the medieval to the modern age.

He concentrated more on education and decided to remain out of politics. "So, to this education", remarks Pandit Jawaharlal Nehru, "he turned all his energy trying to win over his community to his way of thinking. He wanted diversions or distractions from others directions; it was a difficult enough piece of work to overcome the inertia and hesitation of the Muslims. The beginnings of a new nationalism, sponsored by the Hindu bourgeoise, seemed to him to offer such a distraction, and he opposed in this Hindus, half a centure ahead in Western education, could indulge in this pastime of criticising the Government, but he had counted on the full co-operation of that Government in his educational undertakings and he was not going to risk this by any premature step. Sir Syed's decision to concentrate on Western that they could not have played any effective part in the building up of Indian nationalism of the new type, and they would have been doomed to play second fiddle to the Hindus with their better education and far stronger economic position. The Muslims were not historically or ideologically ready then for the bourgeois nationalist movement as they had developed no bourgeoisie, as the Hindus had done. Sir Syed's activities, therefore, although seemingly very moderate, were in the right revolutionary direction."

To conclude, we may say that his decision to keep aloof from politics was correct at that time and not for all times. "Sir Syed's message," rightly remarks Pandit Nehru, "was appropriate and necessary when it came, but it could not be the final ideal of a progressive community. It is possible that had he lived a generation later, he would have himself given another orientation to that message."

22

Mohammad Iqbal (1873-1938)

Sir Mohammad Iqbal, a poet-philosopher has exercised great influence on modern Indian political thought. Iqbal was greatly influenced by poets like Rumi and Ghalib. He never thought of a return to the past and looked to the future. He interpreted the idealist teachings of the past in terms of the needs of the first decades of the twentieth century. In his view the development of human personality is the main aim of life of an individual. He treated both individual and society as a harmonious whole.

His Life Mohammad Iqbal was born on 22 February 1873 at Sialkot in the Punjab. He graduated from Government College, Lahore where he became a lecturer in Philosophy a few years later. In 1905, he went to England. There he qualified for Bar and also for advanced philosophy. In 1908, he was called to the Bar and started practice as an advocate at Lahore. Before returning to India he was awarded Ph.D. degree from the Munich University for his thesis on Persian Mysticism.

The Government College, Lahore offered him a Professorship in Philosophy, but he refused to accept the offer and continued to take interest in law and literature. From his college days, Iqbal took keen interest in poetry and often took part in symposiums. In fact, he was a born poet. He wrote and published *Bang-i-Dira* (The sound of the Caravan Bell) in 1924. This publication gave Iqbal a permanent fame as a poet of very high standard. He had also written Persian poetry. He died on March 8, 1938.

His works Iqbal was a great poet and philosopher. His works were appreciated not in India but throughout the world. His important works are as under :

1. *Bang-i-Dira* (The Sound of Caravan Bell),
2. *Assar-i-Khudi* (Secrets of self),
3. *Ramaz-i-Bekhudi* (Mysteries of self denial),

4. *Payam-i-Mashriqi* (Message of the East),
5. *Tabur-i-Azam* (The Psalms of Persia),
6. *Jawid Nama* (named after his son) and
7. *Bal-i-Jibril* (Wings of Gabriel).

His Political Ideas Sir Mohammad Iqbal was the radiant star of Urdu literature. He wrote numerous patriotic poems exhorting the people to fight against the foreign rule and appealing to all forms of mystical passivity, quiet resignation, withdrawal from mundane activities and a negative attitude toward life. The mystical poets, he said, "have destroyed the capacity for action. Capacity for action depended on the conviction that selfhood of personality was real and not an illusion. He glorified action as life and condemned inaction death.

His Views on Capitalism and Socialism Iqbal was critical of capitalism and socialism.

Iqbal felt that God made the earth for his creatures and any monopolistic claim to it by a capitalist or landlord is unjust. As such he denounced capitalism altogether.

Iqbal never became a socialist. He looked at all the problem from the stand-point of Koran. He criticized the doctrines of Karl Marx. He also decried the evils of capitalism. In one of his poems, he said : "Man is still a miserable prey to exploitation and imperialism; is it not a grievous calamity that man should prey on man?"

The glitter of the modern civilization dazzles the eyesight; but this is merely an artistry of fall beads?...

His Views on Freedom He passionately exhorted the youth to fight for the freedom of their country. In a poem, he writes :

'The freeman's veins are firm as veins of granite;

The bondman's weak as tendrils of the vine'

Again, in another poem he writes;

"If thou would'st drink clear wine from thine own grapes needs wield authority over thine own earth!"

He was against imperialism and narrow nationalism. He said that both imperialism and narrow nationalism rob us of paradise, destroy the feelings of brotherhood and sow the seeds of war.

His Views on Theocracy Dr. Iqbal who in the initial stages stirred his countrymen by his patriotic songs, turned a Muslim patriot. He praised that government which was based on religion. He found the remedy of all problems in religion, he meant Islam. He says, "Asia cannot comprehend modern western capitalism with its undisciplined individualism. The faith which you represent (*i.e.*, Islam) recognises the worth of the individual, and disciplines him to give away his all to the service of God and man. Its possibilities are not yet exhausted. It can still oreate a new world where the social rank of man is not determined by his caste or colour, or the amount of dividend he earns, but by the kind of life he lives; where the poor tax the rich, where human society is founded not on the equality of stomachs but on the equality of spirits, where an untouchable can marry the daughter of a kind, where private ownership is a trust and where capital cannot be allowed to accumulate so as to dominate the real producer of wealth. This superb idealism of your faith, however, needs emancipation from the medieval fancies of theologians legists".

His Views on International Organization Iqbal said that all Muslims in the world are brethren. As such he did not support international organizations which indirectly encouraged the idea he gave an idea of Pan-Islamism which was international in outlook. This is based on the idea that Islam was an international organization spread all over the world. He said, "China, Arabia and India are ours. Moslems, and the whole world is ours". He said that Islam is the real league of nations. He said that when he realized that the conception of nationalism based on the differences of race and country, was beginning to overshade the world of Islam also and that the Muslims were in danger of giving up the university of their ideal in favour of a narrow patriotism and false nationalism, he felt his duty as a Muslim and as a well wisher of humanity to recall them back to their true role in the drama of human evolution. Iqbal writes, "No doubt, I am intensely devoted to Islam but I have selected the Islamic community as my starting point not because of any national or religious prejudice but because it is the most practicable line of approach to the problem".

Iqbal, gave the slogan, 'Back to Islam'.

His Ideology of Pakistan Iqbal was in favour of a consolidated Muslims State. He supported the demand for 'Muslim India within India'. He said, "I would like to see the Punjab, the North-West Frontier Province, Sind and Baluchistan amalgamated into a single state. Self government within the British Empire, the formation of a consolidated North-West Indian Muslim State appeared to me to be the final destiny of the Muslims, at least of North India". In 1937, Iqbal suggested that in order that Muslims in modern India could solve their problems it would be necessary to redistribute the country and to provide one or more Muslim states with absolute majorities. As such Iqbal was a great protagonist of the Pakistan separation.

To conclude we may say that Iqbal is recognized as a great poet in West Asia. His poems brought him great recognition. But as a political thinker, he was not original. He is regarded as the spiritual father of the Pakistani ideology. We agree with Prof. Damodaran: "However, Iqbal's contribution to Indian thought and literature and the progressive role he played in rousing the patriotic consciousness of the people in general and of the Muslims in particular, cannot be overlooked in any objective study of his life and works".

23

Rabindranath Tagore (1861-1941)

Rabindranath Tagore, "the great Sentinal" as Gandhiji called him, in the early twenties, made a deep impression on the contemporary society. He travelled all over the country; travelled beyond the country to the East and to the West as the cultural ambassador of our heritage. He explained, the essence of it, to all. He talked of humanism, universalism and of the oneness of man. He was, as Count Keysirling said : "the most universal, the most encompassing, the most complete human being", this embodiment of peace, goodwill and progress made notable contribution to the contemporary politics without being a politician : to the political thought without being an academician and to the international understanding without holding any official position. His contribution remains of the universal order.

1. Various Influeness on Tagore

Gurudev was born great. Nature had invested him with good physic, excellent mind and positive attitude to life. He was no pedestrian, sectarian or the type of cynic, sometime called "intellectual". In his making ages appear to have contributed their best. He was a man with a mission. He worked to achieve the high objectives, he set before himself. His spiritual experiences were enlightening and elevating. For this extraordinary complexity of the Tagore phenomena, it is difficult to analyse, what constituted him. A surface analysis, and nothing more than that can be attempted, reveals the strong hereditary influence, the deep impact of the contemporary conditions and the abiding influence of the national heritage on him. He was this all, plus the Divine Gifts he had.

Rabindranath came from great parentage with a high family tradition. His father, Devendranath (1817-1905), for his piety, religiousness and learning was known as the Maharishi. He was a towering personality in his own right. His contribution to the intellectual growth and to the spiritual modelling of his son, Rabindranath was significant. His grandfather, Dawarkanath, the merchant prince, philanthrophist and public man of the classical order, had left behind high tradition of public service to inspire anyone; and great fortune to ensure the economic security of his children and grand children. The house of Tagore for all this was recognized as the Centre of religious, philosophical, literary and of artistic activity. Here, the ancient heritage coupled with modernity and liberalism flowed freely. The environment was highly conducive to all creative intellectual activity. In these abundantly available facilities, Rabindranath nursed, the gifts the nature had endowed him with, to their perfection.

Tagore, sprang up when the old order was wearing out and the new was emerging forth. Bengal was bubbling with fresh energy and the people were looking for new ideas and better life. The religious movement initiated by Ram Mohan Roy, had greatly energized the people. It received a forceful stimulus at the hands of Debendranath, the Maharishi. He gave it a new direction, when the movement was whimpering out. The religious renaissance greatly influenced Rabindranath. He was highly impressed by Ram Mohan Roy, and no less by the work of his father the Maharishi. Politics, as yet was in its springing state. Surendranath Banerjee. The moving spirit behind it, initiated the youth in it. He advised them to imbibe the spirit of sacrifice for and service to the country from the Italian leaders like Mazzini. The literary movement, which was now guided by Bankim Chandra Chatterji provided the moral fibre to the men involved in public activity. The three currents religious, political and literary found their Sangam in Rabindranath. He came up as the perfect embodiment of the three.

Rabindranath drank deep at the ever bubbling spring of the ancient heritage of spirituality as embodies in the Upanishads. From his childhood, he had listened to their renderings and recitations as it was the daily routine in the Tagore house. From, these he got his lesson in humanism and universalism. The Buddha, the embodiment of peace, truth and kindness was to him the "Soul of Infinite Sanctity" which "cleans the earth of her stains". In his teachings, Tagore saw, the best fulfilment of Hinduism. The Vaishnav philosophy as presented by Jayadev, Vidayapati and Chandidas had marked impact on him. The words of Chandidas : "listen, Oh brotherman, the truth of man is the highest truth, there is no other truth above", Or, the words of Kabir, "God is within your heart where you will find him easily. Otherwise you will tire yourself out by treading the path of the scripture, holy places, rituals and logic", had much influenced him. This all had become, very much, part of his existence. The simple and spontaneous Baul songs of Bengal too are said to have influenced his thinking. The heritages of the ages, had thus left full impact on him. He detested formal religion, sectarianism and the castism.

2. Early Life

Rabindranath was born on May 7, 1861, in his ancestral house, Jorasanko, on the bank of the holy Ganga, in Calcutta. One of his ancestors Panchanan Kushari, in the closing decades of seventeenth century, had moved from Khulna, now in Bangladesh, where they originally lived, and settled in Govindpur, then a fishing village, on the back of Ganga. Here, he took up, the work of supplying the provisions to the foreign ships which sailed up the river for commerce. The locals, infiding a Brahman amongst themselves, addressed him as 'Thakur', 'the holy lord' after the prevailing practice. Its mispronunciation as 'Tagore', by the Europeans in whose close contact, he came due to the nature of his work, gave to the family a new name.

The acquisition, by the British of the sites of Govindpur, Sutanti and Kalikata on lease from the local authority and the subsequent rise of the modern city of Calcutta, brought fortune to Tagores, Soon after, in the life time of Dawarkanath (1794-1846), it touched the meridian. He rose to be a merchant prince. He was generous : philanthropic and made rich contribution to the public institutions. He played significant role in the establishment of the Hindu College at Calcutta, which later grew into the Presidency College. He was first Indian member and patron of the Asiatic Society of Bengal. He went to England twice, and died in London.

Eldest of his three sons was Dabindranath (1817-1905), born to and brought up in luxury, he rose to be a religious man. At the age of eighteen, he had a spiritual experience when he felt his mind "awakened to joy unfelt before". It induced him to search for more such joy. While, attuned to it, he once stumbled on a leaf of a Sanskrit text, on which was found printed the first Verse of the Isopanished, meaning : "All this, whatever moves in this moving world, is enveloped by God. Therefore, find your enjoyment in renunciation; do not covet what belongs to others". This he felt, satisfied his desire. Feeling enriched, his "faith took deep roots". He got, seized, soon after, by a strong desire to preach the true religion. Being, already impressed, by the Brahma Sabha, of Ram Mohan Roy (1772-1833) he devoted himself to it. He gave it a new breath. This brought into existence the Brahma Samaj. He devoted his energy to the preaching of its tenets, other religious works and to the study of the Upanishads. He lived, his life, the saintly way. He often retired to the Himalayas for mediations. For his honesty and truthfulness and for his purity of thought and belief, he was respectfully known as the Maharishi.

Devindranath and his wife Sarda Devi had several children Rabi, as Rabindranath was known in his childhood, was their fourteenth. The large family she was already looking after, left her hardly time and energy to attend to the new born. He was, therefore, left to the care of his elder sister Saudamin. This denial of the motherly affection to him, left a deep mark on the springing boy. The poems of childhood, he wrote later, reveal his thoughts on this deprivation.

The Jorasanko house had the characteristics of its own. Here lived young and old, learned and not so learned in gaiety and discipline. One could find anything to draw upon : the ancient classics and the modern ideas : literature, poetry and music. In this environment, on the insistence of his older cousin, Rabi was made to write his first verse. He was at this time in his eighth year. From now onwards, both the poet and his muse grew along.

Rabi, in his eleventh year had the first opportunity to accompany his father, on his usual sojourn to the Himalayas. Their destination was Bakrota, in Dalhousie. On their way from Calcutta, they made their first halt at Shantiniketan. This site, for its enchanting beauty had been purchased earlier by the Maharishi and had been so named. Reaching Dalhousie, the father and the son found themselves at ease in the very lap of nature. Here, the father, attended to the education of his son; gave him lessons in Sanskrit, Astronomy and English. Rabi, besides listened to the recitation of the Upanishads and to the Valmiki Ramayan from his father. This association with his father, and schooling at his hands had the modelling effect on the young child.

The following year, the father performed the *Upanayana* ceromony of Rabi. At this time, the great *Gayatri mantra, Tat Savitar Varenyam bhargo devasya dhimahi, dhiyo yonah prachodayat* (May we attain that excellent glory of Savitur the God that he may stimulate our thoughts), was given to the boy. It made deep impression on him, learning remained his occupation. It stimulated his thoughts and he lived, the learned way.

Rabi showed unhappiness with his formal schooling. The school routine was to him dwarfing and its walls engaging. He was feeling, increasingly uneasy with it. Finally, in 1875, in his fifteenth year, he bade good bye to it.

The poet in Rabi had began to peep out. And, this year too he recited a patriotic poem at the Annual Hindu Mela. The poem was successively published under his name in the *Amrit Bazar Patrika* which was then an *Anglo-Bengali* weekly. It whispered confidence in him.

But monotony was creeping over him. His uneasiness made him feel to be "useless, helpless and bereft of his wisdom". This, however, was not all. His other side never lost its brilliance. His ambition guided him and his perseverence sustained him. He was determined to leave his "unfading signature on the scroll of time". While this mental struggle kept the son engaged, the father was thinking to provide him with a career. One of his sons, Satyendranath one of the first Indian members of the Civil Service, who was then a district judge in Ahmedabad, suggested to his father that he would take Rabi, who was younger to him, alongwith him to London to be an I.C.S. or a Barrister. The father agreed to the proposal. Soon after, on September 20, 1878, he alongwith his younger brother, sailed to England. Rabi stayed there for a while; did not pick up a carêer, and had to come back on the summers of his father.

Back in the country, Rabi joined his another elder brother, Jyotirindranath and his family, at Chandernagar. They, later on, came to reside at the Sudder street residence, in Calcutta. Early one morning, here, as he was standing on the varanda of the house watching the rising sun, "All of a sudden a covering seemed to fall away from my eyes, and I found the world watched in a wonderful radiance, with waves of beauty and joy selling on every side". At the end of it he felt, relieved of his gloom. This spiritual experience invested him with a capacity to see all things and all men in their "ultimate significance". He felt new love for living and faith in life. Such was his first spiritual experience.

At the age of twenty-five, Rabindranath was married. But, he was yet without a formal career. It must have been cause of much worry to his father. Therefore, he was made to look after the family estates in Bengal and Orissa. The youngman accepted the position. This situation opened new vistas of experience to him. He came in close contact with the meek and helpless peasantry. They had been over the time denied everything, and deprived of everything. He saw them in bone and skin; laid low in material adversity, hedged in superstition, bound by encumbrances and living in an annihilated social consciousness. This painful sight and this odd experience did enkindle in him the rich humanism. He, successively adopted measures to help them out of this distress.

(3) The Shantiniketan

The span of time, that comes to the share of each one of us, called life, has its stages; and each stage has its pleasures and pains; satisfactions and anxieties. Exception to this law are almost forbidden. The great Buddha experienced it, and spoke of it; and all others high and low have had the experience of it. Our Tagores, had grown into a family; they had five children; three daughters and two sons. Rabindranath was keen to provide them good education. He had the fears : he remembered well his bad experience at his school. This problem, he felt could well be resolved by the ancient method of putting the children under the watching eyes and the guiding hands of Guru. This child of Vedas and Upanishads, therefore, established an *ashram* on December 22, 1901, in the midst of the Silvan freshness of Shantiniketan, and named it the Brahmacharya Asharam. Here, his children, were the first pupils. The aim of education here was that "the young mind should be saturated with the idea that it has been born in a human world which is in harmony with the world around it". The institution steadily grew into eminence.

The Gitanjali

The *Gitanjali,* the offering a songs, reveals Rabindranath's reaction of life's challenge and to its blooming beauty. These poems unfold his intellectual flowering and the spiritual fullness. His communion with beauty and truth is seen here at its best.

It was composed in Bengali and was published in 1910. Nobody at that time seemed to have taken notice of its inherent worth. The country then was, dead enough to awaken to the reality in it; and the alien government too disinterested to recognise the exceptional. Long ago, once, after listening to a poem of his son, Debendranath had rightly felt the disadvantage, of the absence of state patronage and the lack of appropriate response from other quarters to the talented. The position had remained unchanged since.

Subsequently, Rabindranath translated the *Gitanjali* into the English. This script, he carried alongwith, when in 1912, he went to London. Here, he called upon Sir William Rothenstein, a painter of renown, whom he knew since 1910. When he was here he had visited the artist brothers Abanindranath and Gaganendranath during his stay in Calcutta. Later, he had come across the English translation of one of his short stories. He had thus good impression of Rabindranath. Sir William, now went through the translation of the Gitanjali. It attracted him most. Quickly, he sent the script, to W.B. Yeats, the contemporary English poet, who felt it to be the work of "Supreme Culture". It soon got pushed through the circle of the select. And, this was instrumental in securing to; Rabindranath, the Nobel Prize.

The Visva Bharti

Rabindranath, the pilgrim on the endless road of life, turned, literally a globe trotter. Beginning with his father, the successful sojourn to the Himalayas, his travels never came to an end.

His short stay (September 1878 to February 1880) in England, where he had gone with the intent to pick up a career, he described "two day" sojourn, as his first contact, with the civilization beyond the sea.

His second voyage to England in 1912, as indicated above, was a great success. It gave him a deeper peep into the British character.

He voyaged to U.S.A. and delivered there a series of lectures on the ideals of Ancient' India, which were published subsequently as the Sadhana.

He also visited the countries of the European continent.

In Japan, he impressed upon his listeners not to accept the Western ideas wholesale.

'Europe is supremely good in her beneficence where her face is turned to all humanity : and Europe is supremely evil in her maleficent aspect where her face is turned upon her own interest, using all her power of greatness for ends which are against the infinite and the eternal in Man'. He was resentful of the racist policy that was then followed in Canada, and declined their invitation at first; later when he went there his words, made deep impression on the knowing people.

He lectured in China and Iran as well. By his words and personal contact, Rabindranath demonstrated in himself, the full import of the ancient saying : *Yatra visvam bhavati eka nidam* "Where the whole world meets in one nest", which had, over the time, seized his mind.

Having shown that the spirit of the East was alive, he wished the West to draw the advantage out of it; he wanted the East, as well to draw upon the experience of the West. To give full meaning to his concept of universal humanism and to make its realization possible, he established the Visva Bharti, as the meeting place of the western and the eastern minds.

But this effort to bring the East and the West closer, and to build on the foundation of peace, progress and oneness of man, received a grievous jolt when the Balkan. War (1912-13) and the Great War (1914-18) that followed it, broke out in Europe. It made him unhappy. This coupled with his physical agony, due to his aliment caused steady deterioration of his health. At the ripe age of eighty, this August man felt his life receding. He ceased to be on August 7, 1914, six years before the sun of freedom dawned over the country.

(4) Tagore and Contemporary Politics

Rabindranath belonged to the era of compelling politics. No thinking individual then could keep himself away from it. Our poet was no exception. The Sedition Bill of 1898 and the arrest of Bal Gangadhar Tilak, who was then a force in his own right, brought forth a strong protest from him. The repressive measures of the government stirred him to action. He supported the 'Defence of Tilak Fund' Collection drive. The partition of Bengal (1905) brought him out to lead the street procession; and composed patriotic songs. He gave full support to the idea of National Education, which had then seized the mind of the leadership. He supported the Swadeshi movement as well. Presiding over the Bengal Provincial Conference at Patna in 1908, he pleaded strongly for social service and the Hindu-Muslim Unity.

On hearing about the Jalianwala massacre (April 13, 1919) he came to Calcutta to organise the protest meeting but found the people too terror-striken, to assemble. It disgusted him. He, therefore communicated his resentment to the viceroy, Lord Chelmsford; and along with it conveyed to him, his decision to renounce his knighthood. He wrote : 'I for my part wish to stand, shorn of all special distinctions, by the side of those of my countrymen who for their so called in significance are liable to suffer a degradation not fit for human beings'.

This was a passing phase in the life and career of Tagore. He was soon dominated by the poet and the universal man in him. Politics, he felt successively to be, too petty. "My mind refused to respond to the cheap intoxication of the political movements of those days, devoid as they seemed of all strength of national consciousness, with their complete ignorance of the country, their supreme indifference to real service of the motherland. I was tormented by a furious impatience, an intolerable dissatisfaction with myself and all around me". He could not identify with the non-co-operation movement (1921), though "for injustice and insult heaped upon my motherland", he was feeling anger in his heart.

The Communal Award (1932) which aimed to separate the depressed classes from the Hindus caused him immense distress, and, when in protest Gandhiji resorted to fast unto death, Tagore extended full moral support to him. He appreciated the true import of the fast. He felt convinced of Gandhiji's action and observed : "It is worth, sacrificing precious life for the sake of India's unity and social integrity."

(5) His Belief

Rabindranath believed in life as it unfolds itself. "Life is original, it is adventurous : it seeks itself in endless experiments : it is the outcome of its spontaneous creative impulse. The people who passively lend themselves to imitation prove that life has lost its best claim on their hearts. That is why, when we try to imitate some other people's history, we remain so pathetically unaware of the absurdities that are produced". He believed in growth, progress and self-realization leading to the humanism. For the realization of the self he felt, one has to relieve oneself of the limitations of matter and mind. One has to rise above the ordinary and then alone one may have the taste of "the infinite at every point". It is not to be discovered but to be realized "through expansion of sympathy". One has not to alienate oneself from the world or to dominate it. The realization comes by "comprehending and uniting it with ourselves in perfect union."

Faith in life and in its concomitant Karma reveals the strength in man. To lose faith in ones-self is a poor demonstration of mental feebleness. This is held to be contrary to our heritage "Our ancestors", he emphasised, "progressed through mistakes, made discoveries through experiments and gained truth from striving."

He recognized the conflict in society of castes, sects, and of civilization; and of haves and have-nots; but, he held that the role of civilization is to resolve these conflicts. Taking recourse to the Indian way of assimilating the new ideas, he felt that the synthesis of ancient belief and of new experience is the right approach to resolve the conflict. To him "the history of man is the history of the building up of a human universe, as has been proved by the fact that everything great in human activity inevitably belongs to all humanity". He saw harmony in oneness and the Supreme in the collectivity. He expected, individual, to make the offering of service. "Rise, O poet, and give voice to these dumb, haggard and stupefied faces, bring hope to these tired, emptied and broken hearts. Teach them to raise high their heads and stand united."

(6) His Thought

Tagore is a many dimensional thinker. He has expressed himself on matters political, economic, social and religious, in his voluminous writings consisting of poetry, plays, novels and essays. He expressed himself from time to time on the vital issues confronting the society and that too sometimes "much ahead of others". He visualised a new age and a new social order being essentially a poet, his poetic sensitiveness kept him away from the practical business of life. His ever soaring spirit earned him often, away from matters material as his humanism and universalism made him look beyond the national concerns. This gave a peculiar character to his ideas.

Political Ideas

Meaning of Freedom

Tagore did not believe in mere political freedom. The shakles of slavery with which the country had been laid low did not interest him ordinarily. He wanted the larger freedom, the freedom of soul. He wanted men to imbibe the spirit of Independence. "If political freedom be achieved by us, well and good. But even if that does not happen, let us not, with heap of tainted political rubbish, obstruct our own way to larger freedom of the Soul."

He was largely influenced by the ancient Indian political thought. This made him the great exponent of the individual freedom. The ancients had given greater importance to society than to the State; to individual than to the Society. They were totally resentful of a system that could be the cause of injustice and of social suppression of individuals. The Varnadharma recognized the position of individual, made the society interdependent, and the State dependent on it. To Kautilya, "the happiness of the subjects is the happiness of the King; their well being his. The King's welfare lies not in his own pleasure but in that of the subjects."

State is the result of expediency. Its origin is explained in terms of Matsyanyaya or the conflict between the Asuras and Devas. The legendary king Manu symbolises state. He is given a definite role. It is intended to protect mamalva (the property), impose danda (the punishment) and to sustain the Dharma (the balancing righteousness). The postulation that obedience is due not to the organized force, the state; but to the moral instinct alone, is not necessarily in agreement with the heritage, he draws upon. It is different, however, that he wanted, men to depend least on the state. Dr. Edward Thomson points out that he had deep distrust of all Government machinery. He did not like, the people to be dependent on the State. "Let ryots be strong, so that even the temptation to oppress them may not exist". He wanted men to be free from fear and bondage. He wished them to be free to shape their destiny. Hence, he emphasised on national heritage, scientific outlook, social service and the nation building activity.

The Concept of Democracy

Democracy implies the participation of the people in exercising the sovereignty of the body politics. It assumes the political equality of all in the Society. Political equality is, however, only one of the several aspects of civic life. It is dependent on several other aspects such as economic and cultural which according to Tagore are essential for the successful working to the democratic system. Democracy, can never be true in a Society. "Where greed grows, uncontrolled, encouraged even admired by the populace". He wished people to abide by Dharmas, to be self reliant and resourceful. He felt that it was time to "renew the life" of the people, and they "learn to look after their own affairs". True freedom is possible, if there exists "a perfect harmony of relationship". Democracy to be real, has to be relieved of the politics without ethics, governments from the grip of the few and leadership from the clutches of self indulgence.

This is possible according to Tagore, once the right of Service is accepted by all. Every body should render service to the community in the interest of the community. "No one can" he emphasised "take away the blessed task of service to the country — It is god given — It is all to our shame if we lose the natural right of service and throw blame on others for the non-discharge of our duties. Once that is realized, them it is clear that in the Society, there are only two classes : One which is disciplined and serves the great ends the 'upper class'; and the other consisting of the self-centered, the 'lower class'. Therefore, to make democracy real, emphasis should be on service. The habit of being self-centered need be given up. The mere satisfaction of having political rights and the manifest exercise of the same at the elections is not enough and does not serve the real purpose".

Nation, Nationalism, Patriotism and Civilization

The concepts 'nation' and 'States' Tagore held were not of Indian origin. These he considers to be of the European origin. To him state is an "organization for power". The concept of Nation state may have been of advantage to some, but others have suffered due to it. The "Nation is the greatest evil for the nation". They "trade on the feebleness of the rest of the world". It aims at success and not goodness. It is collective selfishness at the cost of morality. In its organic form, it reduces individual to a mere cog. Nationalism, he felt has hindered the growth of humanism. Both Nation and Nationalism have a very narrow scope. He considered Nation to be opposed to the social interest of man. The "ideal of the social man is unselfishness, but the ideal of the Nation, like that of the professional man, is selfishness". The belief in Nation state and Nationalism have raised barriers between the societies. "The basis of Hindu civilisation is society; the basis of European civilisation is the State. Man can attain greatness either through society or through the State. But if we ever think that to build up the Nation after European pattern is the only way open and the only aim of humanity, we shall be wrong."

Patriotism means completely identifying with one's country, its tradition and its heritage. It is the supreme attribute to nationhood. It is the first of religions. Tagore had deep love for the national heritage and for the country. He felt anger in his heart "for injustice and insult heaped upon my motherland". He wanted every one of his countrymen to be so strong as stand on his own. This he emphasised most- in his patriotic songs. His prayers was :

Make us strong that we may not
insult the weak and the fallen,
That we may hold our love high when
all things around us are —
Wooing the dust.

But he could not agree with the patriotism that caused conflict : racial bitterness, religious bigotry and political discord. For this, he did not support the non-co-operation movement. He protested against the Communal Award as it recognized the discrimination and was against the interest of the country. He loved all men irrespective of their racial labels. "In small minds, patriotism dissociates itself from the higher ideal of humanity. It becomes the magnification of self, on a stupendous scale-magnifying our vulgarity, cruelty, greed, dethroning God, to put up this bloated self in its place". Hence : "Pride of patriotism is not for me. I earnestly hope that I shall find my home anywhere in the world before I leave it. We have to fight against wrongs, and suffer for the cause of righteousness : but we should have no petty jealousies or quarrels with our neighbours merely because we have different names". He believed in doing the right thing for the country and humanity. His patriotism was not bound to the geographical limits. He identified himself with all humanity.

But, he did not underestimate the differences in civilization. To him each civilization was a "kind of mould" that each people make "to shape its men and women according to its best ideals". Taking, recourse to the history of India, he held that in the interest of social integration and progress, there should be no effort to keep up a separate existence. All should join the national main stream. "The section which is unable to unwilling to the entire scheme, but struggles to keep up a separate existence, will have to drop out and be lost, sooner or later. And tire component which realising its dedication to the ultimate ideal, acknowledges its own individual unimportance, will lose only its pettiness and find permanence for its greatness in that of the whole". He wished the West and the East to follow his Indian manner of synthesis in regard to one anothers civilization and to make the best of the both in the interest of progress.

Internationalism and Universalism

Tagore drank to his full from the Vedic and the Upanishadic heritage. It made him believe in the unity of man, good for all and in the interdependence of the universe. Our ancestors were earnest for the happiness and good for all.

"May all be happy. May all be free from disease,

May all realise what is good. May none be subject to misery."

Tagore made this belief his own. He expounded the spiritual unity of man and of universalism on this basis. The true freedom according to him is, the freedom of soul. Since, the common spirit is present in all : all men, therefore, are equal. For this he held that the barriers of race, nationalism, religion and caste should not be taken as more than the paper walls. These, whatever, their worth, otherwise, are indicative of the decline in the social values. Once this is understood, the beliefs and practices disparaging the spirit of humanity and discriminating among the nation, communities and of castes would lose their spell. Men must learn to draw, he emphasised, on their spiritual self. Men in the dark are always exploited. He wants every individual to contribute to the welfare of the society and wishes good life for all. This can be a step towards the realization of "the spiritual unity of man."

Economic Ideas

Economic needs are a reality. These are ever present. Man has never been above these. None could disregard them; and Tagore was no exception. The existing economic system he described as the exploitative; and based on exploitation of the weak for the benefit of the strong. Profit motive is its dominant attribute. It has yet to secure an ethical base. It is not wholly contributory to the total growth of individual. This system, has also left "the great multitude, the common people, who bear the burden of civilization" unprovided. This is the greatest weakness of the profit motivated civilization. When the masses remain desolate there cannot be a real civilization. This desolate state, he attributes to the diminution of the spiritual values in the society. He, therefore, held that the awakening of man by organized social action is essential. For this moral decline, Tagore, held greed to be the real cause. The contention that contention advancement is the sole aim of human pursuit, was not acceptable to him. He did not take man to be a mere "catalogue of endless wants." He is not just a "living money-bag jumping from profit to profit, and breaking the backbone of human races in its financial leap-frog". Man is much more than this. He has creative impulse; he can gain his fullness and express his truth. Therefore, "the economic life of a nation is not an isolated fact, and today side by side with economic poverty, we are faced with a cultural poverty which puts us to shame- shame that it in no was lessened when we consider what we once were."

For thé helpless and hungry, Tagore was always full of deep concern. After, he came face to face with the stark poverty of the peasants, he initiated reforms based on the principle of self-help. He introduced co-operative system in their economic life and established the Agricultural Co-operative Bank to relieve them from the clutches of the moneylenders. He invested part of the Nobel Prize money in it. It helped to relieve the distress of the peasantry.

Social Reconstruction

Decline of Indian society Rabindranath attributed to the failure of its social institutions. Their disorganization caused the social disputation. The existing social order, he took to be undervicable. Its worse aspect according to Tagore, is its dependence on the government. In the reconstructed society, he wished not the state but the society to be the centre of power. To make this possible, he wishes every individual to be strong in his own place. Emphasing the point, at a public speech, he impressed upon the students, to teach the downtrodden and the despised "to be strong and to protect themselves". He advised a student gathering: "take each of you charge of some village and organise it. Educate the villagers and show them how to put forward their united strength". He wished the ryots to be strong and the Zamindar to play their traditional role. "Let ryots be strong, so that even that temptation to oppress them may not exist. Is the Zamindar a shop-keeper that he should calculate only his petty takings? Unless he seriously cultivates his ancestral privilege of giving, he will soon find the remnants of his power lost."

His social reconstruction programme included the destruction of the social barriers. Along with it should be undertaken the construction work in the midst of the masses. The people who so contribute to the society are to him the upper class. He wants all to be service rendering so as to make leisure available for all. Civilization cannot survive if only few have the leisure. "Unless all are wealthy no man, however rich, can have real wealth". According to him, society must have spiritual ideal to follow for the "true happiness" of all. Our social system depended upon mutual obligation, upon ethical ideals accepted by all the people.

In the West political life is concentrated in a particular group of men or in some machine, and its obligations are borne by come special group. For this reason the moment that the political life is threatened, the whole life is threatened. In the East whilst the military and the ambitious men fought their battles the people as a whole remained unmolested, and therefore, their civilisation survived for centuries and is still living. He wanted, therefore, to revitalise the society irrespective of its political character and to restore physical and intellectual opportunities to those who have been deprived of it, so as to open the path of inner communication, "with other nations for the purpose of establishing perfect human relationship which is the real goal of civilization."

On Education

Tagore was a rebel and a saint rolled into one. He was resentful of the school system : as a student he found his spirit encaged in it, and gave it up at the first available opportunity. But his response to learnings was remarkable. The Gayatri and the Savitur stimulated his thought. He attained, "that excellent glory" for which he had prayed as a child long ago. Having realized the glory of Vidya, in himself, he wished to make it available for all. His experiment at Santiniketan, was to implement an ancient idea based on a long tradition for the common good. Here, he wished to bring up, the full man : cultured, aesthetic and economically self-reliant : spiritually well conditioned, free from fear and devoted to vigorous activity : full of sympathy, with a spirit of sacrifice and social service. The saint in Tagore through education primarily, wished to dispell avidya, ignorance and give to individual a life style based on culture, with openness of mind to learn all the best anywhere available. Education was to be "the direct fruit of a living and growing knowledge". It was the good, he wished for all.

Education must be purposeful which is the highest realization in one's life. It must set one free "from avidya", which is the beginning of the true growth. It must enable one to know one's "True soul and be saved from the grasp of the self which imprisons you". Education should have a philosophy for the good of the individual and for the advancement of the society. In doctrination is not philosophy. Fulfilment of the immediate political purpose does not make for the richness of life. Politics should be kept out of education. Philosophy is not one man's creation : it is not the result of a momentary out-burst. It is, the eternal in tradition, the good for the totality after, the transitory has got skimmed out of it. As one proud of his heritage, Tagore pointed out in the Sadhna that "the true deliverance of man is the deliverance from avidya, from ignorance". This would provide for training and development of mind to make individual a good citizen; provide the base for good social order, strengthen the sense "of national obligation" and render the citizen capable of "serving the state needs". It must guide the individual to constructive work.

The modern school system is not the proper apparatus to achieve this high aim. It is too circumscribed on arrangement and too impersonal a system to turn out a better class of citizens for the social advancement. Tagore had the experience of this system and described it "the educational factory — lifeless, colourless, dissociated from the context of the universe, within bare white walls staring like eyeballs of the dead". He wished, school to be a place "where the children might be free in spite of the school". Deep in his mind, there was the feeling — "We had the God-given gift of taking delight in the world, but such delightful activity was fettered and imprisoned, stilled by a force called discipline which kills the sensibility of the child mind, the mind which is always on the alert, restless and eager to receive first-hand knowledge from Mother nature. We had to sit inert, like dead specimens of some museum, whilst lessons were pelted at us like hailstones on flowers". In Santiniketan, he gave full attention to the natural setting of the school and to the free atmosphere within it.

> "The young mind should be saturated with the idea that it 'was born in a human world which is in harmony with the world around it. And this the regular type of school ignores with an air of wisdom, severe and disdainfull. It forcibly snatches away children from a world full of the mystery of God's own handiworks, full of suggestiveness of personality. It is a mere method of discipline which refuses to take into account the individual. It is a manufactory specially designed for grinding out uniform results for, according to the school, life is perfect when it allows itself to be treated as dead, to be cut into symmetrical convenience."

The medium of instruction, in school is of vital significance to a child. It should be the appropriate vehicle to communicate ideas, in a manner as not to demand much effort from him. His should be an effortless response. It should enable him to understand, appreciate or reject that what is communicated to him. This sensitive role can be performed only through the mother tongue to which child gets' habituated as he grows. English is not substitute to it. Learning it takes too much time. It does not inculcate in the child the "power of assimilation and rejection" of ideas. Besides, the education imparted in English is, "inadequate to the life that we shall live". The mother tongue in communicating the ideas which are part of the language and of the social life has the advantage of its naturalness.

The books should be in agreement with the social texture. These should present a picture of the household, in which the growing child as a member of the family will live his life; and of society to which he is bound in diverse ways. The literature, he is taught should instill in the child social values and virtues, ethical norms and standards and train him to live, as is the society. Modern education does not fulfil this aim. It is the "topsyturvydom in Education — 'Siksher her pher'. It is deculturizing.

"Cultural conquest was, with Tagore, a tragedy of infinite magnitude. That tragedy must be somehow prevented."

University education is deficient in content and unaccomplishing in purpose. Students should be introduced to the Indian history, philosophy, literature and religion. The university community must take interest in things Indian. "Educational institutions in our country are India's alms-bowl of knowledge; they lower our intellectual self-respect; they encourage us to make a foolish display of decoration composed of borrowed feathers". True education must have national way of life. "True education is to realise at every step how our training and knowledge have organic connection with our surroundings."

The Three Aspects of Education

Education must attend to the cultural, aesthetic and economic development. English is no substitute for mother tongue and is deculturing. Westernization goes with it. He did not agree with those who believe that our ancestors have left no legacy to us. They talk of modernism which to them is synonymous with westernism. He points out : "The time has come for us to break open the treasure grove of our ancestors and use it for our commerce of life. Let us with its help make our future our own-never continue our existence as the eternal rag-picker at the other people's dustbins." He warned the people against the "exaggerated West." He wished the people to understand that there is the Eastern mind. He emphasises that, "it is in your blood, in the marrow of your bones, in the texture of your flesh and in the tissue of your brains."

In absence of due importance being given to the aesthetic aspects of culture, culture has been narrowed down to the vanishing point. Art and Music must be given the rightful place as these "are the highest means of national expression."

Men eats to live. Economic aspects in education is essential. Tagore held that, "education should be a part of life itself, and must not be detached from it and be made into something abstract". It "should not be dragged out of its native element, the life-current of the people. Educational institutions must have close association with the economic life. They must co-operate with the village round it, cultivate land, breed cattle, spin cloth, press oil from oil-seeds : they must produce all the necessaries, devising the best means, using the best material and calling science to their aid. Their very existence should depend upon the success of their industrial activities carried out on the co-operative principle, which will unite teachers and students and villagers of the neighbourhood in living and active bond of necessity. Our ancient tapovands (forest schools) were not shout off from the daily life of the people."

Meeting of the East and West

True to his idea of humanism, universalism and oneness of man, Tagore wished for the meeting of the East and the West. With this is mind, he established in 1921, the Visvabhrati with the object; "To seek to realise in a common fellowship of study the meeting of the East and the West and thus ultimately to strengthen the fundamental conditions of world peace through the establishment of free communication of ideas between the two hemispheres".

This followed from his faith in the unity of man. His feeling was that to explore and expound this unity is the mission of history. "Man, wherever he might be, if he produced something that was of eternal value, he could not claim it exclusively for himself or his own people, because it belonged, as their birthright as human beings, to everyone. All the great literatures, work of art, religious preachings of great men, and their lives, were for every one of them." He, therefore, pleaded for synthesis of cultures. The East should accept the scientific attitude of mind and the gift of science from the West; and the West too should accept for its own sake our concept of unity in diversity. In ancient India, Tagore points out, it was held."

His Religious Belief

Born in the glaze of Renaissance, brought on the Upanishadic thought and modelled by the Maharishi, Rabindranath, a man of Dharma, believed in the infinite living presence of God. He was no blind follower and no believer in the absurdities popularly labelled religious. Spirituality came to him in heritage and no less as a matter of experience. He was unhappy with the formal religion : the worship of image, chanting of prayer, telling of beads and the observance of ritual obligations. The religions discard fanaticism and conversions did not make sense to him. Religion, he held, must help maintain "the true standard of value". This lead him to the acceptance of Dharma. "Our Dharma is not religion : it is not divorced from politics, separated from work, cut off from business, dissociated from daily conduct. It does not confine itself within in the walls of a particular portion of society and keep a sentry over its boundaries to prevent the encroachments of recreations and amusements, poetry and literature, science and art. The stages of *Brahmacharya, Garhastha, Vanaprastha,* etc., are so many means of fulfilling religion completely in life, in this world. Religion is not for the satisfaction of our partial needs: the whole world exists for its fulfilment". At another place he explains: "dharma is the innermost nature, the essence, the implicit truly, of all things. Dharma is the ultimate purpose that is working in our self. When any wrong is done we say that *Dharma* is violated, meaning that the lie has been given to our true nature."

He was a believer in Karma. He abhored renunciation as understood ordinarily. Cheap asceticism, he described as the way to allow ones energy to waste. The feeling, that "there is something glorious in such submission" is just the assumed consolation. So also, the desire of deliverance had no place in his religious thinking.

"Leave this chanting and singing and telling of beads! Whom dost thou worship in this lonely, dark corner of a temple with doors all shut? Open thine eyes and see, thy God is not before thee!

"He is there where the tiller is tilling the hard ground and where the path-maker is breaking stones. He is with them in sun and in shower, and His garment is covered with dust. Put off thy holy mantle and even like him come down on the dusty soil!

"Deliverance! Where is this deliverance to be found? Our Master Himself has joyfully taken upon him the bonds of creation. He is bound with us all for ever.

Come out of they meditations and leave aside thy flowers and incense? What harm is there if thy clothes become tattered and stained? Meet Him and stand by Him in toil and in sweat of thy brow" (*Gitanjali*).

Rabindranath had the feel of God in all things and in all actions. "There is no higher religion than that of sympathy for all that lives. Love is the foundation of all religion." "My religion has no geographical units. I have a living faith in it...."

24

Sarvapalli Radhakrishnan (1888-1975)

Life Sketch

Dr. Sarvapalli Radhakrishnan, a noted philosopher and statesman was born on 5th September 1888 at Tiruttani in Madras. He received his early education in Missionary Schools. He passed his M.A. in the year 1909 and was appointed Lecturer in Philosophy in the same year in Presidency College, Madras. In 1918 he became Professor of philosophy. He joined Calcutta University in 1921 as Professor of philosophy. He became Lecturer of Manchester College, Oxford in 1926. He served Andhra University in 1938 and Banaras Hindu University in 1948. On attaining freedom by the country he was appointed Indian Ambassador to U.S.S.R. in 1952. He remained Chairman of the Council of States and also was the ex-officio Vice-President of India. He was awarded Bharat Ratna in 1954. He became President of India in 1962.

Dr. Radhakrishnan became fellow of all Souls College Oxford, honorary fellow of Royal Asiatic Society of Bengal; then Professor of Eastern religion and Eicsth at Oxford. He was the member of the executive of UNESCO in Paris (1948). He presided over the Silver Jublee Session of the Indian Philosophical Congress Calcutta in 1950 and was the President of All Asia Education Conference at Banaras. He became Chancellor of Delhi University in 1953. He became honorary fellow of British Academy on 11th July 1962. He visited several countries in his capacity as President of India.

Tributes by the Eminent Scholars

In the words of Professor Humayun Kabir, "Essentially a self made man, Radhakrishnan has achieved national and international fame through sheer merit. Starting his life as Assistant Lecturer, he rose steadily till he reached the highest position in the university in the world. He was the first Indian to hold Achairat Oxford. A teacher in five and Vice-chancellor in two universities, he was appointed Chairman of the First

University Education Commission in free India." The personality of Dr. Radhakrishnan is inspired by its immense humanity. He has impressed the great men of our age, who are through contracts, in their temperaments and outlook.

B.L. Atveya says "God has given him in abundance everything that any man can desire and aspire for. He is deep thinker, eloquent speaker, fascinating writer, and an inspiring teacher. He has been recipient of innumerable doctorate degrees without having supplicated for any. He is immensly rich. He is at the top of political greatness without having undergone any throves of selection."

In the words of Prof. Charles A. More, "In his spirit Radhakrishnan resolves the traditional opposition between the absolute and non-absolute God and world, appearance and reality, international and reason, philosophy and religion and philosophy and life as well as contradictions and opposition among the various religions and philosophical system. Radhakrishnan stands as a profound critic of all forms of exclusiveness. One sided perspective, dogmatism and intolerance, he supports this with a philosophical perception which avoids more electicism through a truly enlightened integration."

Prof. C.E.M. Joad writes "Professor Radhakrishnan possesses the rare gift of being able to make righteousness readable, and I know of no work which while so fairly and crisply presenting the modern criticism of religion, presents also with such an eloquence of passionate conviction the modern reply. The result is one of the profound by moving religious books of our time."

As Politician

1. He believed in full freedom of both body and mind. He writes, "the freedom that human desire is not the unreal negative absence of restraint, but the real positive freedom to use the full one natural endowments physique and branches."
2. He considered that Parliamentary democracy and Marxism are not incompatible. He never considered Marxism a workable proposition.
3. He was staunch supporter of nationalism.
4. He pleaded very strongly the right of self-determination.
5. He believed that the entire world should enjoy peace. For this purpose he advocated that democratic functioning should be adopted by all countries. The Imperialistic domination and colonialism should be totally abolished. He believed in justice and treatment of equality for all.

6. He was a very successful diplomat. K.P.S. Memon says that Radhakrishnan was an exceptional man. The service of his success as diplomat lay in his personality, often, it is what a diplomat is rather than what he does which counts, Genius has been defined to be courage to be truly one's own self. He lacked the technique of career diplomat but he had two virtues, without which all other qualities are as thinking brass and sounding cymbal namely, sincerity and detachment.

His writings Dr. Radhakrishnan is a renowned writer who has written various books on tough subjects. Being a scholar of top grade his writing won the praise of one and all and made him an international figure. Tagore has said, "I consider the book an idealist view of life" to be one of the most original and significant contribution in modern thought. Personally I am deeply grateful to him for the benefit. I have derived from the beauty and lucidity as wide as the Urdu range of the philosophical insight.

He has written the following books :

1. *The Essentials of Philosophy* (1911).
2. *Indian Philosophy* (1923), 2 vols.
3. *An Idealist View of Life* (1929).
4. *The Hindu View of Life* (1926).
5. *The Ethics of Vedanta and its Metaphysical* (1908) pre-suppositions.
6. *East and West in Religion* (1933).
7. *Freedom and Culture* (1936).
8. *Religion and Society* (1947).
9. *The Bhagwad Gita* (1948) English translation.
10. *East and West — some Reflection* (1954).
11. *Eastern Religion and Western Thought* (1948).
12. *The Dhammapada* (1950-English translation).
13. *India and China* (1944).
14. *Kalki or the Future of Civilisation* (1920).
15. *The Philosophy of Upanishads* (1924).
16. *The Principal Upanishads.*
17. *Introduction to Mahatma Gandhi* (1939).
18. *History of philosophy Eastern and Western* (1936).
19. *Contemporary Indian Philosophy* (1936).
20. *The philosophy of Ravindra Nath Tagore* (1918).
21. *The Religion in Contemporary Philosophy* (1920).

22. *The Religion We Need* (1928).
23. *Gautma, the Buddha* (1938).
24. *Education, Politics and War* (1944).
25. *Brahma Sutra* (1960).
26. *The Recovery of Faith* (1936).
27. *Is This Peace?* (1945).
28. *The Heart of Hindustan* (1936).
29. *Great Indians* (1949).
30. *My Search for Spirit* (1956).
31. *Fellowship of Spirit* (1961).

Dr. S. Radhakrishnan was a deep thinker, eloquent speaker, fascinating writer and an inspiring teacher. He rose from the post of lecturer to the highest post of President of India. He was immensly rich in thoughts and remained at the top of political greatness.

His Political Thoughts He believed in the Hegelion conception of freedom. He writes "The freedom which human being desire is not the unreal negative absence of restraint but the real positive freedom to use to the full one natural endowments physique and brains."

(2) He was deadly against the principles of Marxism. He held that Parliamentary democracy and Marxism are not incompatible.

(3) He believed that world peace would usher in if (i) we set up social democracies, (ii) elimination of Imperialistic domination and colonialism and (iii) International control over the exercise of sovereign power by nature-states.

His Spiritualism

He is original thinker of the first order. His philosophy is of absolute idealism. In the words of More, "Radhakrishnan resolves the traditional opposition between the absolute and non-absolute God and world, appearance and reality, intention and reason, philosophy and religion and philosophy and life as well as contradictions, and opposition among the various religions and philosophical systems. Radhakrishnan stands as a profound critic of all forms of exclusiveness and one sided perspective, dogmatism and intolerance. He supports with his philosophical perspective which avoids mere electicism through a truly enlightened Integration."

Radhakrishnan believed that religion is not a creed or code but an insight into reality. He is a modern prophet of spiritual religion.

His Views on Education According to Dr. Radhakrishnan, "the aim of education is not the acquisition of information, although important, or acquisition of technical skills, though essential in modern society, but the development of that bent of mind, that attitude of reason, that spirit of democracy which will make us responsible citizens. The goal is commitment to knowledge and advancement of learning." Further, "Education is the process of giving the individual, knowledge and skills which he should apply in his life. Inculcating noble traditions, compassion and love in the individual in order to help him lead a full life should be the aim of education." Before making an attempt to study the unfathomable knowledge in diverse fields of Dr. Radhakrishnan, let us know, in brief, the meaning and importance that he had given to the "teacher" and his "profession".

Who is a Teacher?

Dr. Radhakrishnan said, "Until and unless we have dedicated and committed teachers who take to teaching as a mission in their lives, we cannot have a good educational system." He spent many years of his life teaching. He was an embodiment of varied qualities, so ideal to a teacher. That is the reason he is still respected by all sections of people in general, and the teaching community in particular.

The teachers should be the best minds of the country, he said. They should not merely instruct but should gain the true love of pupils. He was of the opinion that "respect for the teachers cannot be ordered; it must be earned."

Acquiring and imparting knowledge are like the two eyes for a teacher, said Dr. Radhakrishnan. His heart should be the lamp of knowledge, burning bright all the time. His conduct should be simple with noble ambitions. His river of wisdom should not become stagnant water. It should flow like pure rain water. He should work hard, be broad-minded, and innovative. Distress, ignorance and blind beliefs should be viewed in the bright light of the teacher's wisdom, he said. His service should be devoted to spreading knowledge. These were the ideals which encouraged Dr. Radhakrishnan to choose this noble profession.

It would be appropriate to mention the greatness of a teacher as envisaged in Sutra literature. Guru Bramha, Guru Vishnu, Guru Deva, Maheshwaraha, *Guru Sakshat Para Bramha,* Tasmai Sri Gurave Namaha. A teacher is equivalent to God, and he should be regarded and respected. With noble qualities executed of an ideal teacher, Radhakrishnan used to hold his students spell bound by his felicity of expression and brilliance of exposition, interspersed with humorous anecdotes. He was able to inspire his students to appreciate high human and ethical values.

It was Dr. Radhakrishnan's practice to study in depth before he taught the subject to his students. He used to teach difficult subjects like philosophy and would impress upon all his students by his innovative style.

Thoughts on University

A University, he said, is expected to be a place of higher learning where an individual is helped to acquire more knowledge, refine his culture and master philosophy. He should give up greed and selfishness and work hard with devotion. He, as a seeker of higher knowledge, sets aside his personal desires, and indulges in higher thinking and absorbs himself in nobler endeavours. Men and women besides acquiring knowledge, master various skills in their own disciplines which are going to stand them in good stead later in life. A university encourages those who enter its portals to become refined. It never just encourages one to learn the laws prescribed in books. The teachers, therefore, should provide standing examples in this regard.

A University, said Dr. Radhakrishnan, is essentially a co-operation of teachers and students and the relation between the two is of a sacred, character. Magnificent buildings and equipment are no substitute for the great teacher. A university is not a mere information shop, it is a place where man's intellect, will and emotions are disciplined. The university is a sanctuary of the intellectual life of the country, and pursuit of knowledge is the soul of the university. Dr. Radhakrishnan calls the universities homes of culture and citadels of liberty.

Higher education, he opined, should provide leadership in politics, administration, profession, industry and commerce. The universities should train minds to bring together material resources and human energies. Hence, education should train for self-development, fearlessness of mind, integrity of purpose and strength of conscience. In short, education should be liberating and life-giving.

The following example reflects the regard and respect which the students developed towards the teacher, Dr. S. Radhakrishnan :

On the day he left Mysore University for Calcutta where Sir Asutosh Mookerjee, the then Vice-Chancellor of Calcutta University has offered the King George V, Professorship of Mental and Moral Philosophy Chair, the students brought a coach without its horse, decorated it with flowers to give it the appearance of a chariot, seated Radhakrishnan in it and pulled it to the railway station themselves. Many distinguished citizens of Mysore and Bangalore lined up to bid farewell to Radhakrishnan. The students bid him an emotional and tearful farewell.

In spite of his busy schedule in attending university affairs, Dr. Radhakrishnan had shown keen interest in writing too. Some of his books include *East and West in Religion* (1933); *Freedom and Culture* (1936); *The Heart of Hindustan*; and he Co-edited the book entitled *Contemporary Indian Philosophy.* Apart from these, he had delivered many lectures and presented papers at various meetings and conferences.

Inclination Towards Gandhi

While in Oxford, Radhakrishnan first wrote on Gandhi in 1921 in an article "Gandhi and Tagore" published in the *Calcutta Review.* During the period 1936 to 1939 he edited a felicitation volume in honour of Gandhi, which he planned to present to the Mahatma on his 70th birthday.

He got some of the world's leading minds to contribute to it. Some of the distinguished personalities who contributed articles to the book included, Albert Einstein, Pearl S. Buck and Rabindranath Tagore. "Reflections on Gandhi's life and work" was published and presented to Gandhi on his 70th birthday on October 2, 1939.

Lectures

Radhakrishnan's earlier lectures in the U.K. were so successful that he was invited to take the post vacated by Principal J. Estlin Carpenter in Manchester College, Oxford in 1929-30.

This invitation gave him an opportunity to lecture on comparative religion. In addition to these lectures, he was also invited to give many lectures at various places which included Manchester University and London University.

Bertrand Russel who had attended his lectures in London met him and told him that he had never heard philosophy better espounded than in those lectures.

H.N. Spalding who had also listened to the lectures in London was so fascinated by their content and Radhakrishnan's personality and scholarship that he decided to found a chair at Oxford, for Eastern Religions and Ethics. The Chair, established in 1936 was offered to Radhakrishnan.

Vice-Chancellor of BHU

At the time when Radhakrishnan returned to Calcutta from Oxford in 1939, Pandit Madan Mohan Malaviya, founder and Vice-Chancellor of the Banaras Hindu University, who was not keeping good health, found Dr. Radhakrishnan the most suitable person and requested him to take charge as the Vice Chancellor of BHU.

Though Dr. Radhakrishnan declined the offer at the beginning for some reasons, offer a lot of persuasion he had agreed to become the V.C. of BHU. Malaviya resigned on August 20, 1939 and Radhakrishnan took charge on September 24.

The academicians and dignitaries hailed Malaviya's choice. As in the case of Andhra University, Radhakrishnan made mark as an able administrator and fund mobiliser.

Distinguished President

In 1962, he was elected President of India. He accepted only Rs. 2,500 out of his salary of Rs. 10,000 and like Dr. Rajendra Prasad, he donated the remaining amount to the Prime Minister's National Relief Fund every month. Even though he occupied the highest office of the country, he remained a simple person.

Dr. Radhakrishnan's intellectual capabilities were such that in spite of his deep involvement in various activities at higher levels, his contribution in the field of education is monumental. Dr. Radhakrishnan died of cardiac arrest on April 17, 1975.

Estimate

Dr. Radhakrishnan is an internationally eminent philosopher who attempted to symthasize Eastern and Western thoughts in an idealistic perspective. An eloquent speaker, an eminent writer, a diplomat, sincere in thought and action and truly religious man. He is a versatile genious, a distinguished scholar, a great administrator and a clear sighted statesman. He is the greatest interpreter of Indian philosophy and religion and his philosophy is full of Idealism.

Dr. Sarvapalli Radhakrishnan's contribution to education in unique though he was a multi-faceted personality — scholar, renowned professor, orator, able administrator, prolific writer, well-known philosopher, diplomat, statesman, patriot — his contributions towards education is stupendous, irrespective of the positions he held later in his life. Dr. Radhakrishnan was of the opinion that the right kind of education only could solve many ills of society and the country.

INDEX

A

Abdulla, 153
Aberdeen University, 132
Abidharma Kosha, 293
Acharya Narendra Dev, 292-99
Achyut Patwardhan, 298
Act of 160, 264
Advaitism, 89
Afro-Asian Unity, 282
Afzal Khan, 101
Aga Khan, 61, 76
Agarkar, 79-80
Age of Consent Bill, 80, 94-96
Ahimsa, 170
AICC, 293
Akbar, 36
Albert Einstein, 350
Alexander, Mr., 166
Alexander, Sir, 45
Aligarh Conspiracy case, 131, 134
All India Voters Association, 240
Allan Octavian Hume, 22, 32
Amarkosh, 292
Amrita Bazar Patrika, 105, 328
Amritsar Tragedy, 158
Andhra University, 351
Annie Basent, Mrs., 24, 157, 262, 265
Ansari, M.A. Dr., 91
Appollo Bunder, 157
Arctic Home and the Vedas, 85
Aristotle, 10
Arjuna, 101
Arms Act, 48
Arnot, Mr., 10
Arthasastra, 123
Aruna Asaf Ali, Shrimati, 291
Arya Samaj, 94, 116, 119, 122
Arya, 137
Arys Bhushan Press, 79
Ashok Mehta, 286, 294, 299, 304-305
Asiatic Registration Act, 155
Asiatic Society of Bengal, 327
Asutosh Mukerjee, 349
Atmakatha, 119
Atraya B.L., 345
Attlee, Clement, 166
Aung San, 268
Aurangzeb, 37
Aurobindo Ghosh, 1, 104, 106, 113, 132-49, 246, 293
Austine, 15-16
Ayrton, 45
Aziz-Un-nisa Begum, 311

B

Baden Weiler, 267
Baisakhi Day, 159
Balkan War, 331
Banaras Hindu University, 298, 351
Banarjee, S.N., 1, 3, 8, 11, 18, 52-60
Bande Mataram, 105, 107, 119, 135, 138, 143
Bankim Chandra Chatterjee, 133
Bardoli, 160
Barinder Kumar Ghosh, 135
Barker, 216
Basic Education, 204
Bengal Public Opinion, 105
Bengalee Journal, 53
Benoy Kumar Sarkar, Prof., 104, 106
Bhagavad Gita, 170-71, 262, 267, 292
Bhandarkar, Prof., 208
Bhanumati, 7
Bhoodan, 215, 221-23; Movement, 224, 227
Bipin Chandra Pal,1, 11-12, 17, 52, 104-114, 135, 138
Birla House, 167
Black Law, 155

Bluntschelli, 293
Bolshevism, 182, 185; Revolution, 243
Bombay Association, 21
Bombay Corporatin, 46
Bondaref, T.M., 195
Bontham, 16
Borsuet, 49
Boycott, 66, 78, 87, 91
Brahma Samaj, 8, 9, 94, 327
Braja Binod Roy, 5
Brajendranath Seal, 18
Branbon, 93
Bread Labour, 195
British Communist Party, 306
Brooks. Mr., 262
Buckingham, 12
Buddhism, 6, 170-71, 223
Buddha, 56, 57, 102, 211, 293
Buke, 54, 56, 57

C

Cabinet Mission, 268-69
Calcutta Corporation, 3, 53, 54
Calcutta University, 349
Cama & Co., 21
Cambridge, 262
Carlyle, 151, 189
Chagla, M.C., 290
Chamberlain, 155, 182
Chandidas, 326
Charles Bradlaugh, 129
Charter Act of 1833, 14
Chauri Chaura, 160, 263
Chengiskhan, 191
Chintamani, C.Y., 53
Chirol, 93
Chitpavan Brahmin, 32, 61-63
Chou-En-Lai, 258
Christiantiy, 173
CIE, 62
Cicero, 57
Civil disobedience, 161-162, 169, 229, 266
Class War, 182
Co-education, 124-25
Collect, Miss., 18
Comintern, 244
Commonwealth, 273-74
Communal Award, 162-63, 212, 332
Communal Triangle in India, 304
Communal Unity, 120
Communism, 199-200, 225, 229, 243
Communist Manifesto, 182
Communist party, 243
Compte, 39
Condorcet, 49
Conference of Democrats, 30
Congress Organisation, 1;
Indian National Congress, 3, 22-23, 45-46, 49-51, 62, 78, 80, 97, 133, 244, 264-66
Congress Socialist Party, 229
Congress Socialist weekly, 304
Constituent Assembly, 271
Contemporary Hindu Philosophy, 350
Coomaraswamy, A.K., 293
Corporate Boards of Trade, 44
Council of State, 253
Count Keysivling, 325
Cow Protection, 204
CPI, 308
CPM, 308
Curzon, 3, 77

D

Dabindranath, 327
Dada Dharmadhikari, 236
Dadabhai Naoroji, 1, 3, 19-31, 32, 34, 45
Dandi March, 161-62
Dange, S.A., 307-08
Das, C.R., 134, 161
Dawan, 163
Dayanand Anglo-Vedic College, 116
Dayanand, Swami, 116, 242
Deccan Education Society, 62, 78, 80
Democratic Socialism, 304
Depressed Classes Conference, 96
Deshabandhu Das, 117, 131, 134
Deshpande 134, 138
Devendranath, 325, 327
Dharma, 137, 143; Dharmayuddha, 140
Dharma, 2
Dhudhike, 115
Dialectical Materialism, 242
Diderot, 49
Dikshit, Prof., 183, 185, 197, 199
Din-i-Ilahi, 37
Discovery of India, 259, 271, 277, 286
Diwakar, R.R., 77, 231
Dominion Status, 65, 161
Doveton College, 52
Dowry System, 202
Drain Theory, 42
Dunjibhoy, 45

Dunkirk, 136
Durga Charan, 52
Dyer, General, 159

E

East India Association, 46
East India Company, 7, 19
Edward Thompson, 210
Ellen and Roy, 248, 249
Elphinstone, Mount Sturat, 19
Emerson, 129
Euclid, 193
Engels, 182, 226
Erasmus, 245
Erskine Perry, Sir. 20
Eslin Carpenter, J. 350
Extremist, 97, 171, 242
Extremists, 4

F

Father of India Renaissance, 5
Father of the Nation, 150, 210
Fazli Hussain, 160
Federal Assembly, 253
Fergusson College, 62, 80, 116
First World War, 117, 243
Five Year Plan, 218, 290
Foodgrains Induiry Committee, 304
Fox, 56
Francis Young, Sir, 105
Francis, 211
Frank Moraes, 282, 283
Free Church College, 53
Freedom of Press, 9
French Revolution, 48, 89, 293

G

Gandhi and Lenin, 307
Gandhi and Marx, 216
Gandhi-Irwin Pact, 162
Ganeshotsava, 86; Ganapathy Festival, 90
Ganga Saran Sinha, 297
Gangadhar Pant, 78
Ganganath Jha, Pandit, 262
Garibaldi, 293
Ghalib, 321
Gila Rahasya, 82, 101, 140
Gitanjali, 330
Gladsltone, 46, 57
Glimpses of World History, 266
Gnekwar of Baroda, 133
Gokhale and Gandhi, 207-09
Gokuldas Makani, 152
Gold Standard Fund, 72
Golden Age, 37
Gopal Krishna Gokhale, 1-3, 32, 48, 56, 61-77, 157, 208, 212
Gopi Chand Bhargava, 117
Goyal, Dr., 16, 168-69, 219, 237, 249
Gram Mandal, 238
Gram Swarajya, 220
Gramadan, 222-23
Grand Old Man of India, 19, 24
Grant, 14
Great Rebellion of 1857, The, 304
Green T.K., 27
Grotius, 14
Grouping Arrangements, 269
Gupta, K, 290
Guru Dutt, Pt., 116

H

Hafiz, 6
Halit, 319
Halifax, 210
Hampden, 211
Hardayal, 293
Haridas Chaudhri, Dr., 131
Harijan, The, 163
Harrow Public School, 262
Hasan Imam, 91
Hasrat Mohani, 91
'He Ram', 167
Heart of Hindustan, The, 350
Hegel, 39, 49-50
Herder, 245
Hijrat, 179
Hindu Review, 105
Hitler, 132, 136, 182
Hobhouse Decentralisation Commission 62
Home Rule Agitation, 57
Home Rule Party, 82; Home Rule, 85; Home Rule League, 87, 117, 157
Homes, J.H. Dr. Rev., 210
Hotborn Liberal Association, 22
Howrah conspiracy case, 243
Hoyland, 76, 93
Humanism, 245-46
Humayan Kabir, 344-45
Hunter Committee Report, 159

I

I.N.A., 268
Idol worship, 204
Ijtihad, 318
Ilbert Bill Agitation, 46; Bill. 48
Ilion, 137
Imperial Council, 53, 71, 87
Imperial Press Conference, 54
Independent Allahabad, 105
Independent India, 244
India in Transition, 245
Indian Civil Service, 53, 66, 94, 138, 329
Indian Councils Act, 4
Indian Federation of Labour, 244
Indian Independence Committee, 243
Indian Independence, 1, 2
Indian Majlis, 133
Indian National Movement, 52
Indian National Social Conference, 33, 36
Indian Renaissance Movement, 244
Indian Shipping, 304
Indian Unrest, 93
Individual Civil Disobediance, 164
Indu Prakash, 134, 307
Industrial conference, 42, 44
Industrialisation, 44
Interim Government, 269
International Humamist and Ethical Association, 245
Ishwar Dutt, 63
Islam, 173

J

Jacques Maritain, 245
Jainism, 170-71
Jallianwala Bagh, 159
Jaltola, 52
James Fergusson, Sir, 80
James Kellock, 33
Jamnalal Bajaj, 163, 214, 217
Jana Shakti, 227
Jatin Chatterjee, 135
Jayadev, 326
Jayaprakash Narain, 222, 225, 229-41
Jeevandan, 225
Jesus Christ, 210, 211
Jewel of Maharashtra, 77
Jinnah, M.A., 76, 91, 165
Jiten Sen, 113
Joad, C.E.M. Prof., 345
Joint Select Committee, 54
Joseph Mazzini, 54, 108, 116, 133, 211, 293
Joshi, G.V., 38
Journal Swaraj, 105
Jugantar, 137
Jury Act of 1827, 14

K

Kabir, 96
Kalidasa, 133
Kallenback, 156
Kamala Nehru, 262, 265-67
Kant, 37
Karamchand, 152
Karan Singh, Dr., 132, 148
Karmakar, D.P., 85
Karmayogi, 289
Karmayogin, 137
Karve, D.G., 32, 95
Kasturbai, 152, 156, 165
Kesari, 78, 80, 82, 90, 93
Keskar, B.V., 298
Khadi, 196-97; Khadar, 196
Khankhoje, P.S., Dr., 93
Khilafat, 159; movement, 263
King George V., 349
King of Bombay, 45
Kirpal, P.N. Prof., 126
Kirplani, 202-03, 205, 211
Kisan Mazdoor Praja Party, 300
Krishan Chander Banderjee, 5
Krishanantha Ghosh, 132
Krishna, 101
Kropotkin, 292
Kunznu, H.N., 290

L

Lala Lajpat Rai, 1, 3, 115-30, 243
Lal, Bal and Pal, 27
Lala Jagannath, 117
Lama, 6
Latin America, 265
League of Nations, 92, 274
Lenin, 226, 243, 304
Liberal Association (Halborn), 22-23
Liberal Party, 22
List, 72
Lloyd George, 119
Locks, 14
Loghu Kaumudi, 292
Lokmiti, 218-19, 223, 231
London Indian Society, 25, 46

London University, 350
Lord Amherst, 9-11, 16
Lord Bentinck, 17, 94
Lord Betrand Russell, 270
Lord Boyd Orr, 200, 258
Lord Hardinge, 77, 156
Lord Mountbatten, General, 166, 269
Lord Reay, 22
Lord Ronald Shay, 105
Lord Salisbury, 50
Lorretto Convent School, 132
Lotus and Dagger, 133
Louis Fischer, 210
Luilithgow, 164-165

M

Macaulay, 54, 56, 123
Machiavelli, 10
Madan Mohan Malavia, 118, 351
Madhusudan Dutta, 133
Mahabharata, 101, 133, 292
Mahadeo Raoji, 85
Mahadev Desai, 165
Maharaja of Baroda, 133
Mahatma Gandhi, 1, 2, 4, 61, 62, 63, 68, 77, 115, 118, 128, 131, 140, 142, 148, 150-212, 229-30, 233, 259-60, 275, 282-85, 291, 298, 306-07, 325, 350
Mahatma Hanj Raj, 116
Majumdar, B., 12-13, 16
Malttus, 42
Manchester University, 356
Mandalay Jail, 82
Manekboi, 19
Manu, 101
Mao, 183
Maratha, The, 78, 93
Martyrdom, 167
Marx, 181, 225; Philosophy, 229, 242, 245, 255-57, 304
Mashruwala, K., 216
Materialism, 246-47
Max Muller, 5, 81, 260
Mc. Cullough, 42
Menon. K.P.S., 346
Metropolitan Institution, 53
Mill, J.S., 48, 54, 56, 69, 89
Miller, 243
Milton, 12
Mirabeau, 211
Moderates, 4, 97, 171
Modern Review, 105
Mohammad Alam, Dr., 117-18
Mohammad Iqbal, 321-24
Montagu-Chelmsford Reforms, 76
Montesquieu, 11
Mont-Ford Reforms, 91
Moplah Riots, 160-61
More, 245
Mother India, 3
Motilal Nehru, 61, 63, 65, 117, 130, 161, 261, 265, 266
Muhammed Ali, 161
Mulhar Rao, 22
Muslim League, 165; Its Demand, 166-67
Mysore University, 355

N

Nagari Shambhurao, Shri, 213
Nagendranath Gupta, 211
Nanak, 96
Narendra Nath Battacharya, 243
Narsi Mehta, 101
Nasik, 18
Natal, 62, 153
National Education, 123
Nazism, 136, 244
Nehru Report, 117
Nehru, Pt., 1, 9, 84, 117, 129, 131, 229, 244, 245, 258-91; Nehru and Gandhi, 281-85, 300, 303, 309
Nepolean Bonaparte, 132
New India, 105
New Lamps for old, 138
Nihilist Literature, 293
Nizami, 310, 314-17, 319
Non-alignment, 273
Non-Co-Operation Movement, 159-61
Non-Violance, 174-75
Notingham Conference, 92

O

Official Secret Act, 3
Oliver Cronwell, 47, 49
On the Congress Constitution, 245
On the Move, 301
One World, 273, 277
Orion, the, 85
Our Differences, 245
Overstreet, 243
Oxford, 344, 350

P

Palanji Dordi, 19
Palma Dutt, 91
Panchayati Raj, 240-41
Panchsheel, 271-72
Panikkar K.M., 280
Panini, 57
Paramhans Mandli, 33
Paridarshak, 113
Paris Peace Conference, 92
Partition, The, 166
Parvate, T.V., 104
Passive Resistance Association, 155
Passive Resistance, 110
Patanjali, 56
Patel, V.J., 161
Pearl Buck, 270, 290, 350
Penal Code, 101
People's committees, 251
People's Councils, 252; Supreme People Council, 252
Percival Spear, 211
Pherozeshah Mehta, 1, 45-51
Philawati, 7
Phoenix settlement, 155-56
Pilgrim Fathers, 57
Pitt, 56
Planned Economy, 279-80
Planning Commission, 304
Poona Pact, 163
Poston, Mrs., 20
Praja Socialist Party, 304
Prakasha, Shri, 292
Prarthana Samaj, 33 Press Act, 48
Prime Minister's National Relief Fund, 351
Prince of Wales, The, 160
Prince of Workers, 77
Protagorak, 245
Public Service Commission, 50
Purna Swaraj, 162
Putli Bai, 152

Q

Queen Victoria, 81
Queen's Bench, 53
Queen's Proclamation, 25
Quit India Movement, 229

R

Radha Krishan, 115
Radhakrishnan, Dr., 61, 131, 148, 228, 258, 344-51
Radical Democratic Party, 244
Radical Humanism, 242
Raghunath Rao, 34
Raichand Bhai, 101
Raizada Hans Raj, 117-18
Raj Kumar Shukla, 158
Raja Jaikishan Das, 312, 313
Rajendra Prasad, Dr. 211, 277
Rajne Palme Dutt, 306-09
Rajniti, 218-19, 223, 231
Ram Kanta, 5, 6
Ram Manohar Lohia, Dr. 300-03
Ram Mohan Rai, 2, 5-18, 32, 34-35, 38, 45, 94, 326-27
Ramabai Ranade, 33
Ramachandra Pal, 104
Ramcharitramanas, 151
Ramakrishna Paramhamsa, Swami, 85, 131
Ramarajya, 199
Ramaswamy Iyer, 63
Ramatirth, 242
Ramyana, 133, 292
Ramsay Macdonald, 162, 212
Ranade, M.G., 1, 22, 32-44, 45, 46, 61
Ranadiv, 308-09
Rao, V.K.R.V. 290
Rast Goftar, 21
Reay, Lord, 22
Reflections on French Revolution, 64
Revolutionary, 135
Richardo, 42
Rienze, 211
Robespierre, 49
Romain Rolland, 131, 148, 151, 210
Rousseau, 11
Rowlett Bill, 159
Roy, B.C., 104, 106
Roy, M.N. 229, 237, 242-57
Royal Asintic Society of Bengal, 344
Royal Indian Navy, 268
Rumi, 321
Ruskin, 101, 151, 168-69
Russian Revolution, 225, 308

S

Saadi, 6
Sabarmati, 157, 213-14
Sati, 7, 8, 94
Sahay, T.L. 171, 209
Samajwadi Yuwak Sabha, 294
Sampatidan, 223
Sankar Ghose, Prof., 306

rada Devi, 327
rvodaya Samaj, 225, 231, 234
rvajanik, Sabha, 33-34, 62, 73
rvodaya, 2, 188; Sarvodaya Society, 219, 229-232
typal. Dr. 117
varkar, V.D. 243
vitri, 137
yyid Ahmad Khan, 310-20
ience and Technology, 277-78
cond Round Table Conference, 162
n, S.D. 291
rvants of India Society, 62, 67-69, 73-77
vagram, 230
akti, 142
antiniketan, 328-30
arada Act, 94
arma, D.C. Prof. 129, 171, 209, 247
avkat Ali, 91
eikh Mehtab, 152
ivaji, 81-86, 89; Shivaji Festivals, 93-101
ramdan, 224
mon Commission, 117, 130, 163: Report, 163, 265
r Naraian Chandravarker, 24
taramaya, 45, 97, 130
nith, 42
nuts, 155
ocialism, 112-13
ocialism, Sarvodaya and Democracy, 240
ocialist Party, 300
ocialistic Pattern of Society, 279
outh Africa, 62
palding H.N. 350
pencer, 39, 48
piritualisation of Politics, 67-68
afford Cripps, Sir, 164, 210
alin, 258, 310
ate Intervenist, 68-69
atesman, 105
ubhas Chandra Bose, 1, 284
uda J.P., 138
un-Yat-Sen, 211
urendranath Dwivedy, 298
wadeshi, 3, 59, 60; Movement, 66, 100, 120, 198
waraj Party, 117
Swaraj, 3, 65, 78, 86-87, 107-110, 122, 220, 229
Swarajya Shastra, 215, 219
Swarpuarani, 261
Sylhet, 53, 104, 113

T

Tagore, 8, 148, 245, 258, 291, 325-43, 350
Tamerlane, 191
Tawarikh-e-Hind, Technique of Satyagraha, 176-80
Thana Panchayat, 238
Theory of Surplus Value, 236
Tilak and Gandhi, 100-03
Tilak and Gokhale, 97-100
Tilk, B.G. 1, 3, 19, 42, 65, 78-103
Tolstoy, 151, 156, 168
Toynbee, 50
Tribune, The, 105
Tulsidas, 37
Turgenev, 293
Tyabaji, 81, 142

U

U.K. 27
U.N.O. 274-75, 303
U.S.A. 117, 164, 166, 229, 243
Uka, 152, 350
Umesh Chandra Banerjee, 22
UNESCO, 344
Unhappy India, 119
Unity of India, 287
University College, 52
Unto This Last, 169, 230
Untouchability, 121, 200-01
Upanishads, 7, 101, 107, 151, 327, 329
Urban Communities, 240
USSR, 166, 243, 344

V

Vaishnavism, 170, 326
Vallabhbhai Patel, 158
Valmiki, 56, 57
Varna, 203
Varnashramadherma, 2
Vasant Nargolkar, 217, 224-25
Vasavadatta, 137
Vasudev Balwant Phadke, 1
Vanguard of Indian Independence. The, 244

Vedanga Jyotisha, 85
Vedanta Philosophy, 230
Vedanta Sutra, 7; Vedanta, 88
Vedas, 292, 329
Verma Dr. 6, 46, 49, 93, 101, 234
Videshi, 59
Vidyapati, 326
Vikramorvasie, 137
Village Republics, 192-94
Vinoba Bhave, 213-28
Vishnu Bhaskar Lele, 134
VJshnu Krishna Chiplunkar, 79
Visva Bharati, 330-32
Vivekanand, Swami, 85, 131, 242
Voltaire, 49
Vyasa, 57

W

Walter Crocker, 270, 289
Wardha, 214
Washington, 211
Wavell, Lord, 165
Welby Commission, 54, 70
Wellington, Lord, 157
Wheel of History, 300
White paper, 163
Who Owns India? 304
Widow Remarriage Association, 33, 38, 2
William Hunter, 81
Willoughby, 15
Wilson, 89
Winston Churchill, Sir, 164
Women uplift, 201
World Parliament, 303
World War II, 132, 136, 164, 195, 244
Wrold Federation of Trade Unions, 307

Y

Yajur Veda, 7
Yeats, W.B. 330
Yerveda, 162
Yogi, 134, 136, 148; Yoga, 134, 136
Young India, 115, 117, 163, 187, 204, 285
Yusuf Meherally, 299

Z

Zabardust Maulvi, 6
Zaghlul Pasha, 211
Zakarias, 91
Zakir Hussain, Dr. 290
Zoraster, 211
Zorastrain Faith, 21